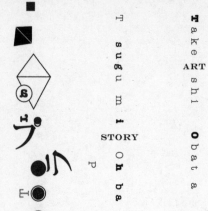

Takeshi Obata
ART

Tsugumi Ohba
STORY

Platinum End

PLATINVM END

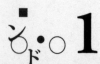

1

CONTENTS

1

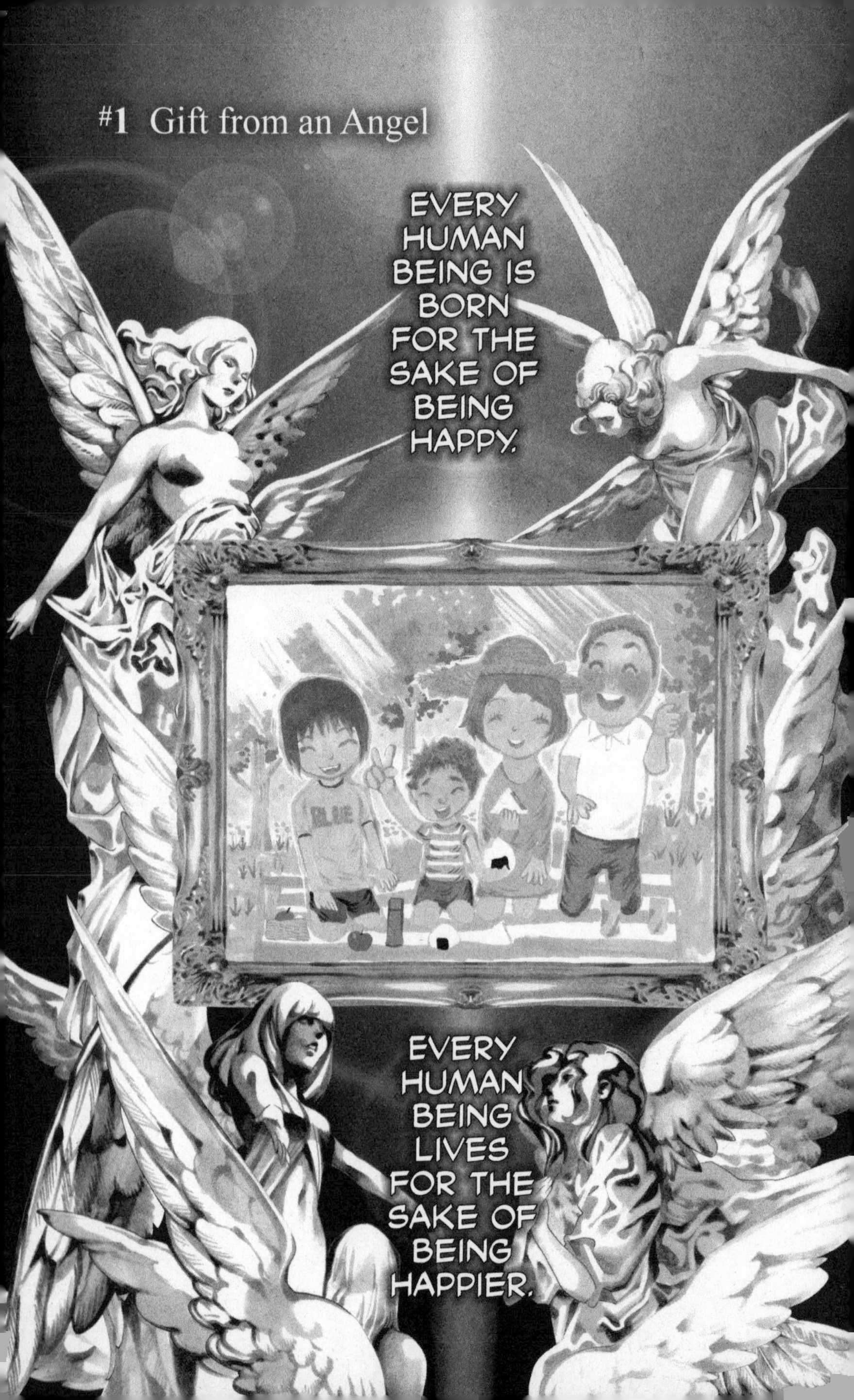
#1 Gift from an Angel
EVERY HUMAN BEING IS BORN FOR THE SAKE OF BEING HAPPY.
EVERY HUMAN BEING LIVES FOR THE SAKE OF BEING HAPPIER.

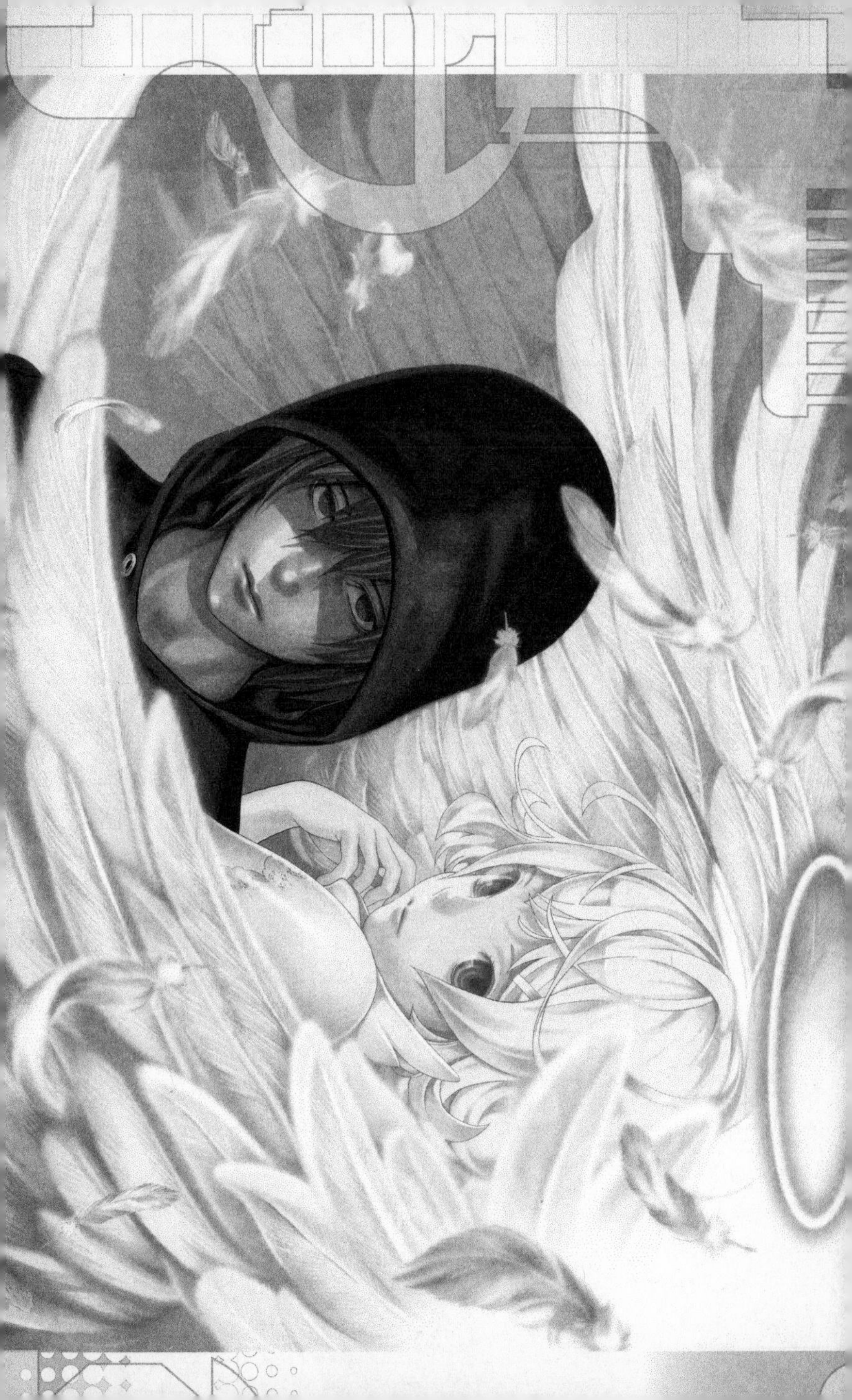

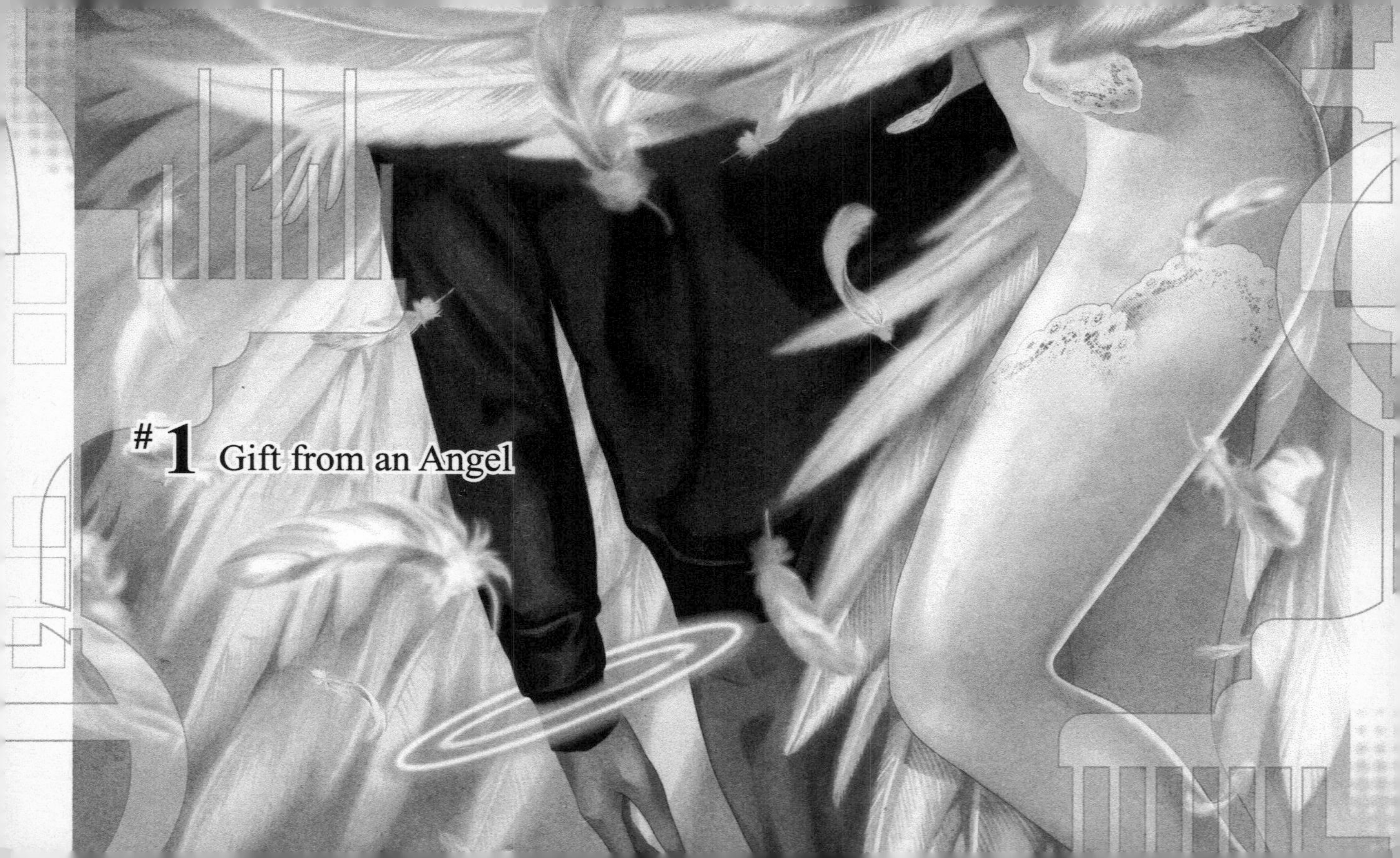
#1 Gift from an Angel

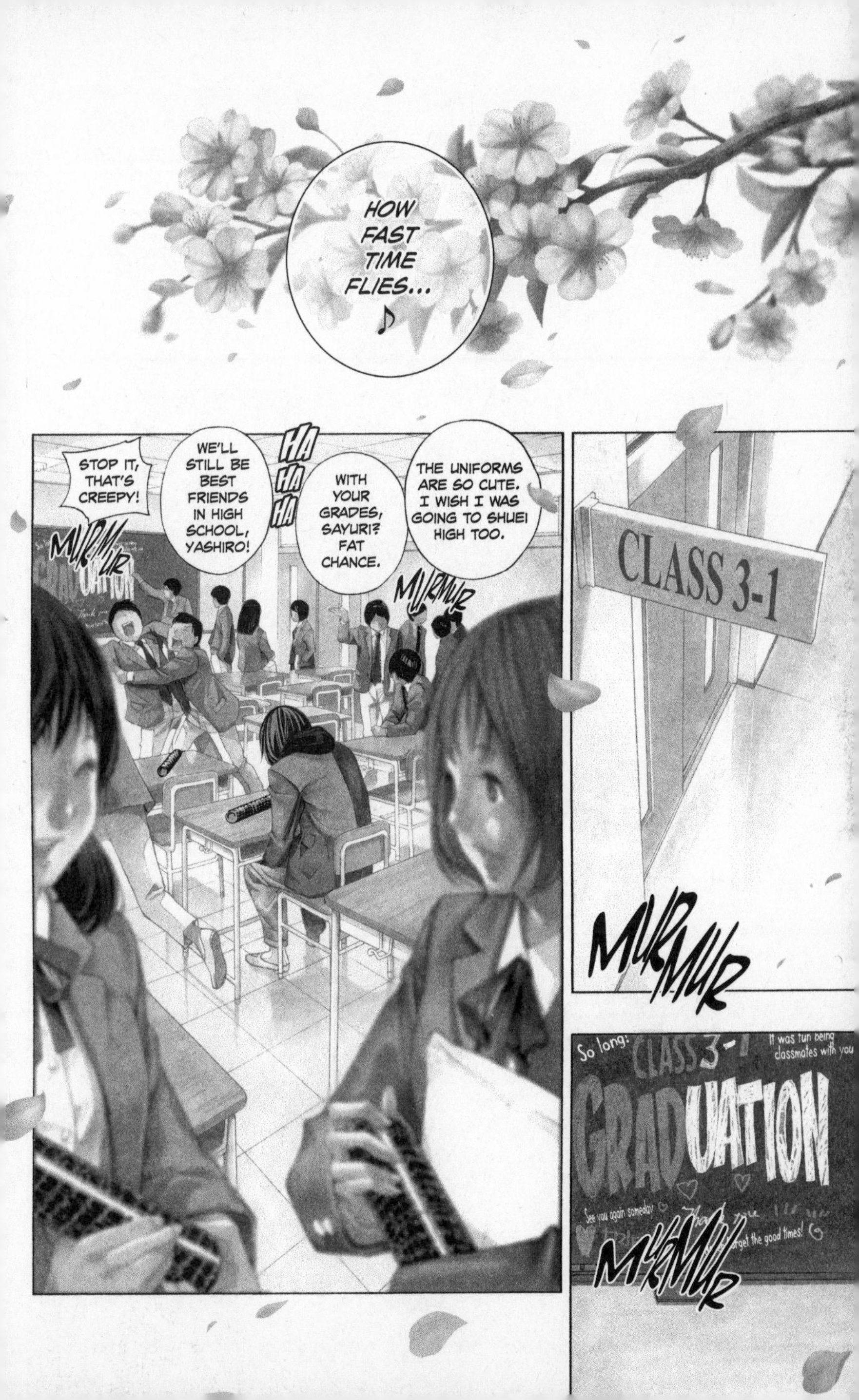
HOW FAST TIME FLIES... ♪
CLASS 3-1
MURMUR
So long: CLASS 3-1
It was fun being classmates with you
GRADUATION
See you again someday
MURMUR
THE UNIFORMS ARE SO CUTE. I WISH I WAS GOING TO SHUEI HIGH TOO.
WITH YOUR GRADES, SAYURI? FAT CHANCE.
HA HA HA
WE'LL STILL BE BEST FRIENDS IN HIGH SCHOOL, YASHIRO!
STOP IT, THAT'S CREEPY!
MURMUR
MURMUR

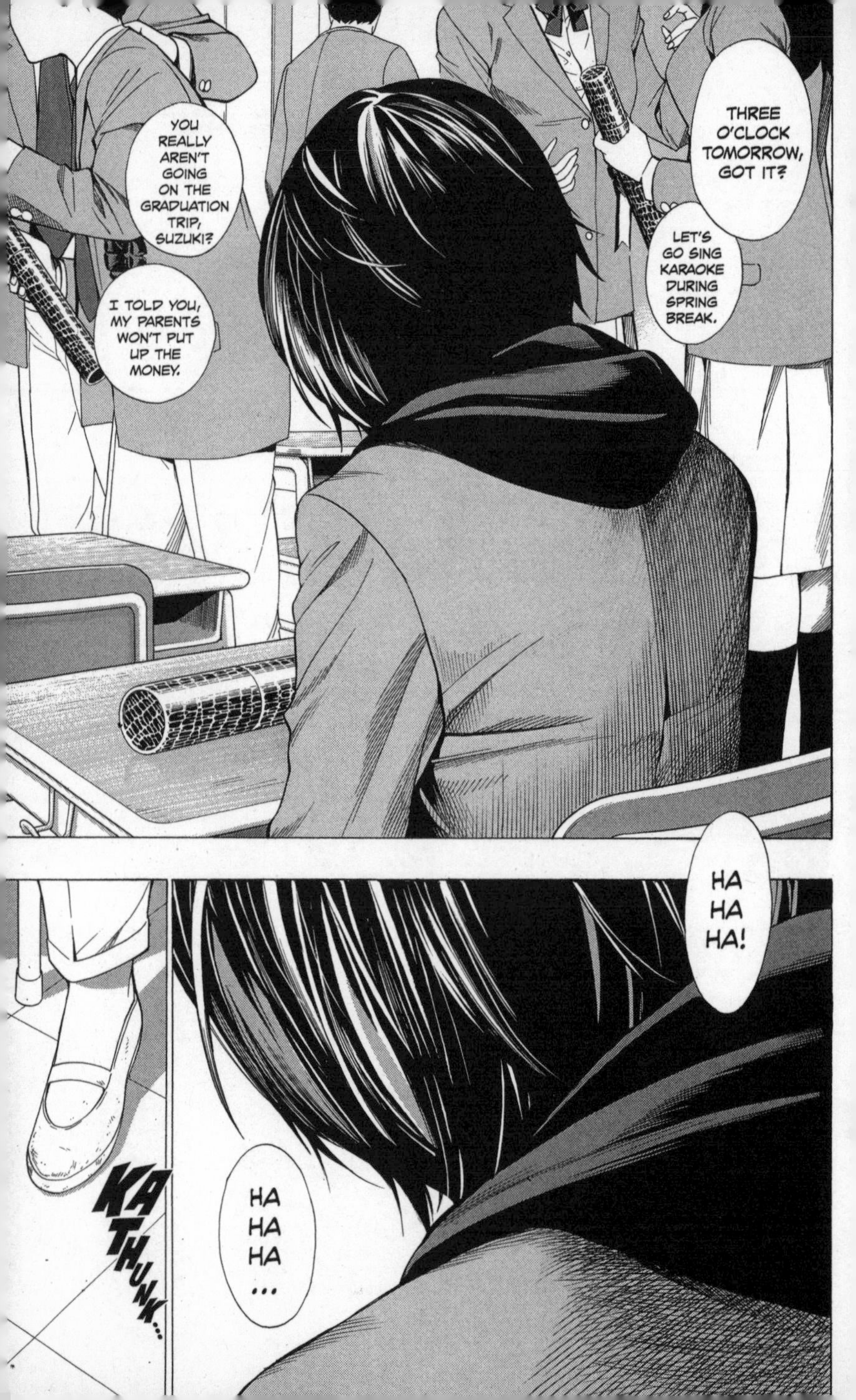
THREE O'CLOCK TOMORROW, GOT IT?
LET'S GO SING KARAOKE DURING SPRING BREAK.
YOU REALLY AREN'T GOING ON THE GRADUATION TRIP, SUZUKI?
I TOLD YOU, MY PARENTS WON'T PUT UP THE MONEY.
HA HA HA!
HA HA HA ...
KATHUNK...

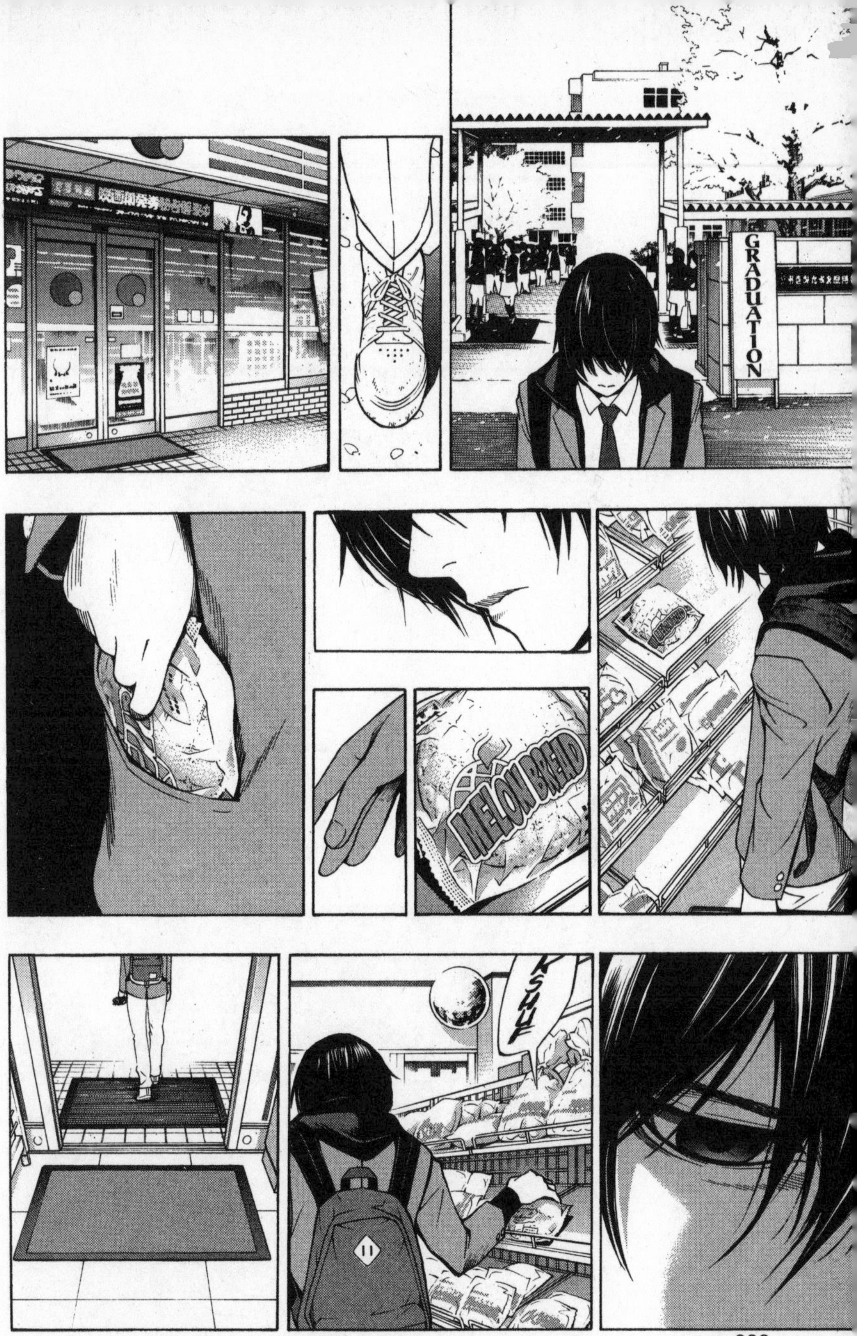
GRADUATION
MELON BREAD
KSHUF

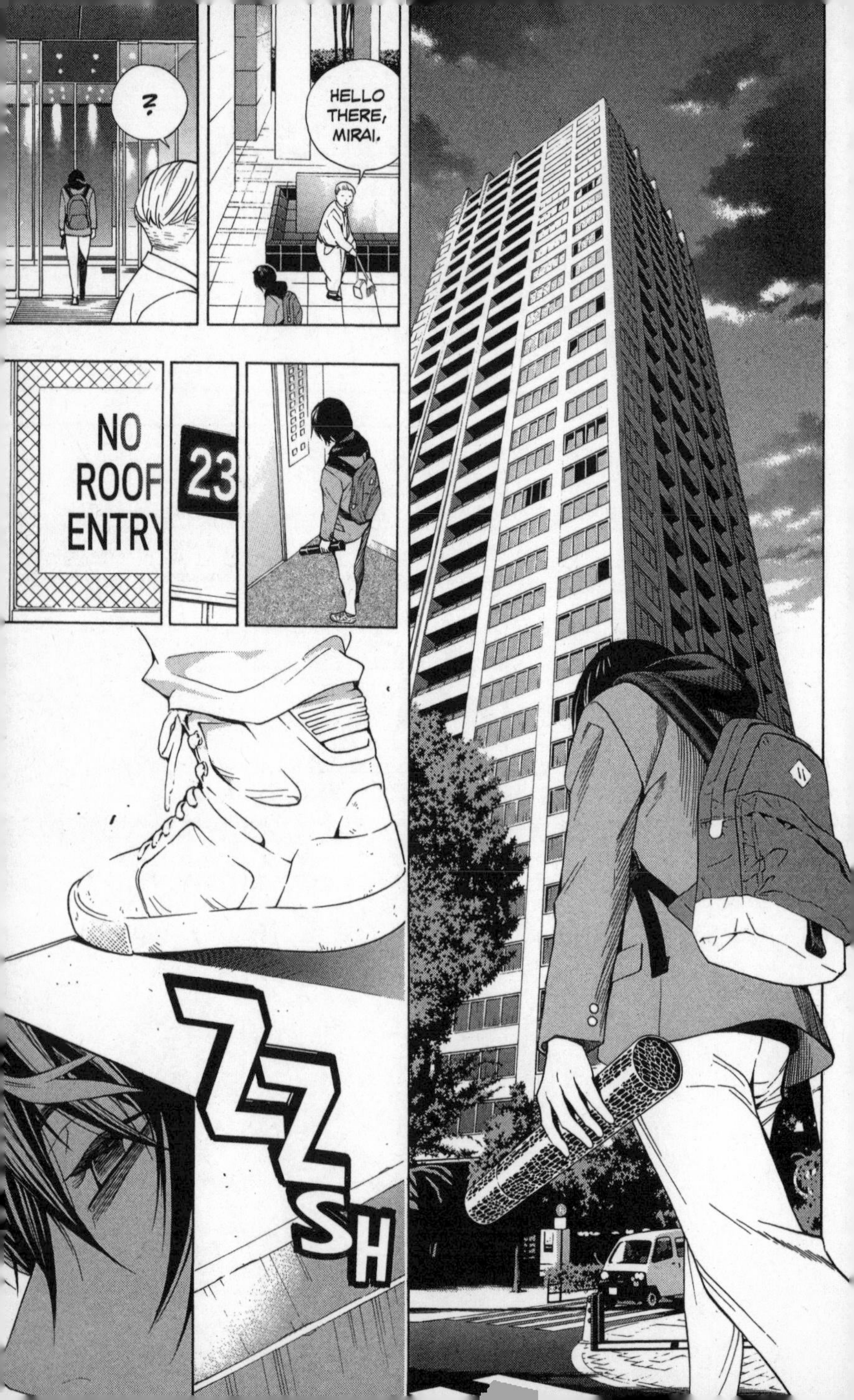
HELLO THERE, MIRAI.
?
23
NO ROOF ENTRY
ZZSH

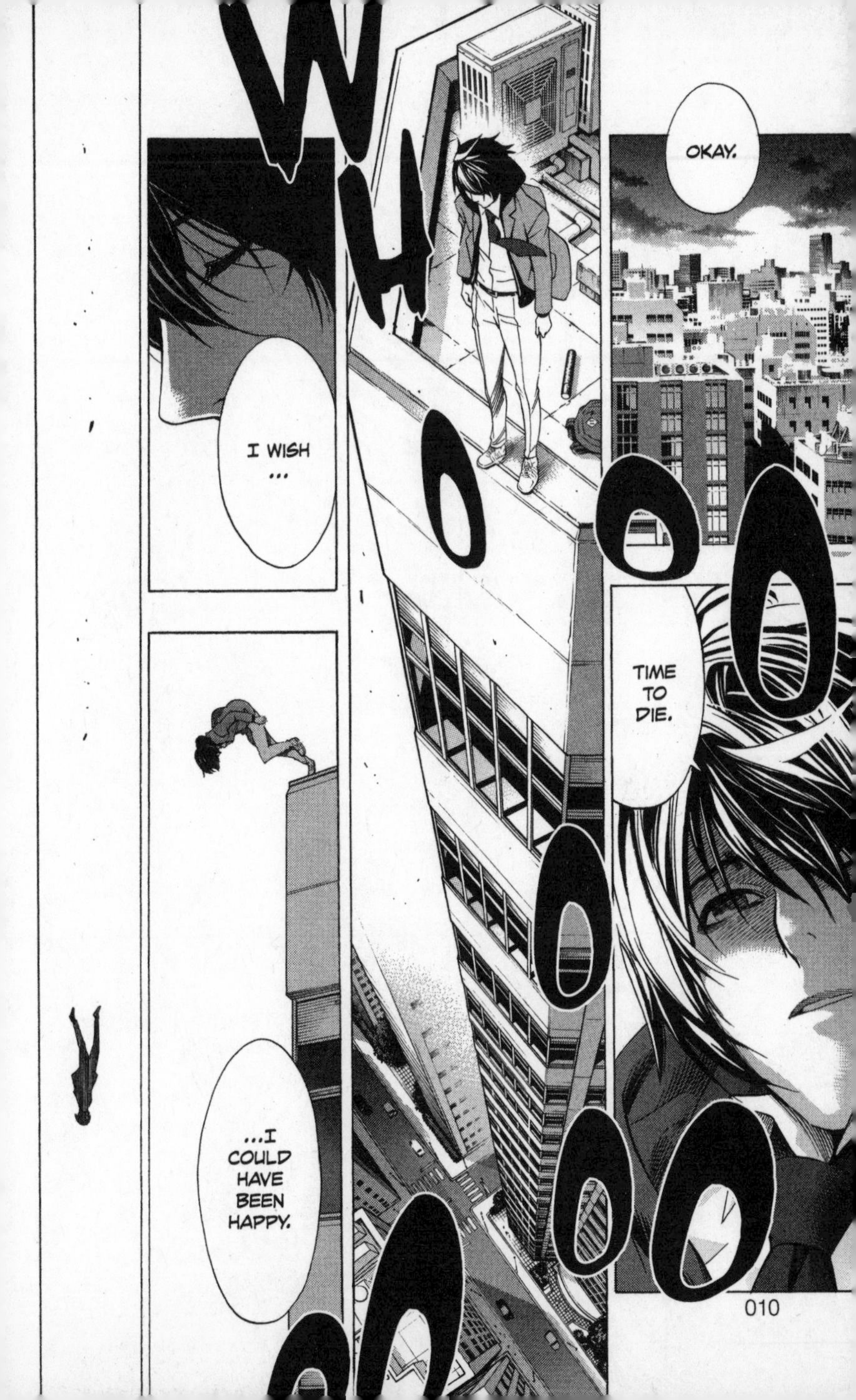
OKAY.
TIME TO DIE.
WHOOOO
I WISH ...
...I COULD HAVE BEEN HAPPY.

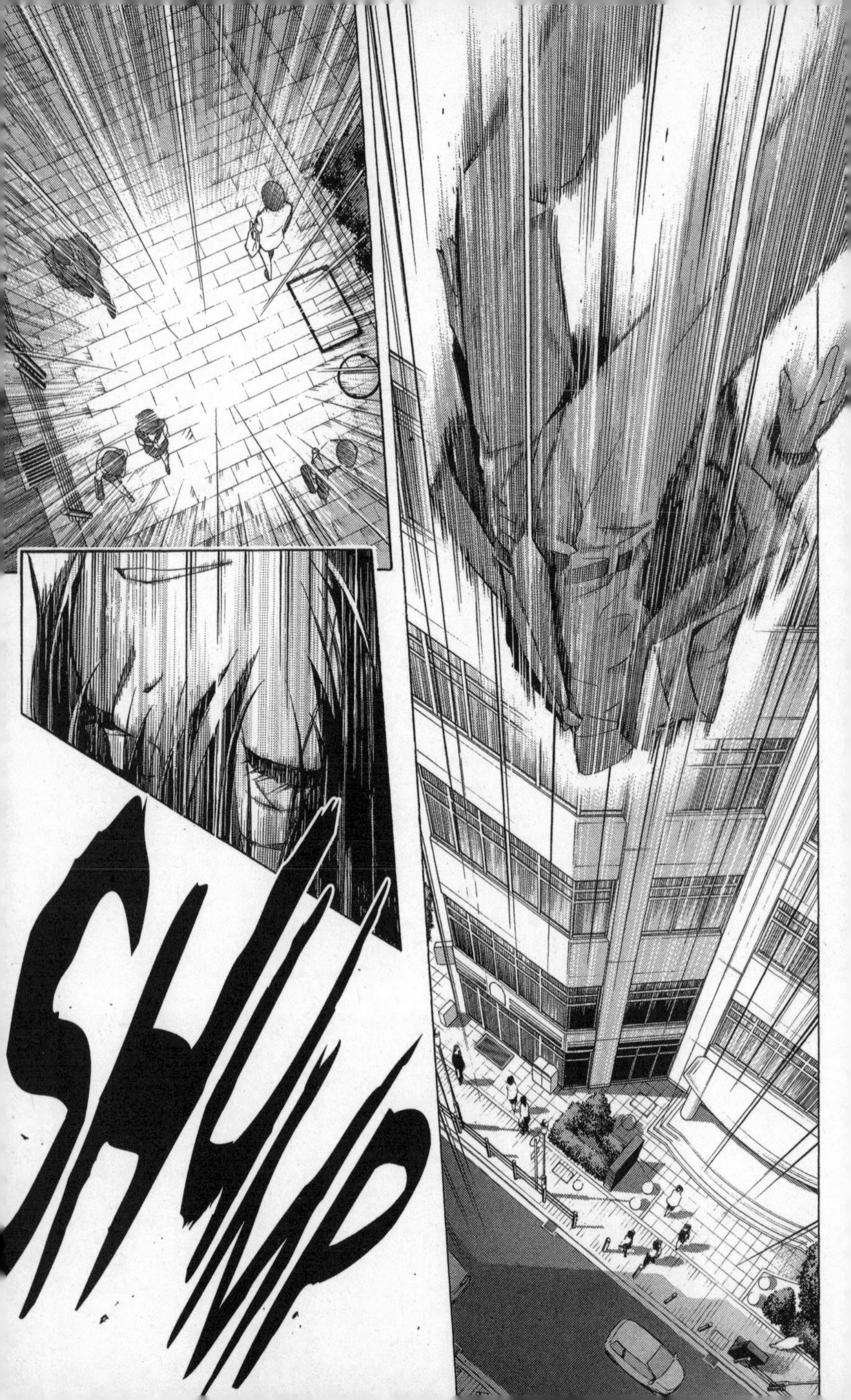
SHUP

I'M STILL ...?

...

...

CONSCIOUS ...

...

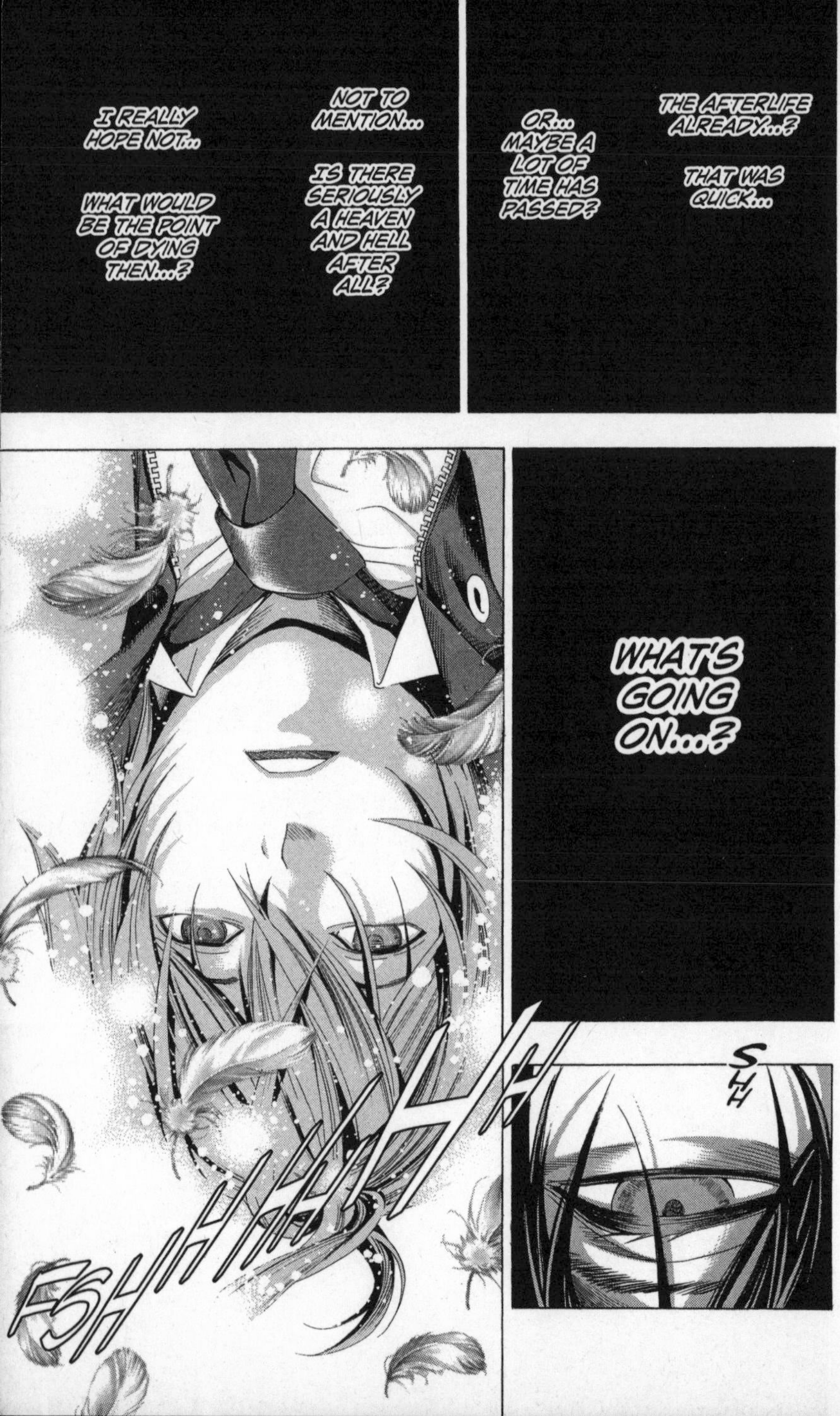
THE AFTERLIFE ALREADY...?
THAT WAS QUICK...
OR... MAYBE A LOT OF TIME HAS PASSED?
NOT TO MENTION...
IS THERE SERIOUSLY A HEAVEN AND HELL AFTER ALL?
I REALLY HOPE NOT...
WHAT WOULD BE THE POINT OF DYING THEN...?
WHAT'S GOING ON...?
SHH
FSHHHHHHHH

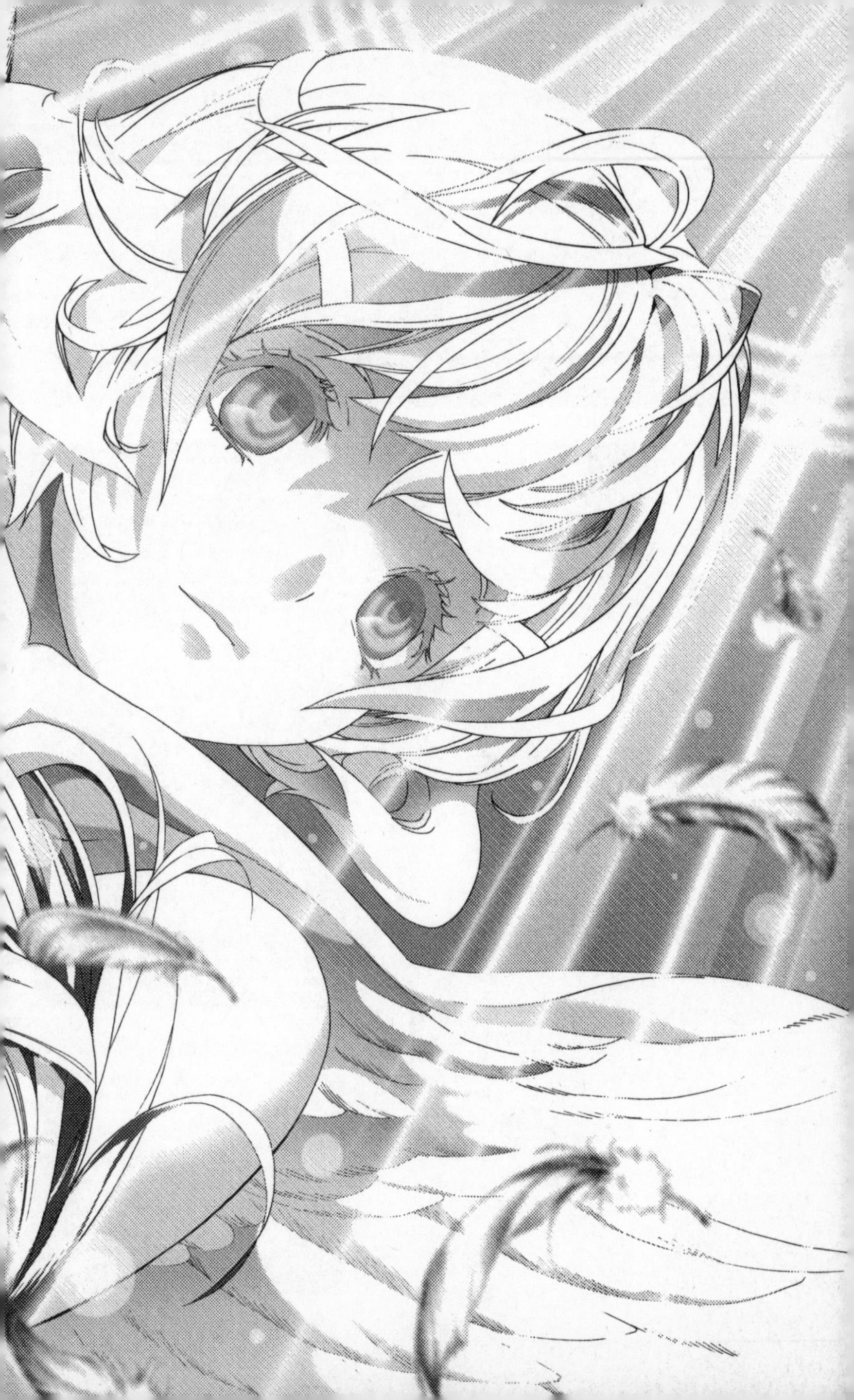

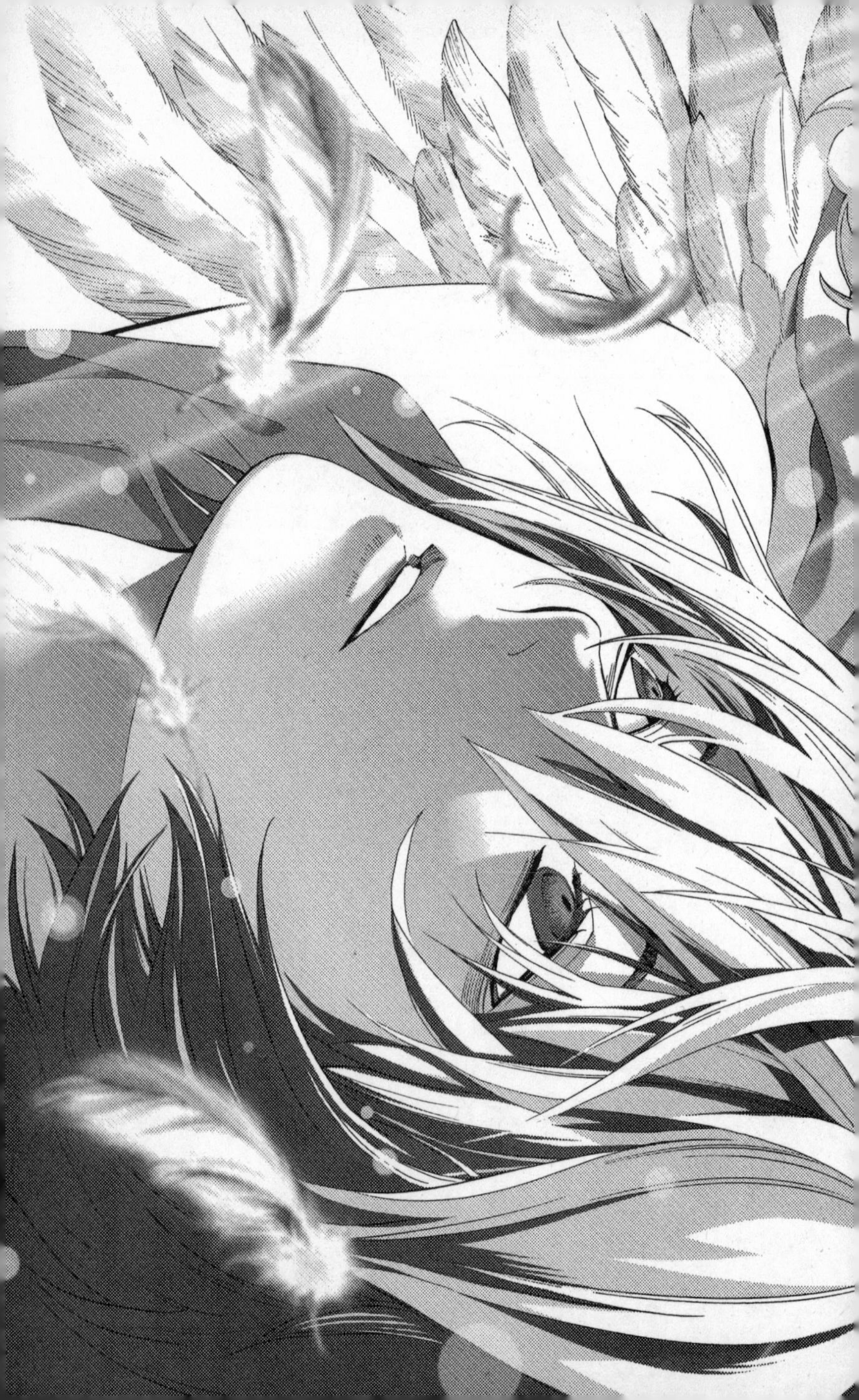

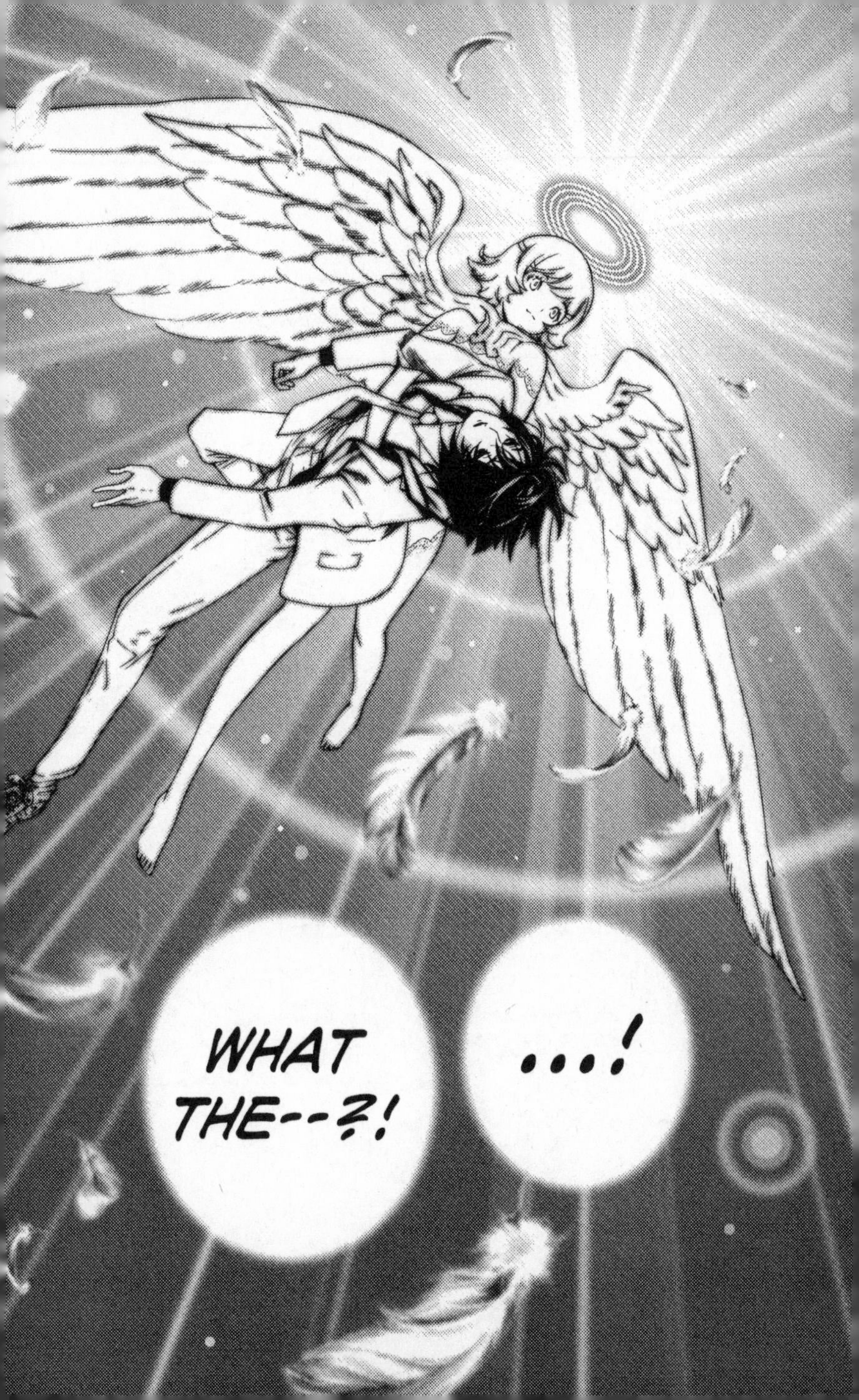
...!
WHAT THE--?!

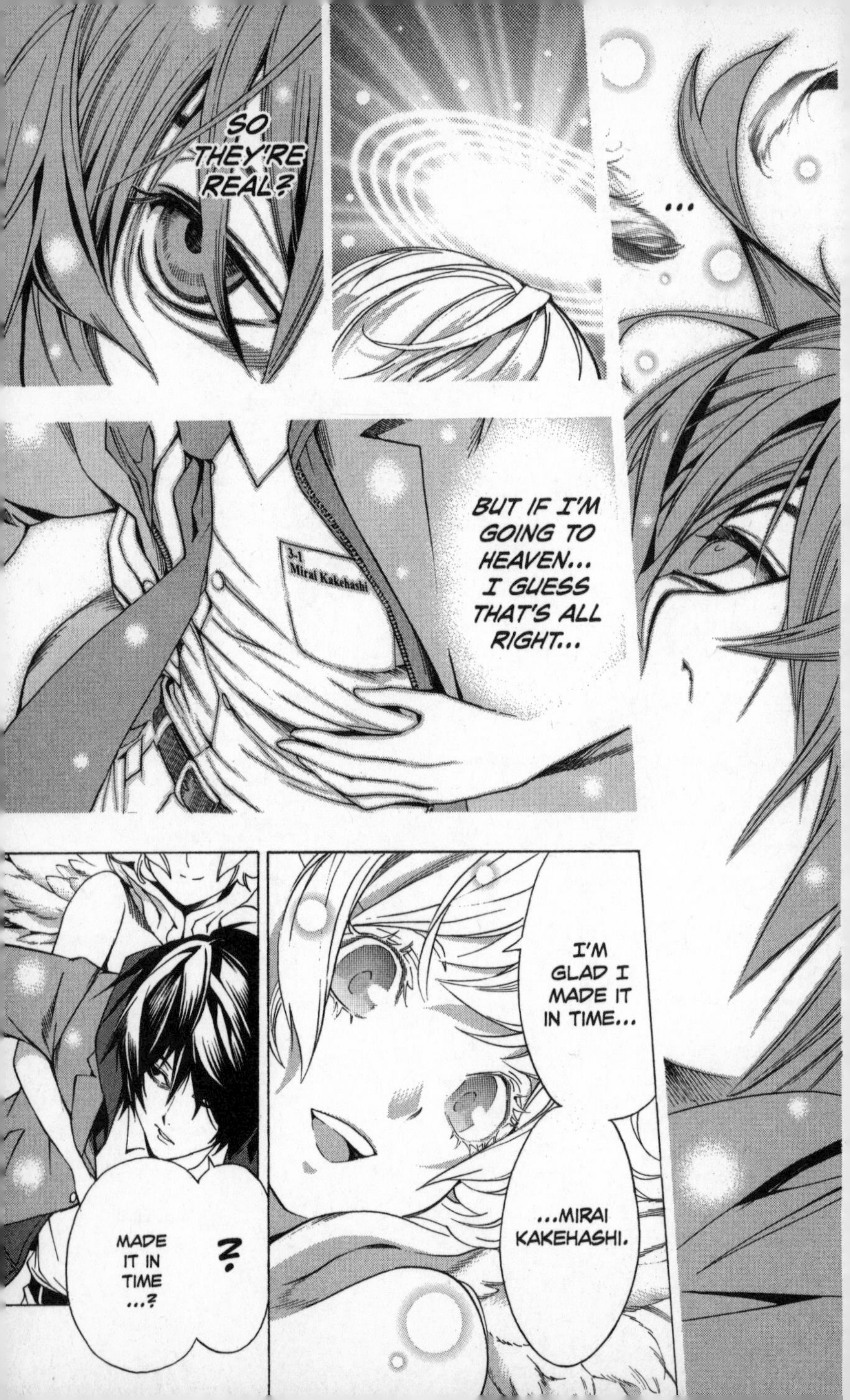
...
SO THEY'RE REAL?
BUT IF I'M GOING TO HEAVEN... I GUESS THAT'S ALL RIGHT...
3-1 Mirai Kakehashi
I'M GLAD I MADE IT IN TIME...
...MIRAI KAKEHASHI.
MADE IT IN TIME ...?

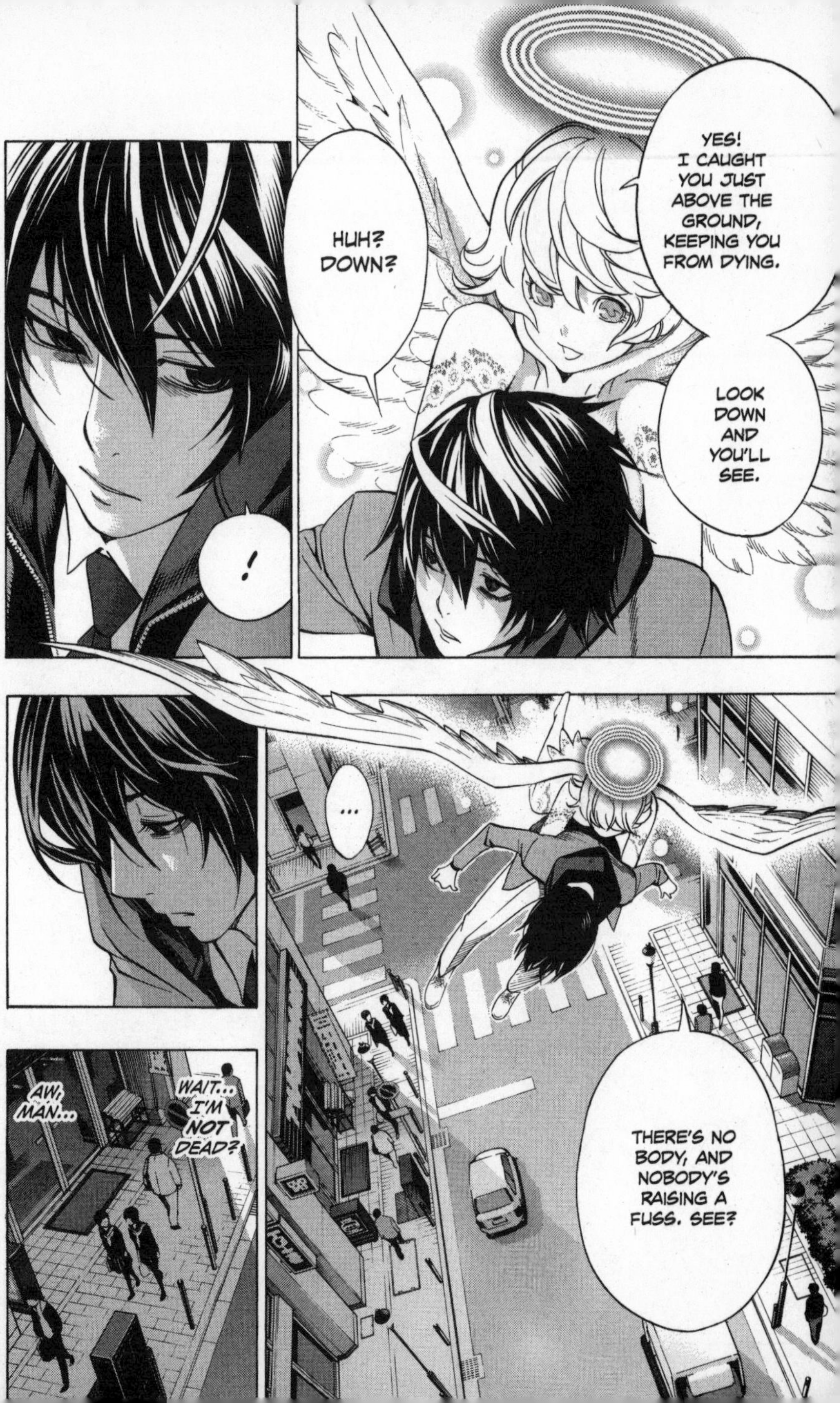
YES! I CAUGHT YOU JUST ABOVE THE GROUND, KEEPING YOU FROM DYING.
LOOK DOWN AND YOU'LL SEE.
HUH? DOWN?
!
...
THERE'S NO BODY, AND NOBODY'S RAISING A FUSS. SEE?
WAIT... I'M NOT DEAD?
AW, MAN...

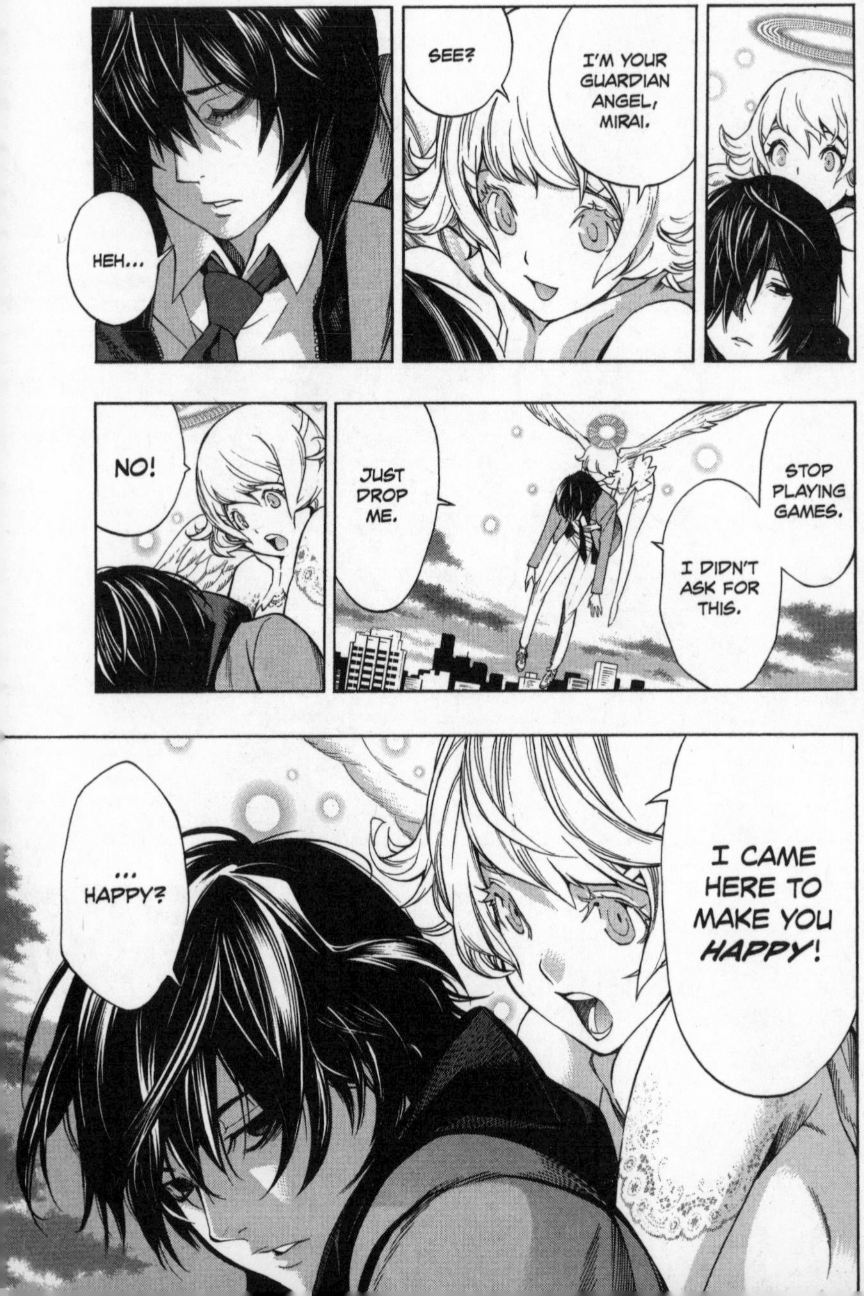
I'M YOUR GUARDIAN ANGEL, MIRAI.
SEE?
HEH...
STOP PLAYING GAMES.
I DIDN'T ASK FOR THIS.
JUST DROP ME.
NO!
I CAME HERE TO MAKE YOU *HAPPY*!
... HAPPY?

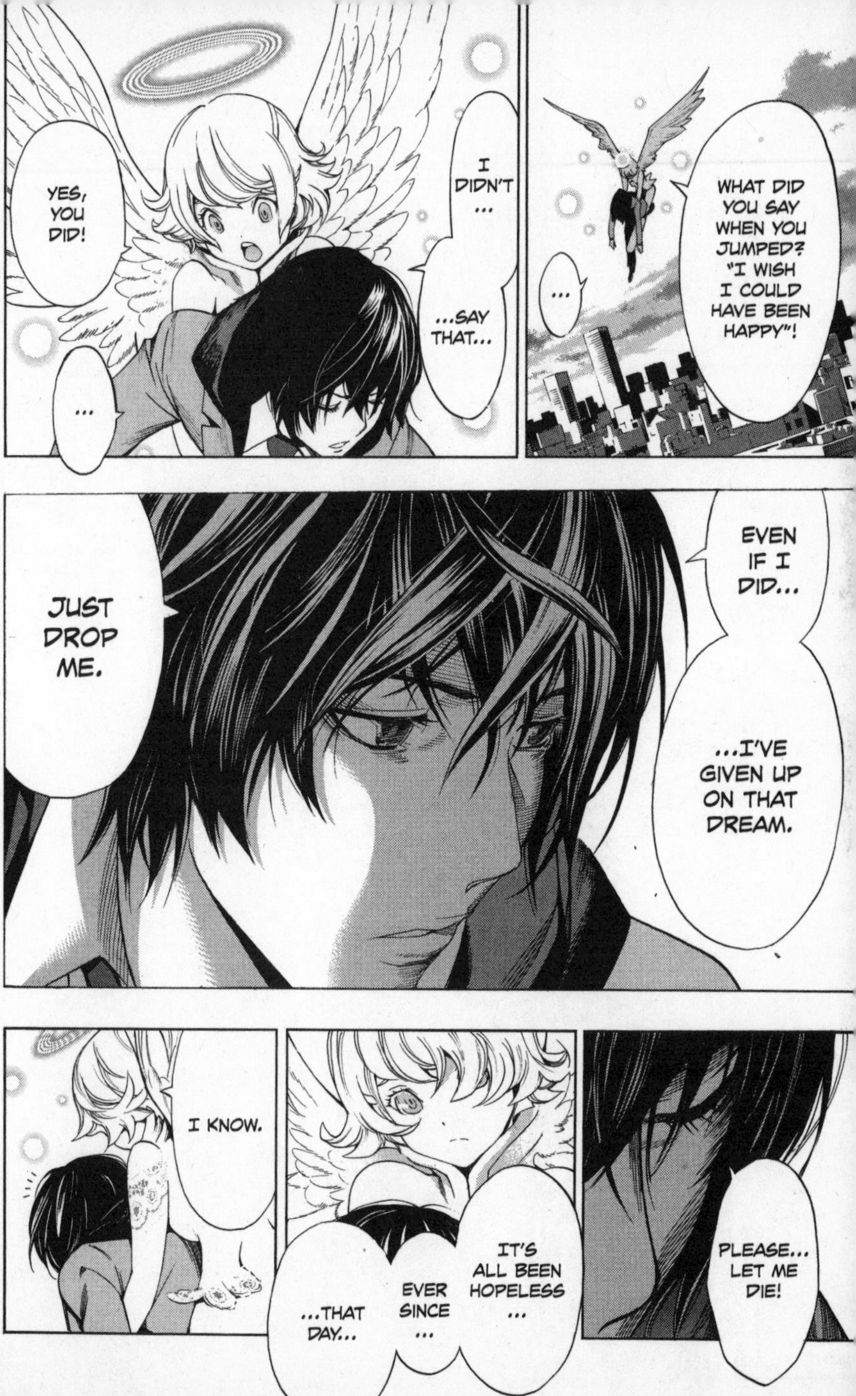
WHAT DID YOU SAY WHEN YOU JUMPED? "I WISH I COULD HAVE BEEN HAPPY"!
...
I DIDN'T ...
...SAY THAT...
YES, YOU DID!
...
EVEN IF I DID...
...I'VE GIVEN UP ON THAT DREAM.
JUST DROP ME.
PLEASE... LET ME DIE!
IT'S ALL BEEN HOPELESS ...
EVER SINCE ...
...THAT DAY...
I KNOW.

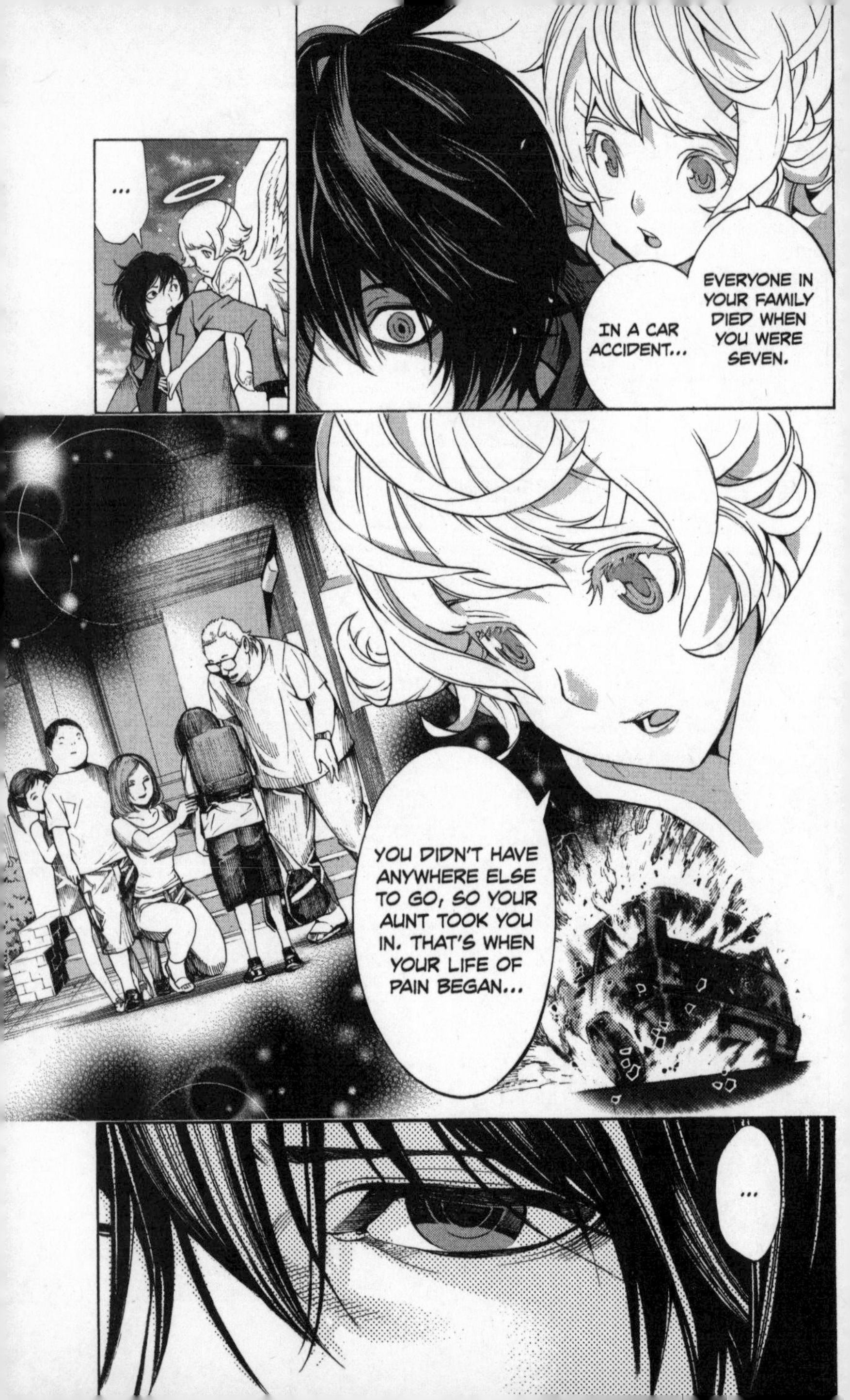
EVERYONE IN YOUR FAMILY DIED WHEN YOU WERE SEVEN.
IN A CAR ACCIDENT...
...
YOU DIDN'T HAVE ANYWHERE ELSE TO GO, SO YOUR AUNT TOOK YOU IN. THAT'S WHEN YOUR LIFE OF PAIN BEGAN...
...

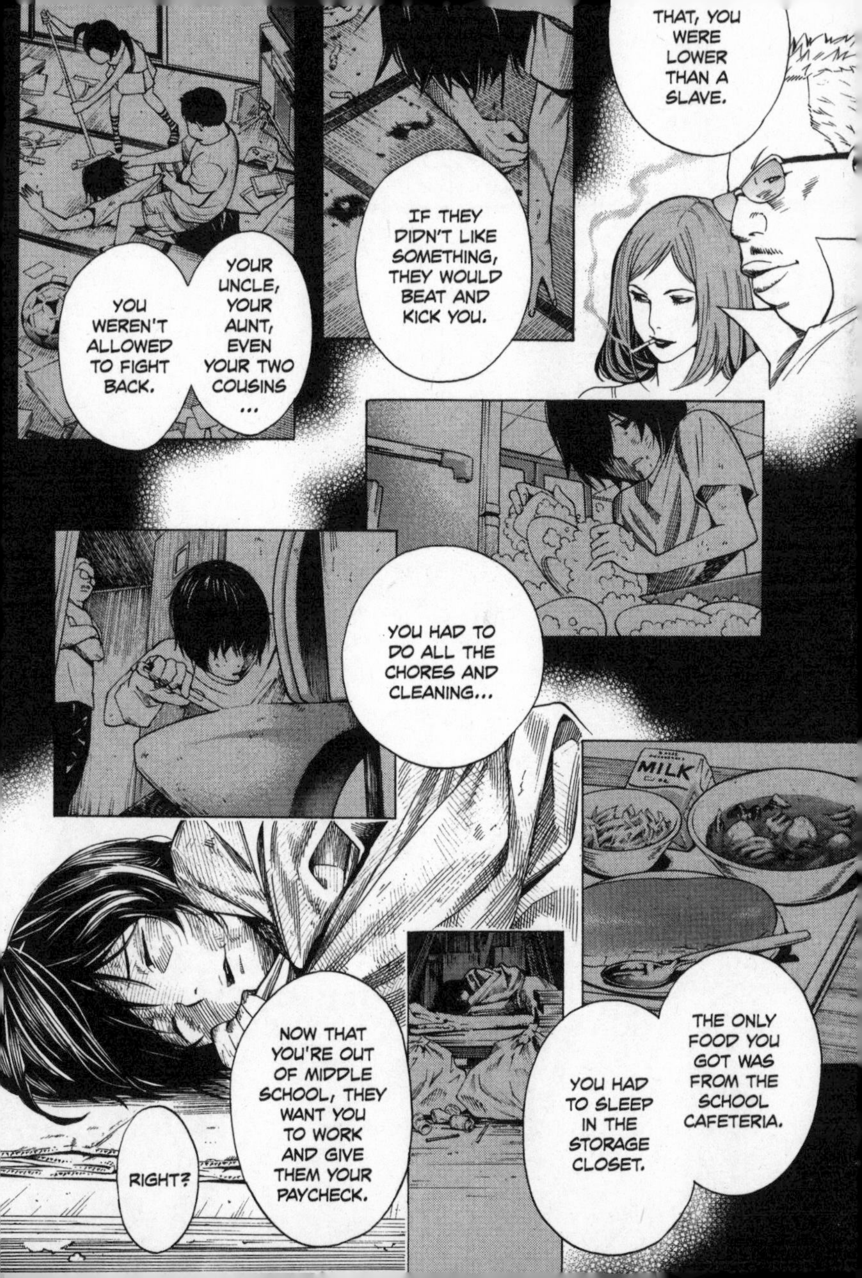
THAT, YOU WERE LOWER THAN A SLAVE.
IF THEY DIDN'T LIKE SOMETHING, THEY WOULD BEAT AND KICK YOU.
YOUR UNCLE, YOUR AUNT, EVEN YOUR TWO COUSINS...
YOU WEREN'T ALLOWED TO FIGHT BACK.
YOU HAD TO DO ALL THE CHORES AND CLEANING...
MILK
THE ONLY FOOD YOU GOT WAS FROM THE SCHOOL CAFETERIA.
YOU HAD TO SLEEP IN THE STORAGE CLOSET.
NOW THAT YOU'RE OUT OF MIDDLE SCHOOL, THEY WANT YOU TO WORK AND GIVE THEM YOUR PAYCHECK.
RIGHT?

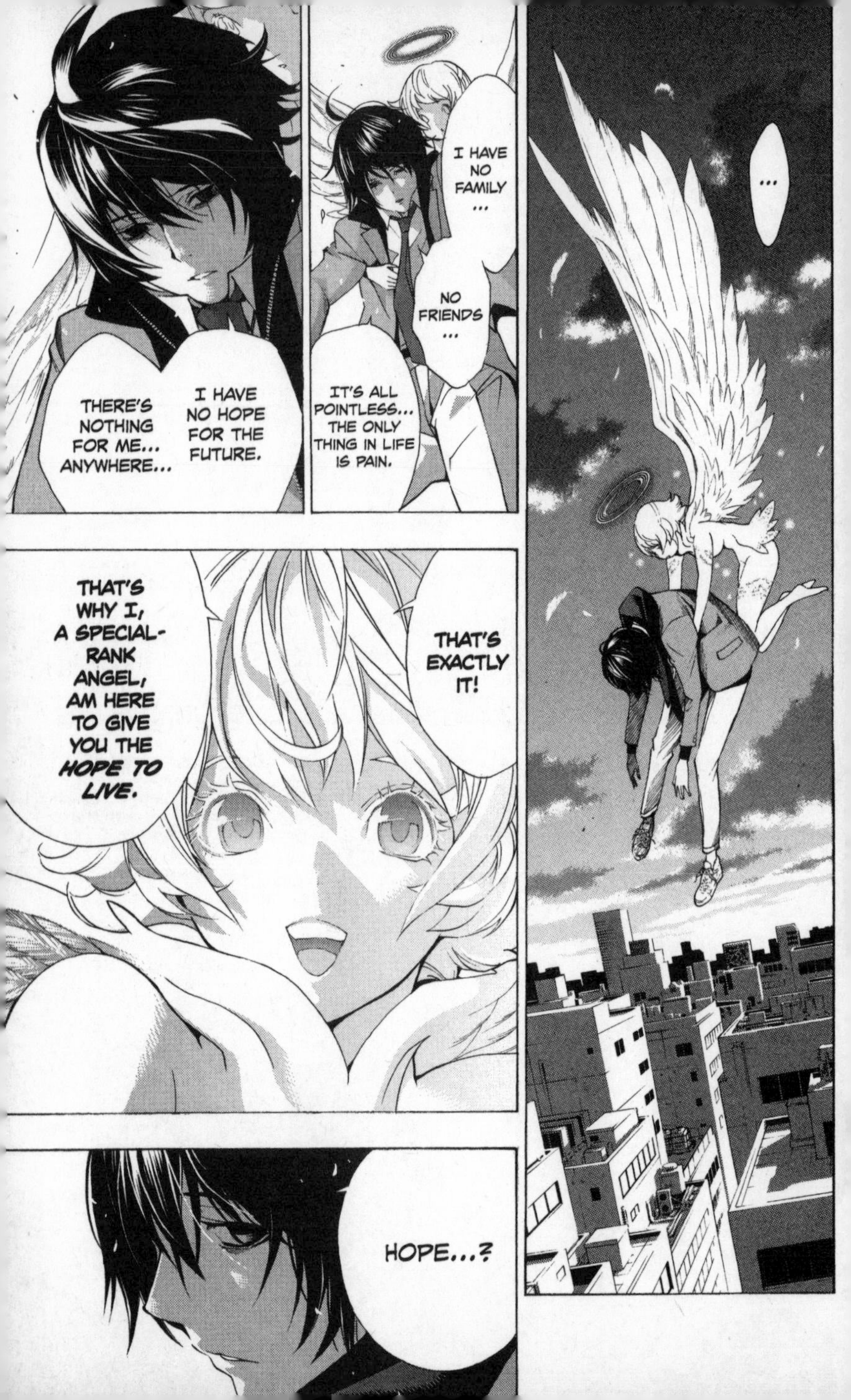
...
I HAVE NO FAMILY ...
NO FRIENDS ...
IT'S ALL POINTLESS... THE ONLY THING IN LIFE IS PAIN.
I HAVE NO HOPE FOR THE FUTURE.
THERE'S NOTHING FOR ME... ANYWHERE...
THAT'S EXACTLY IT!
THAT'S WHY I, A SPECIAL-RANK ANGEL, AM HERE TO GIVE YOU THE *HOPE TO LIVE*.
HOPE...?

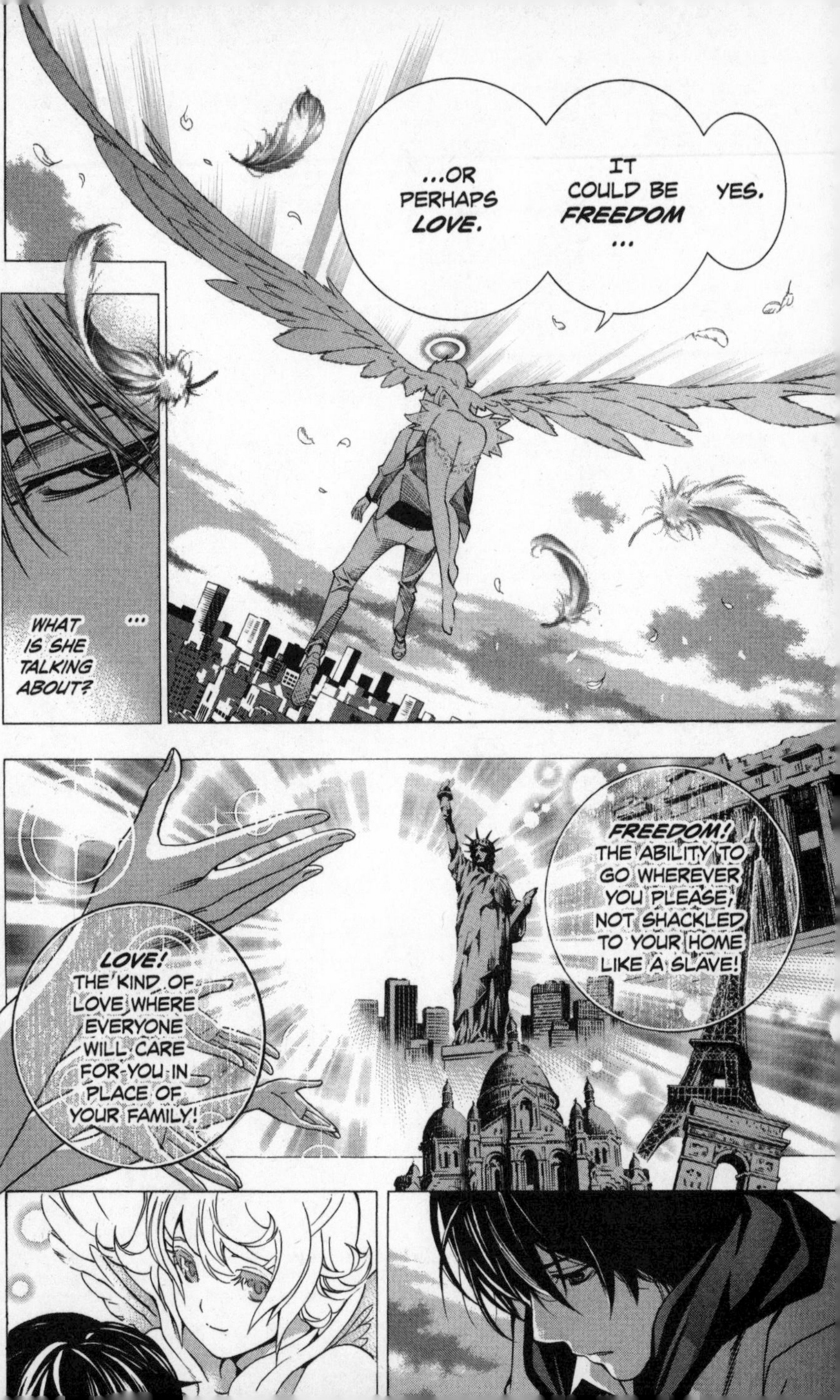
YES.
IT COULD BE FREEDOM...
...OR PERHAPS LOVE.
...
WHAT IS SHE TALKING ABOUT?
FREEDOM! THE ABILITY TO GO WHEREVER YOU PLEASE, NOT SHACKLED TO YOUR HOME LIKE A SLAVE!
LOVE! THE KIND OF LOVE WHERE EVERYONE WILL CARE FOR YOU IN PLACE OF YOUR FAMILY!

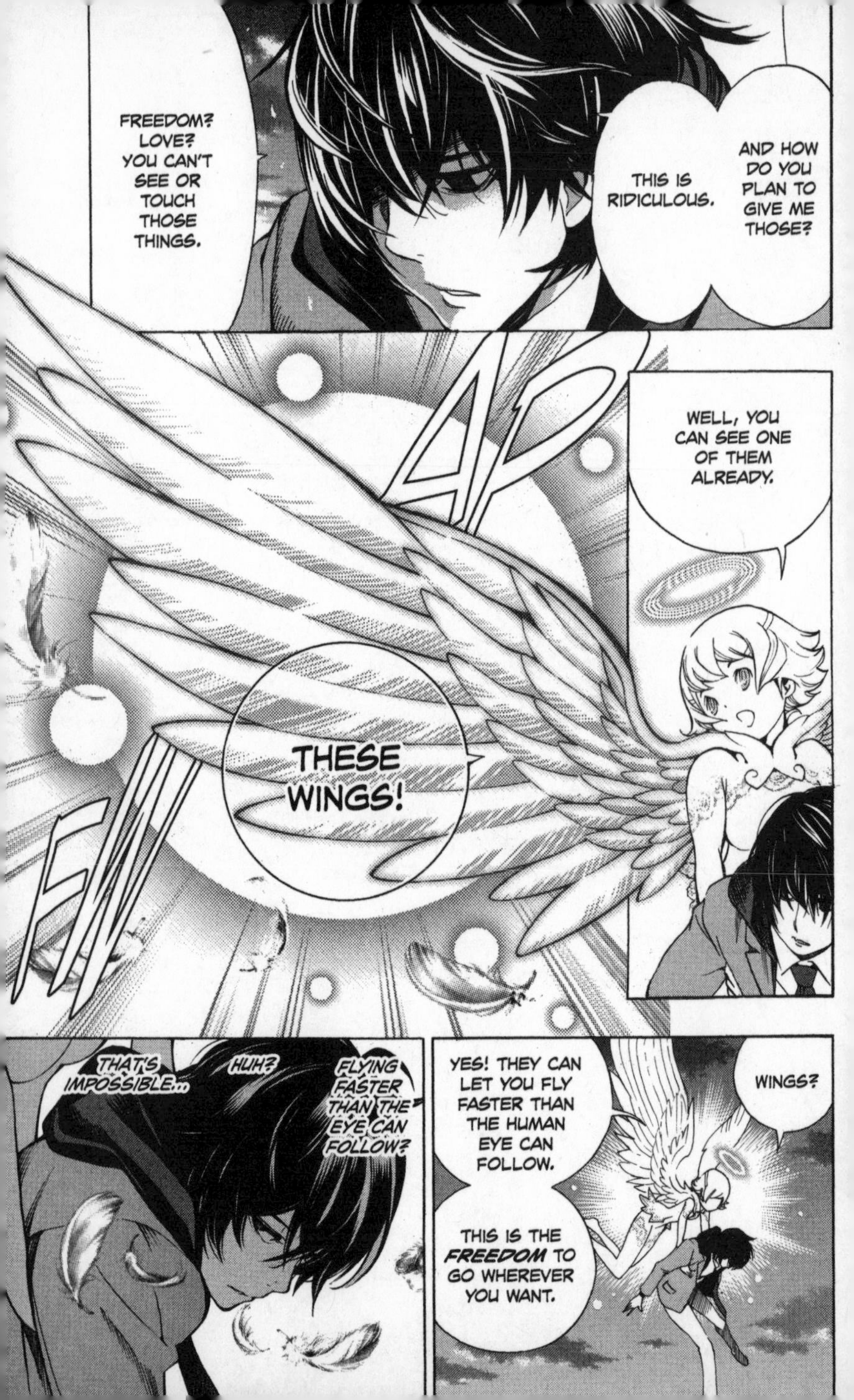
AND HOW DO YOU PLAN TO GIVE ME THOSE?
THIS IS RIDICULOUS.
FREEDOM? LOVE? YOU CAN'T SEE OR TOUCH THOSE THINGS.
WELL, YOU CAN SEE ONE OF THEM ALREADY.
THESE WINGS!
WINGS?
YES! THEY CAN LET YOU FLY FASTER THAN THE HUMAN EYE CAN FOLLOW.
THIS IS THE *FREEDOM* TO GO WHEREVER YOU WANT.
FLYING FASTER THAN THE EYE CAN FOLLOW?
HUH?
THAT'S IMPOSSIBLE...

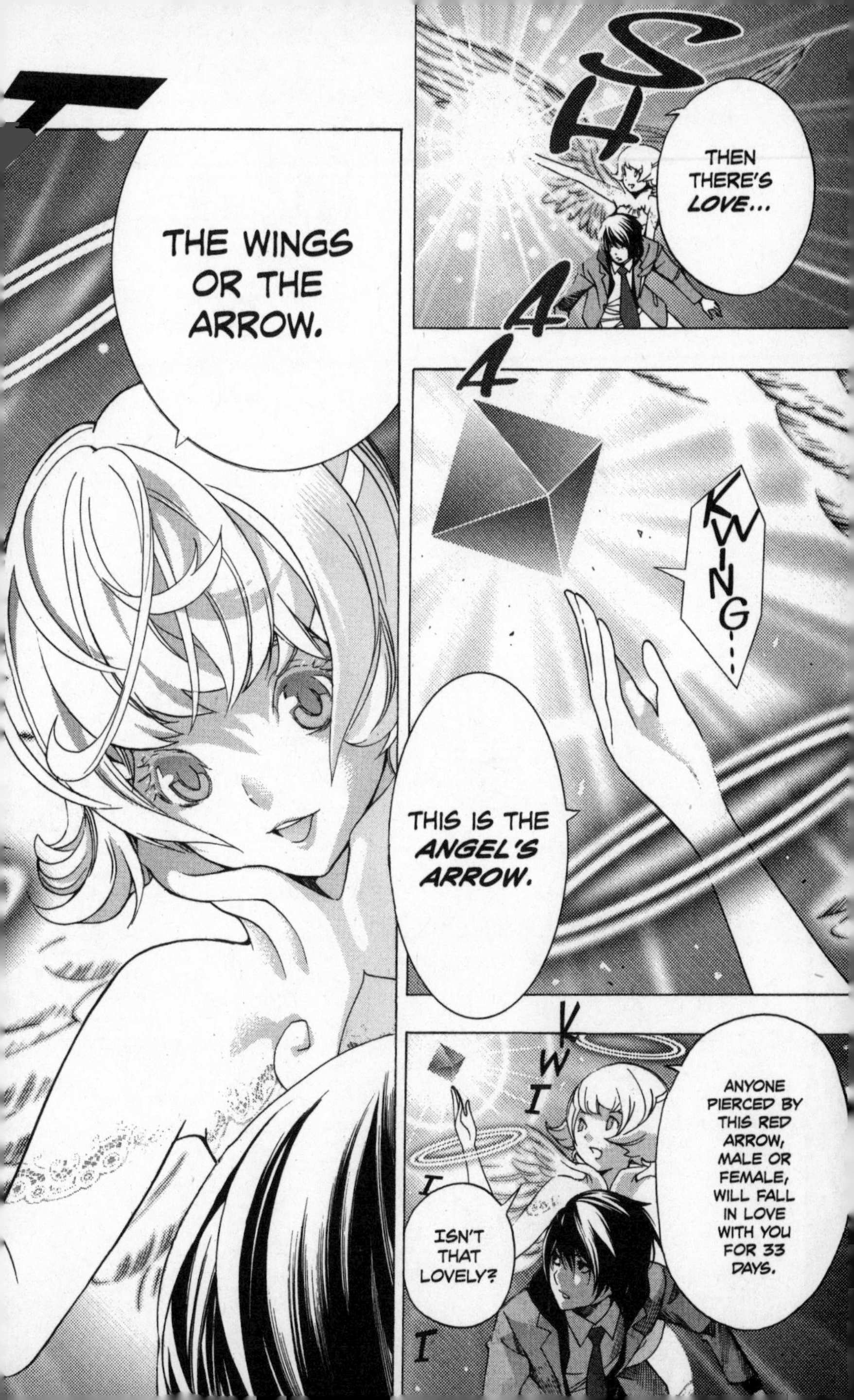

THEN THERE'S *LOVE*...
SHAA
KWING...
THIS IS THE *ANGEL'S ARROW*.
ANYONE PIERCED BY THIS RED ARROW, MALE OR FEMALE, WILL FALL IN LOVE WITH YOU FOR 33 DAYS.
KWIII
ISN'T THAT LOVELY?
THE WINGS OR THE ARROW.

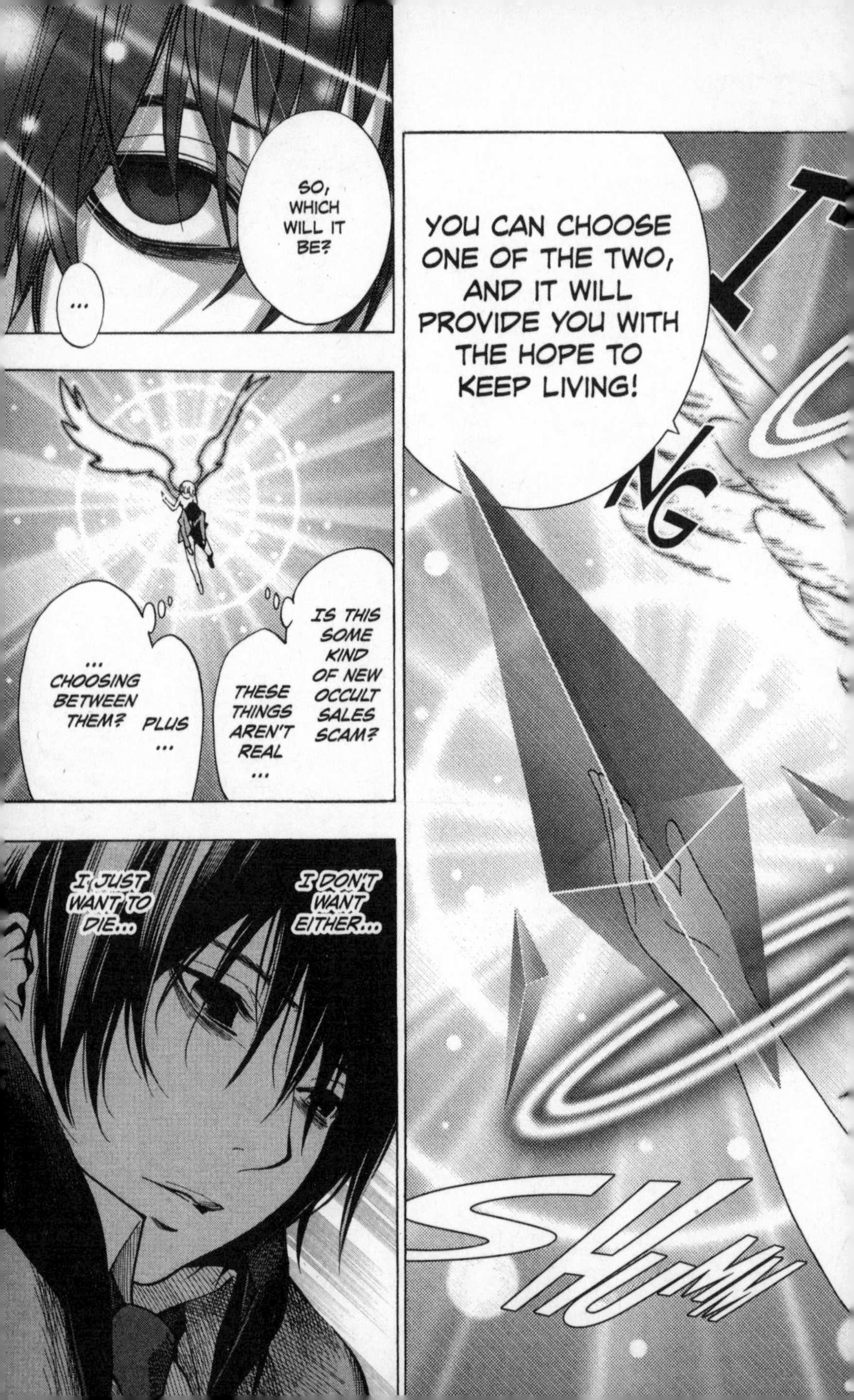
YOU CAN CHOOSE ONE OF THE TWO, AND IT WILL PROVIDE YOU WITH THE HOPE TO KEEP LIVING!
SHUMM
SO, WHICH WILL IT BE?
...
IS THIS SOME KIND OF NEW OCCULT SALES SCAM?
THESE THINGS AREN'T REAL ...
PLUS ...
... CHOOSING BETWEEN THEM?
I DON'T WANT EITHER...
I JUST WANT TO DIE...

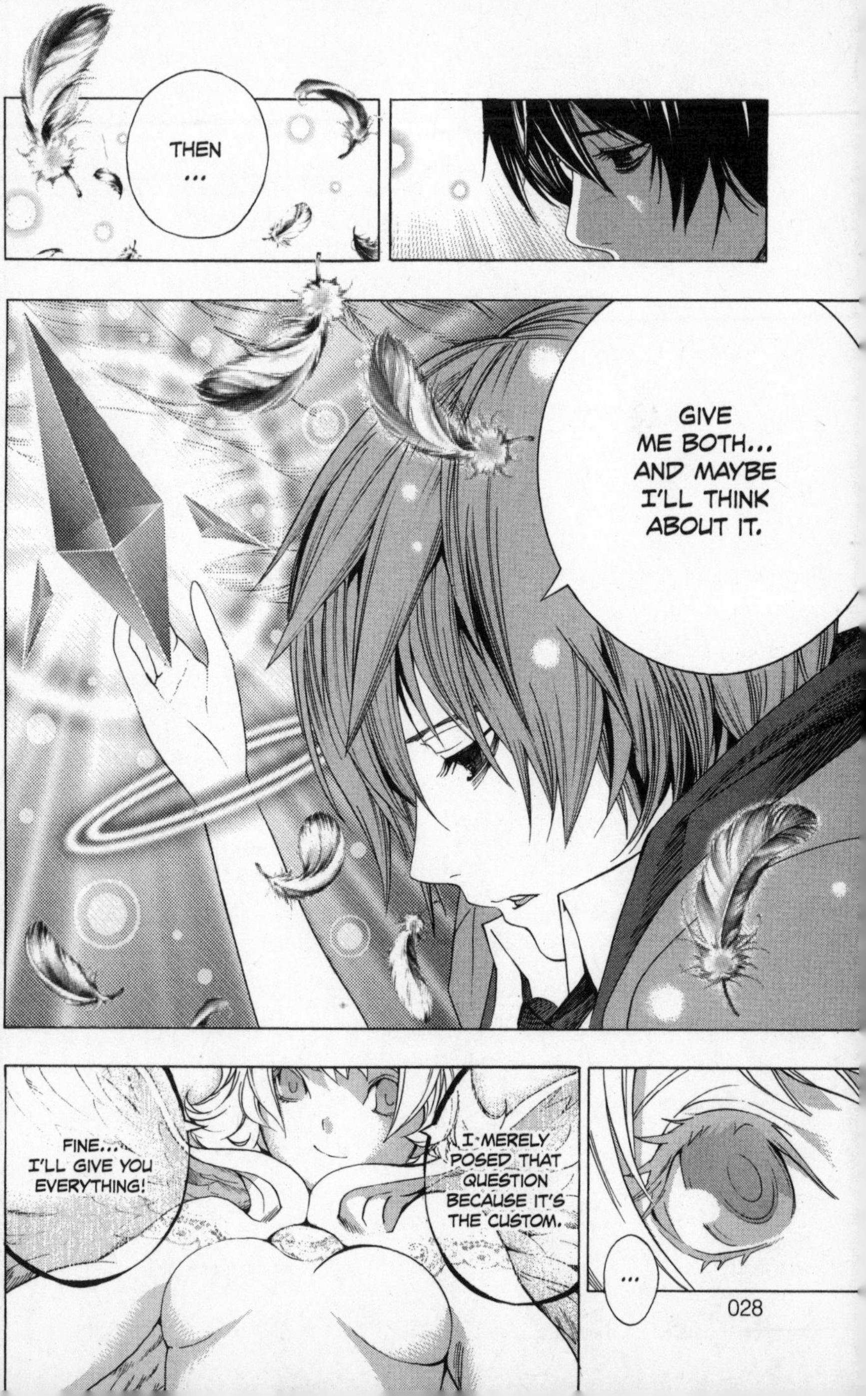
THEN ...
GIVE ME BOTH... AND MAYBE I'LL THINK ABOUT IT.
...
I MERELY POSED THAT QUESTION BECAUSE IT'S THE CUSTOM.
FINE... I'LL GIVE YOU EVERYTHING!

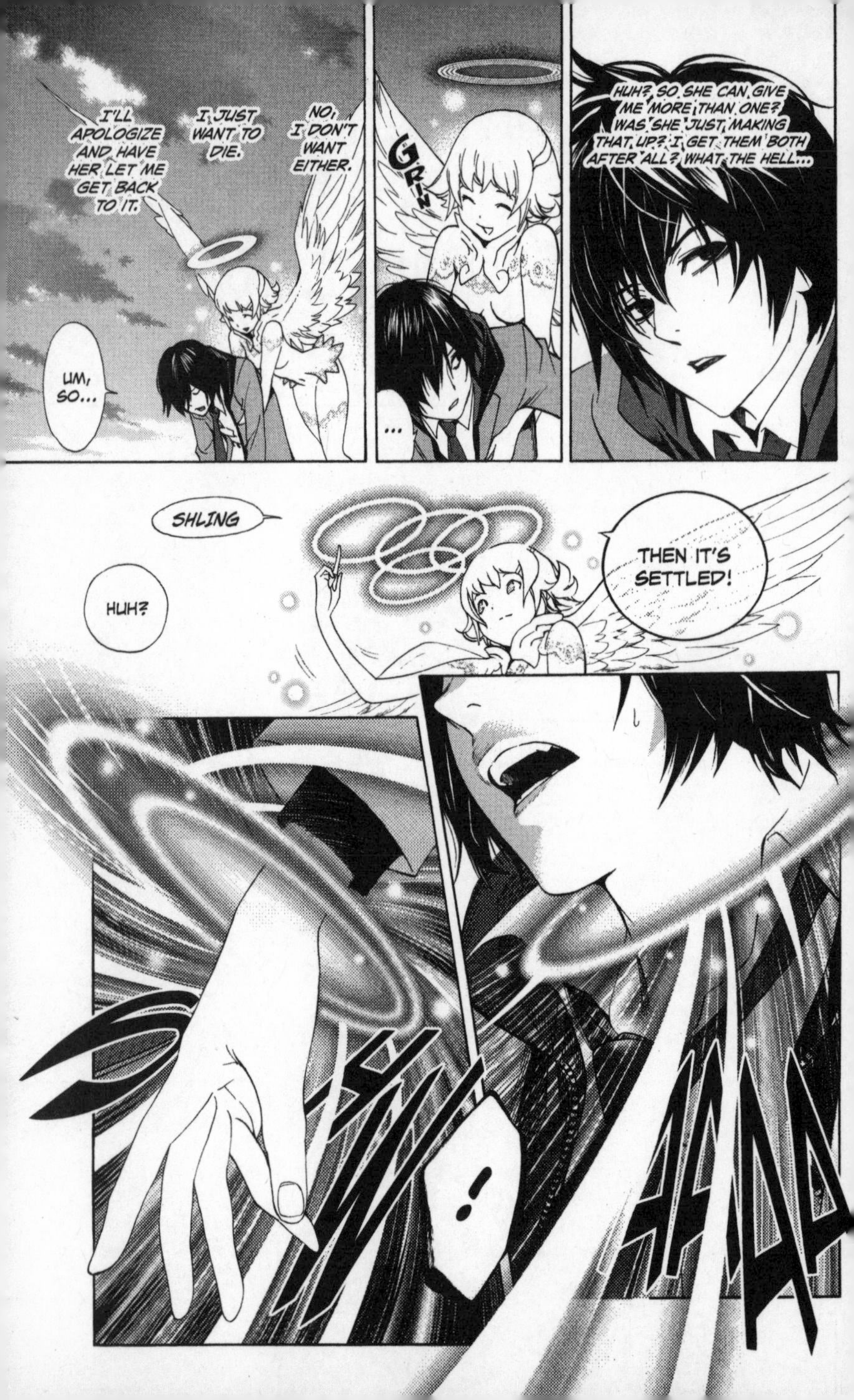
HUH? SO SHE CAN GIVE ME MORE THAN ONE? WAS SHE JUST MAKING THAT UP? I GET THEM BOTH AFTER ALL? WHAT THE HELL...
GRIN
...
NO, I DON'T WANT EITHER.
I JUST WANT TO DIE.
I'LL APOLOGIZE AND HAVE HER LET ME GET BACK TO IT.
UM, SO...
THEN IT'S SETTLED!
SHLING
HUH?
!

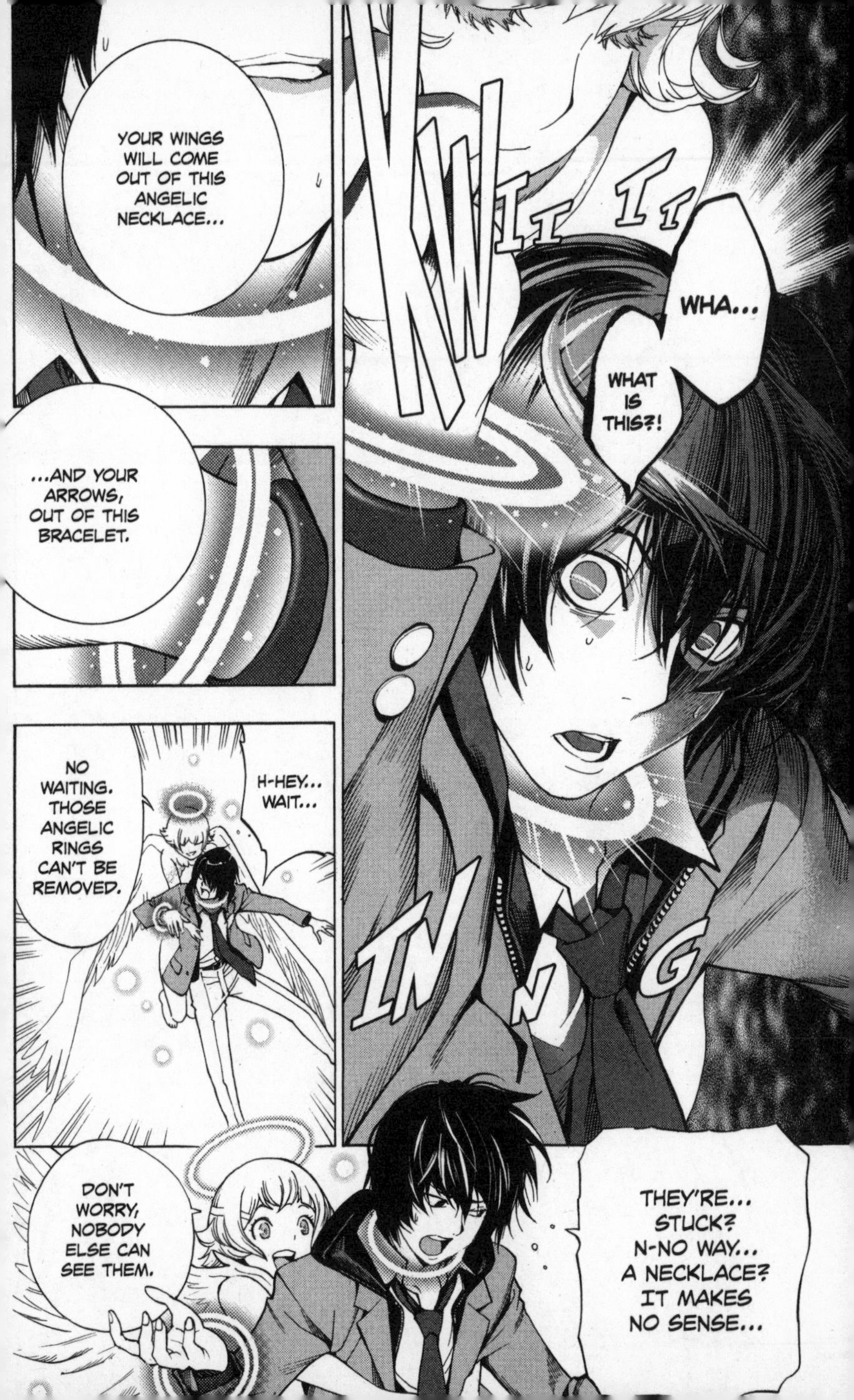
WHA...
WHAT IS THIS?!
INNG
YOUR WINGS WILL COME OUT OF THIS ANGELIC NECKLACE...
...AND YOUR ARROWS, OUT OF THIS BRACELET.
H-HEY... WAIT...
NO WAITING. THOSE ANGELIC RINGS CAN'T BE REMOVED.
THEY'RE... STUCK? N-NO WAY... A NECKLACE? IT MAKES NO SENSE...
DON'T WORRY, NOBODY ELSE CAN SEE THEM.

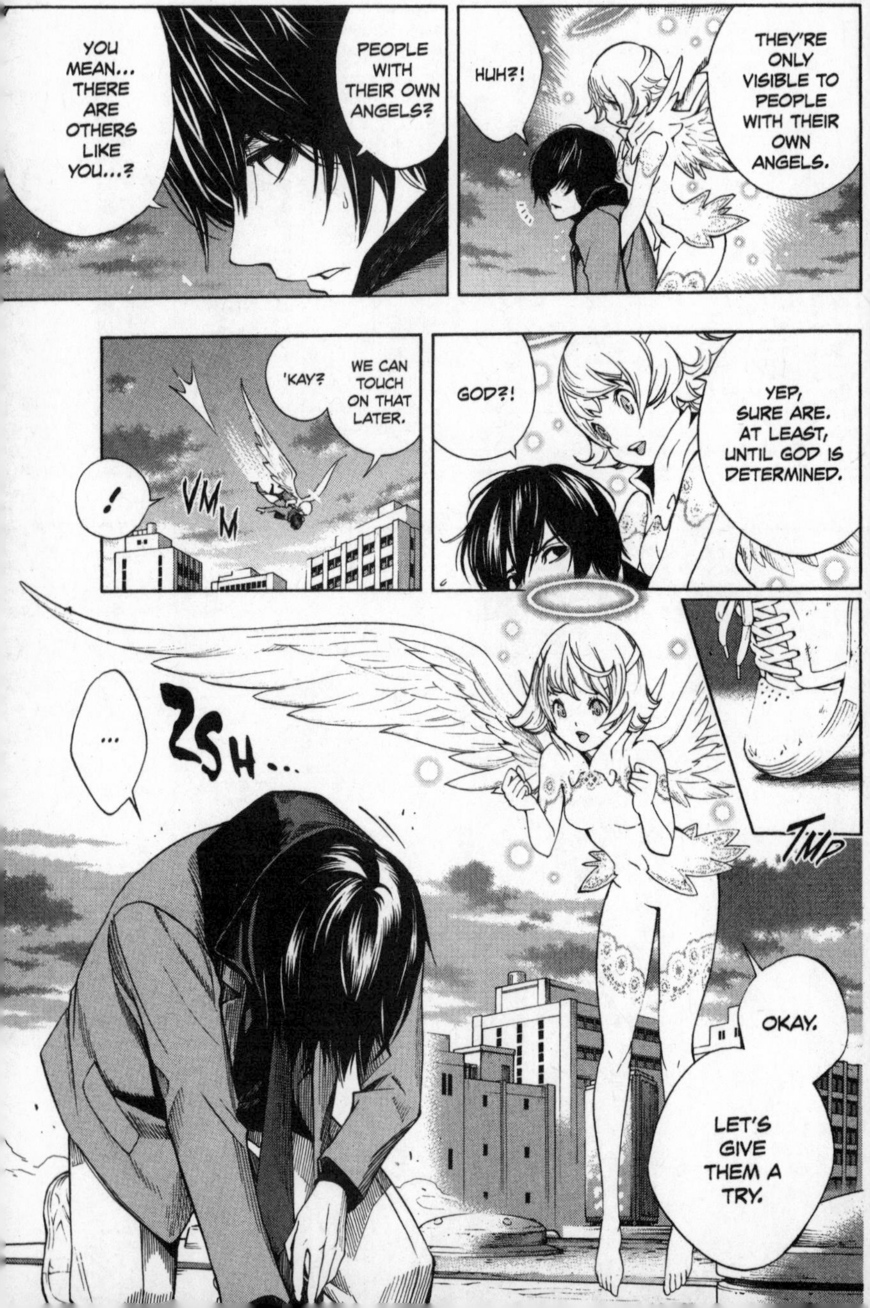
THEY'RE ONLY VISIBLE TO PEOPLE WITH THEIR OWN ANGELS.
HUH?!
PEOPLE WITH THEIR OWN ANGELS?
YOU MEAN... THERE ARE OTHERS LIKE YOU...?
YEP, SURE ARE. AT LEAST, UNTIL GOD IS DETERMINED.
GOD?!
WE CAN TOUCH ON THAT LATER.
'KAY?
VMM
!
TMP
OKAY.
LET'S GIVE THEM A TRY.
ZSH...
...

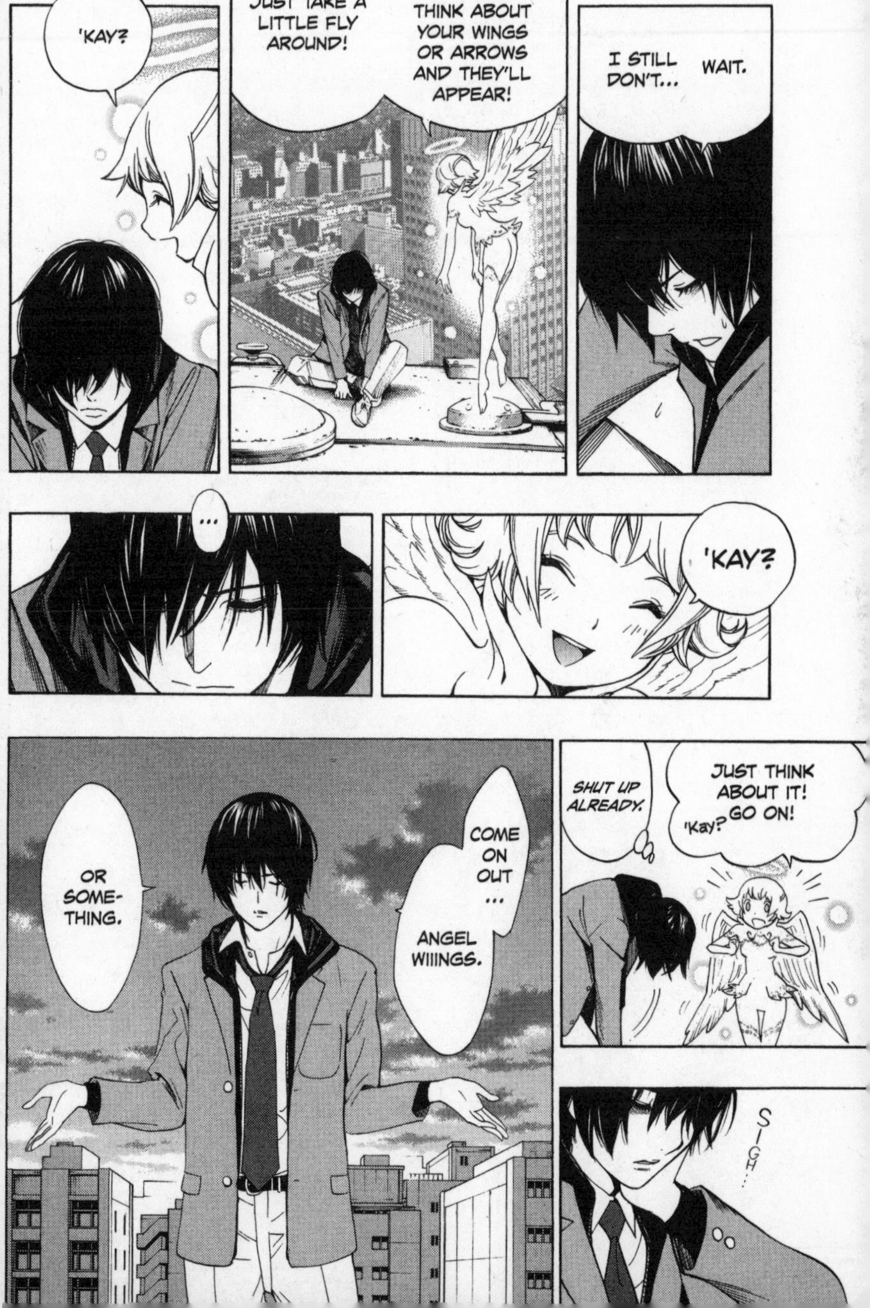
WAIT.
I STILL DON'T...
ALL YOU HAVE TO DO IS THINK ABOUT YOUR WINGS OR ARROWS AND THEY'LL APPEAR!
JUST TAKE A LITTLE FLY AROUND!
'KAY?
'KAY?
...
JUST THINK ABOUT IT! GO ON!
'Kay?
SHUT UP ALREADY.
SIGH...
COME ON OUT ... ANGEL WIIINGS.
OR SOME-THING.

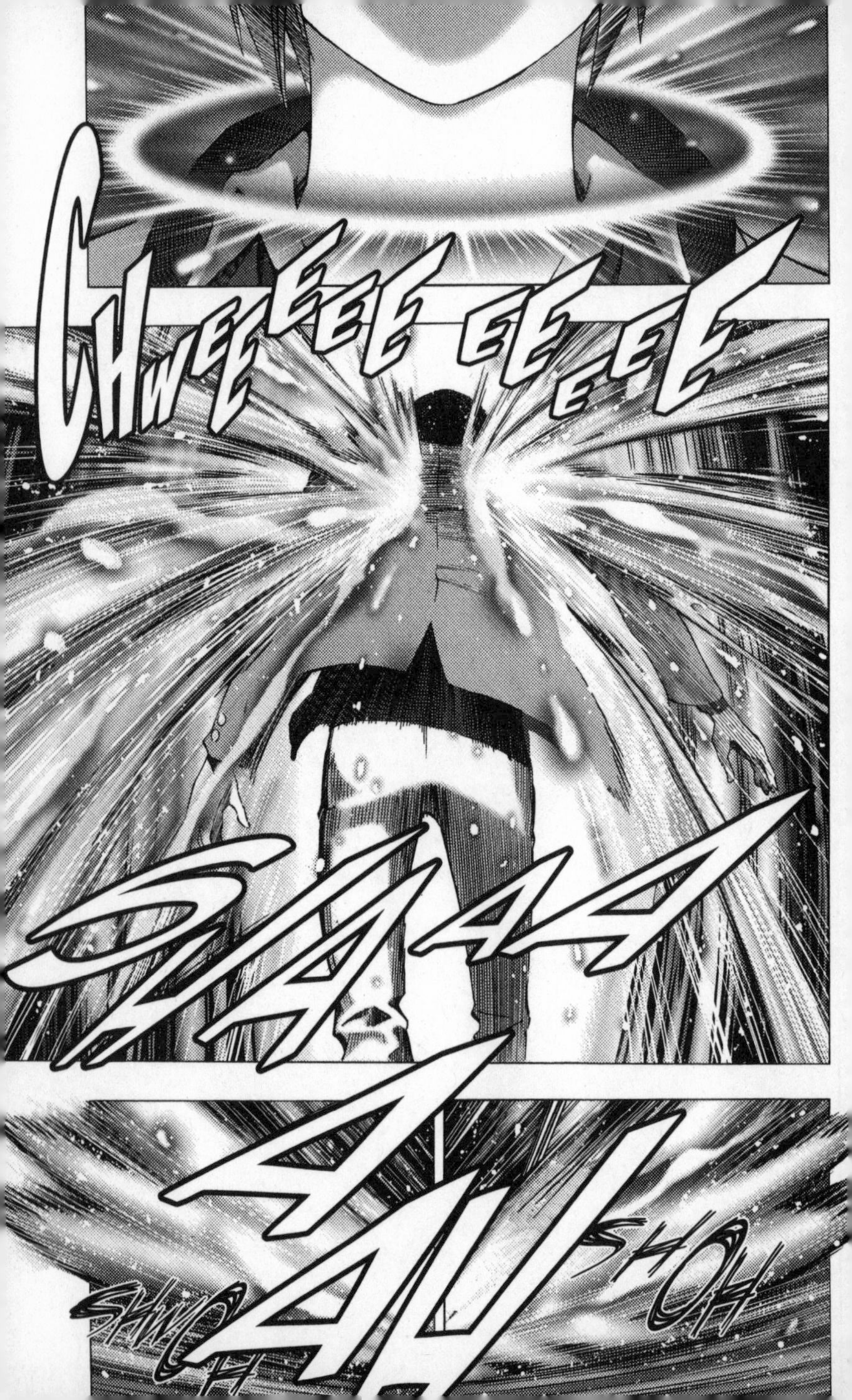
CHWEEEEE EEEEE
SHAAAAAAH
SHOOH
SHWOOH

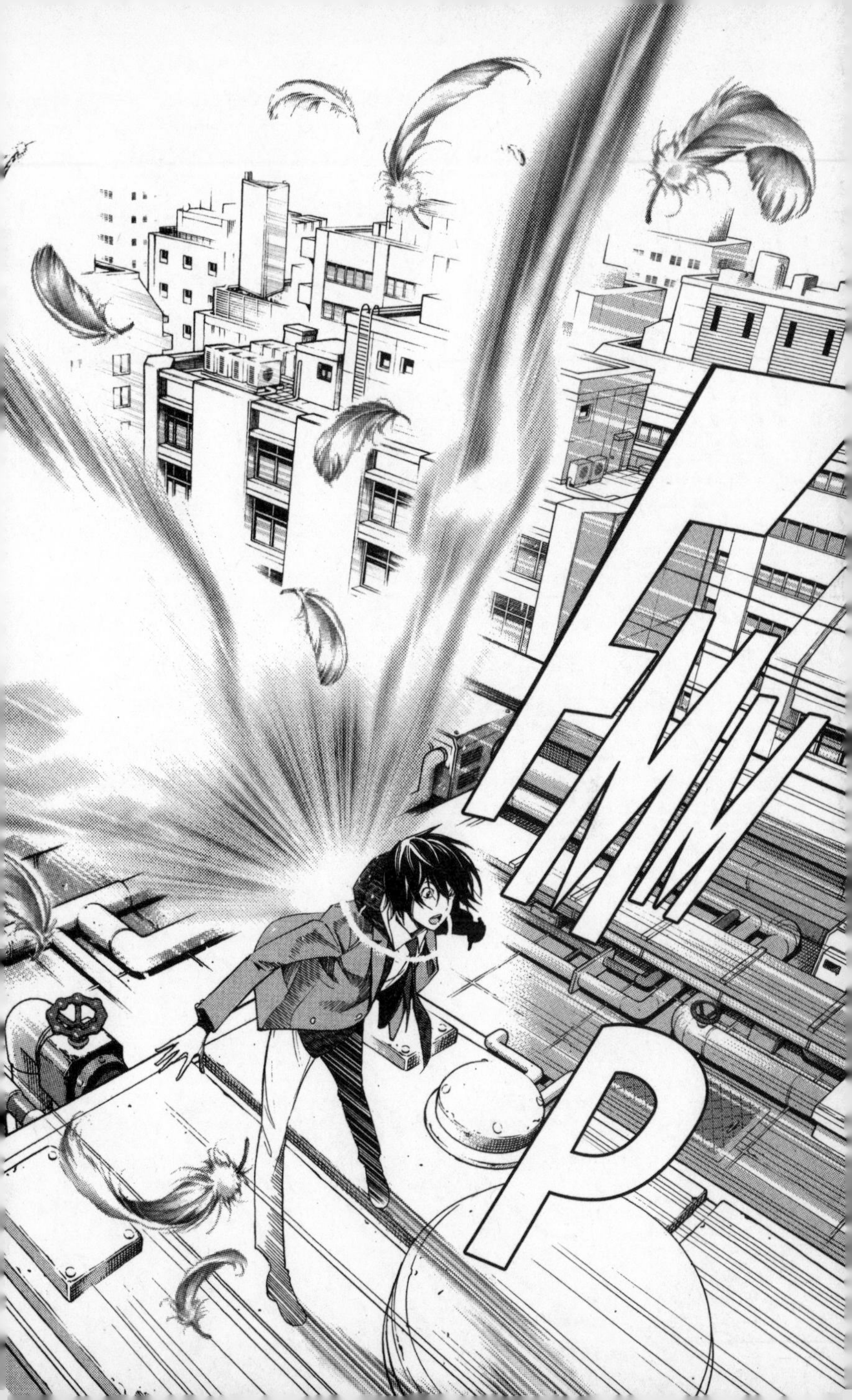
FWMP

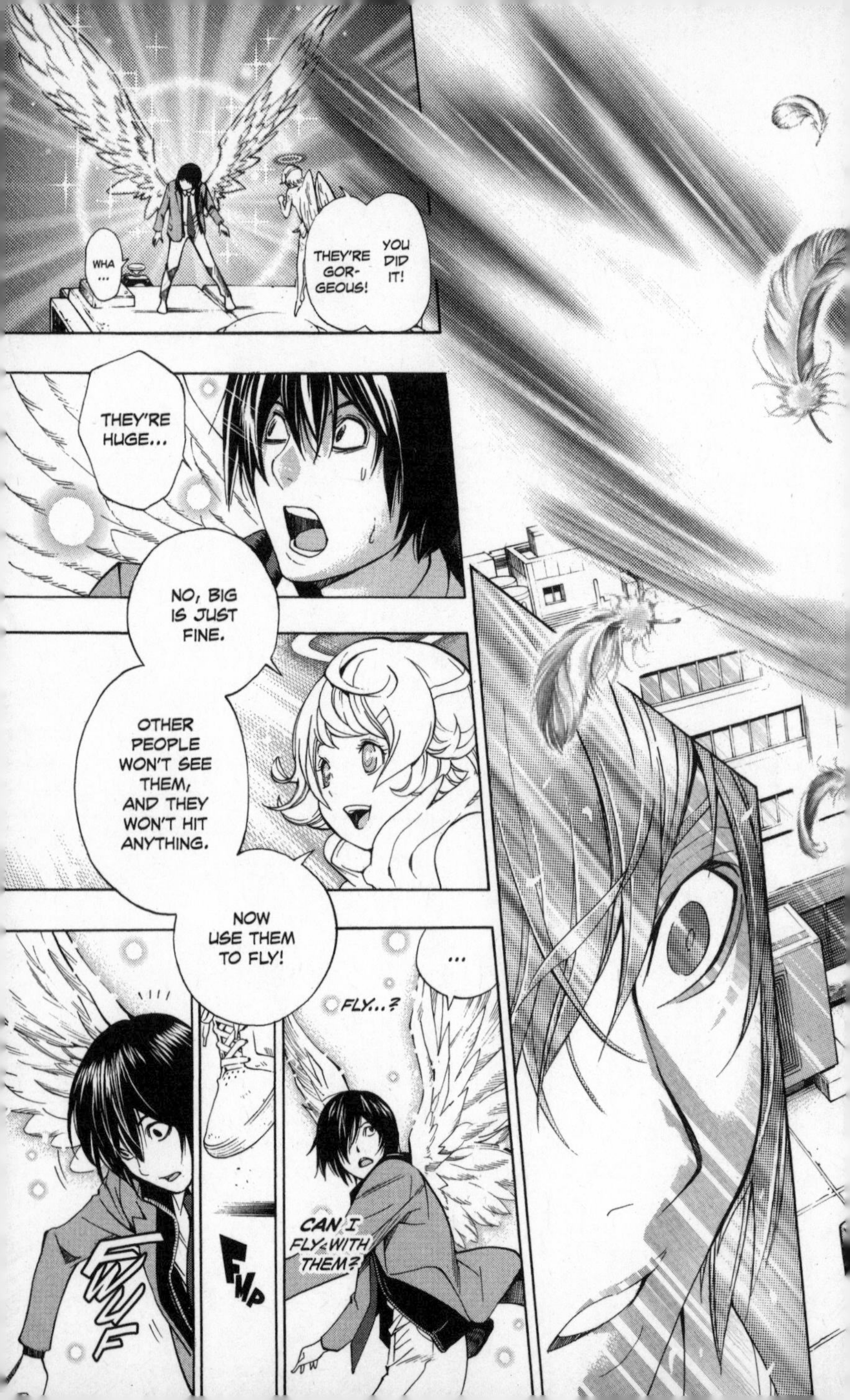
YOU DID IT!
THEY'RE GOR-GEOUS!
WHA...
THEY'RE HUGE...
NO, BIG IS JUST FINE.
OTHER PEOPLE WON'T SEE THEM, AND THEY WON'T HIT ANYTHING.
NOW USE THEM TO FLY!
...
FLY...?
CAN I FLY WITH THEM?
FMP
FWUF

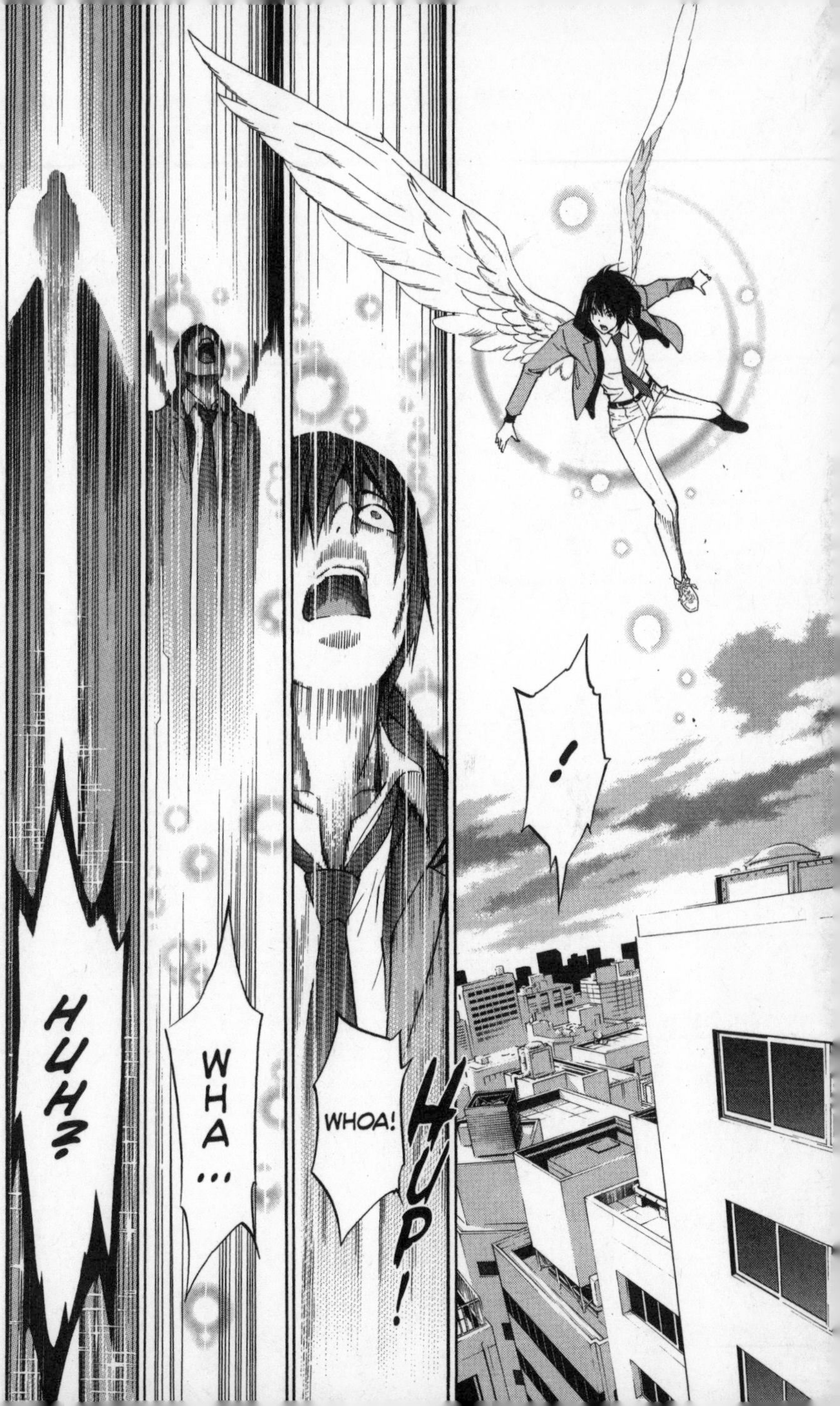
!
HUP!
WHOA!
WHA...
HUH?

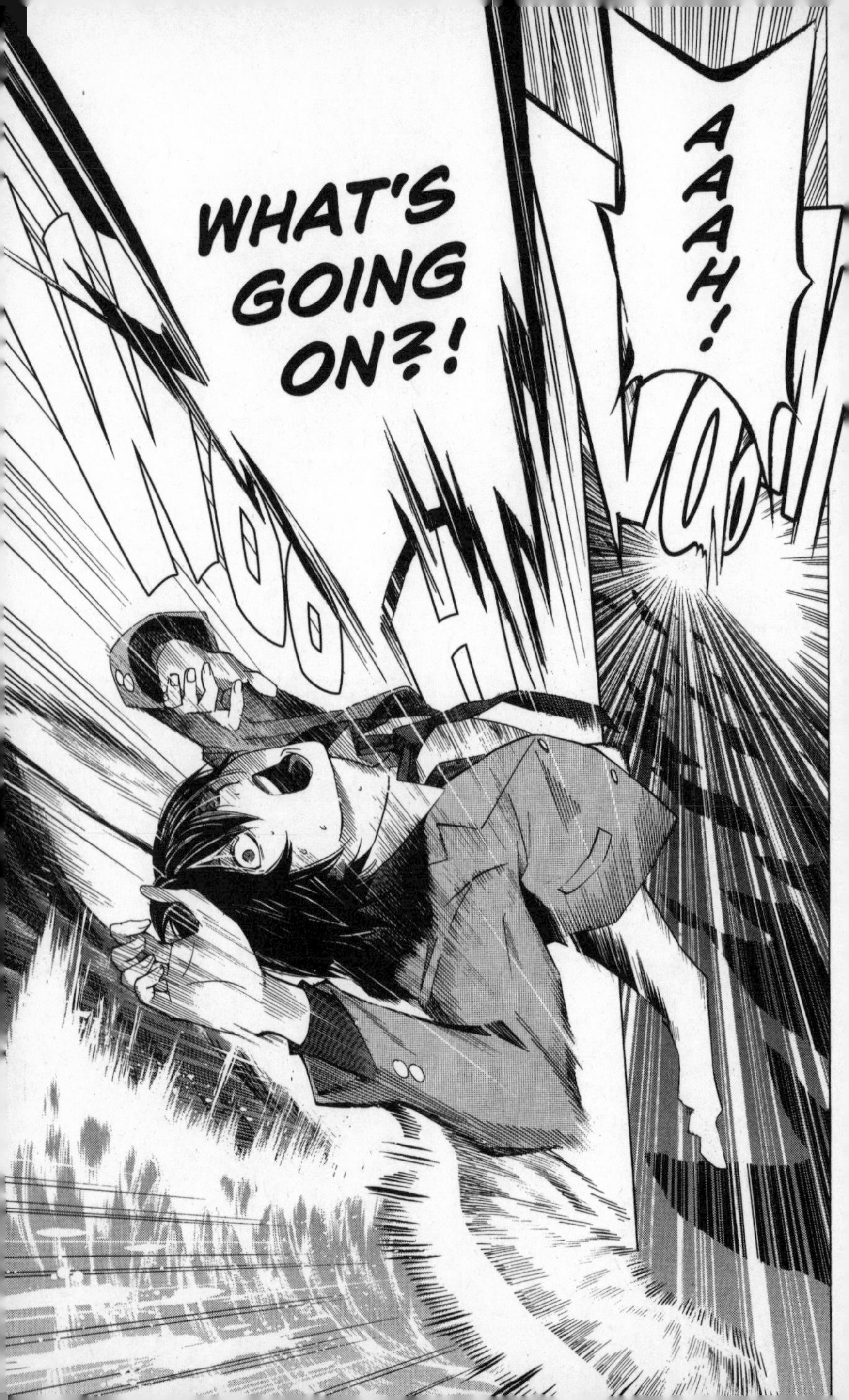
AAAH!
WHAT'S GOING ON?!

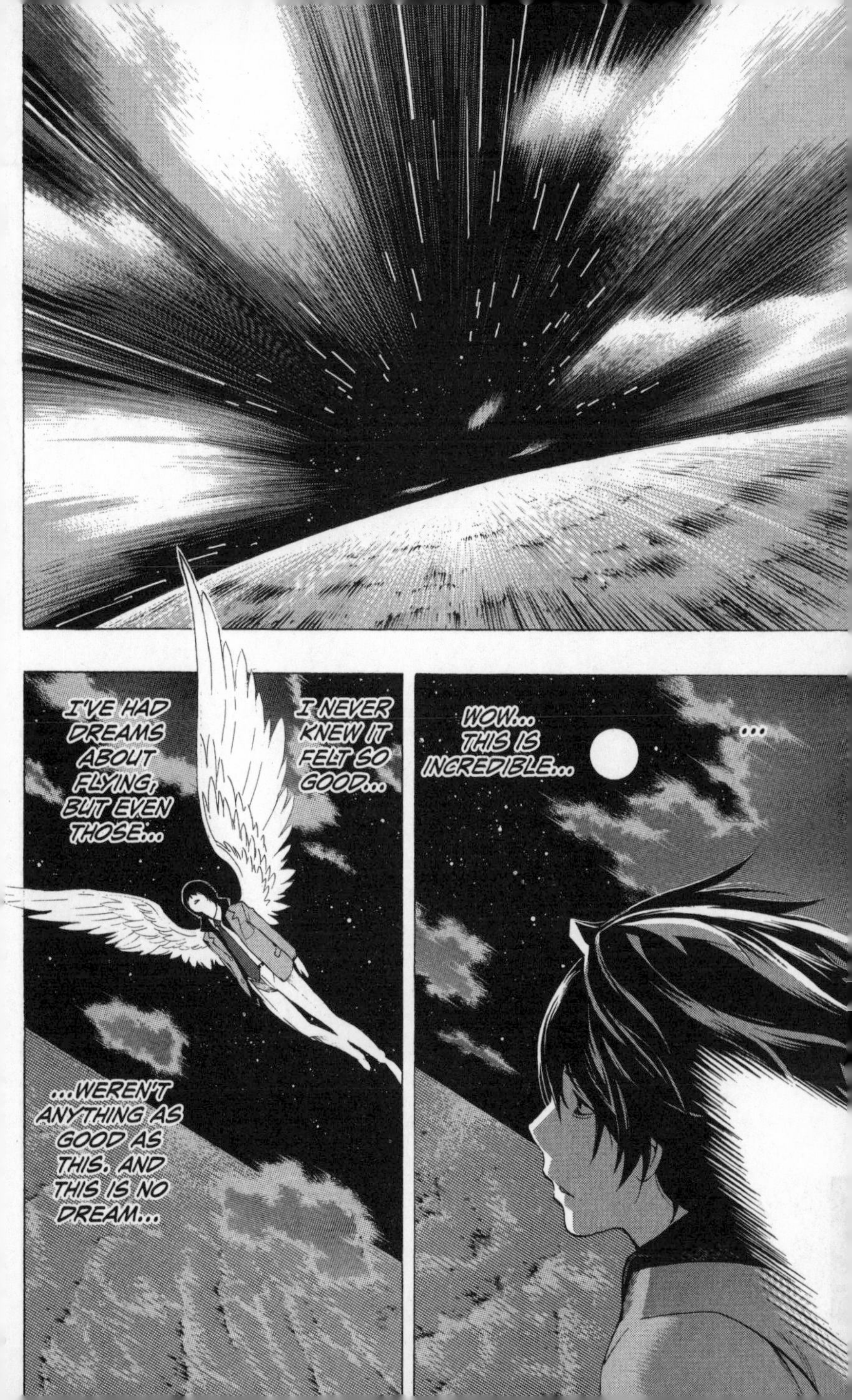
...
WOW... THIS IS INCREDIBLE...
I NEVER KNEW IT FELT SO GOOD...
I'VE HAD DREAMS ABOUT FLYING, BUT EVEN THOSE...
...WEREN'T ANYTHING AS GOOD AS THIS. AND THIS IS NO DREAM...

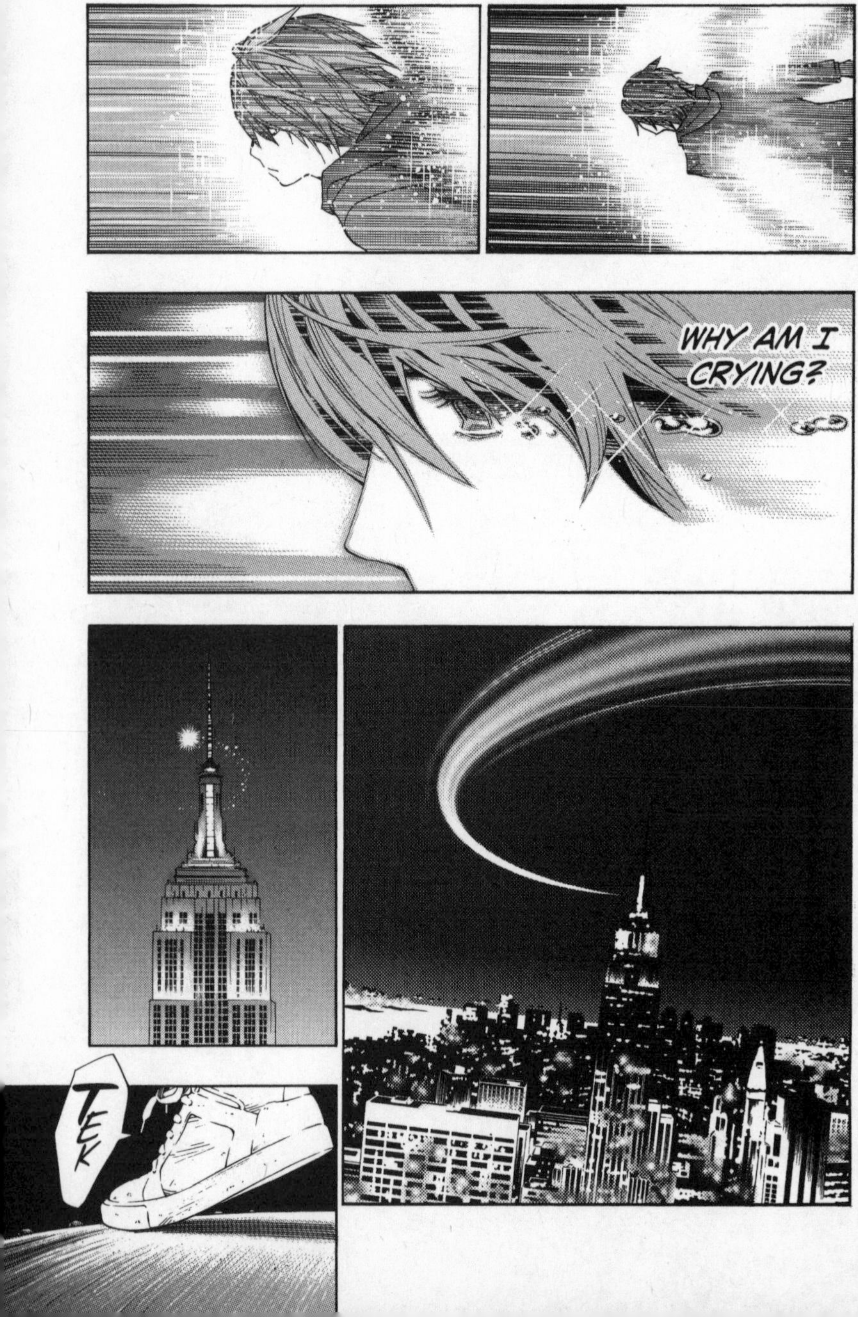
WHY AM I CRYING?
TEK

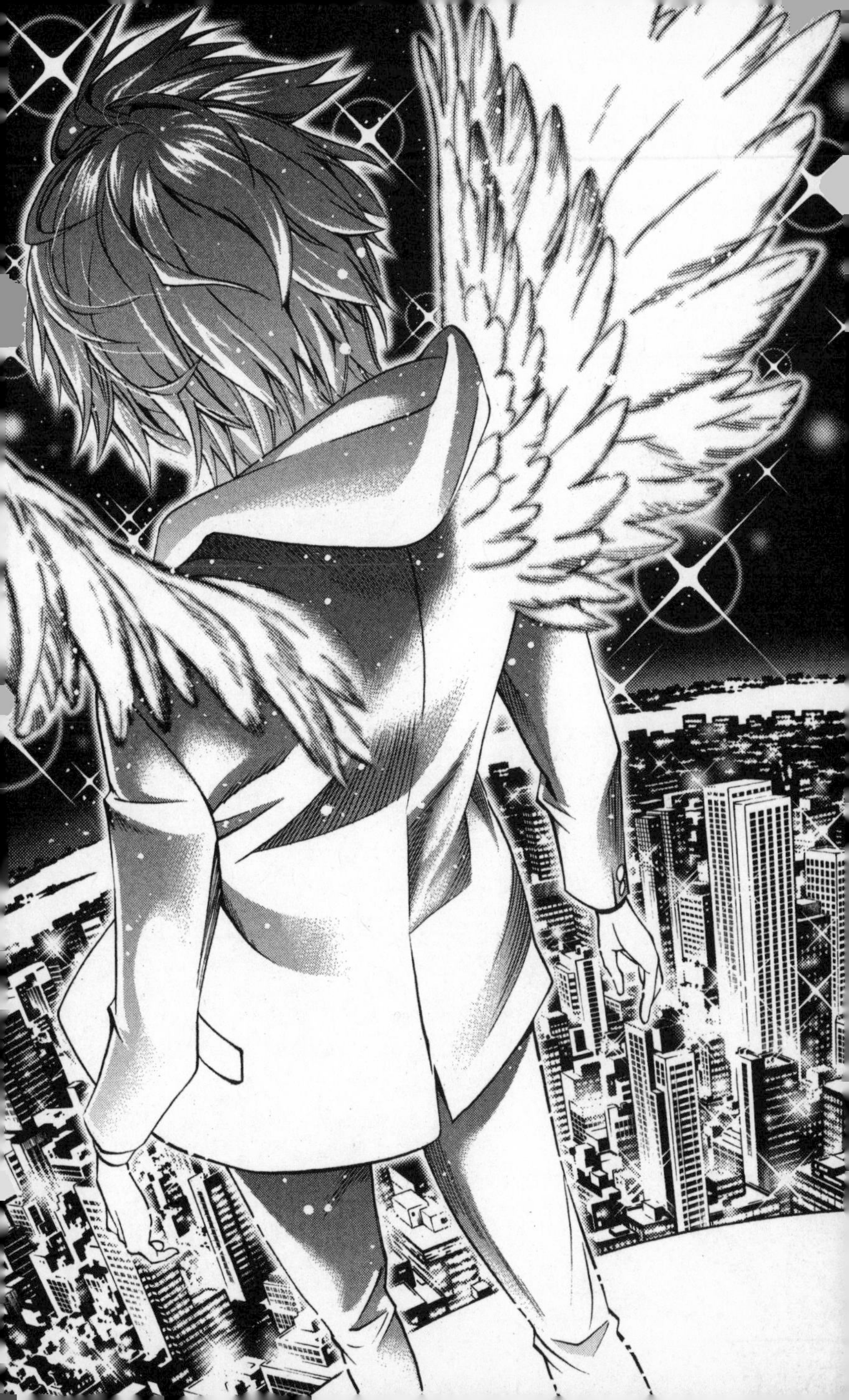

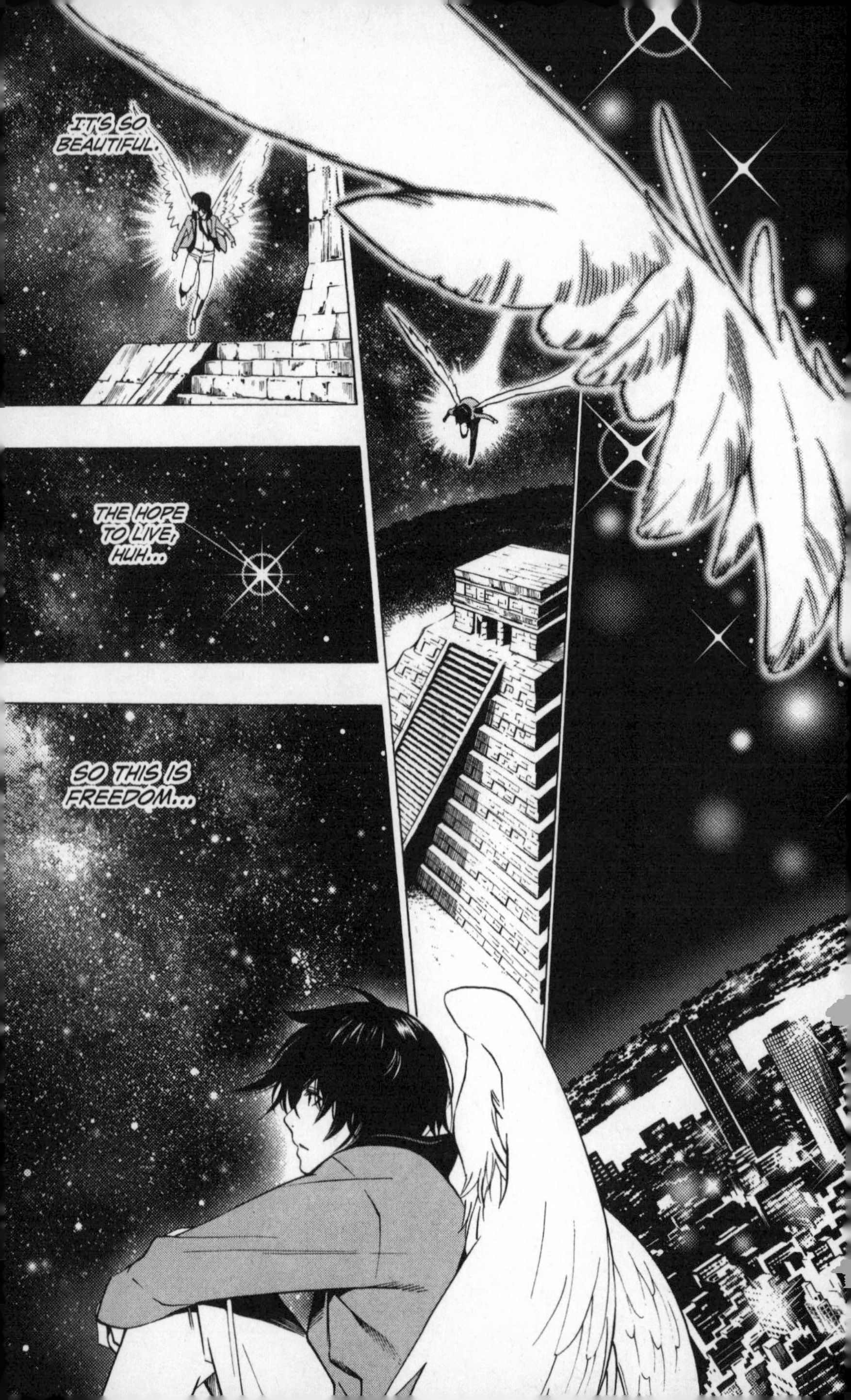
IT'S SO BEAUTIFUL.
THE HOPE TO LIVE, HUH...
SO THIS IS FREEDOM...

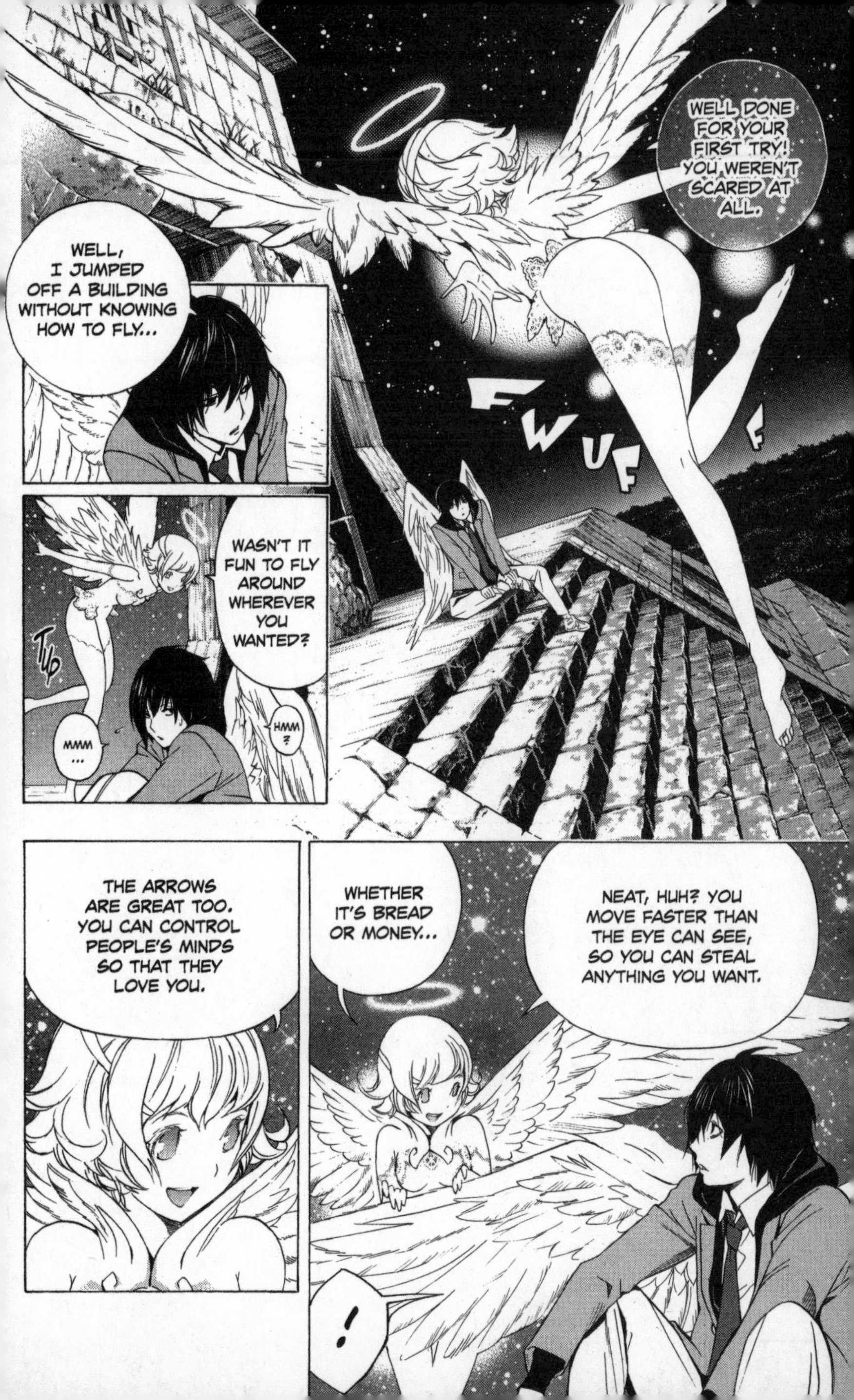
WELL DONE FOR YOUR FIRST TRY! YOU WEREN'T SCARED AT ALL.
FWUFF
WELL, I JUMPED OFF A BUILDING WITHOUT KNOWING HOW TO FLY...
WASN'T IT FUN TO FLY AROUND WHEREVER YOU WANTED?
HMM?
MMM...
TUP
NEAT, HUH? YOU MOVE FASTER THAN THE EYE CAN SEE, SO YOU CAN STEAL ANYTHING YOU WANT.
WHETHER IT'S BREAD OR MONEY...
!
THE ARROWS ARE GREAT TOO. YOU CAN CONTROL PEOPLE'S MINDS SO THAT THEY LOVE YOU.

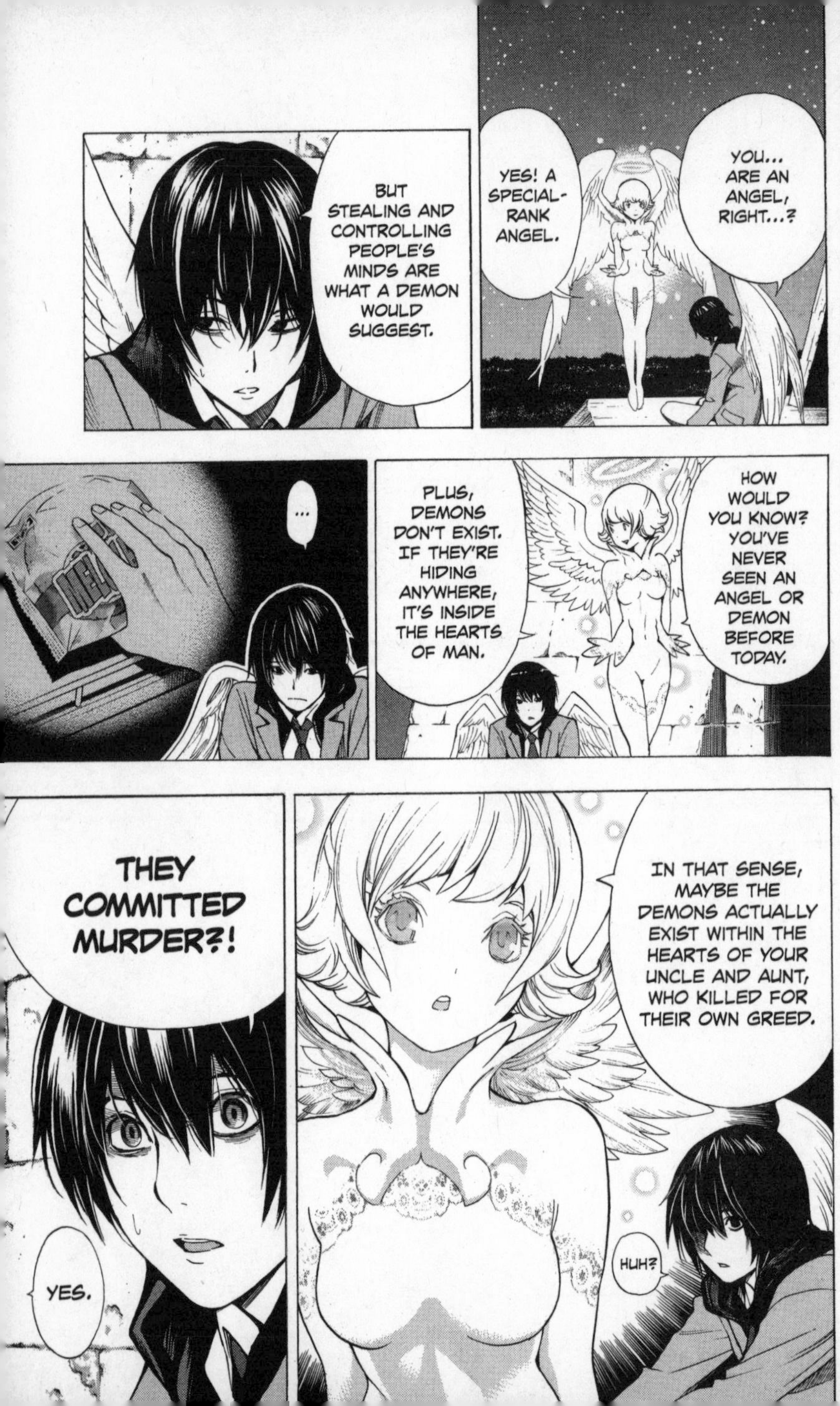
YOU... ARE AN ANGEL, RIGHT...?
YES! A SPECIAL-RANK ANGEL.
BUT STEALING AND CONTROLLING PEOPLE'S MINDS ARE WHAT A DEMON WOULD SUGGEST.
HOW WOULD YOU KNOW? YOU'VE NEVER SEEN AN ANGEL OR DEMON BEFORE TODAY.
PLUS, DEMONS DON'T EXIST. IF THEY'RE HIDING ANYWHERE, IT'S INSIDE THE HEARTS OF MAN.
...
IN THAT SENSE, MAYBE THE DEMONS ACTUALLY EXIST WITHIN THE HEARTS OF YOUR UNCLE AND AUNT, WHO KILLED FOR THEIR OWN GREED.
HUH?
THEY COMMITTED MURDER?!
YES.

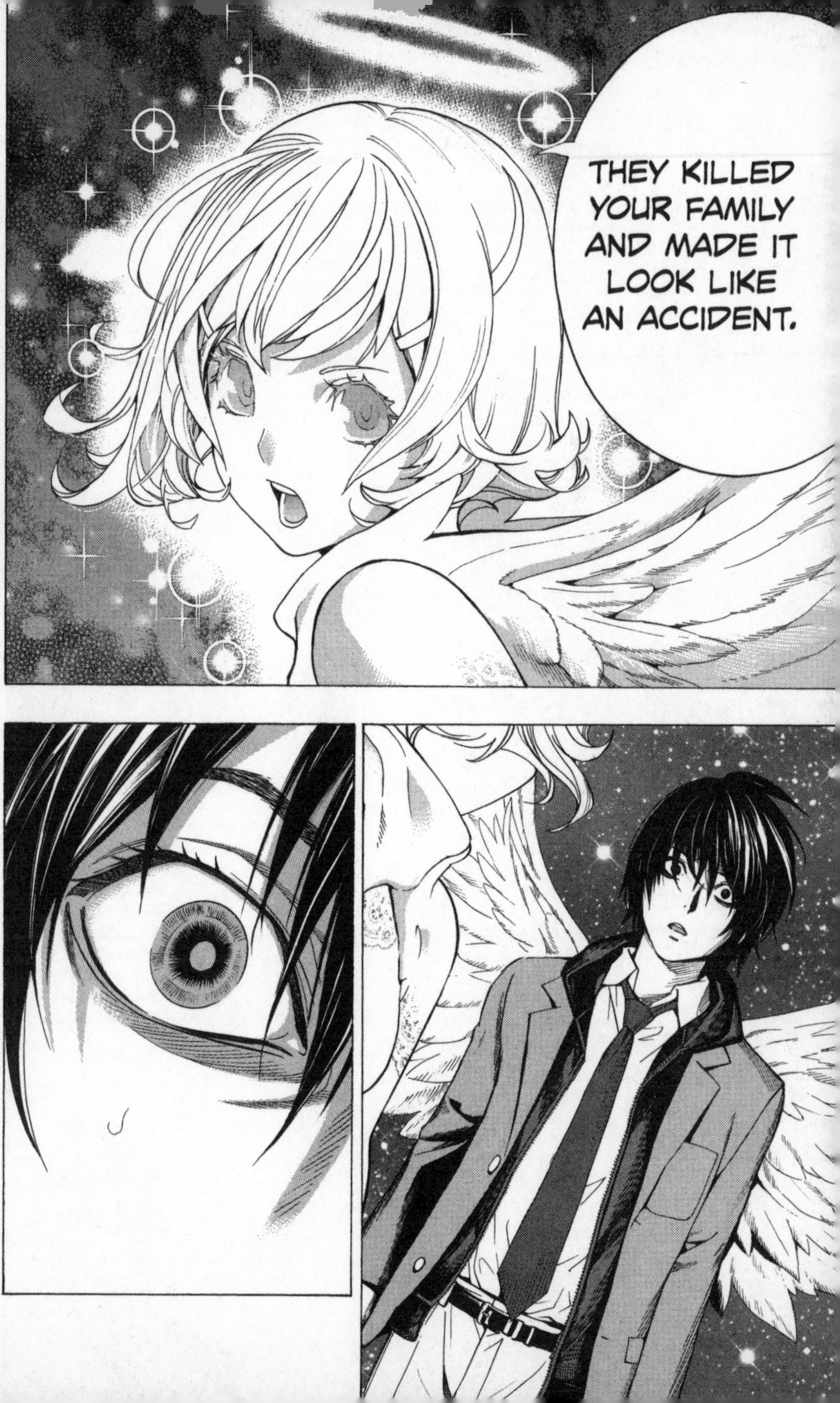
THEY KILLED YOUR FAMILY AND MADE IT LOOK LIKE AN ACCIDENT.

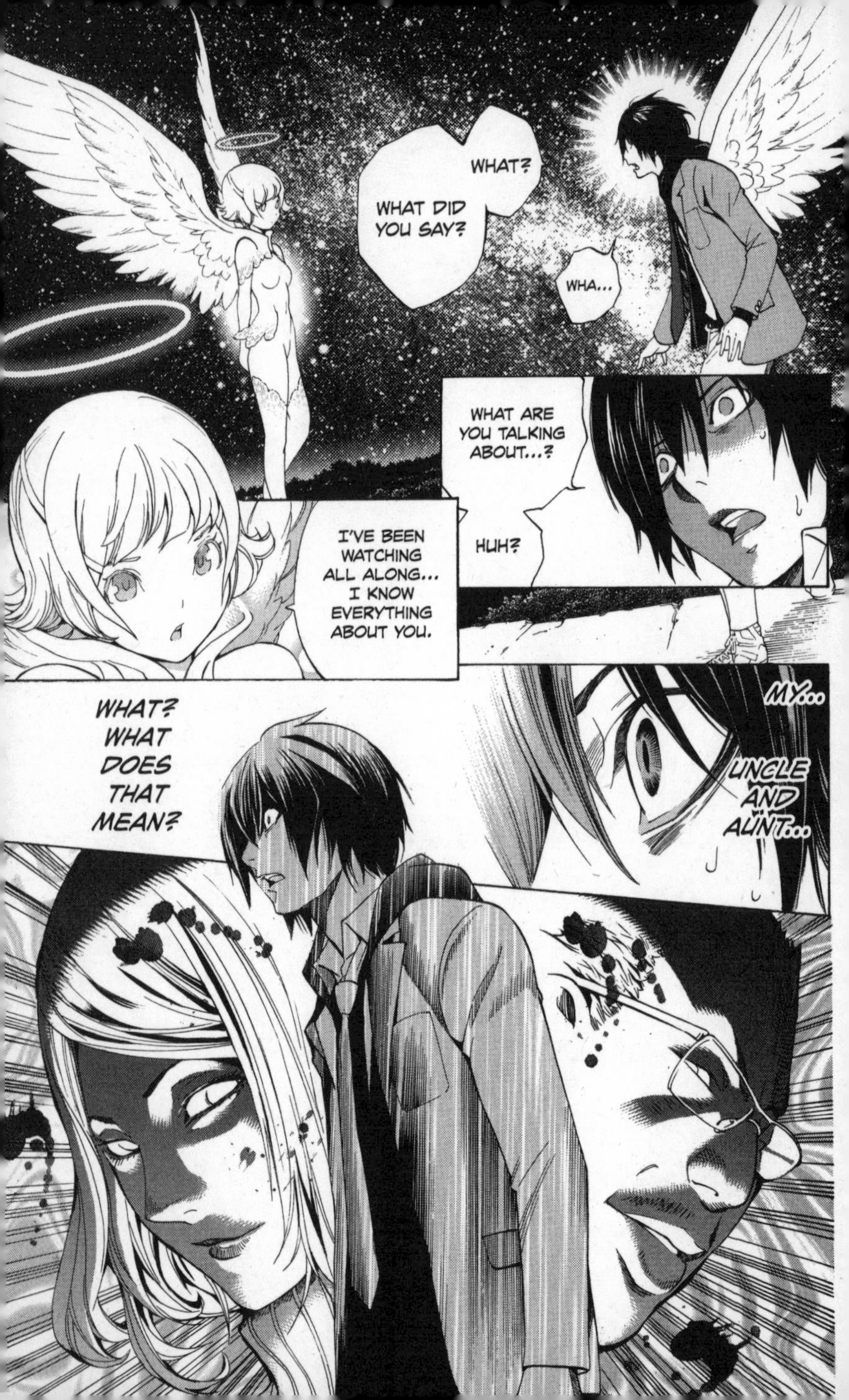
WHA...
WHAT?
WHAT DID YOU SAY?
WHAT ARE YOU TALKING ABOUT...?
HUH?
I'VE BEEN WATCHING ALL ALONG... I KNOW EVERYTHING ABOUT YOU.
MY...
UNCLE AND AUNT...
WHAT? WHAT DOES THAT MEAN?

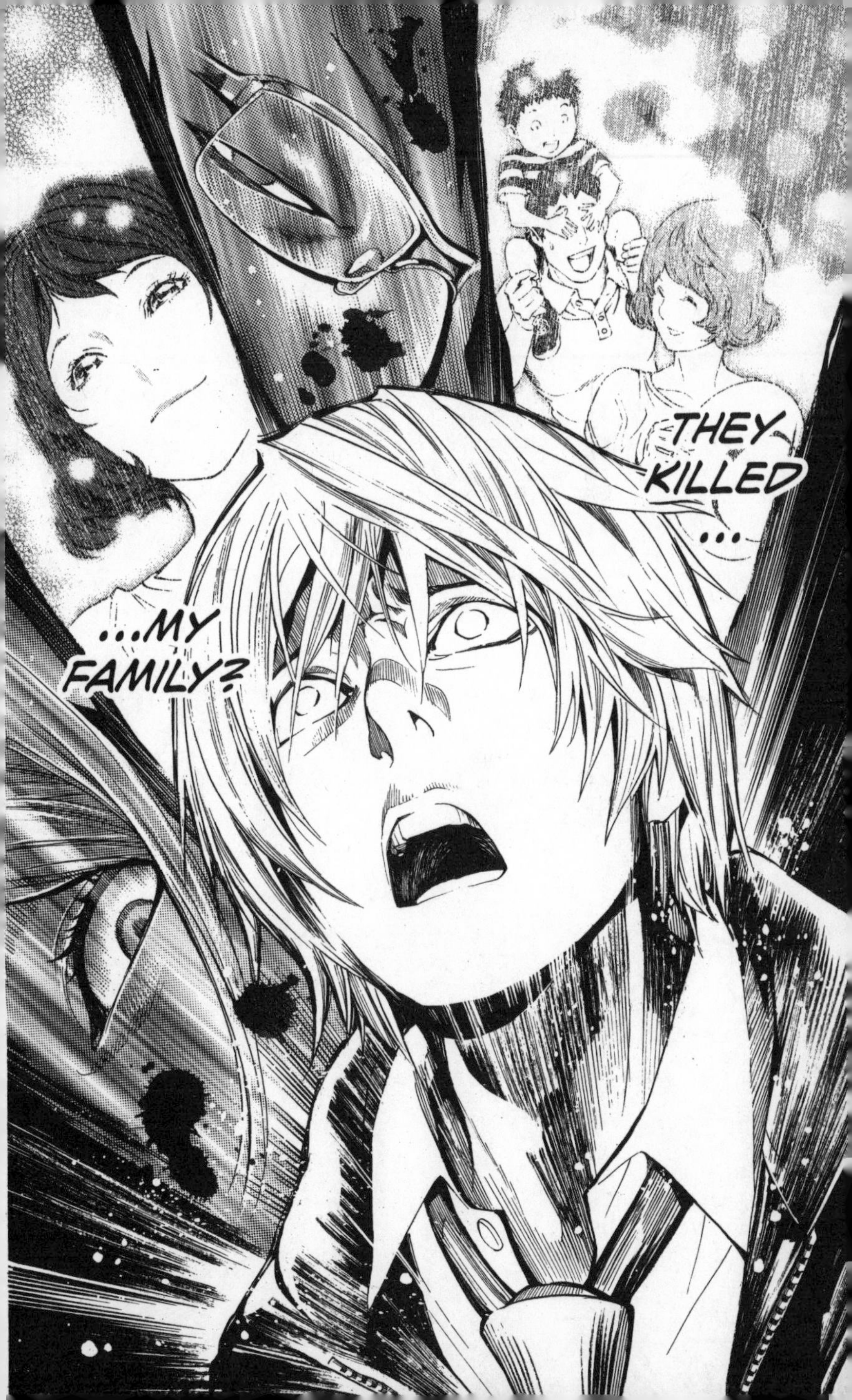
THEY KILLED ...
...MY FAMILY?

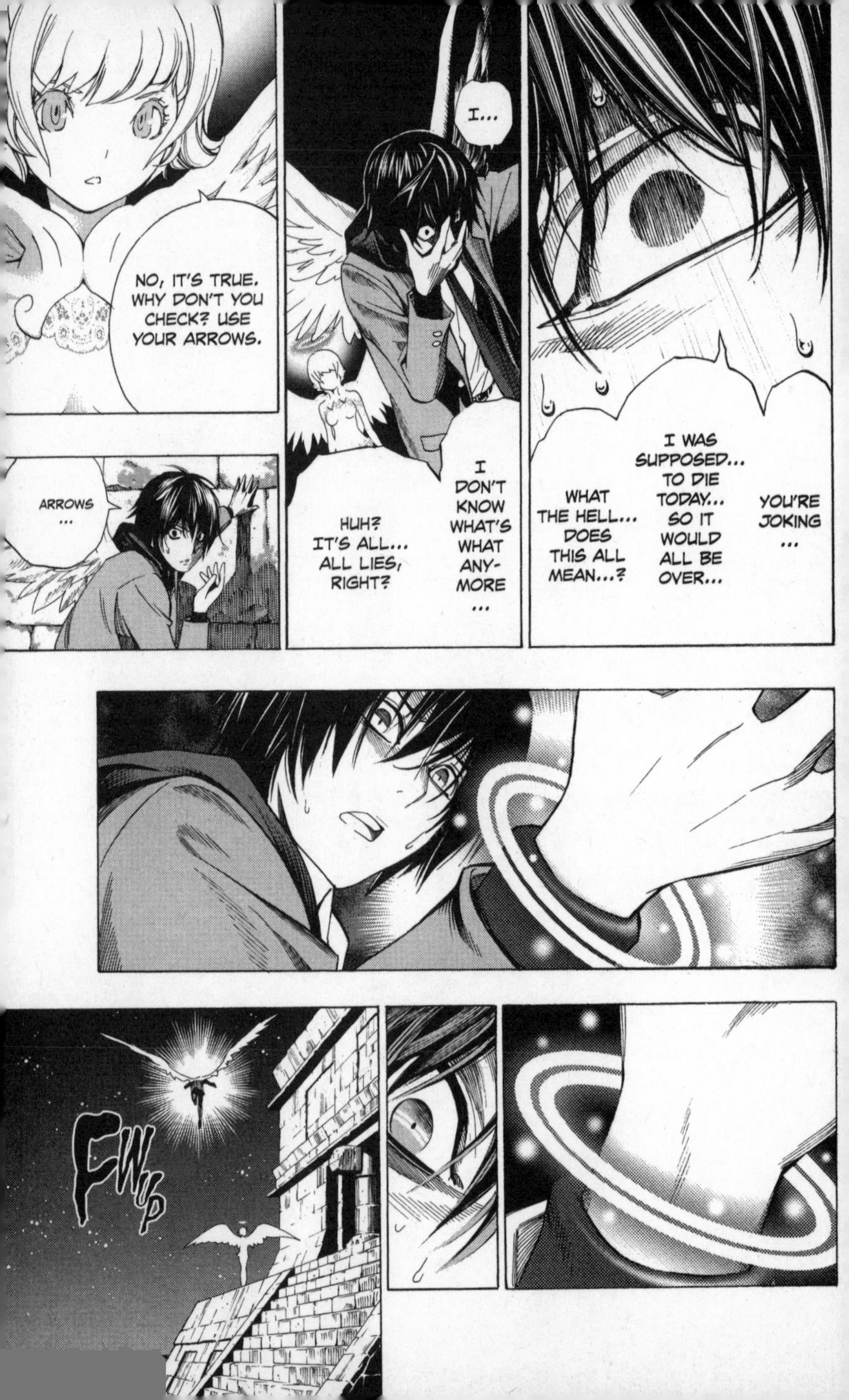
YOU'RE JOKING...
I WAS SUPPOSED... TO DIE TODAY... SO IT WOULD ALL BE OVER...
WHAT THE HELL... DOES THIS ALL MEAN...?
I...
I DON'T KNOW WHAT'S WHAT ANYMORE...
HUH? IT'S ALL... ALL LIES, RIGHT?
NO, IT'S TRUE. WHY DON'T YOU CHECK? USE YOUR ARROWS.
ARROWS...
FWUP

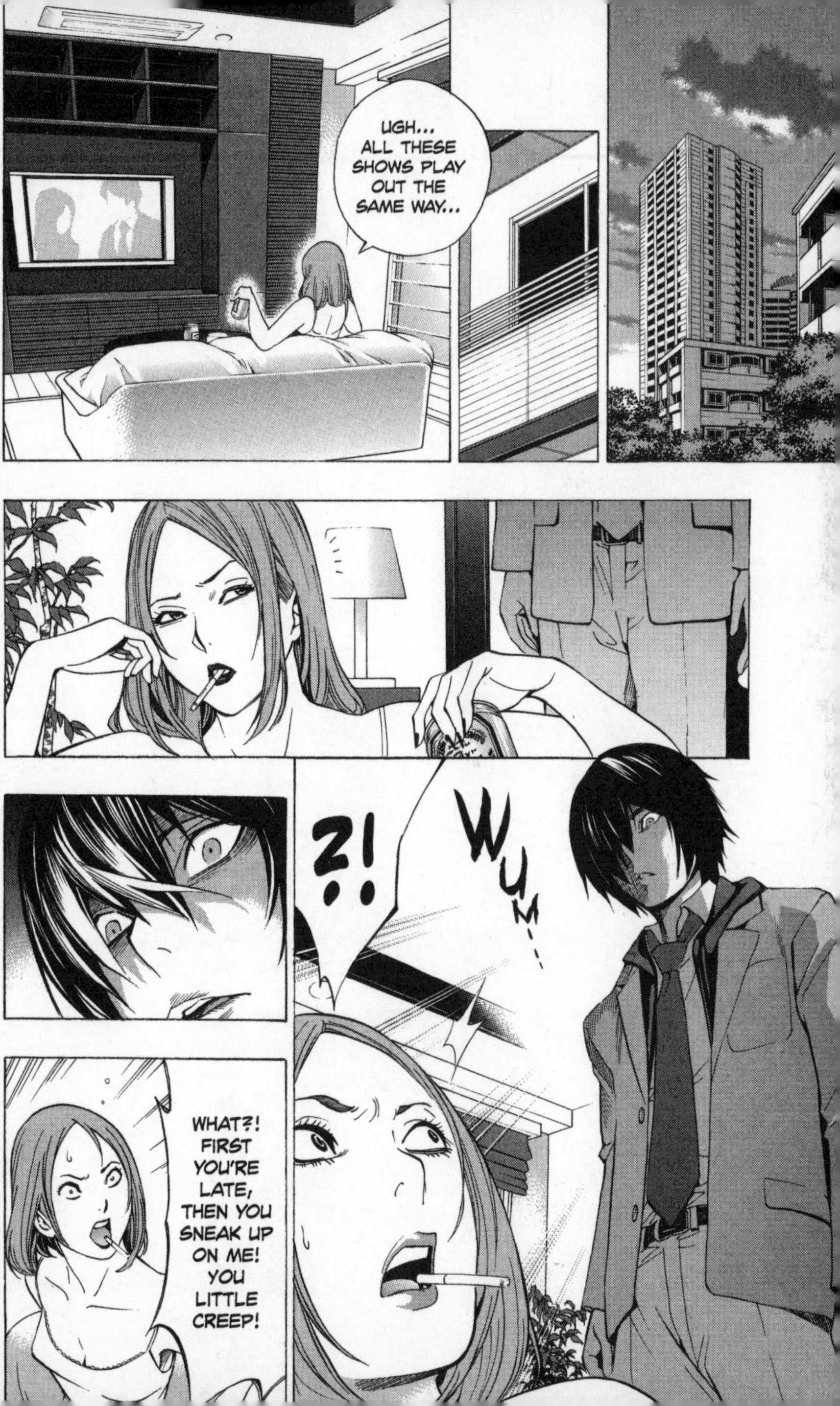
UGH... ALL THESE SHOWS PLAY OUT THE SAME WAY...
WUM...
?!
WHAT?! FIRST YOU'RE LATE, THEN YOU SNEAK UP ON ME! YOU LITTLE CREEP!

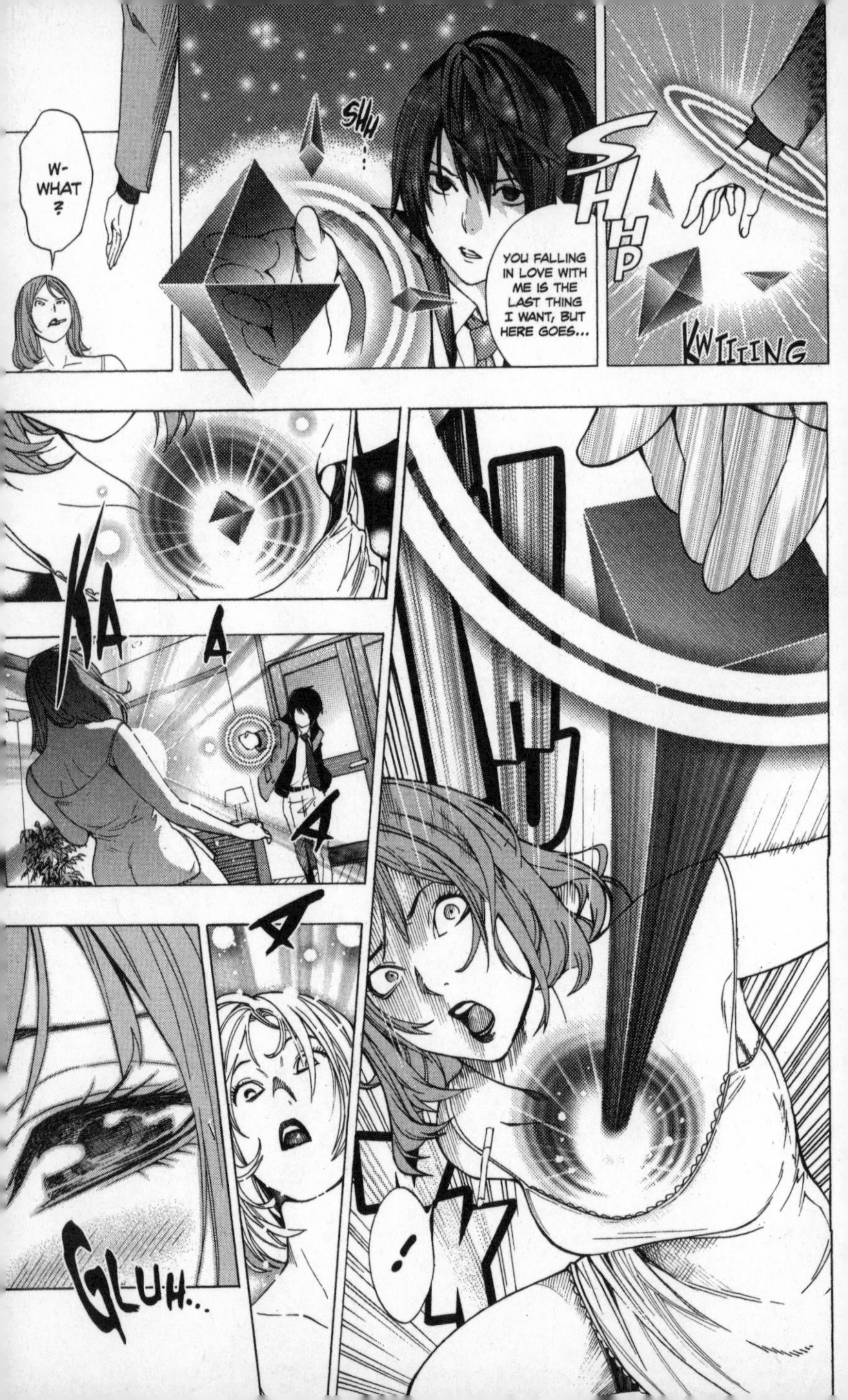
SHHP
KWIIING
SHH...
YOU FALLING IN LOVE WITH ME IS THE LAST THING I WANT, BUT HERE GOES...
W-WHAT?
!
KA
A
A
A
GLUH...

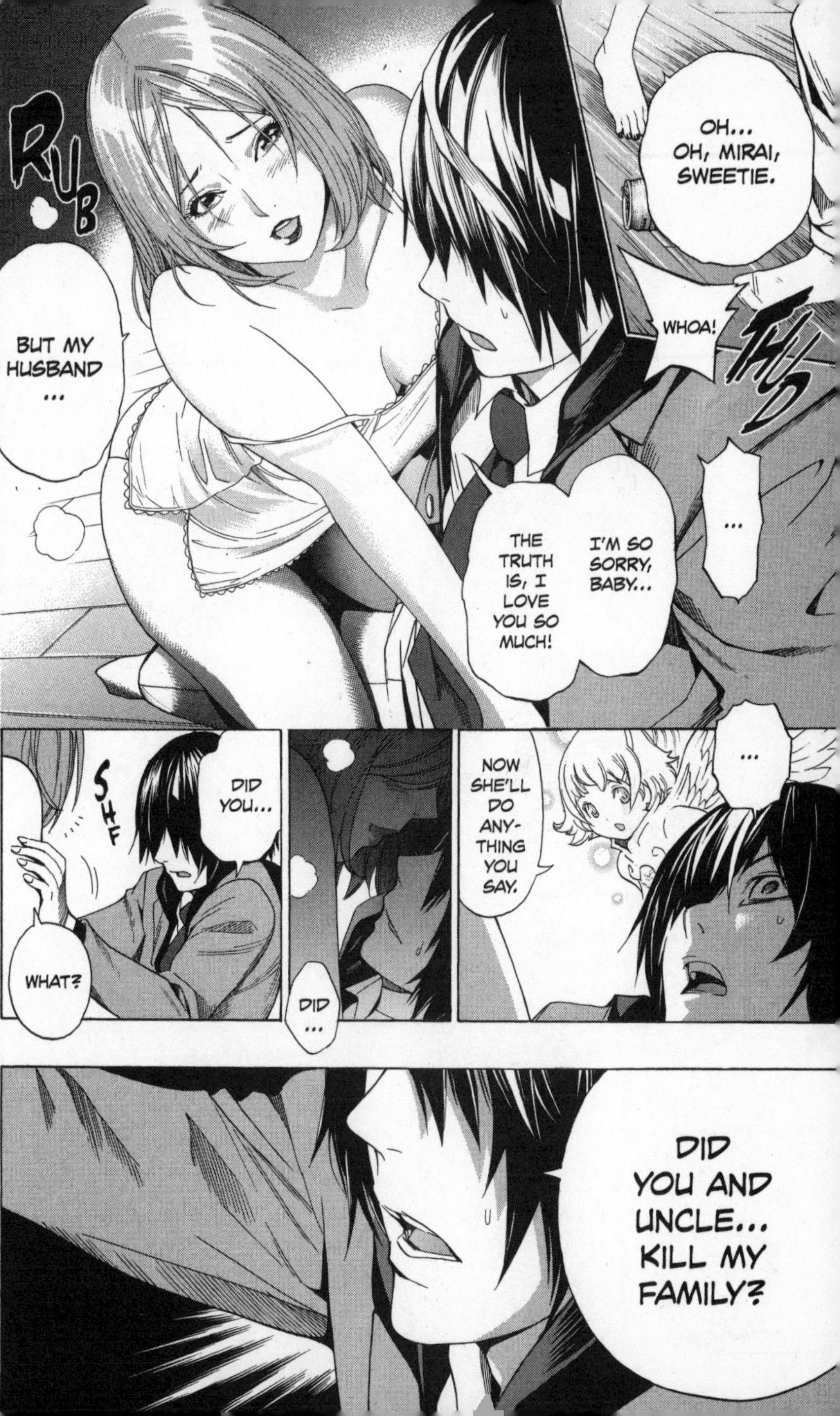
OH... OH, MIRAI, SWEETIE.
WHOA!
THUD
...
I'M SO SORRY, BABY...
THE TRUTH IS, I LOVE YOU SO MUCH!
BUT MY HUSBAND ...
RUB
...
NOW SHE'LL DO ANYTHING YOU SAY.
DID ...
DID YOU...
SHF
WHAT?
DID YOU AND UNCLE... KILL MY FAMILY?

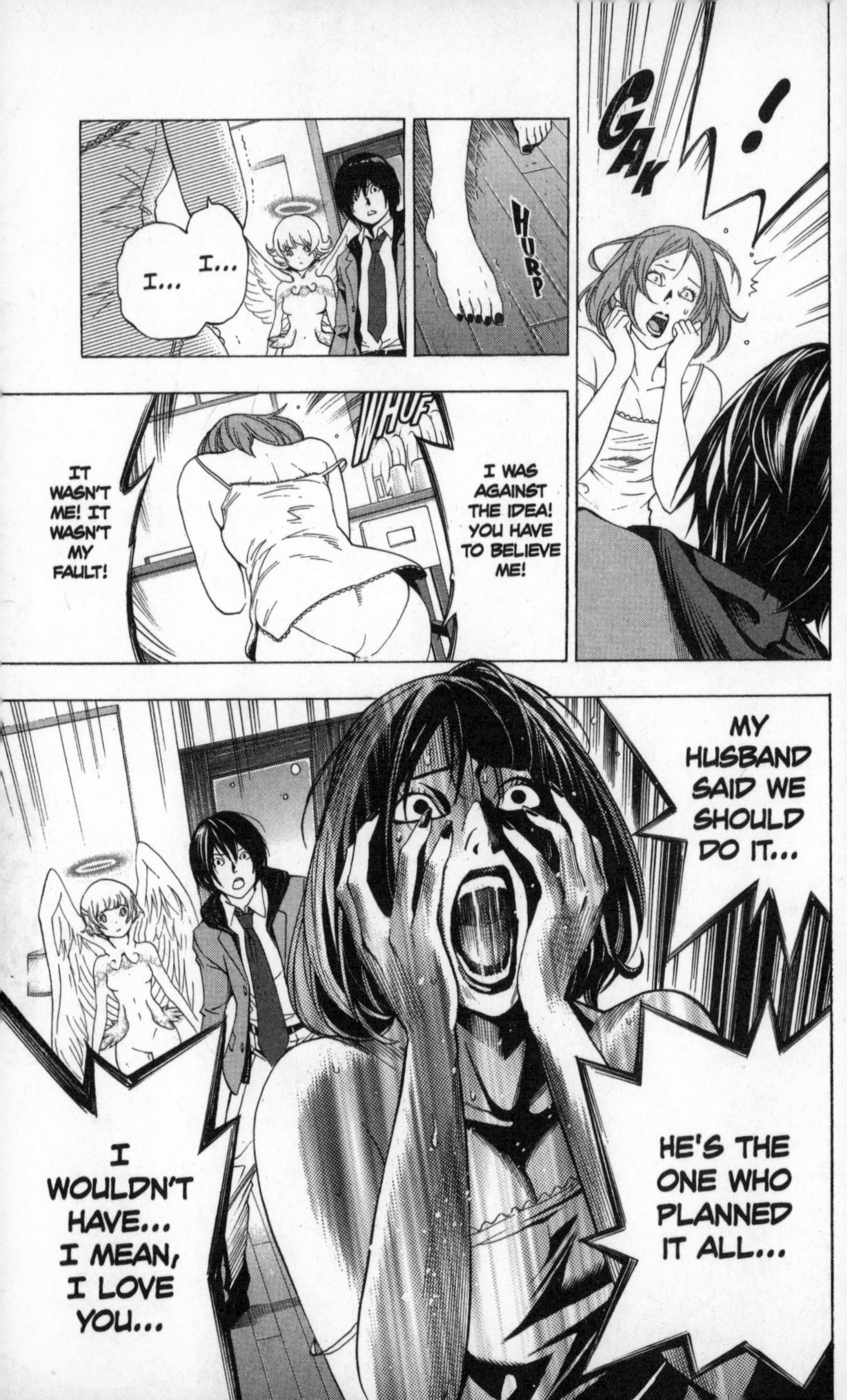
GAK !
HURP
I... I...
WHUF
I WAS AGAINST THE IDEA! YOU HAVE TO BELIEVE ME!
IT WASN'T ME! IT WASN'T MY FAULT!
MY HUSBAND SAID WE SHOULD DO IT...
HE'S THE ONE WHO PLANNED IT ALL...
I WOULDN'T HAVE... I MEAN, I LOVE YOU...

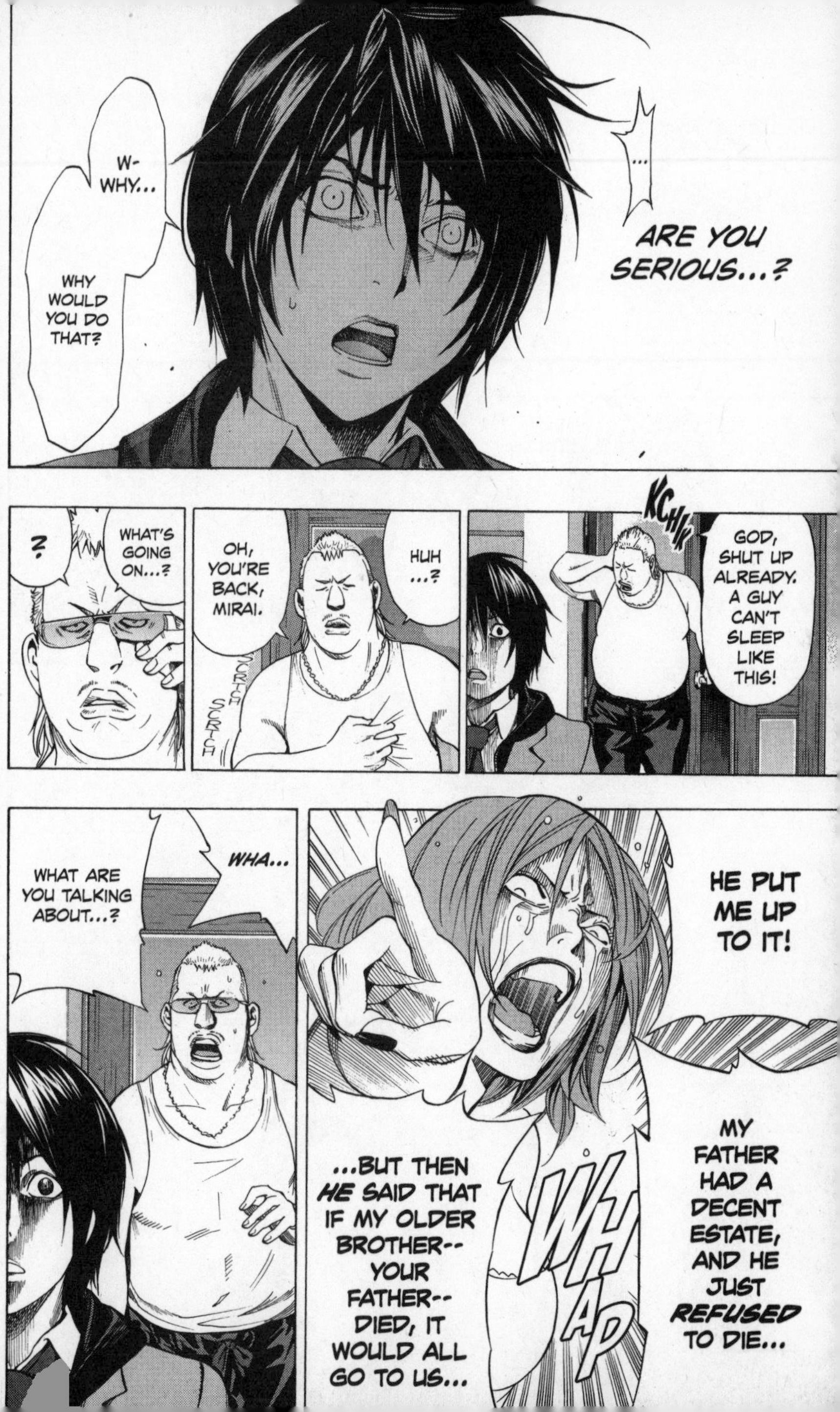
...
ARE YOU SERIOUS...?
W- WHY...
WHY WOULD YOU DO THAT?
KCHIK
GOD, SHUT UP ALREADY. A GUY CAN'T SLEEP LIKE THIS!
HUH ...?
OH, YOU'RE BACK, MIRAI.
SCRTCH SCRTCH
WHAT'S GOING ON...?
?
HE PUT ME UP TO IT!
MY FATHER HAD A DECENT ESTATE, AND HE JUST *REFUSED* TO DIE...
...BUT THEN *HE* SAID THAT IF MY OLDER BROTHER-- YOUR FATHER-- DIED, IT WOULD ALL GO TO US...
WHAP
WHA...
WHAT ARE YOU TALKING ABOUT...?

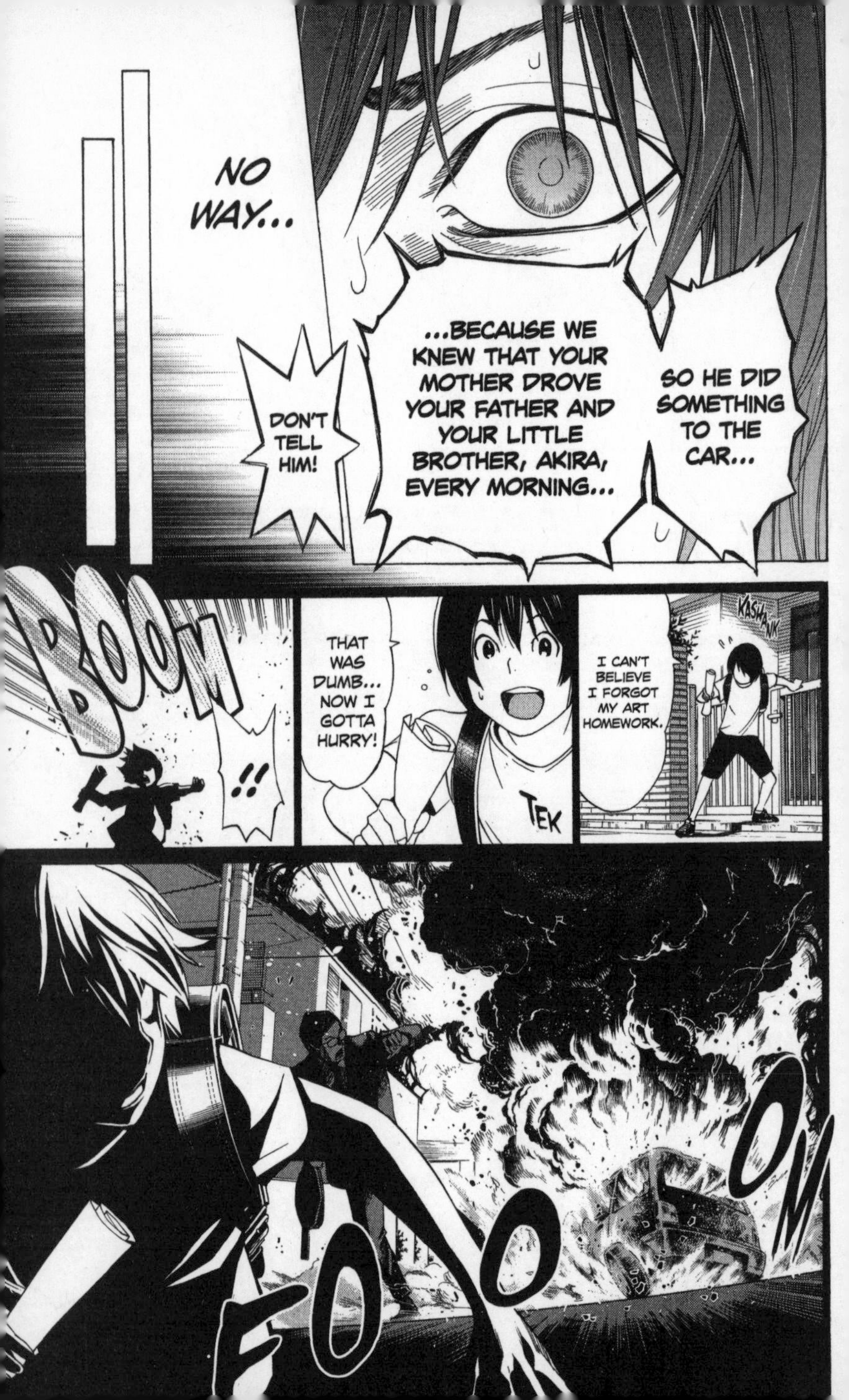

SO HE DID SOMETHING TO THE CAR...
...BECAUSE WE KNEW THAT YOUR MOTHER DROVE YOUR FATHER AND YOUR LITTLE BROTHER, AKIRA, EVERY MORNING...
DON'T TELL HIM!
NO WAY...
KASHANK
I CAN'T BELIEVE I FORGOT MY ART HOMEWORK.
THAT WAS DUMB... NOW I GOTTA HURRY!
TEK
BOOM
!!
FOOOM

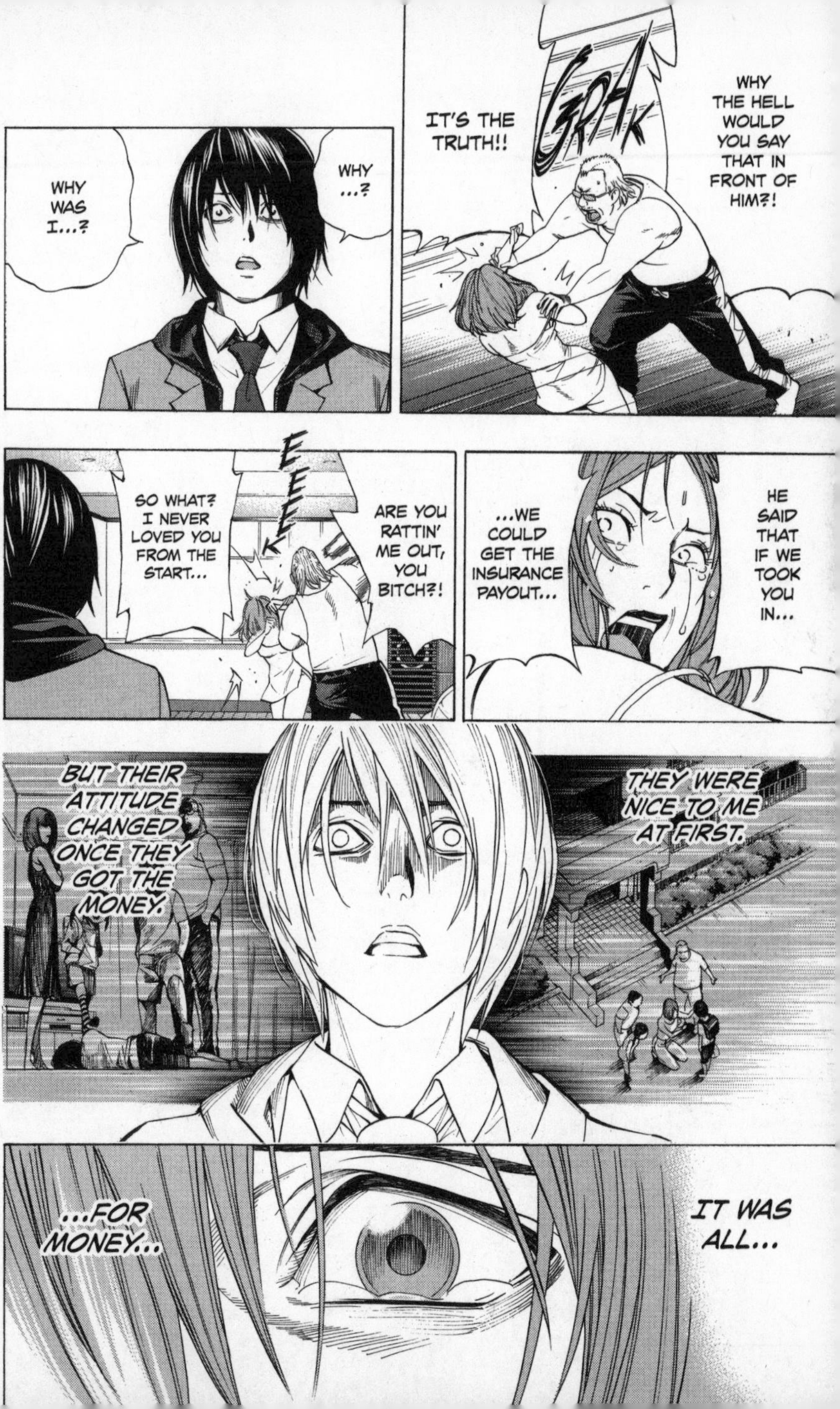
WHY THE HELL WOULD YOU SAY THAT IN FRONT OF HIM?!
IT'S THE TRUTH!!
WHY ...?
WHY WAS I...?
HE SAID THAT IF WE TOOK YOU IN...
...WE COULD GET THE INSURANCE PAYOUT...
ARE YOU RATTIN' ME OUT, YOU BITCH?!
SO WHAT? I NEVER LOVED YOU FROM THE START...
THEY WERE NICE TO ME AT FIRST.
BUT THEIR ATTITUDE CHANGED ONCE THEY GOT THE MONEY.
IT WAS ALL...
...FOR MONEY...

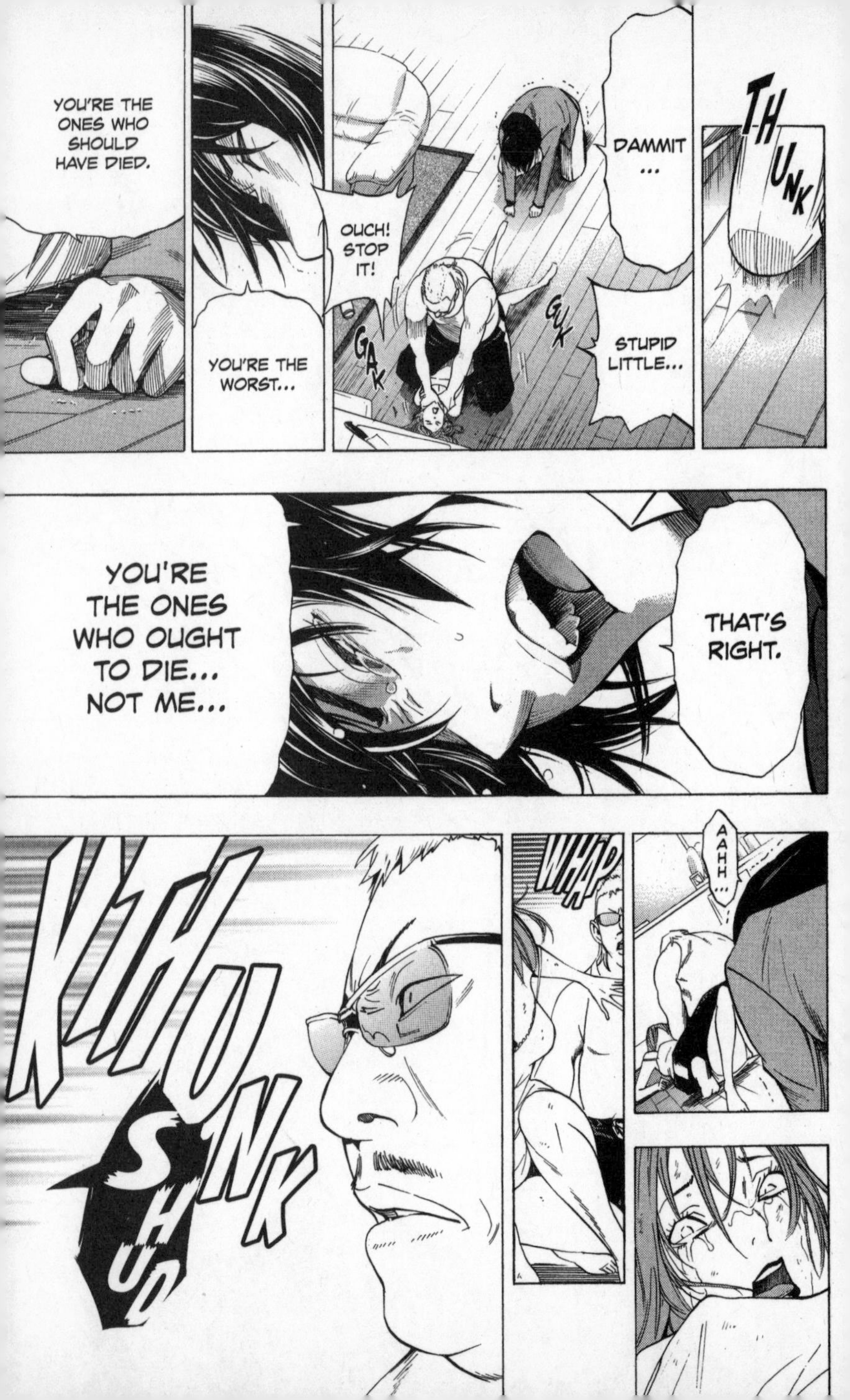
THUNK
DAMMIT...
OUCH! STOP IT!
GUK
STUPID LITTLE...
GAK
YOU'RE THE WORST...
YOU'RE THE ONES WHO SHOULD HAVE DIED.
THAT'S RIGHT.
YOU'RE THE ONES WHO OUGHT TO DIE... NOT ME...
AAHH...
WHAP

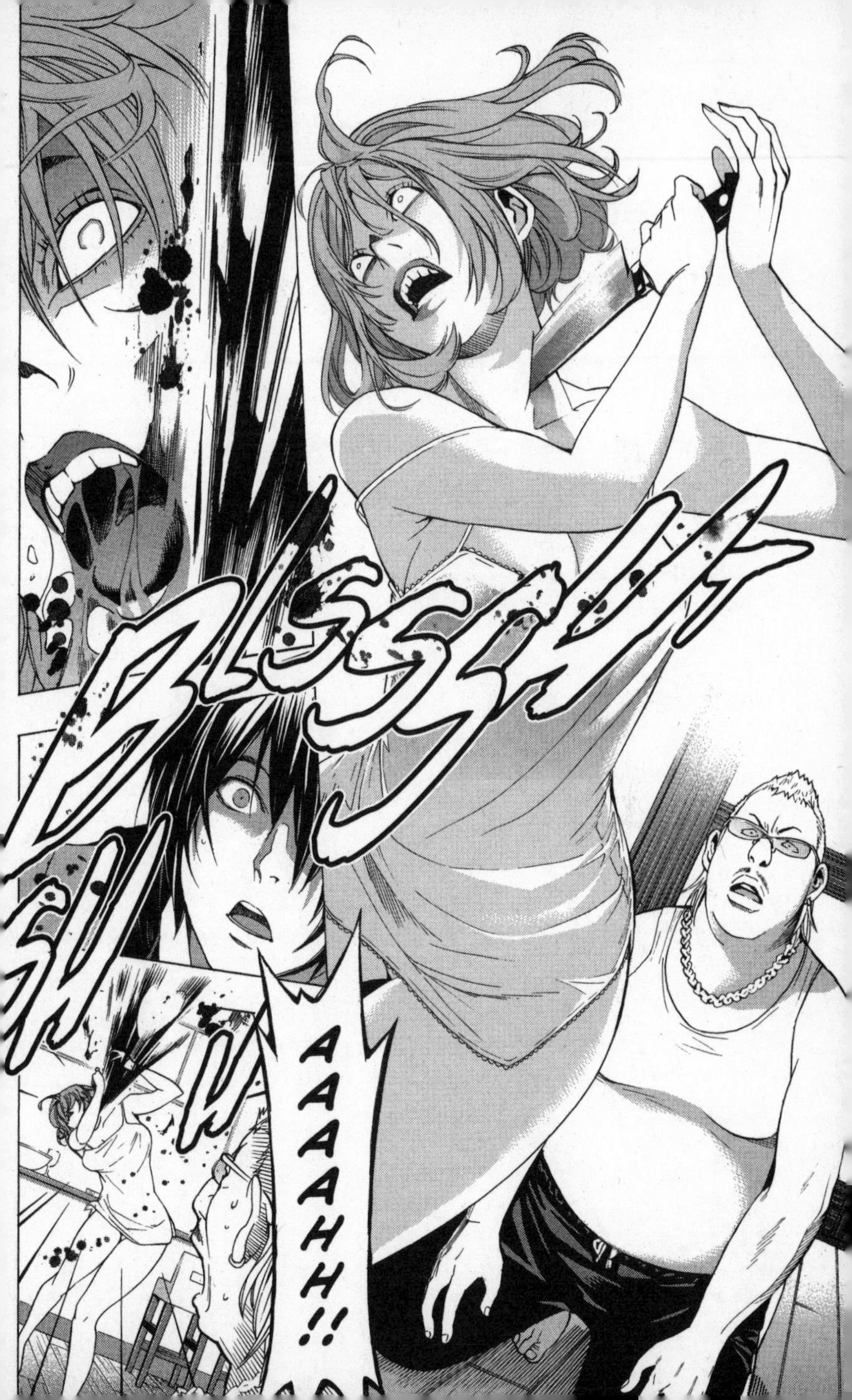
AAAAAHH!!

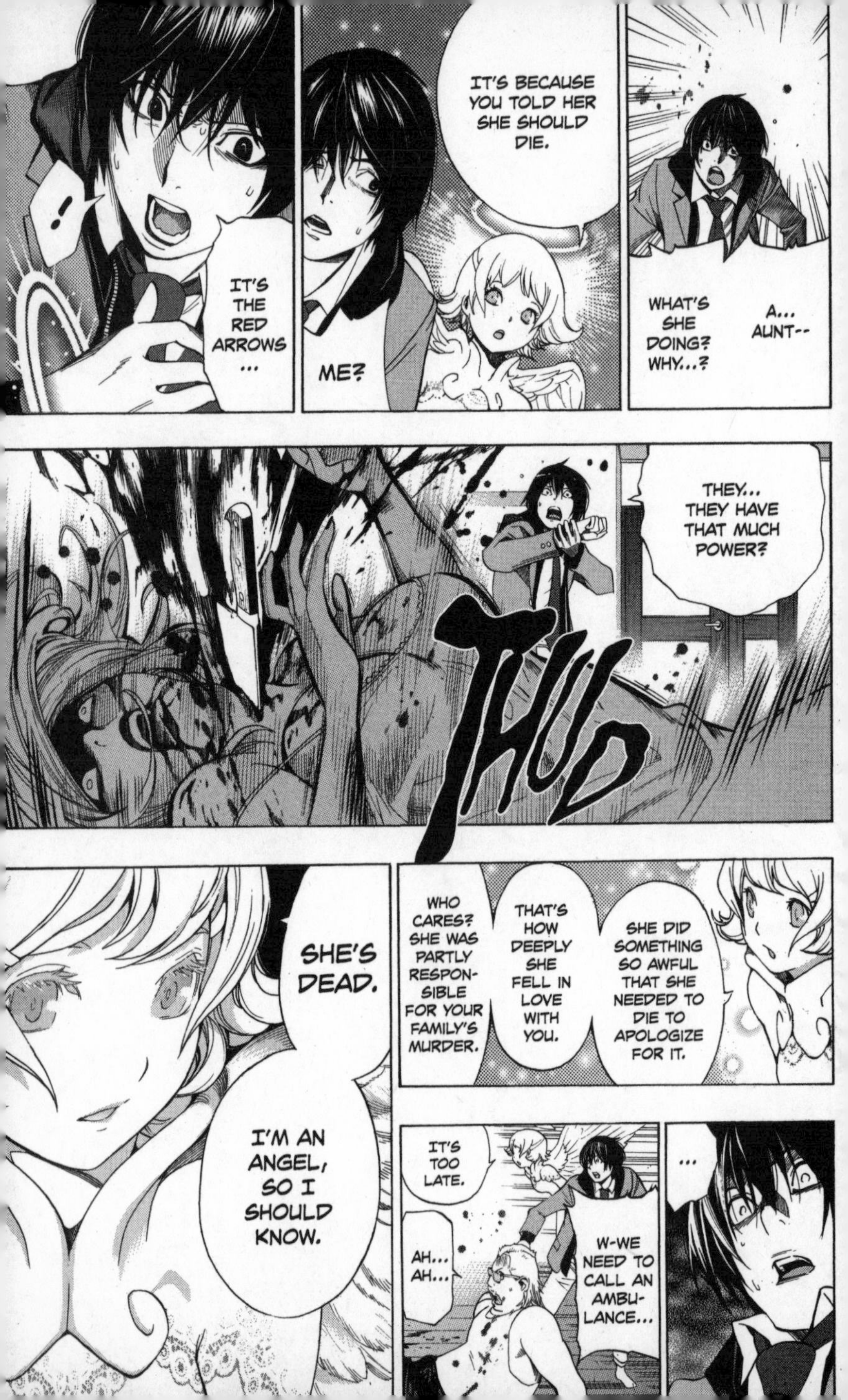
A... AUNT--
WHAT'S SHE DOING? WHY...?
IT'S BECAUSE YOU TOLD HER SHE SHOULD DIE.
ME?
!
IT'S THE RED ARROWS ...
THEY... THEY HAVE THAT MUCH POWER?
THUD
SHE DID SOMETHING SO AWFUL THAT SHE NEEDED TO DIE TO APOLOGIZE FOR IT.
THAT'S HOW DEEPLY SHE FELL IN LOVE WITH YOU.
WHO CARES? SHE WAS PARTLY RESPON-SIBLE FOR YOUR FAMILY'S MURDER.
...
W-WE NEED TO CALL AN AMBU-LANCE...
IT'S TOO LATE.
AH... AH...
SHE'S DEAD.
I'M AN ANGEL, SO I SHOULD KNOW.

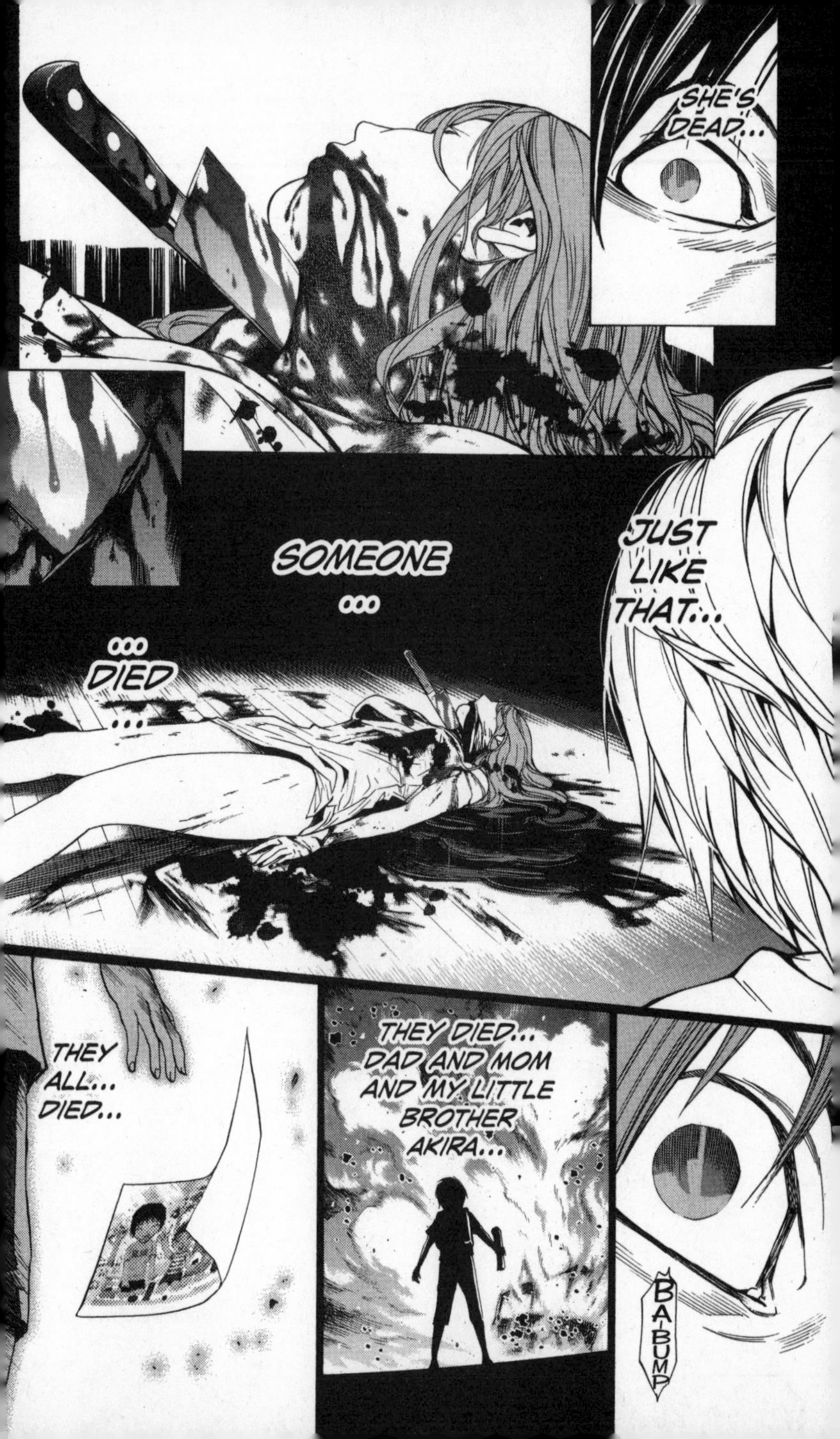
SHE'S DEAD...
JUST LIKE THAT...
SOMEONE ...
... DIED ...
BA-BUMP
THEY DIED... DAD AND MOM AND MY LITTLE BROTHER AKIRA...
THEY ALL... DIED...

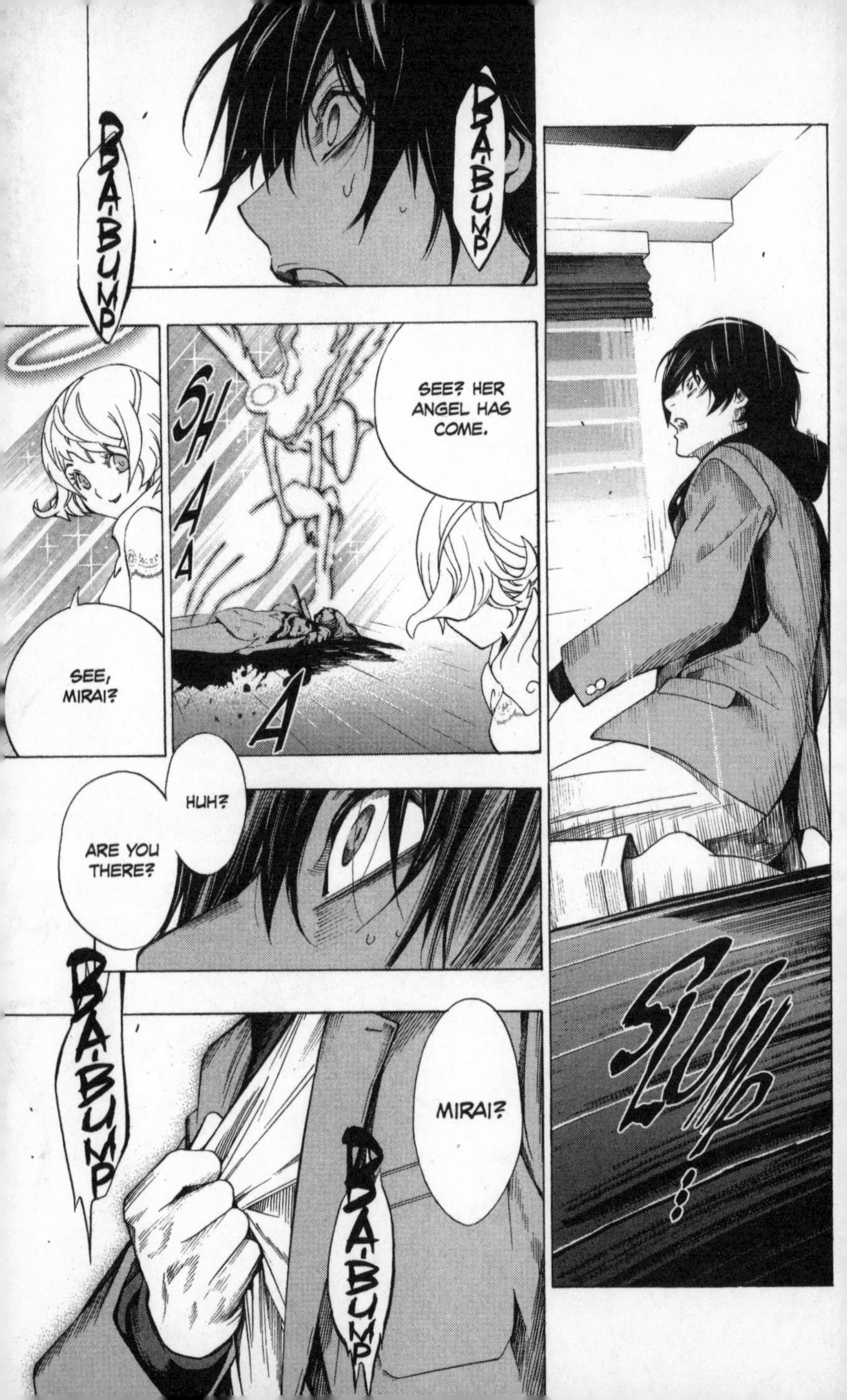
SLUMP
BA-BUMP
BA-BUMP
SEE? HER ANGEL HAS COME.
SHAAAA
SEE, MIRAI?
HUH?
ARE YOU THERE?
MIRAI?
BA-BUMP
BA-BUMP

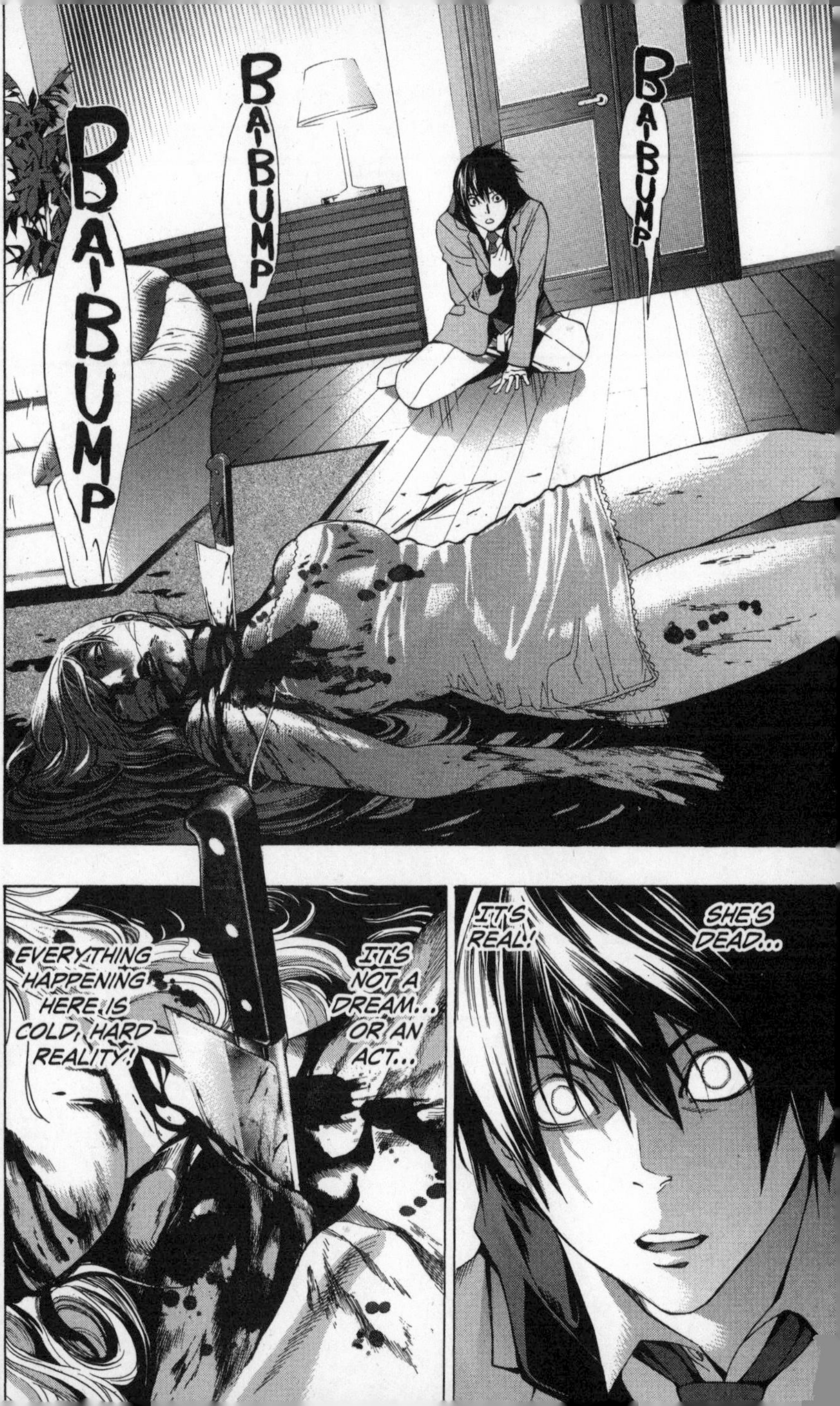
BABUMP
BABUMP
BABUMP
SHE'S DEAD...
IT'S REAL!
IT'S NOT A DREAM... OR AN ACT...
EVERYTHING HAPPENING HERE IS COLD, HARD REALITY!

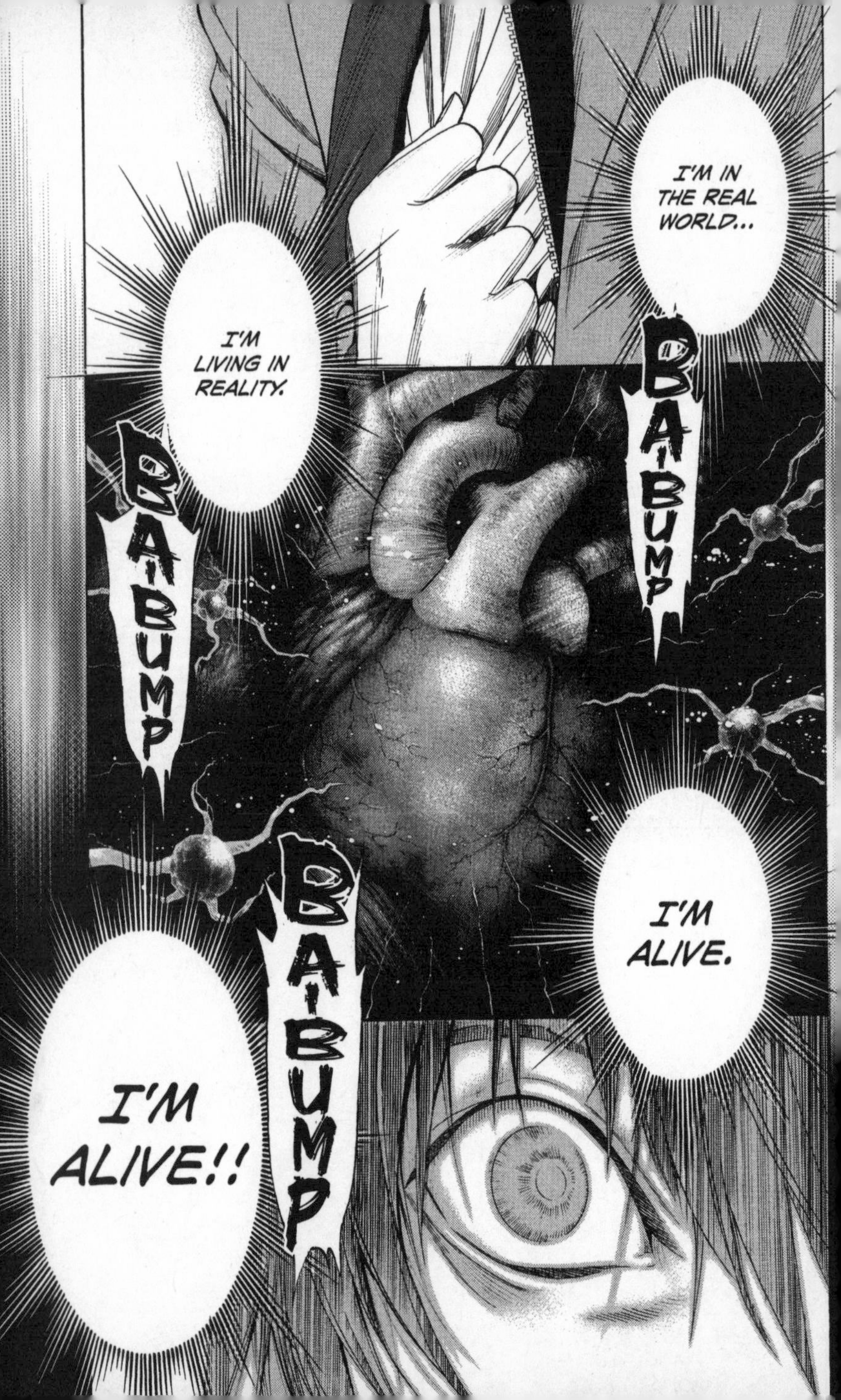
I'M IN THE REAL WORLD...
I'M LIVING IN REALITY.
BA-BUMP
BA-BUMP
I'M ALIVE.
BA-BUMP
I'M ALIVE!!

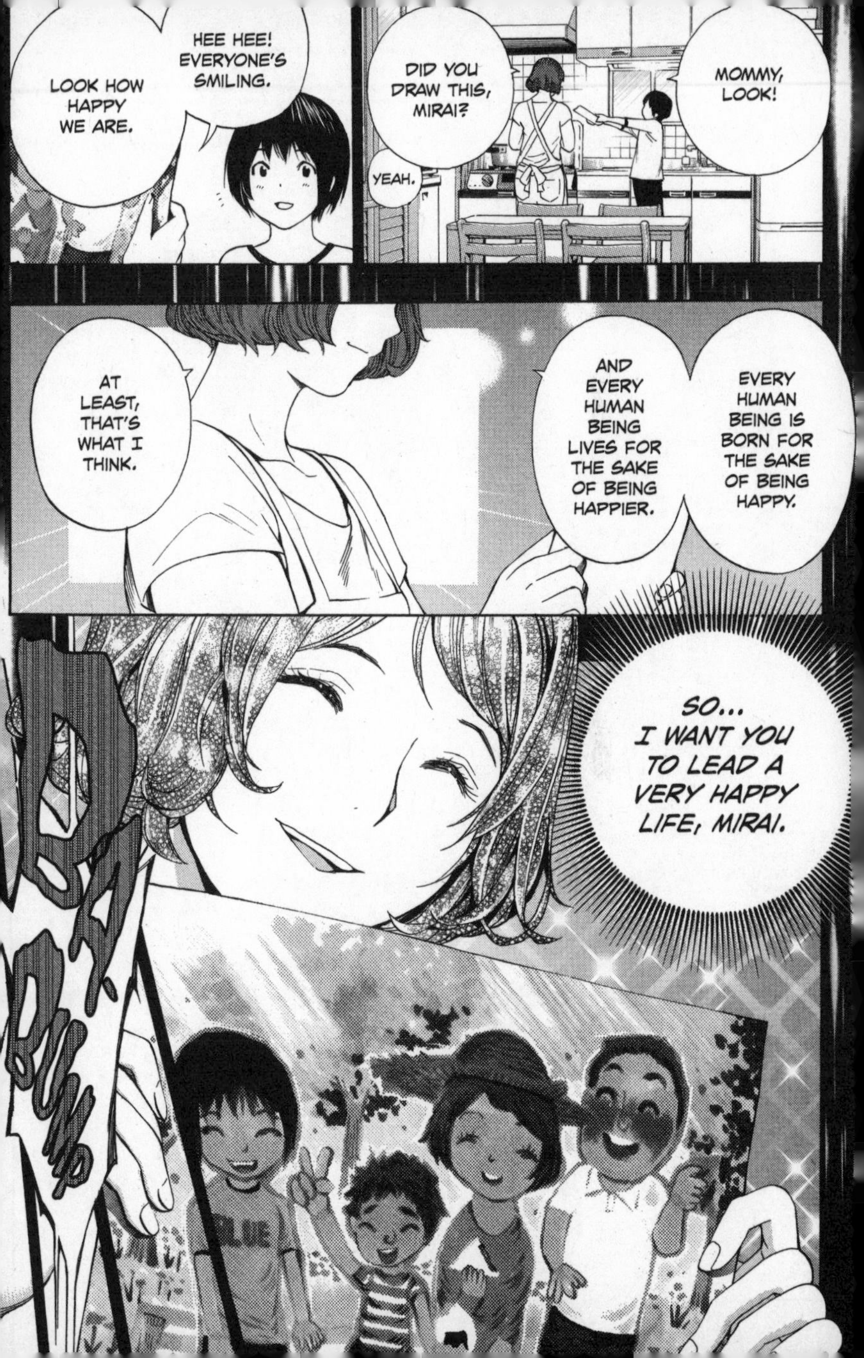
MOMMY, LOOK!
DID YOU DRAW THIS, MIRAI?
YEAH.
HEE HEE! EVERYONE'S SMILING.
LOOK HOW HAPPY WE ARE.
EVERY HUMAN BEING IS BORN FOR THE SAKE OF BEING HAPPY.
AND EVERY HUMAN BEING LIVES FOR THE SAKE OF BEING HAPPIER.
AT LEAST, THAT'S WHAT I THINK.
SO... I WANT YOU TO LEAD A VERY HAPPY LIFE, MIRAI.

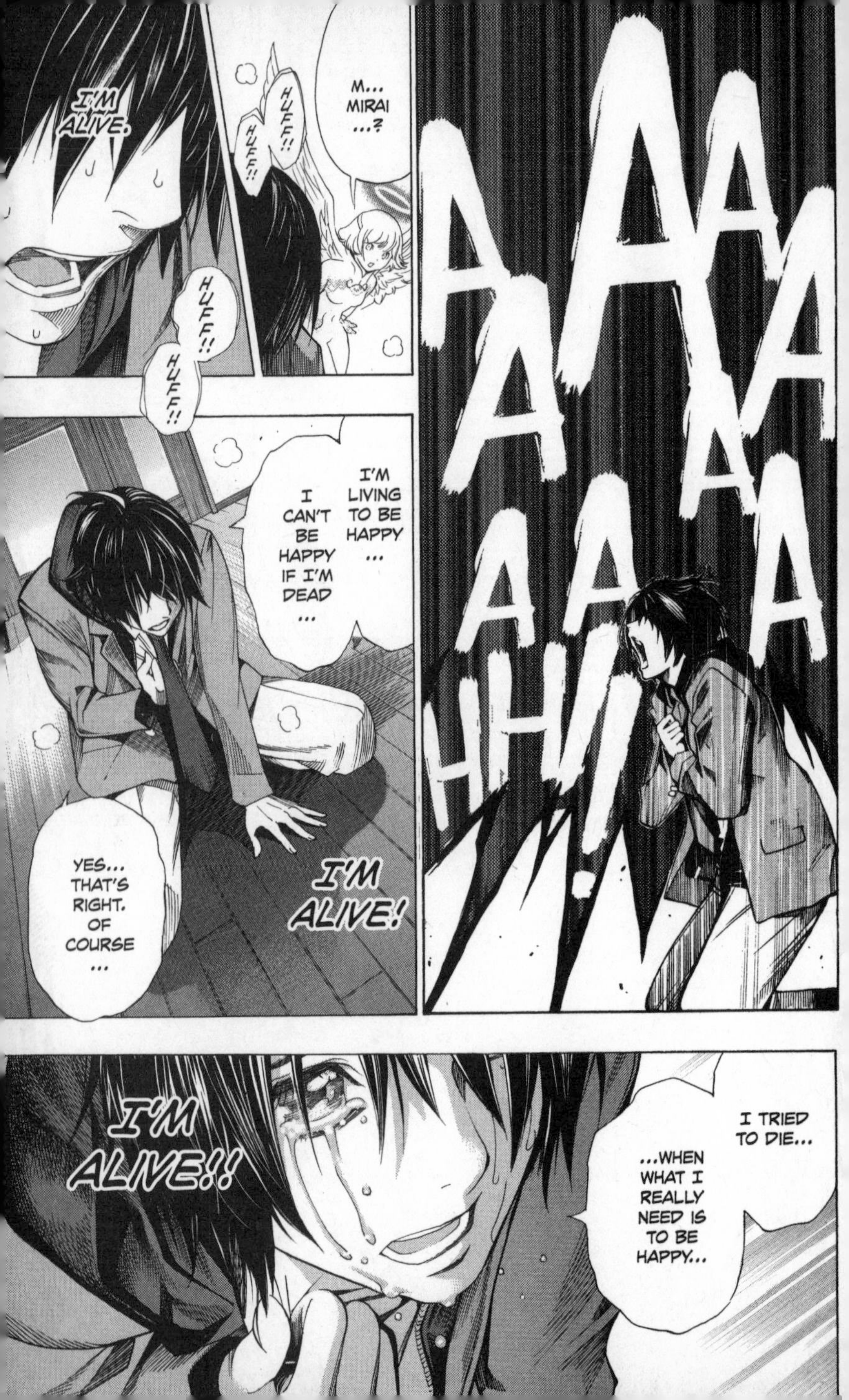
AAAAAAAAAAHH!!
M... MIRAI ...?
HUFF!! HUFF!!
I'M ALIVE.
HUFF!! HUFF!!
I'M LIVING TO BE HAPPY ...
I CAN'T BE HAPPY IF I'M DEAD ...
I'M ALIVE!
YES... THAT'S RIGHT. OF COURSE ...
I TRIED TO DIE...
...WHEN WHAT I REALLY NEED IS TO BE HAPPY...
I'M ALIVE!!

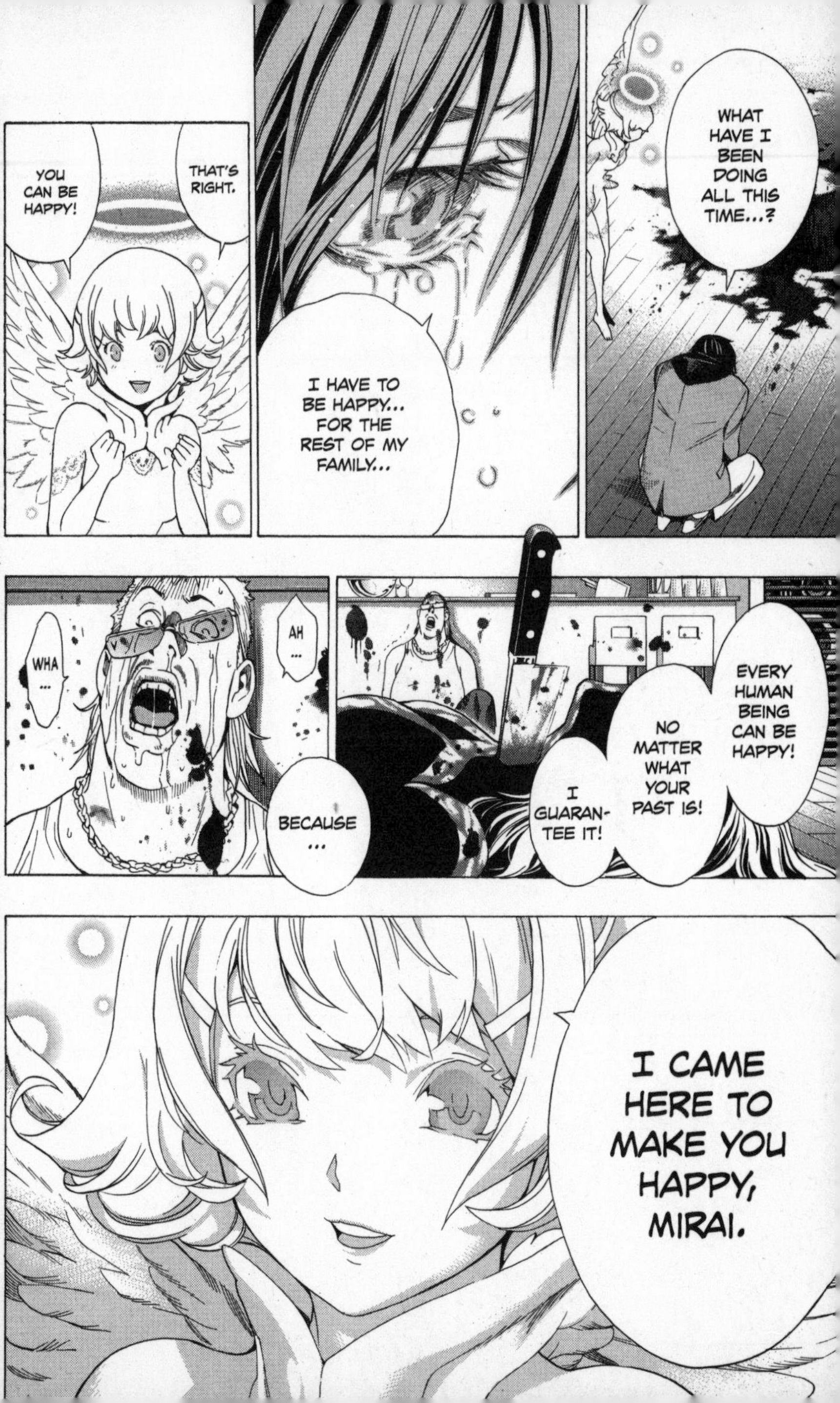
WHAT HAVE I BEEN DOING ALL THIS TIME...?
I HAVE TO BE HAPPY... FOR THE REST OF MY FAMILY...
THAT'S RIGHT.
YOU CAN BE HAPPY!
EVERY HUMAN BEING CAN BE HAPPY!
NO MATTER WHAT YOUR PAST IS!
I GUARAN-TEE IT!
BECAUSE ...
AH ...
WHA ...
I CAME HERE TO MAKE YOU HAPPY, MIRAI.

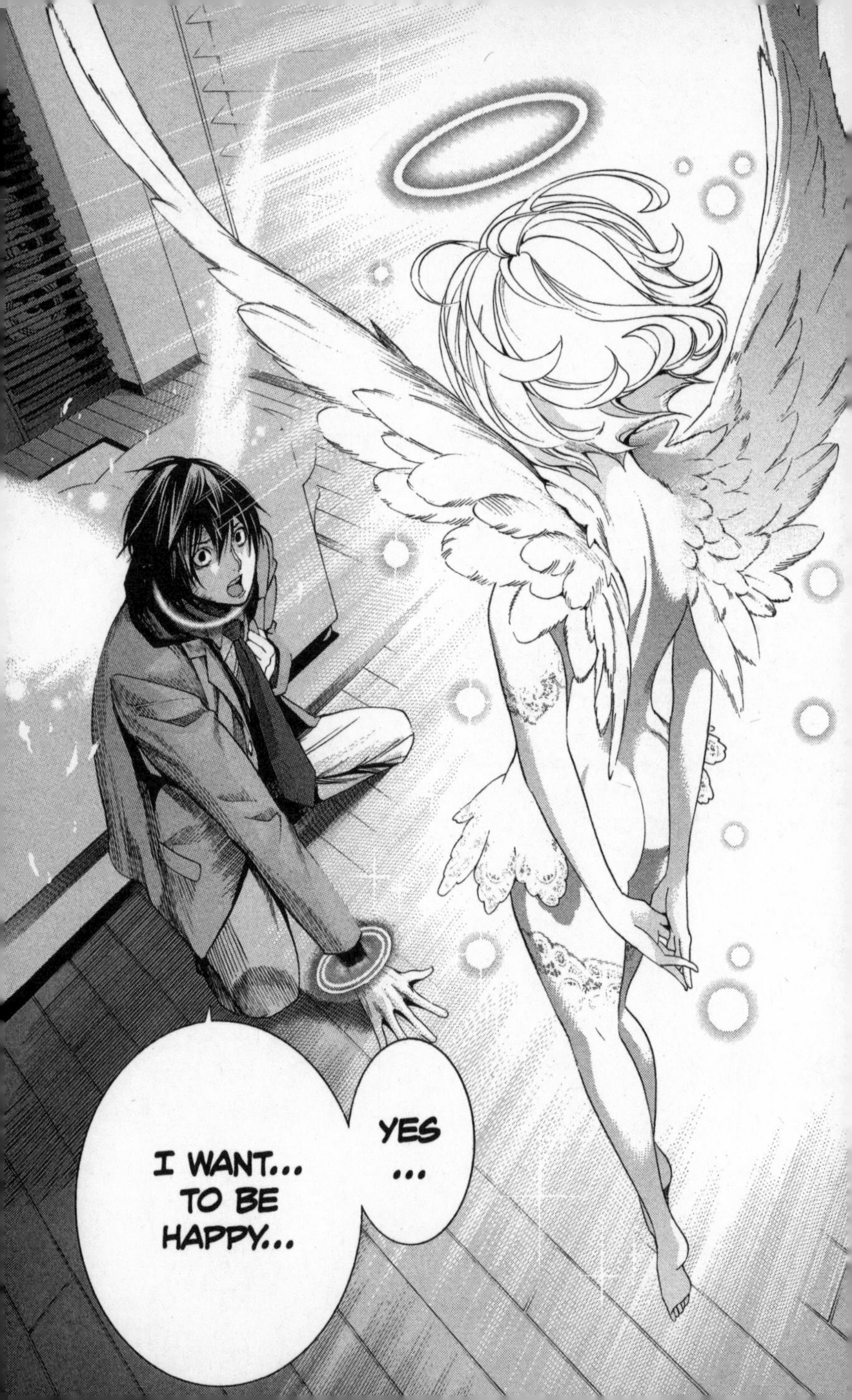
YES ...
I WANT... TO BE HAPPY...

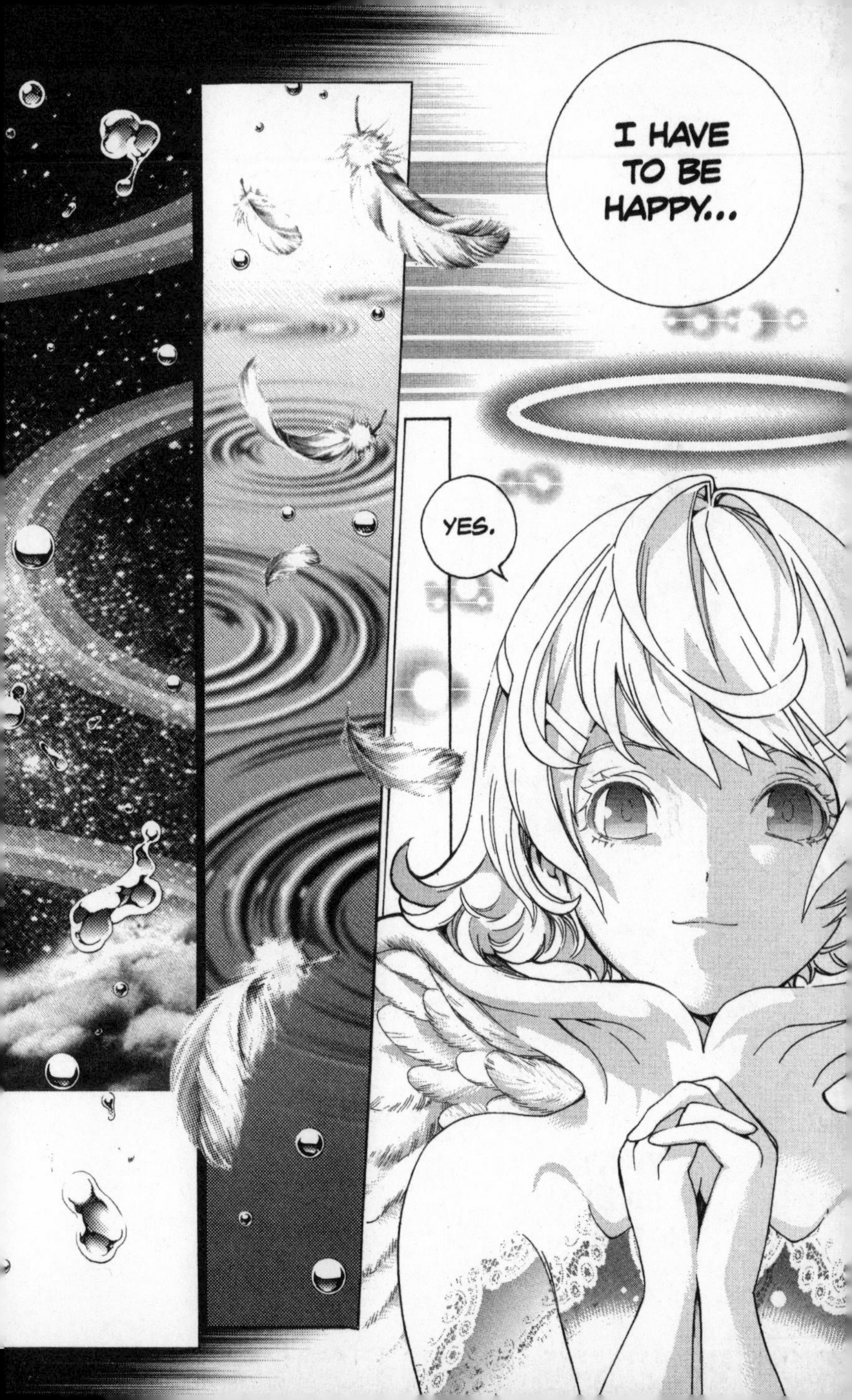
I HAVE TO BE HAPPY...
YES.

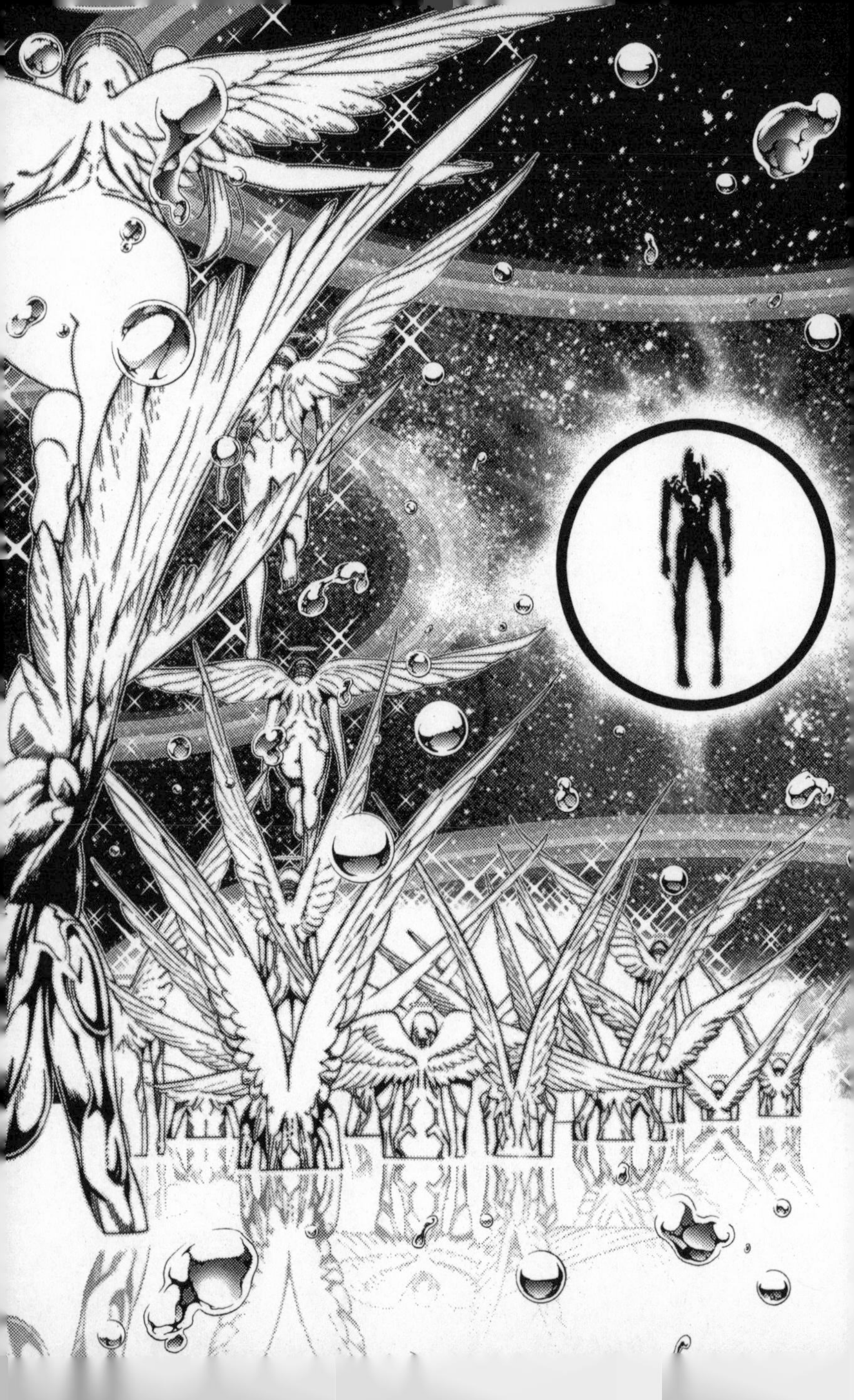

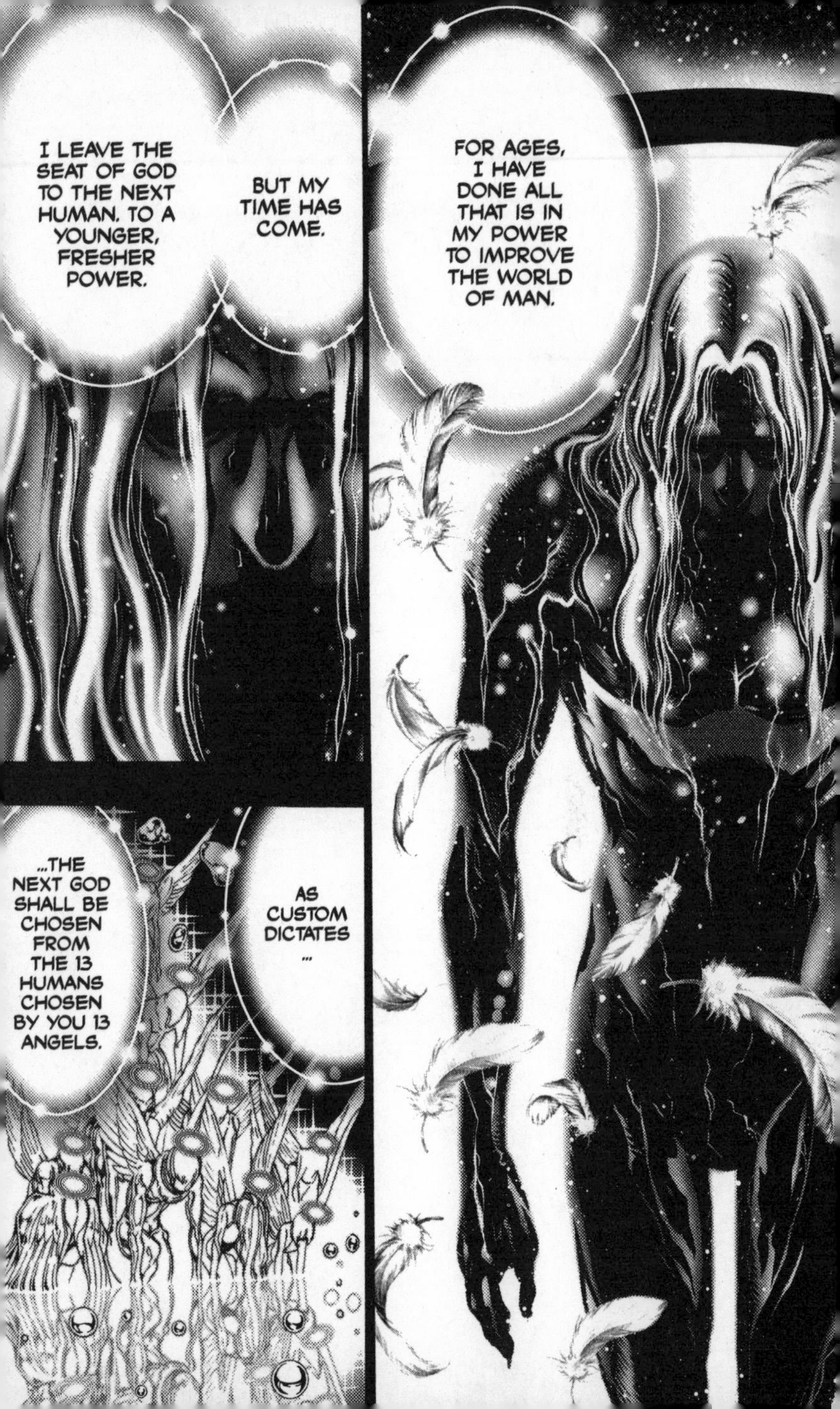
FOR AGES, I HAVE DONE ALL THAT IS IN MY POWER TO IMPROVE THE WORLD OF MAN.
BUT MY TIME HAS COME.
I LEAVE THE SEAT OF GOD TO THE NEXT HUMAN. TO A YOUNGER, FRESHER POWER.
AS CUSTOM DICTATES...
...THE NEXT GOD SHALL BE CHOSEN FROM THE 13 HUMANS CHOSEN BY YOU 13 ANGELS.

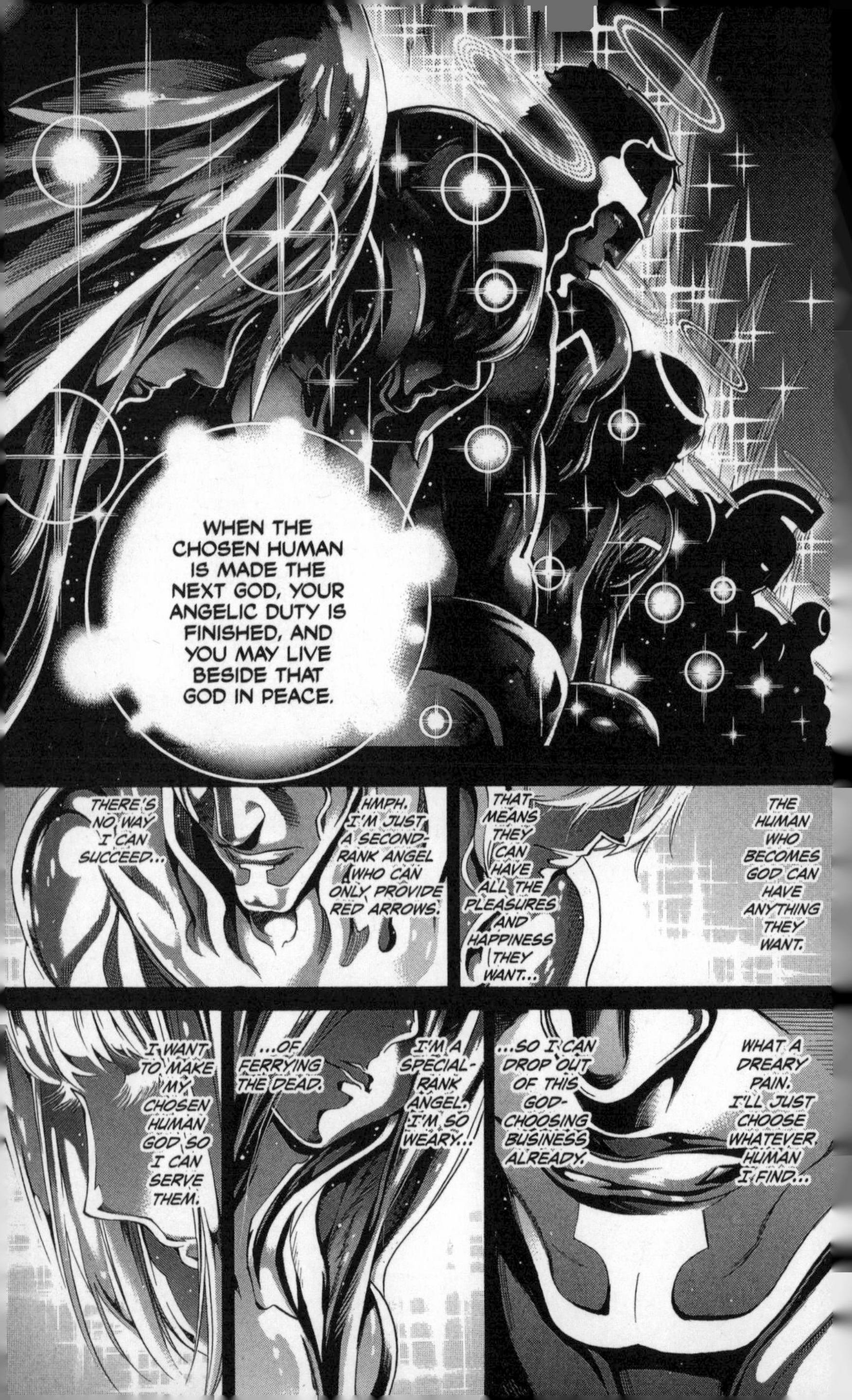
WHEN THE CHOSEN HUMAN IS MADE THE NEXT GOD, YOUR ANGELIC DUTY IS FINISHED, AND YOU MAY LIVE BESIDE THAT GOD IN PEACE.
THE HUMAN WHO BECOMES GOD CAN HAVE ANYTHING THEY WANT.
THAT MEANS THEY CAN HAVE ALL THE PLEASURES AND HAPPINESS THEY WANT...
HMPH. I'M JUST A SECOND-RANK ANGEL WHO CAN ONLY PROVIDE RED ARROWS.
THERE'S NO WAY I CAN SUCCEED...
WHAT A DREARY PAIN. I'LL JUST CHOOSE WHATEVER HUMAN I FIND...
...SO I CAN DROP OUT OF THIS GOD-CHOOSING BUSINESS ALREADY.
I'M A SPECIAL-RANK ANGEL. I'M SO WEARY...
...OF FERRYING THE DEAD.
I WANT TO MAKE MY CHOSEN HUMAN GOD SO I CAN SERVE THEM.

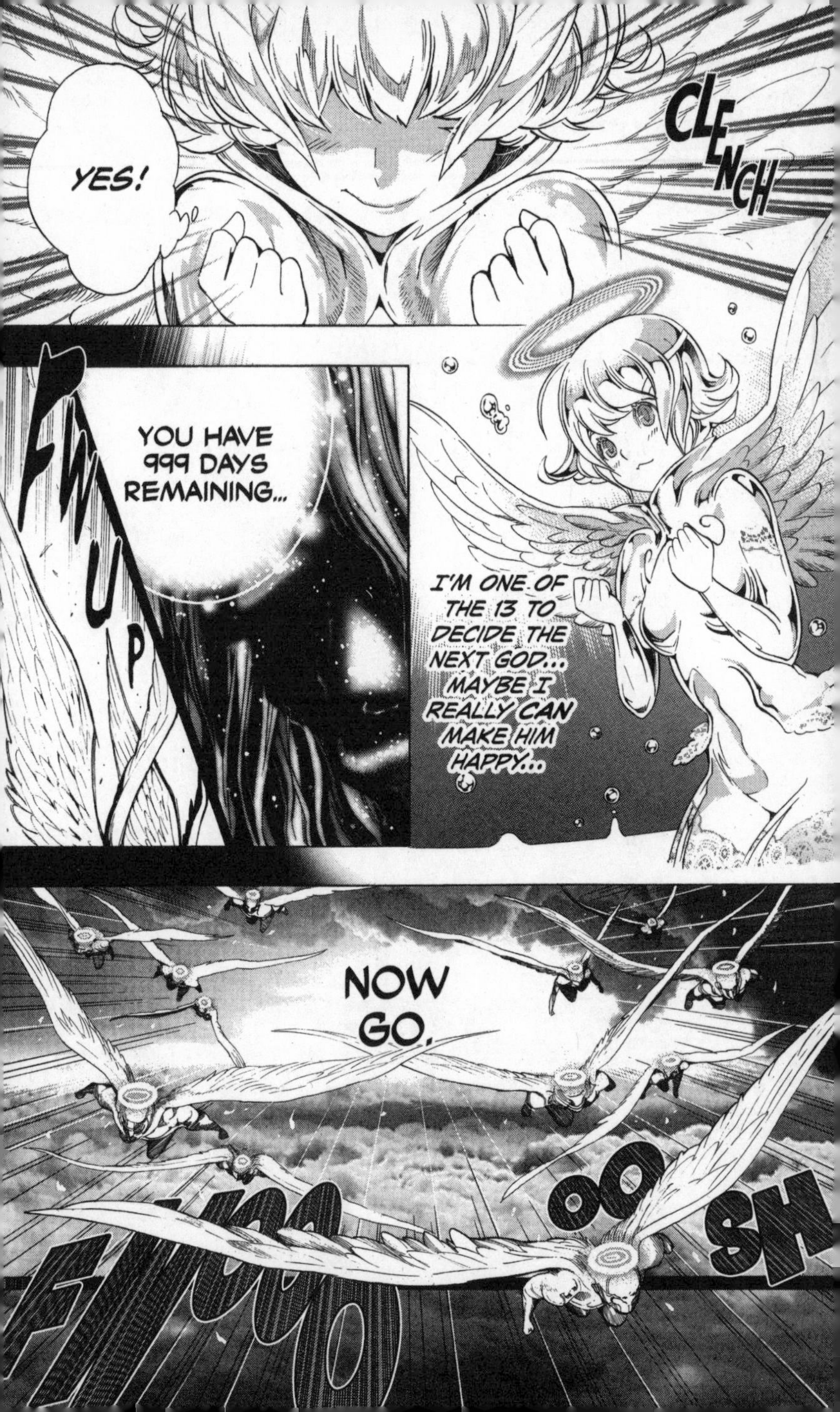
CLENCH
YES!
I'M ONE OF THE 13 TO DECIDE THE NEXT GOD... MAYBE I REALLY CAN MAKE HIM HAPPY...
YOU HAVE 999 DAYS REMAINING...
FWUP
NOW GO.
FWOOO
OOSH

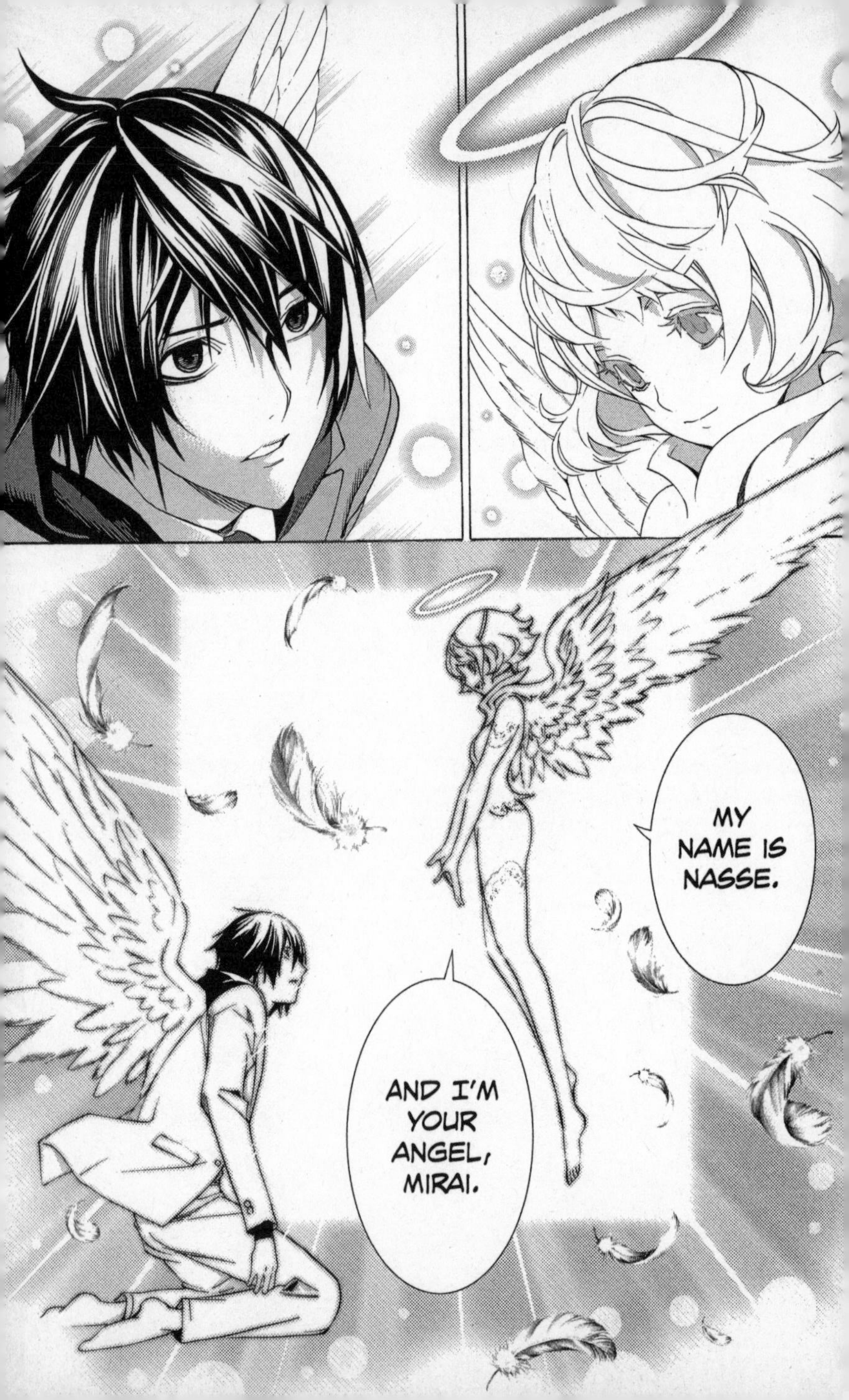
MY NAME IS NASSE.
AND I'M YOUR ANGEL, MIRAI.

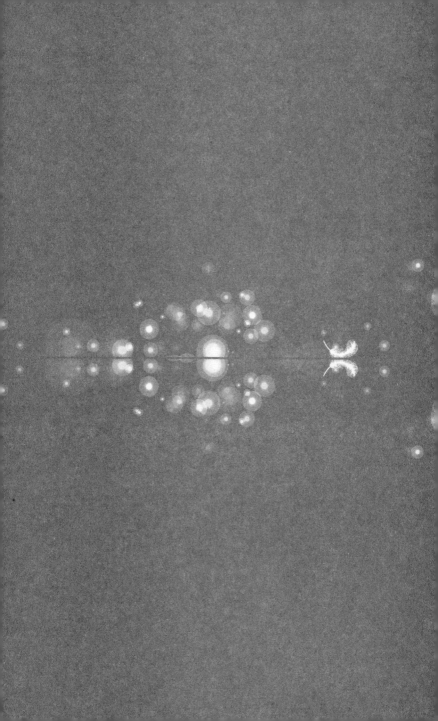

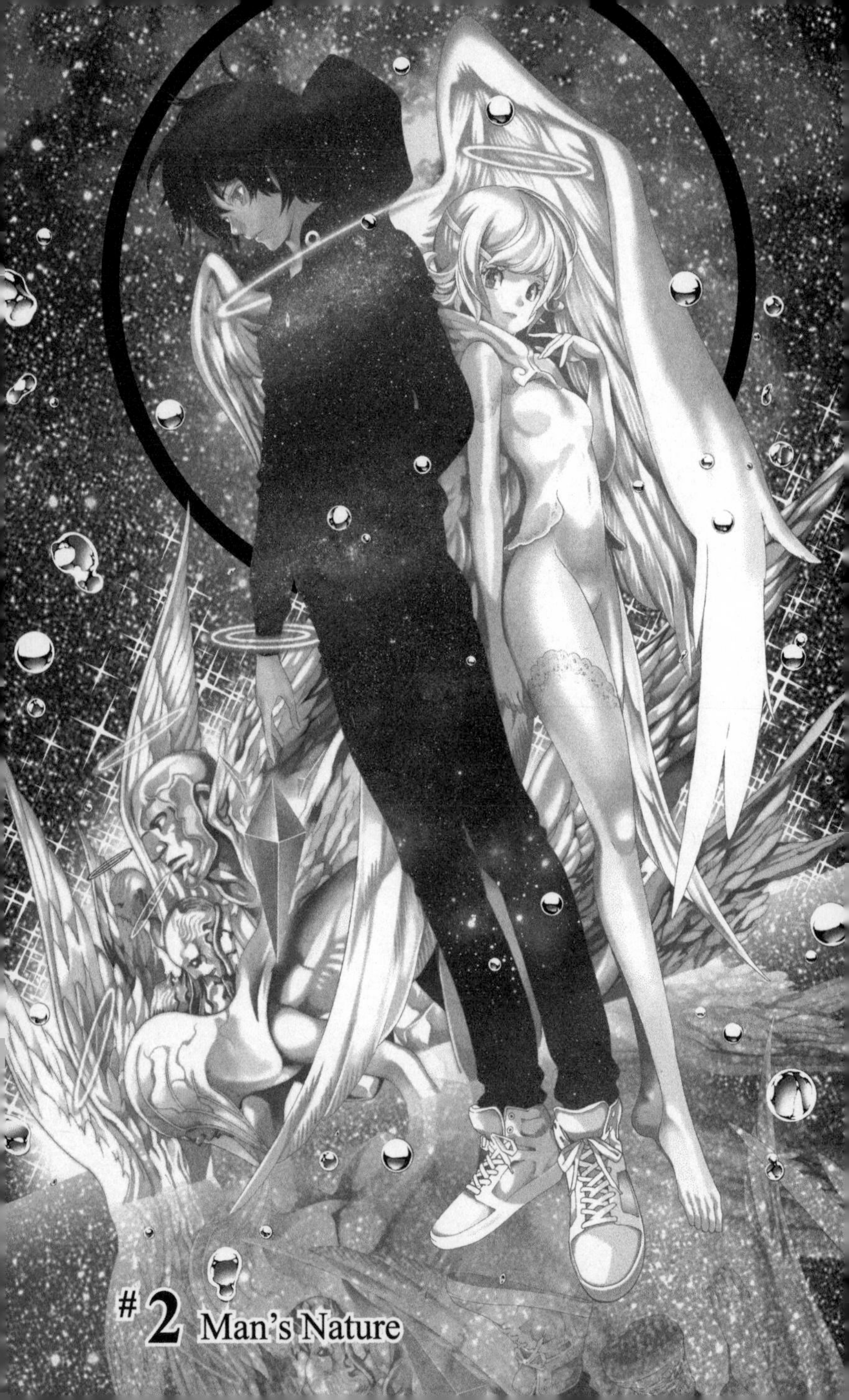
#2 Man's Nature

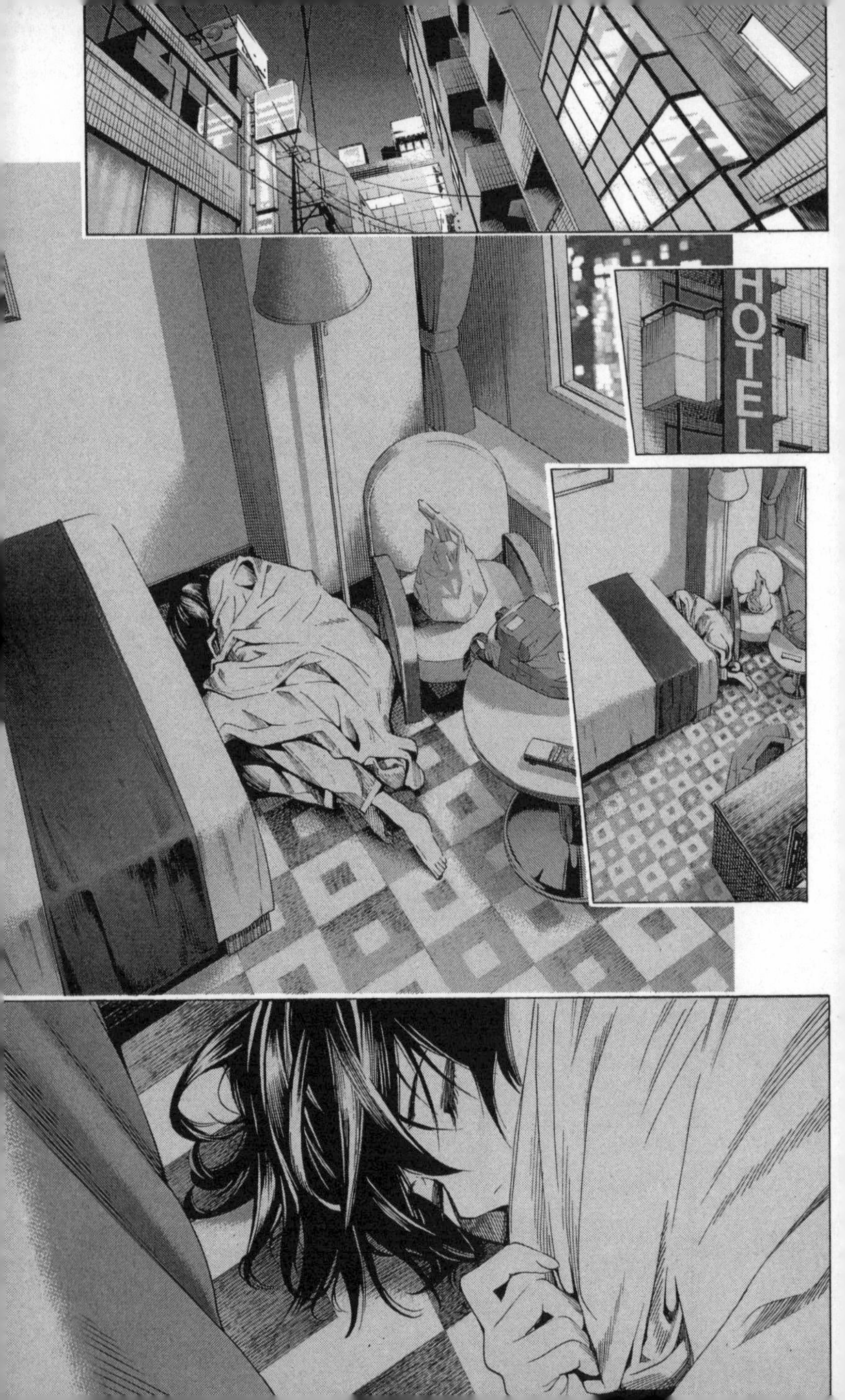
HOTEL

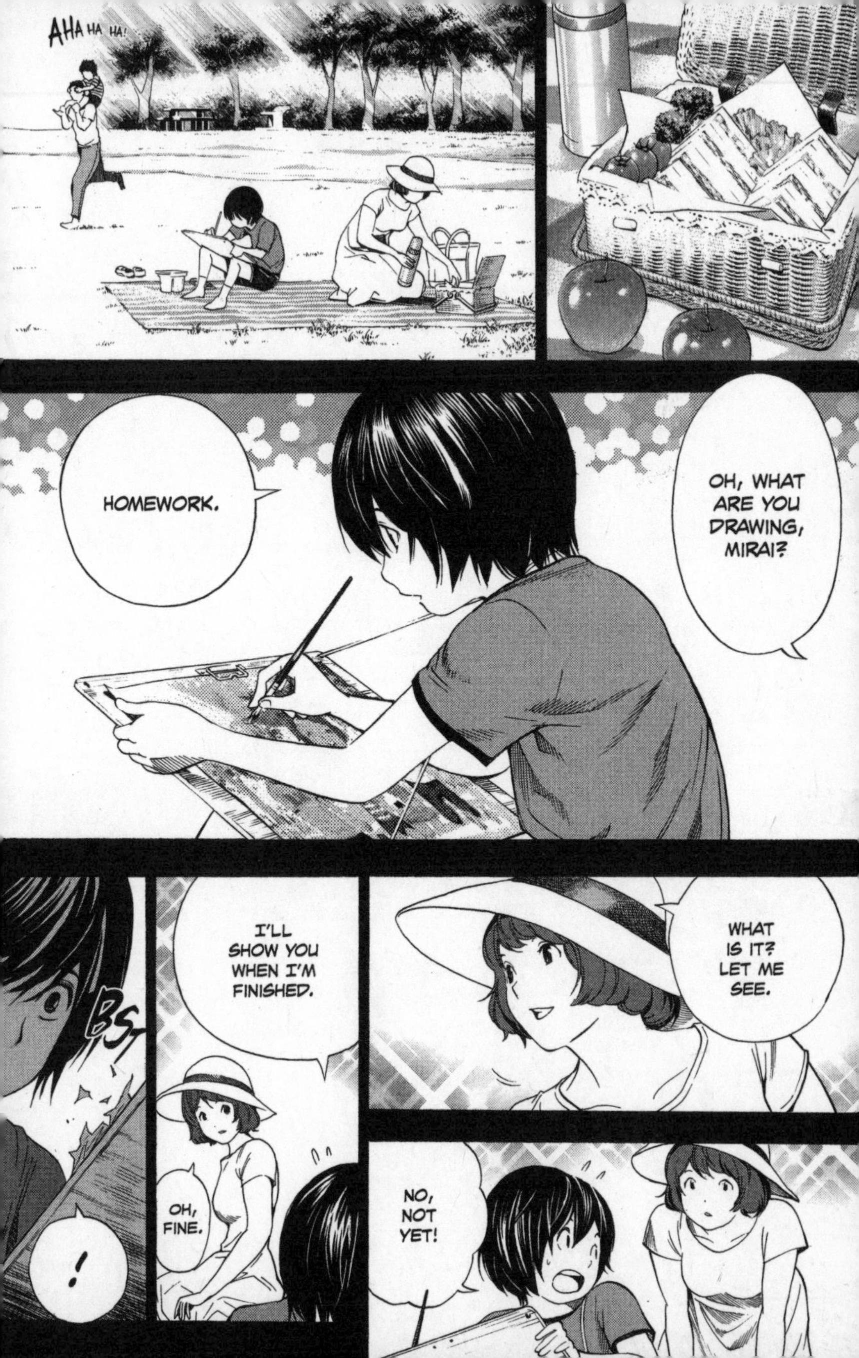
AHA HA HA!
OH, WHAT ARE YOU DRAWING, MIRAI?
HOMEWORK.
WHAT IS IT? LET ME SEE.
NO, NOT YET!
I'LL SHOW YOU WHEN I'M FINISHED.
OH, FINE.
BST
!

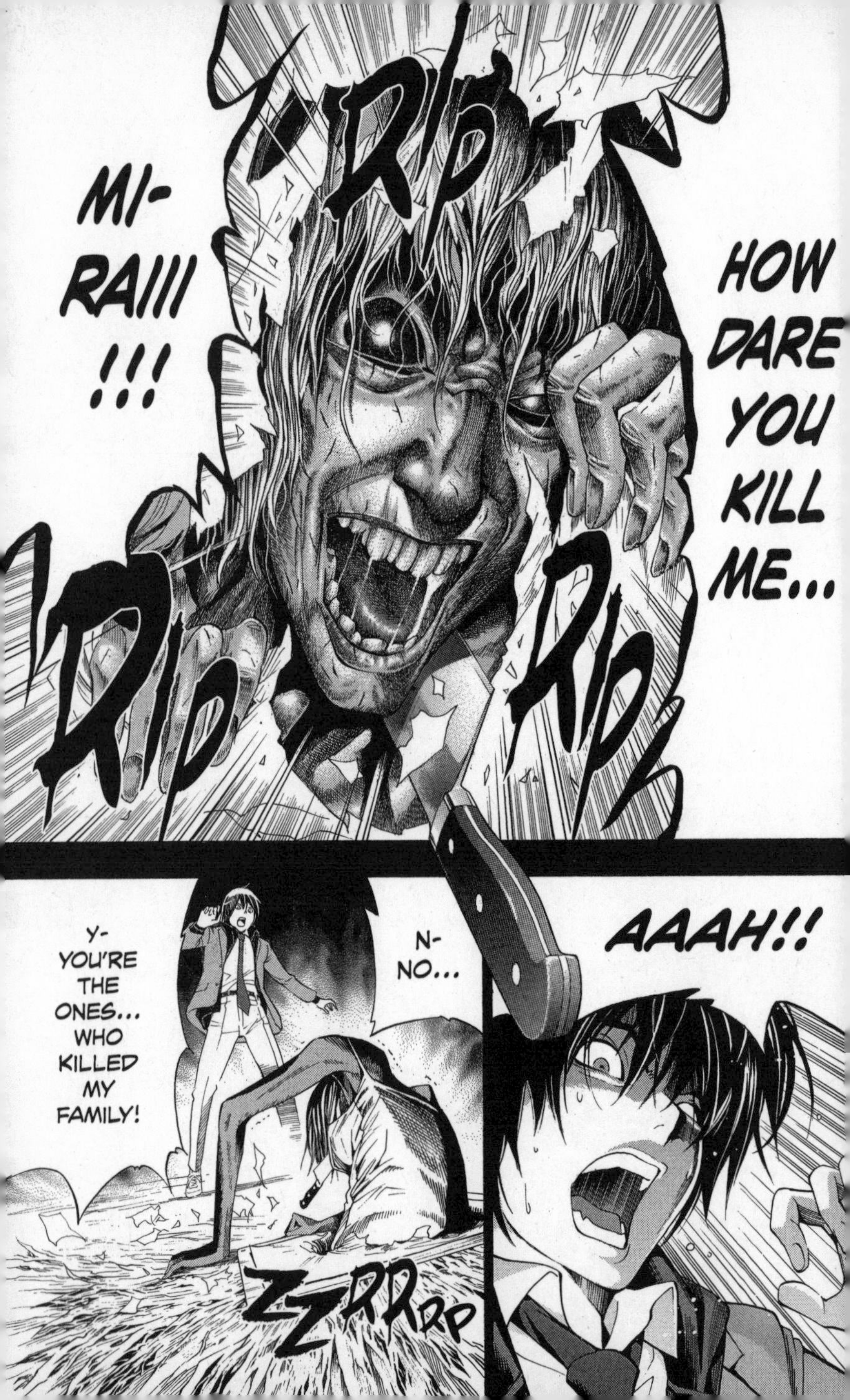
RIP
HOW DARE YOU KILL ME...
MI-RAIII!!!
RIP
RIP
AAAH!!
N-NO...
Y-YOU'RE THE ONES... WHO KILLED MY FAMILY!
ZZRRDRP

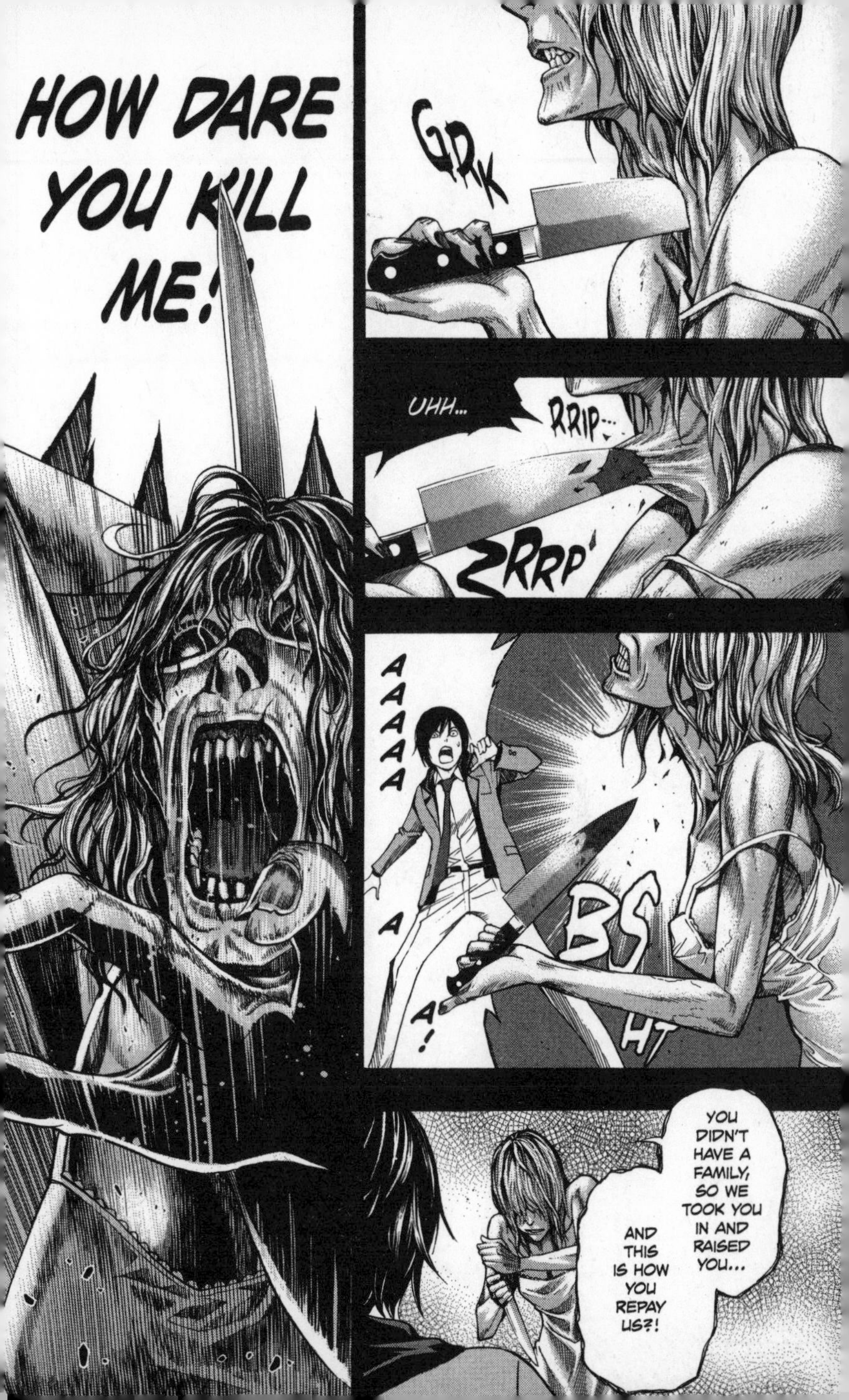
GRK
UHH...
RRIP...
ZRRP
AAAAAA
A
A!
BSHT
YOU DIDN'T HAVE A FAMILY, SO WE TOOK YOU IN AND RAISED YOU...
AND THIS IS HOW YOU REPAY US?!
HOW DARE YOU KILL ME?!

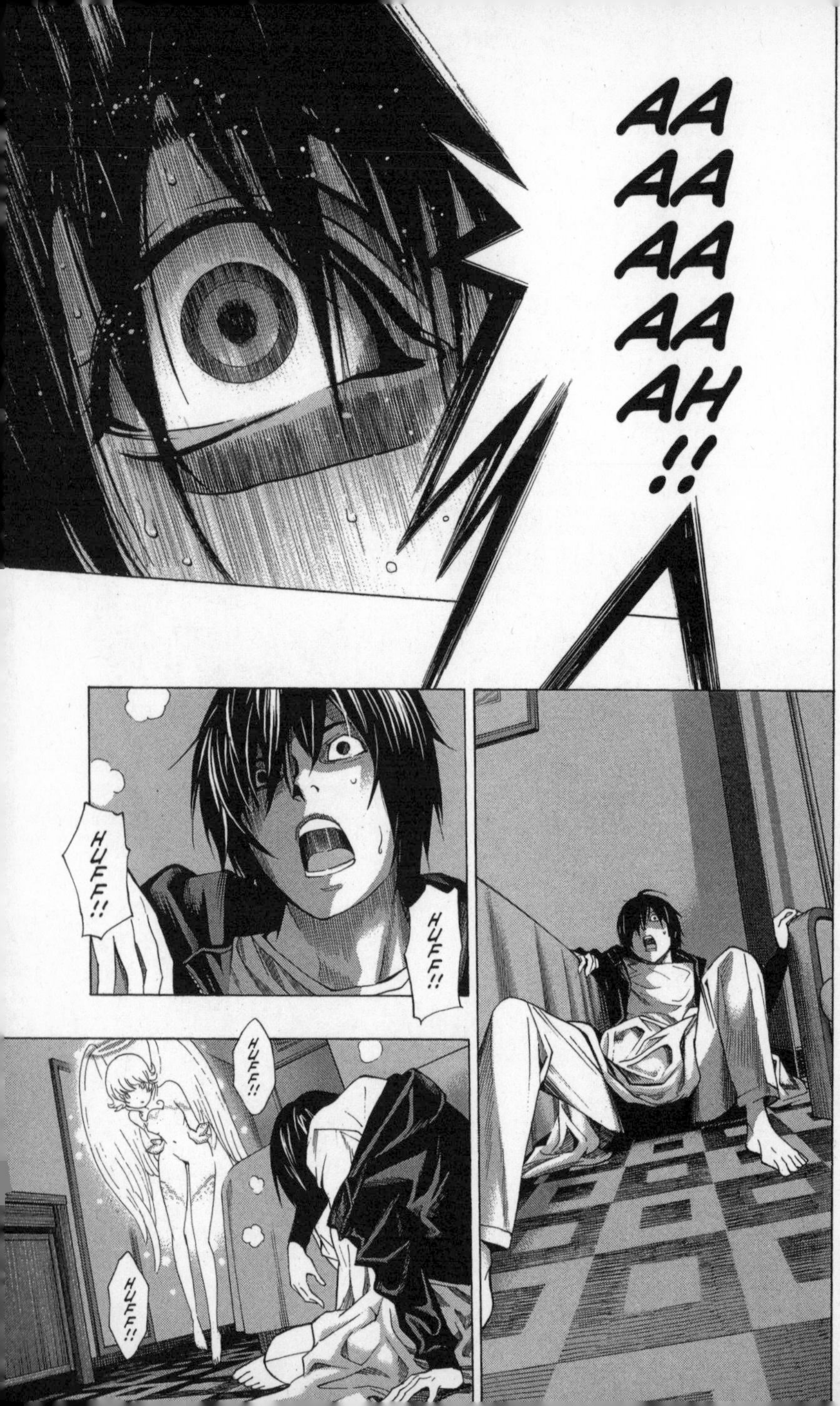
AAAAAAAAAH!!
HUFF!!
HUFF!!
HUFF!!
HUFF!!

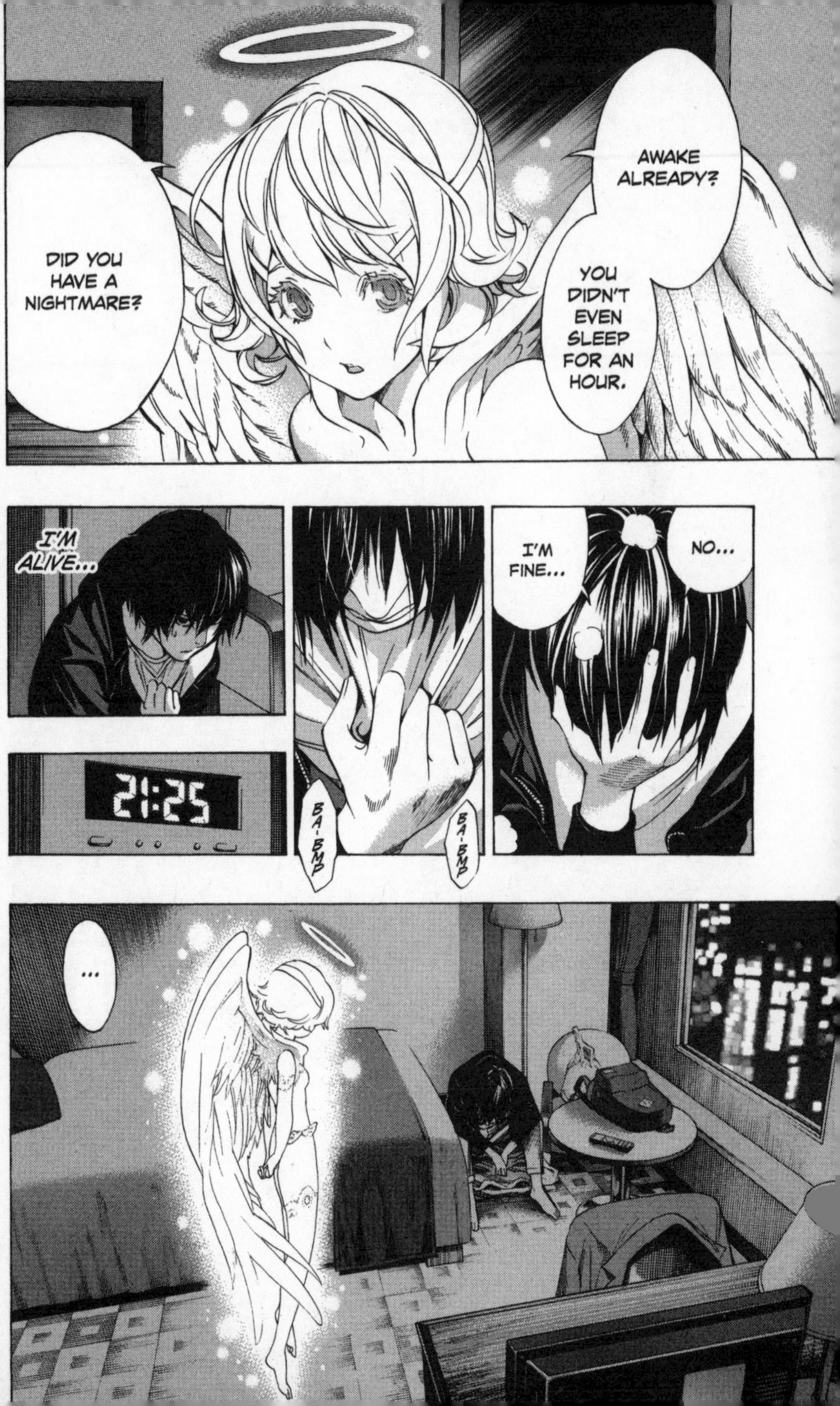
AWAKE ALREADY?
YOU DIDN'T EVEN SLEEP FOR AN HOUR.
DID YOU HAVE A NIGHTMARE?
NO...
I'M FINE...
BA-BMP
BA-BMP
I'M ALIVE...
21:25
...

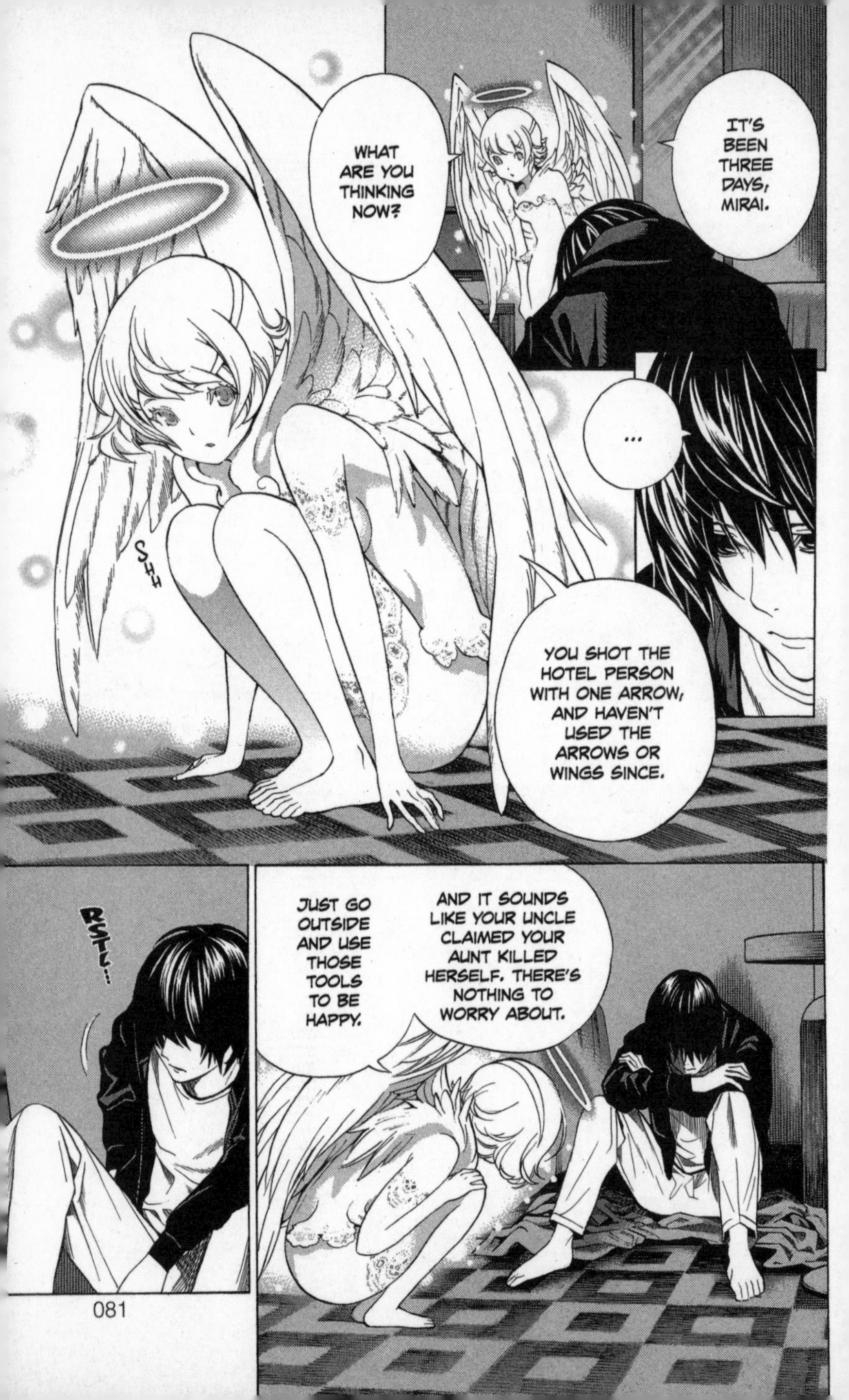
IT'S BEEN THREE DAYS, MIRAI.
WHAT ARE YOU THINKING NOW?
...
YOU SHOT THE HOTEL PERSON WITH ONE ARROW, AND HAVEN'T USED THE ARROWS OR WINGS SINCE.
SHH
AND IT SOUNDS LIKE YOUR UNCLE CLAIMED YOUR AUNT KILLED HERSELF. THERE'S NOTHING TO WORRY ABOUT.
JUST GO OUTSIDE AND USE THOSE TOOLS TO BE HAPPY.
RSTL...

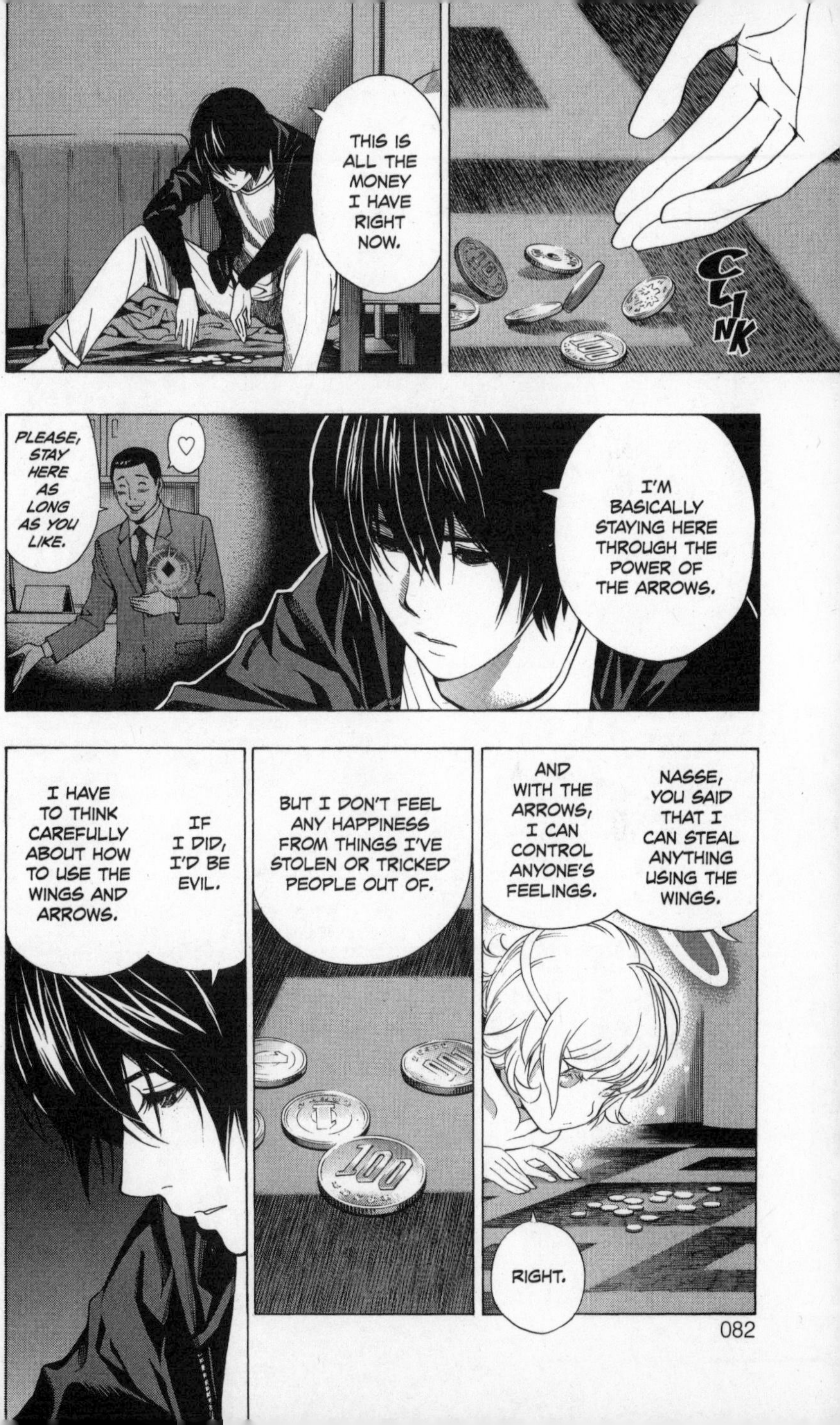
CLINK
THIS IS ALL THE MONEY I HAVE RIGHT NOW.
I'M BASICALLY STAYING HERE THROUGH THE POWER OF THE ARROWS.
♡
PLEASE, STAY HERE AS LONG AS YOU LIKE.
NASSE, YOU SAID THAT I CAN STEAL ANYTHING USING THE WINGS.
AND WITH THE ARROWS, I CAN CONTROL ANYONE'S FEELINGS.
RIGHT.
BUT I DON'T FEEL ANY HAPPINESS FROM THINGS I'VE STOLEN OR TRICKED PEOPLE OUT OF.
IF I DID, I'D BE EVIL.
I HAVE TO THINK CAREFULLY ABOUT HOW TO USE THE WINGS AND ARROWS.

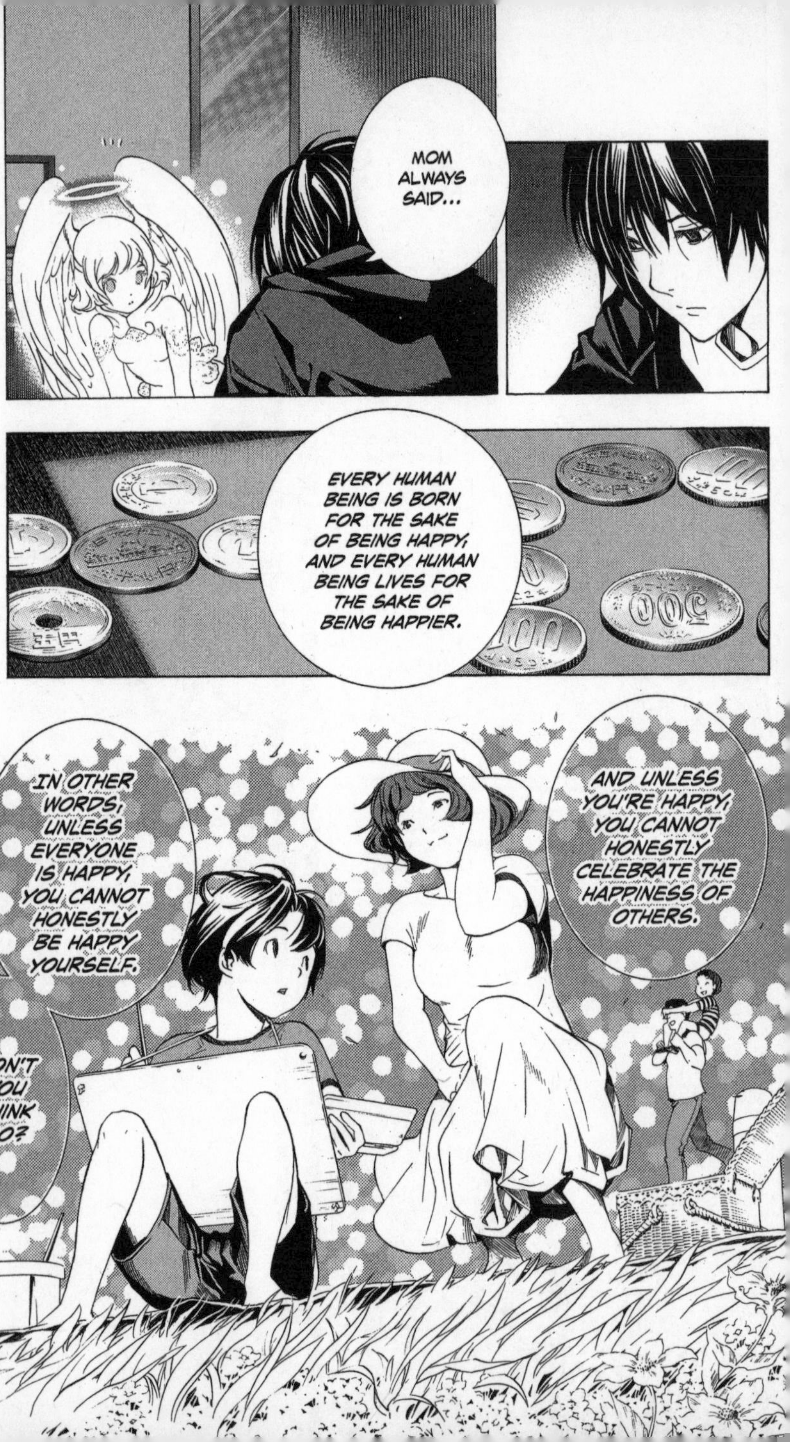
MOM ALWAYS SAID...
EVERY HUMAN BEING IS BORN FOR THE SAKE OF BEING HAPPY, AND EVERY HUMAN BEING LIVES FOR THE SAKE OF BEING HAPPIER.
AND UNLESS YOU'RE HAPPY, YOU CANNOT HONESTLY CELEBRATE THE HAPPINESS OF OTHERS.
IN OTHER WORDS, UNLESS EVERYONE IS HAPPY, YOU CANNOT HONESTLY BE HAPPY YOURSELF.
DON'T YOU THINK SO?

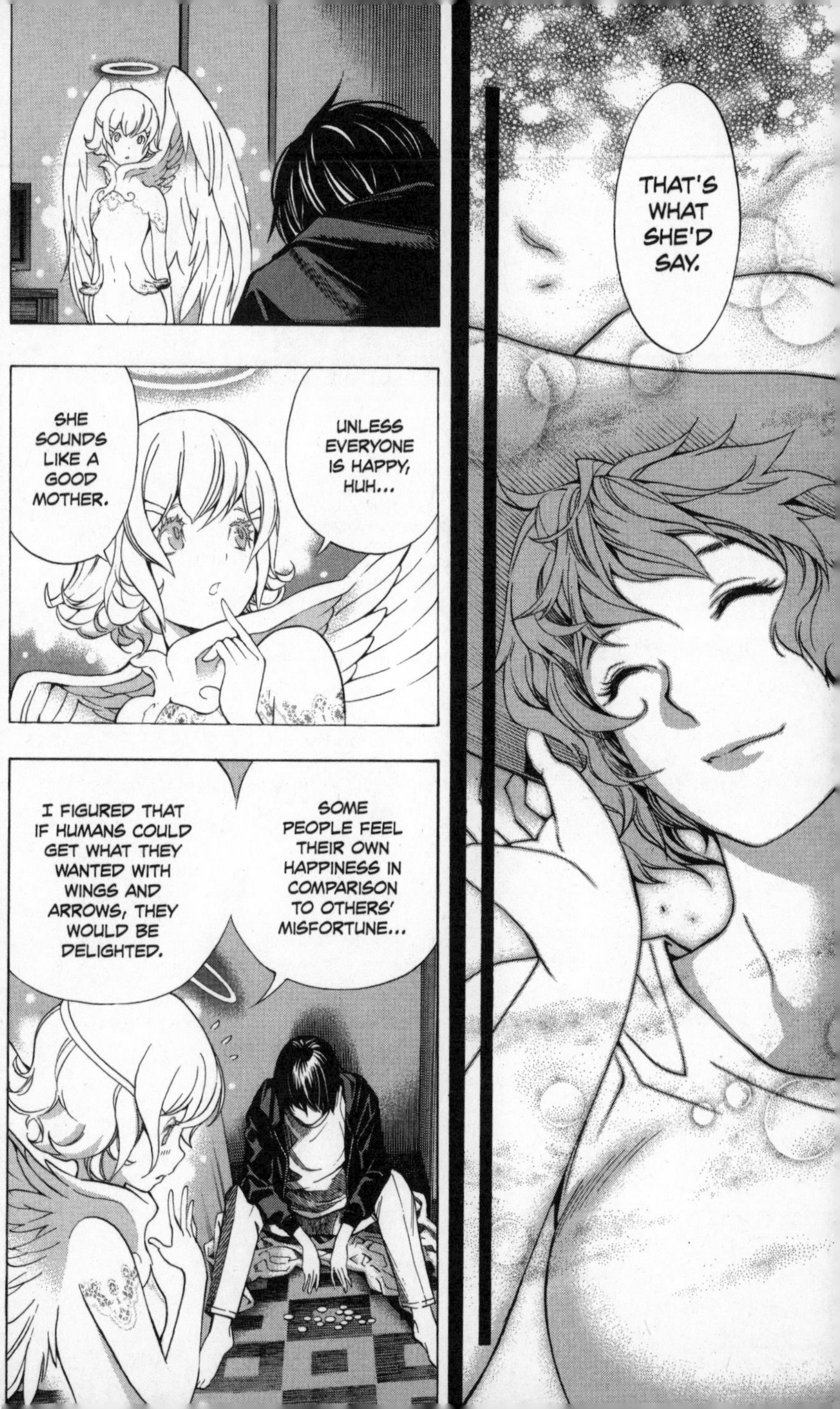
THAT'S WHAT SHE'D SAY.
UNLESS EVERYONE IS HAPPY, HUH...
SHE SOUNDS LIKE A GOOD MOTHER.
SOME PEOPLE FEEL THEIR OWN HAPPINESS IN COMPARISON TO OTHERS' MISFORTUNE...
I FIGURED THAT IF HUMANS COULD GET WHAT THEY WANTED WITH WINGS AND ARROWS, THEY WOULD BE DELIGHTED.

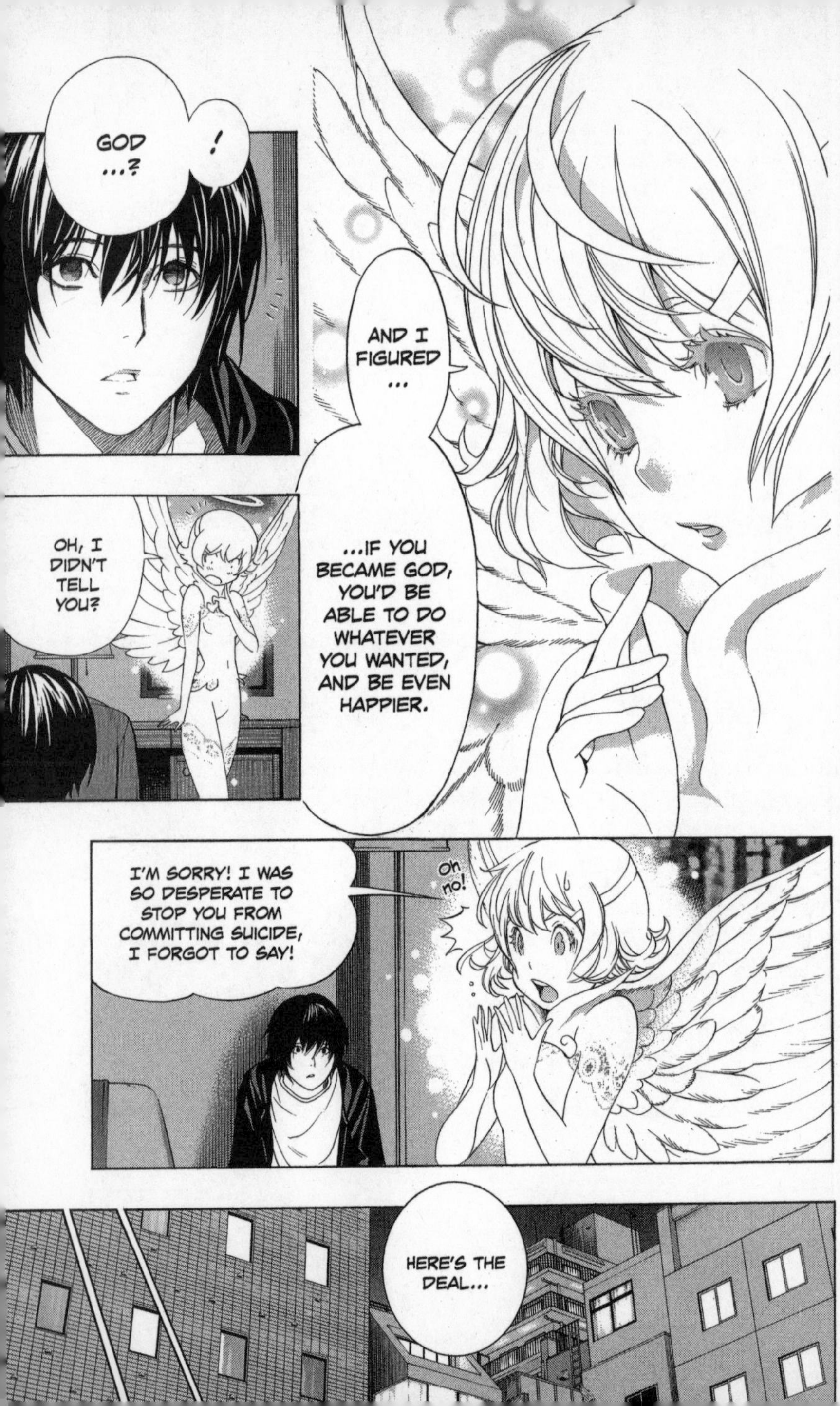
AND I FIGURED ...
...IF YOU BECAME GOD, YOU'D BE ABLE TO DO WHATEVER YOU WANTED, AND BE EVEN HAPPIER.
GOD ...?
!
OH, I DIDN'T TELL YOU?
Oh no!
I'M SORRY! I WAS SO DESPERATE TO STOP YOU FROM COMMITTING SUICIDE, I FORGOT TO SAY!
HERE'S THE DEAL...

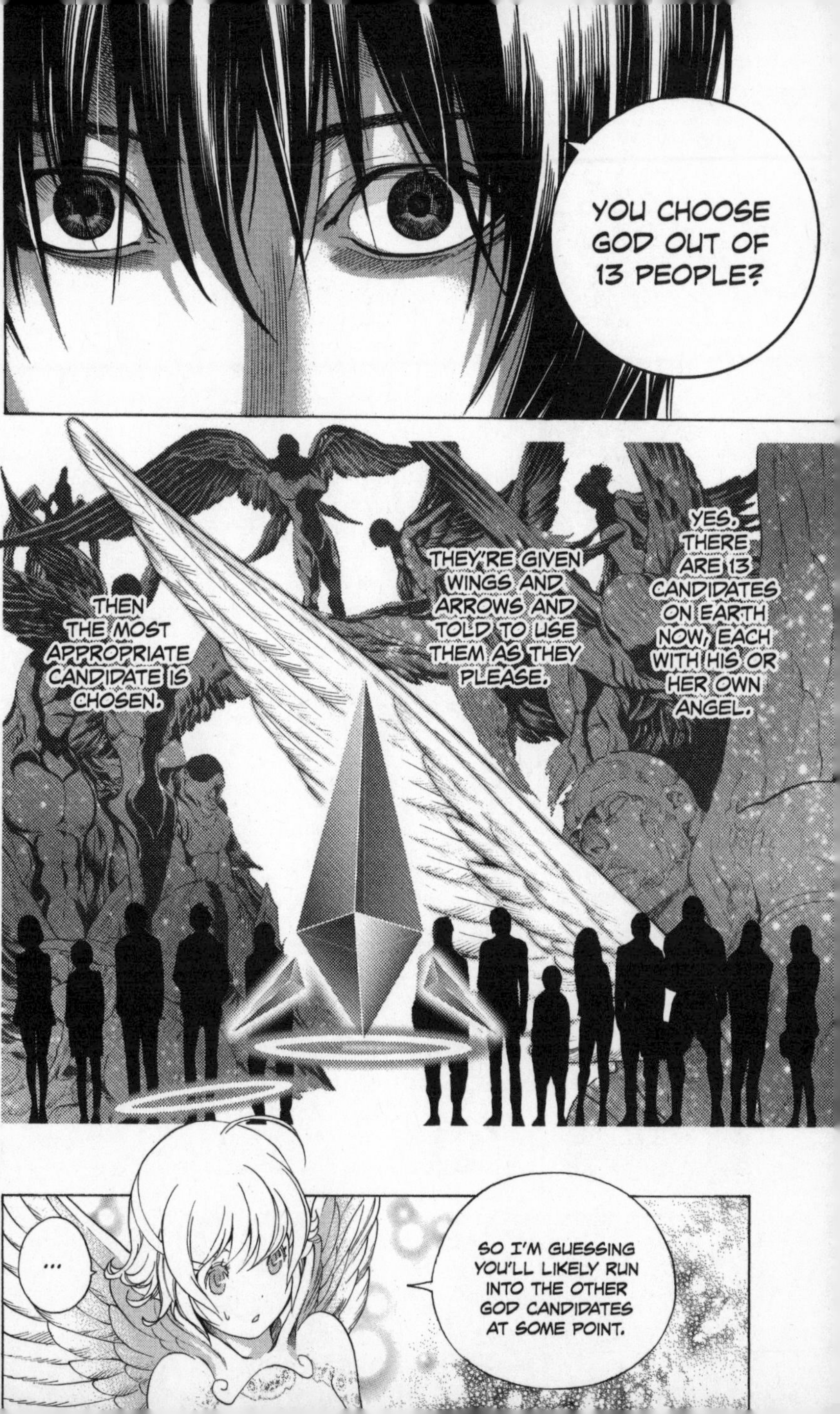
YOU CHOOSE GOD OUT OF 13 PEOPLE?
YES. THERE ARE 13 CANDIDATES ON EARTH NOW, EACH WITH HIS OR HER OWN ANGEL.
THEY'RE GIVEN WINGS AND ARROWS AND TOLD TO USE THEM AS THEY PLEASE.
THEN THE MOST APPROPRIATE CANDIDATE IS CHOSEN.
SO I'M GUESSING YOU'LL LIKELY RUN INTO THE OTHER GOD CANDIDATES AT SOME POINT.
...

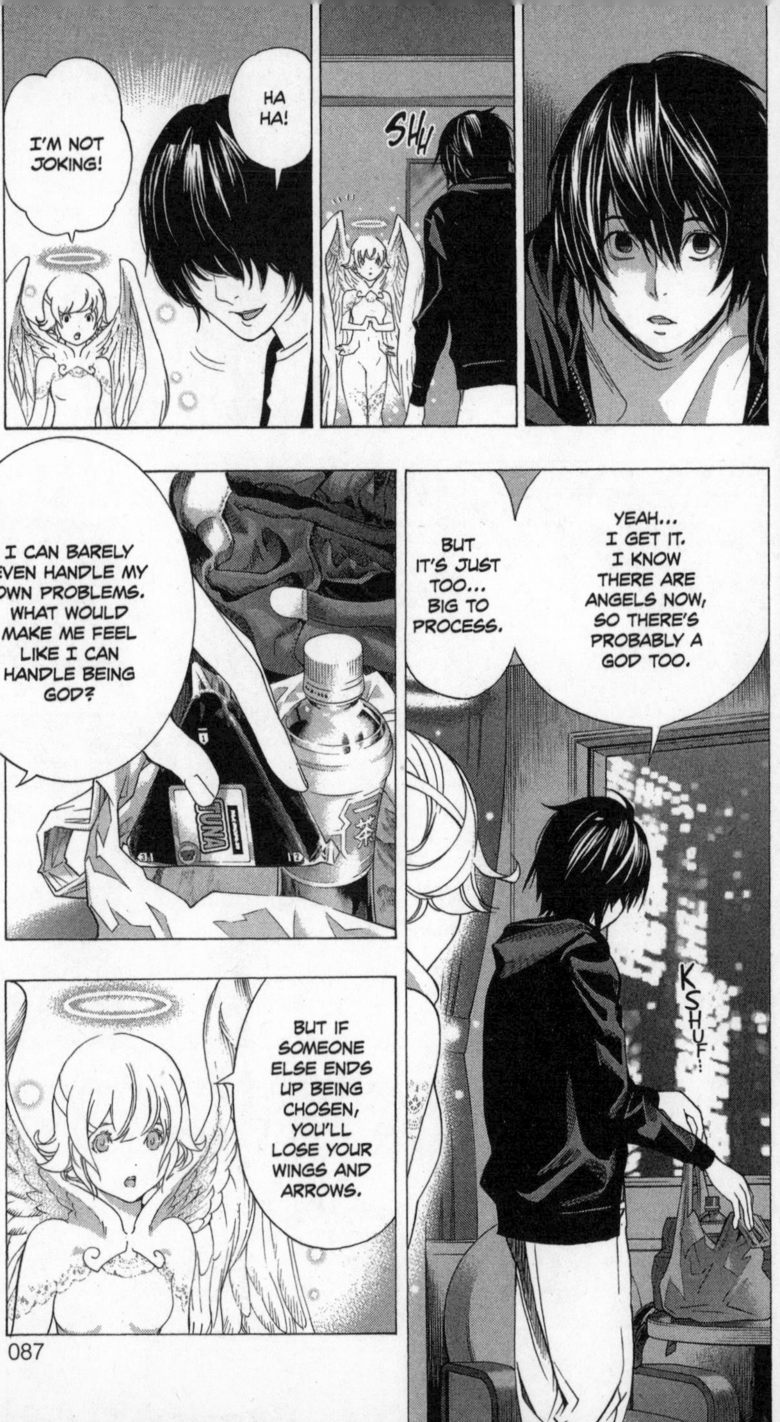
SHH
HA HA!
I'M NOT JOKING!
YEAH... I GET IT. I KNOW THERE ARE ANGELS NOW, SO THERE'S PROBABLY A GOD TOO.
BUT IT'S JUST TOO... BIG TO PROCESS.
KSHUF...
I CAN BARELY EVEN HANDLE MY OWN PROBLEMS. WHAT WOULD MAKE ME FEEL LIKE I CAN HANDLE BEING GOD?
TUNA
BUT IF SOMEONE ELSE ENDS UP BEING CHOSEN, YOU'LL LOSE YOUR WINGS AND ARROWS.

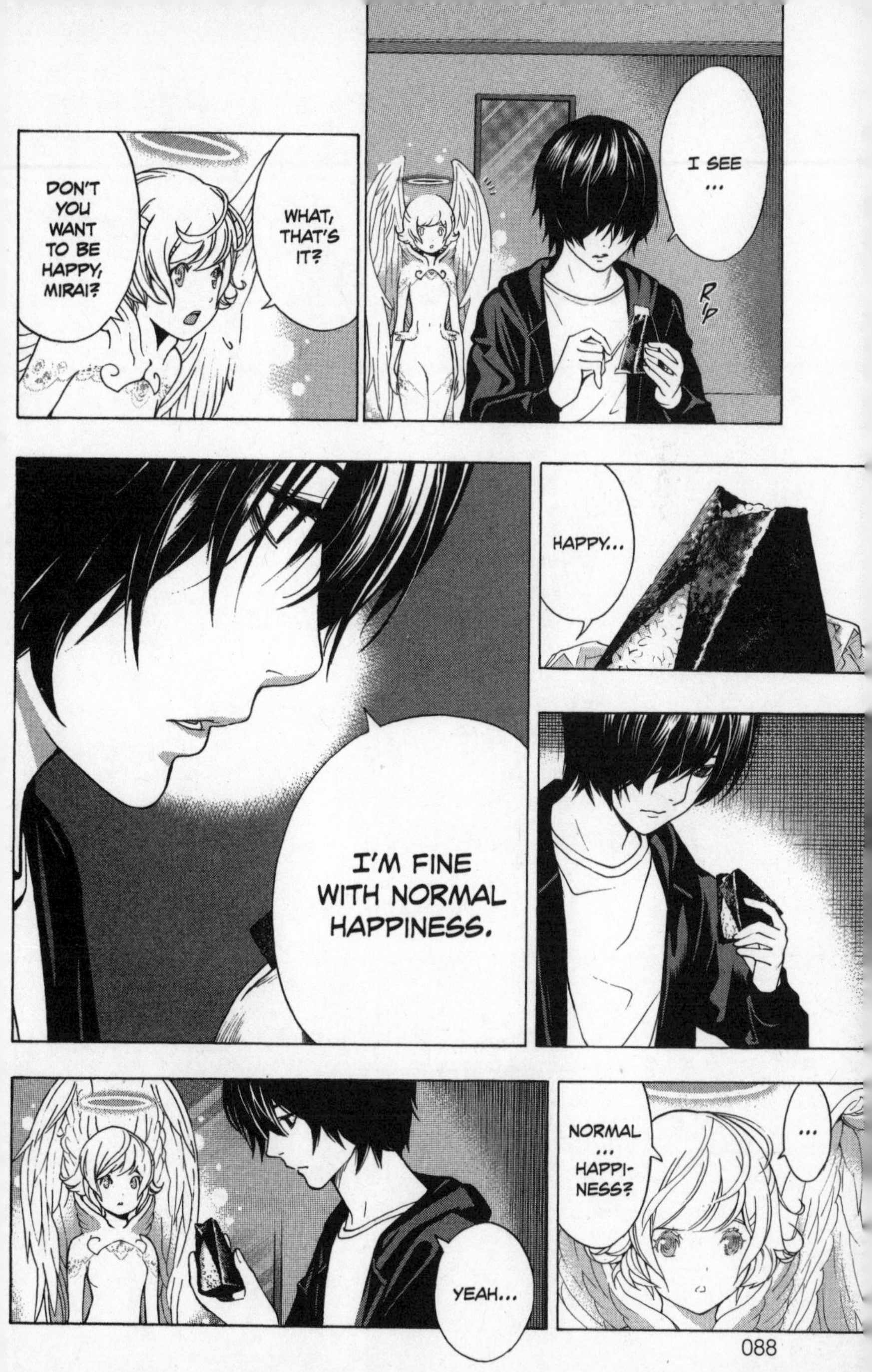
I SEE ...
RIP
WHAT, THAT'S IT?
DON'T YOU WANT TO BE HAPPY, MIRAI?
HAPPY...
I'M FINE WITH NORMAL HAPPINESS.
...
NORMAL ... HAPPI-NESS?
YEAH...

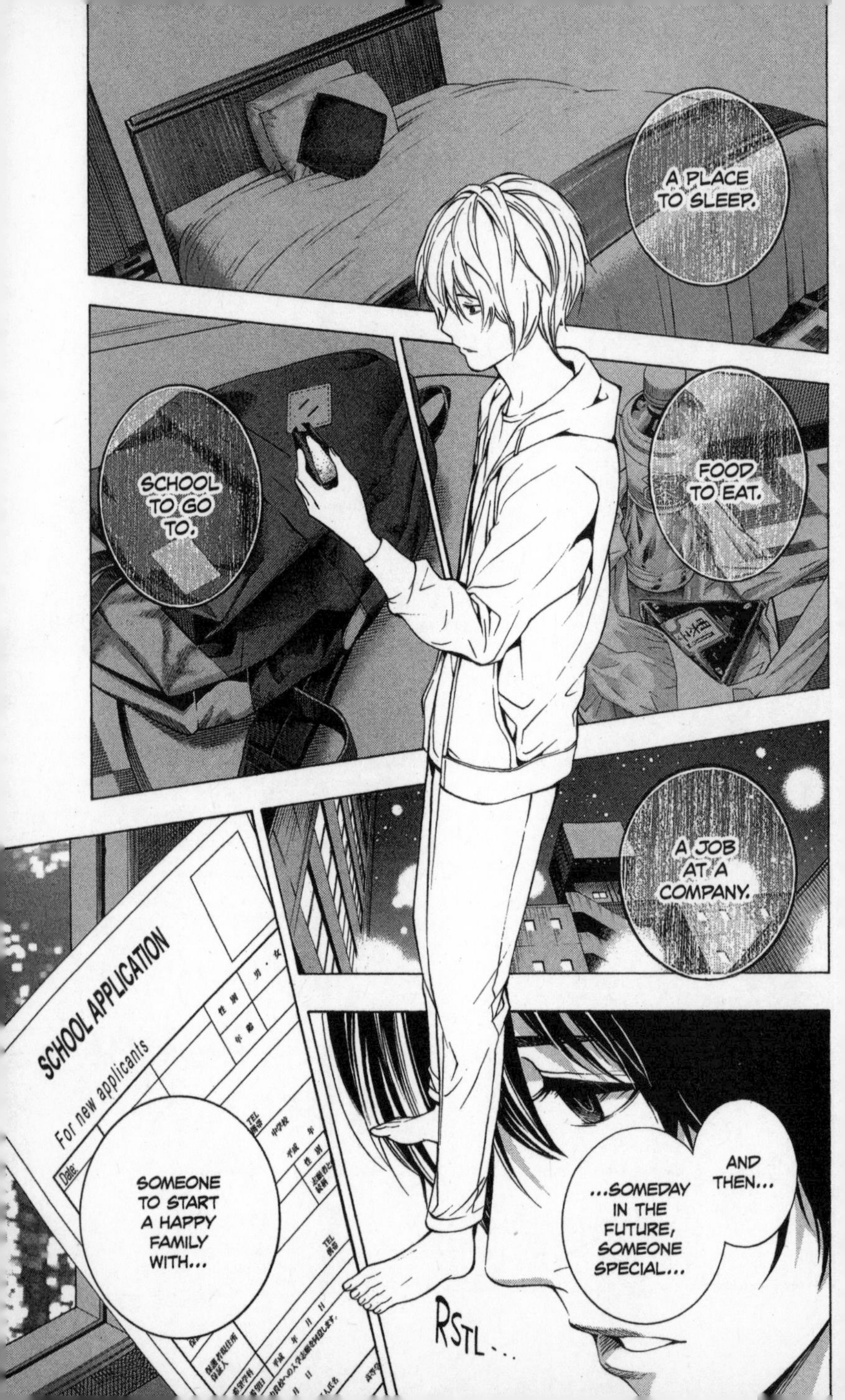
A PLACE TO SLEEP.
FOOD TO EAT.
SCHOOL TO GO TO.
A JOB AT A COMPANY.
AND THEN...
...SOMEDAY IN THE FUTURE, SOMEONE SPECIAL...
RSTL...
SCHOOL APPLICATION
For new applicants
Date:
SOMEONE TO START A HAPPY FAMILY WITH...

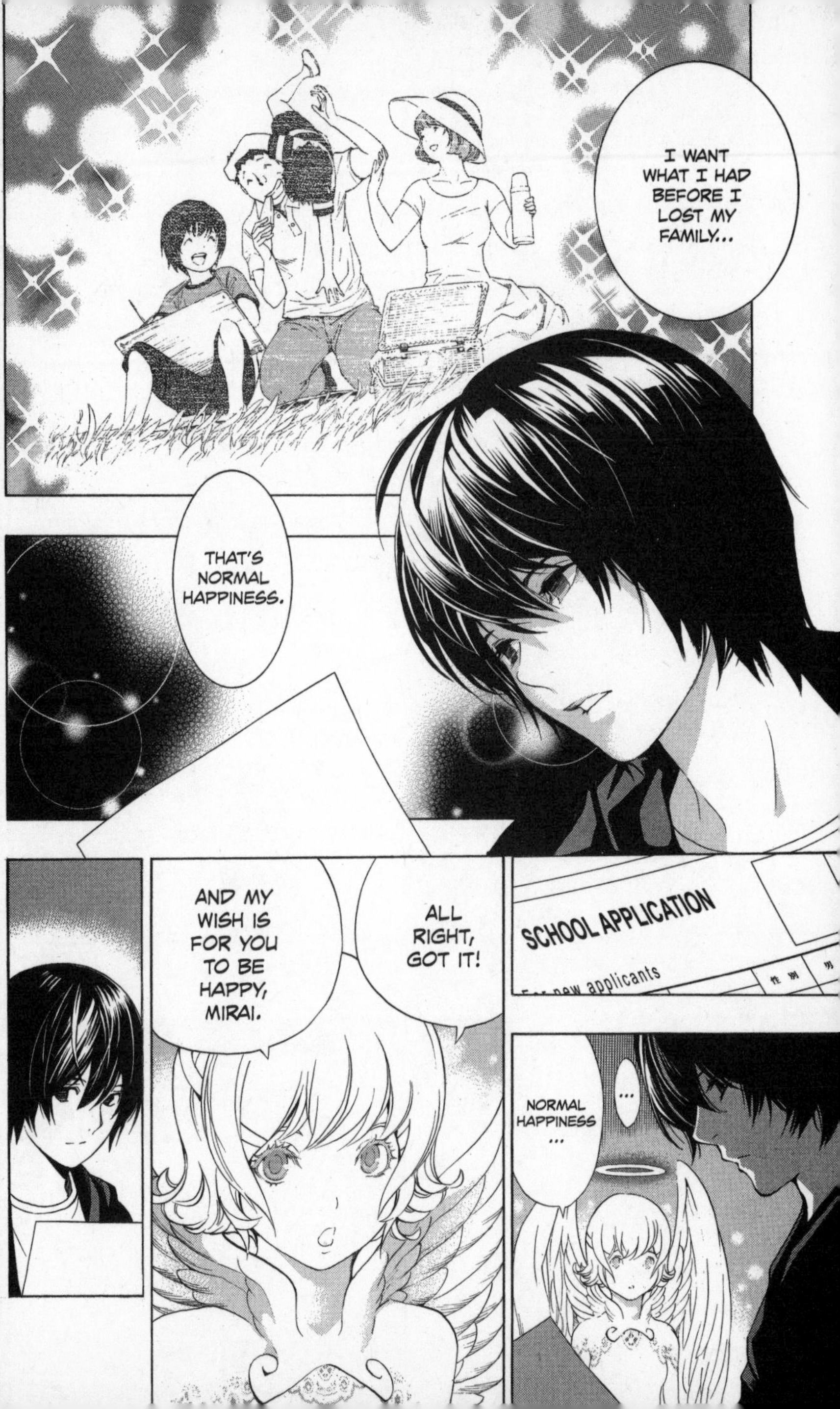
I WANT WHAT I HAD BEFORE I LOST MY FAMILY...
THAT'S NORMAL HAPPINESS.
SCHOOL APPLICATION
For new applicants
性別 男
...
NORMAL HAPPINESS...
ALL RIGHT, GOT IT!
AND MY WISH IS FOR YOU TO BE HAPPY, MIRAI.

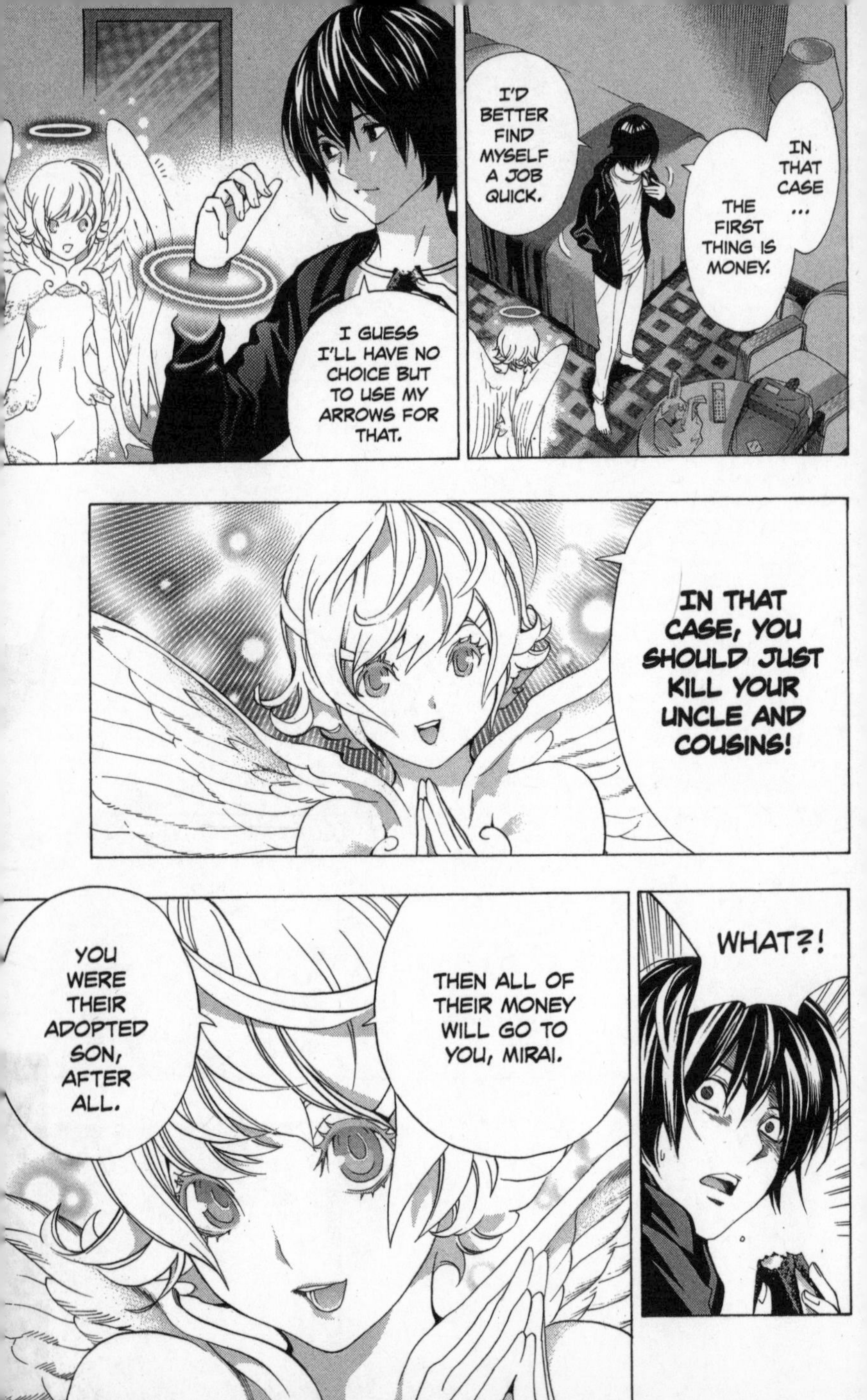
I'D BETTER FIND MYSELF A JOB QUICK.
IN THAT CASE ...
THE FIRST THING IS MONEY.
I GUESS I'LL HAVE NO CHOICE BUT TO USE MY ARROWS FOR THAT.
IN THAT CASE, YOU SHOULD JUST KILL YOUR UNCLE AND COUSINS!
WHAT?!
THEN ALL OF THEIR MONEY WILL GO TO YOU, MIRAI.
YOU WERE THEIR ADOPTED SON, AFTER ALL.

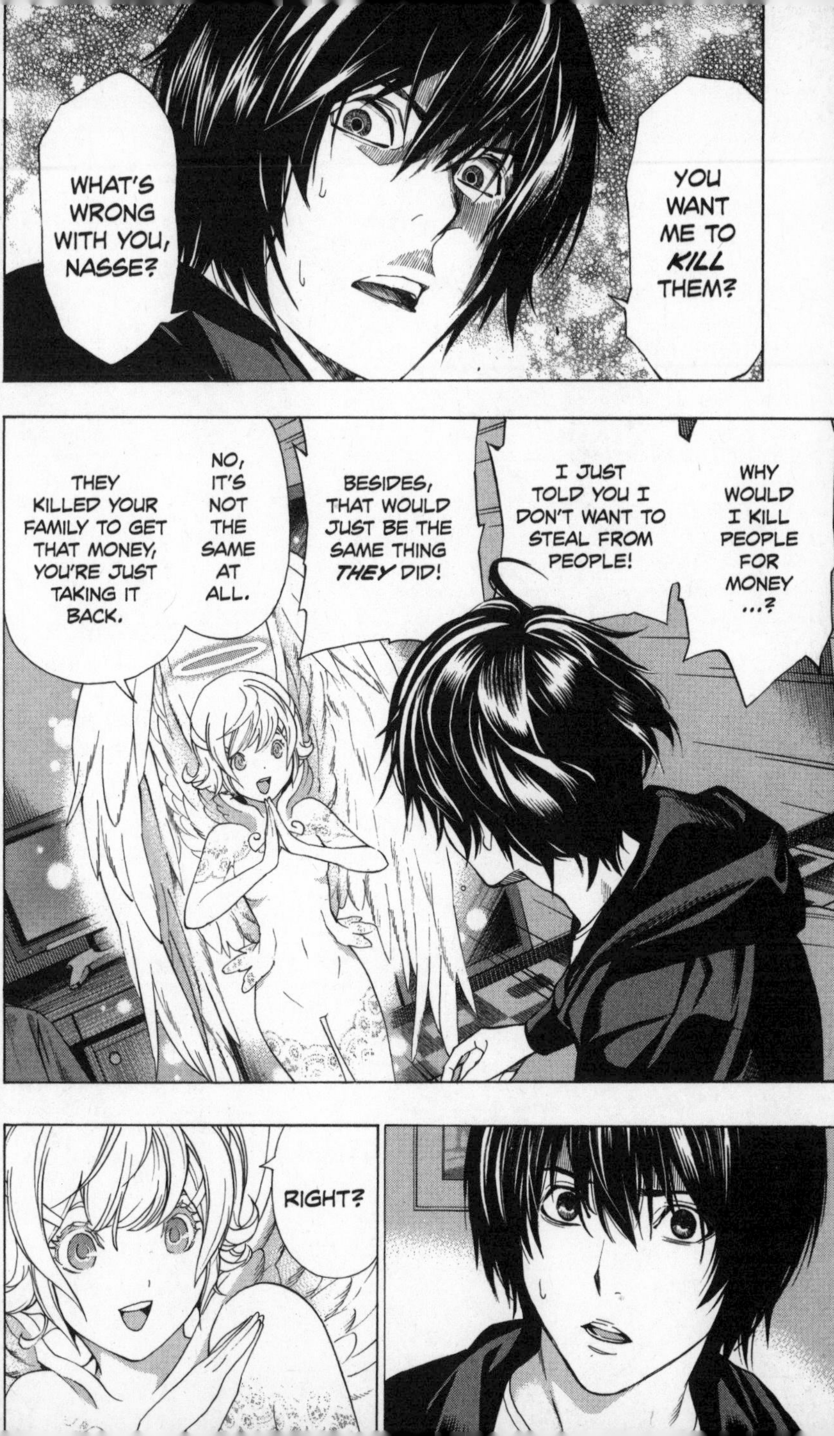
YOU WANT ME TO KILL THEM?
WHAT'S WRONG WITH YOU, NASSE?
WHY WOULD I KILL PEOPLE FOR MONEY ...?
I JUST TOLD YOU I DON'T WANT TO STEAL FROM PEOPLE!
BESIDES, THAT WOULD JUST BE THE SAME THING THEY DID!
NO, IT'S NOT THE SAME AT ALL.
THEY KILLED YOUR FAMILY TO GET THAT MONEY, YOU'RE JUST TAKING IT BACK.
RIGHT?

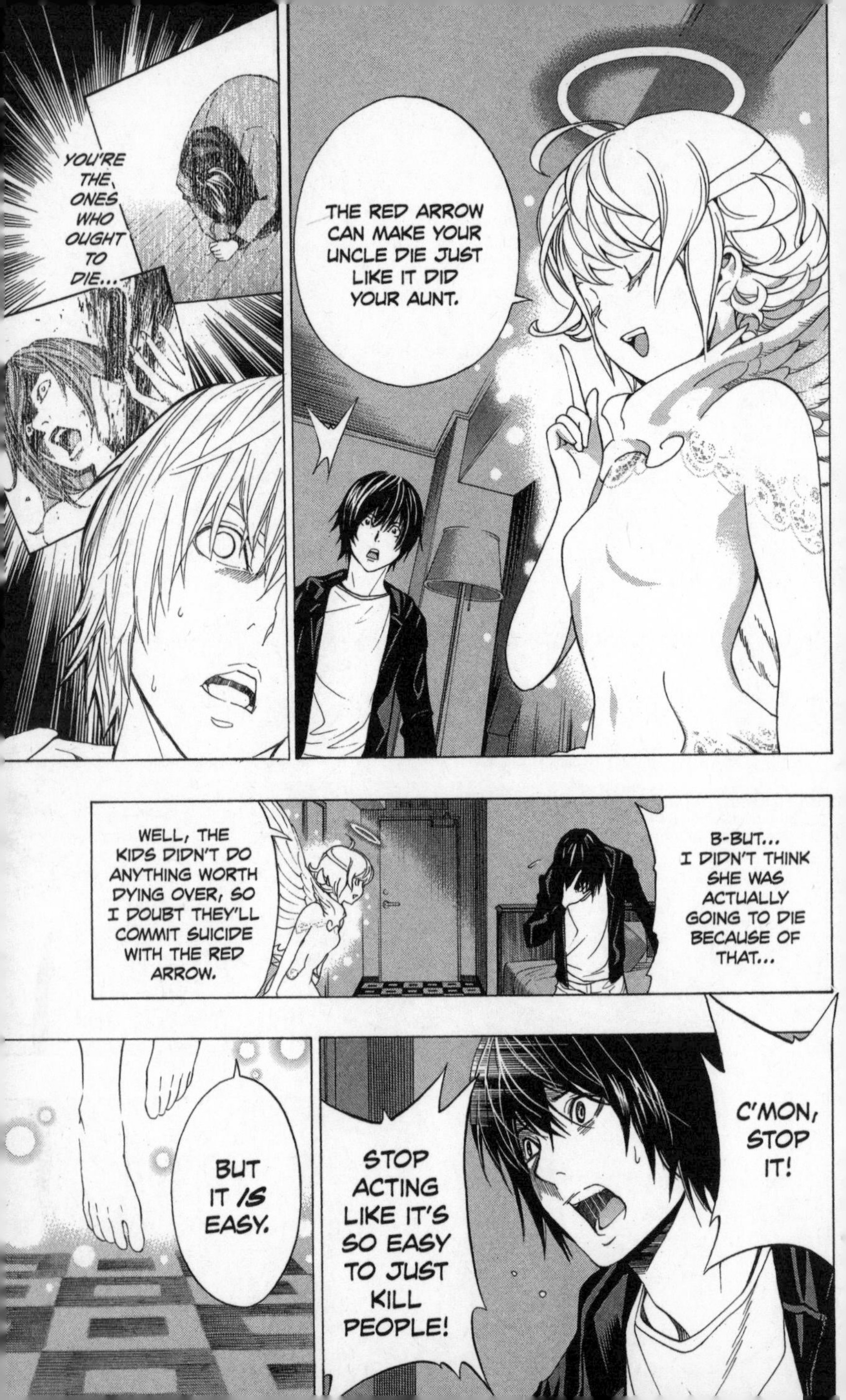
THE RED ARROW CAN MAKE YOUR UNCLE DIE JUST LIKE IT DID YOUR AUNT.
YOU'RE THE ONES WHO OUGHT TO DIE...
B-BUT... I DIDN'T THINK SHE WAS ACTUALLY GOING TO DIE BECAUSE OF THAT...
WELL, THE KIDS DIDN'T DO ANYTHING WORTH DYING OVER, SO I DOUBT THEY'LL COMMIT SUICIDE WITH THE RED ARROW.
C'MON, STOP IT!
STOP ACTING LIKE IT'S SO EASY TO JUST KILL PEOPLE!
BUT IT *IS* EASY.

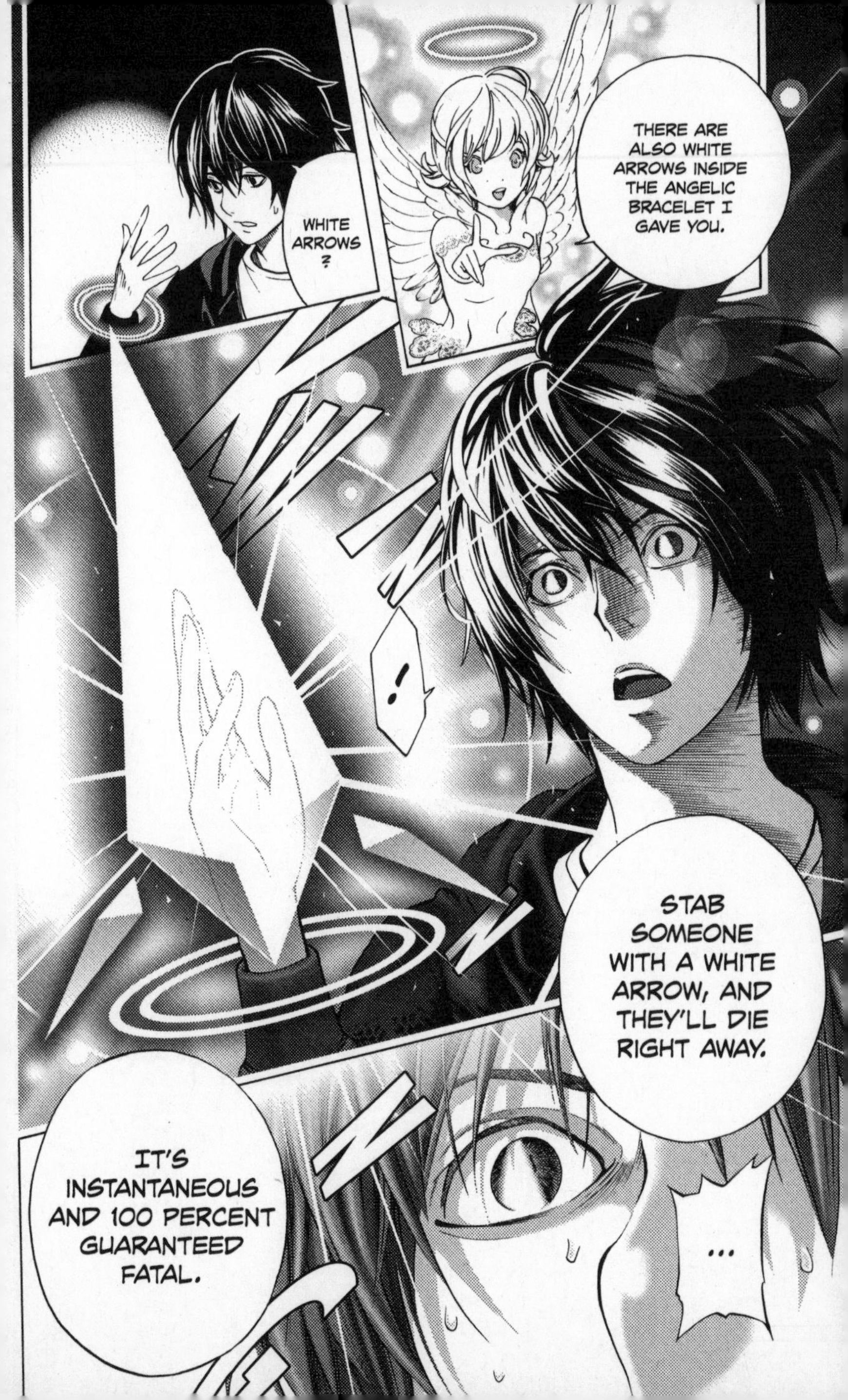
THERE ARE ALSO WHITE ARROWS INSIDE THE ANGELIC BRACELET I GAVE YOU.
WHITE ARROWS?
!
STAB SOMEONE WITH A WHITE ARROW, AND THEY'LL DIE RIGHT AWAY.
...
IT'S INSTANTANEOUS AND 100 PERCENT GUARANTEED FATAL.

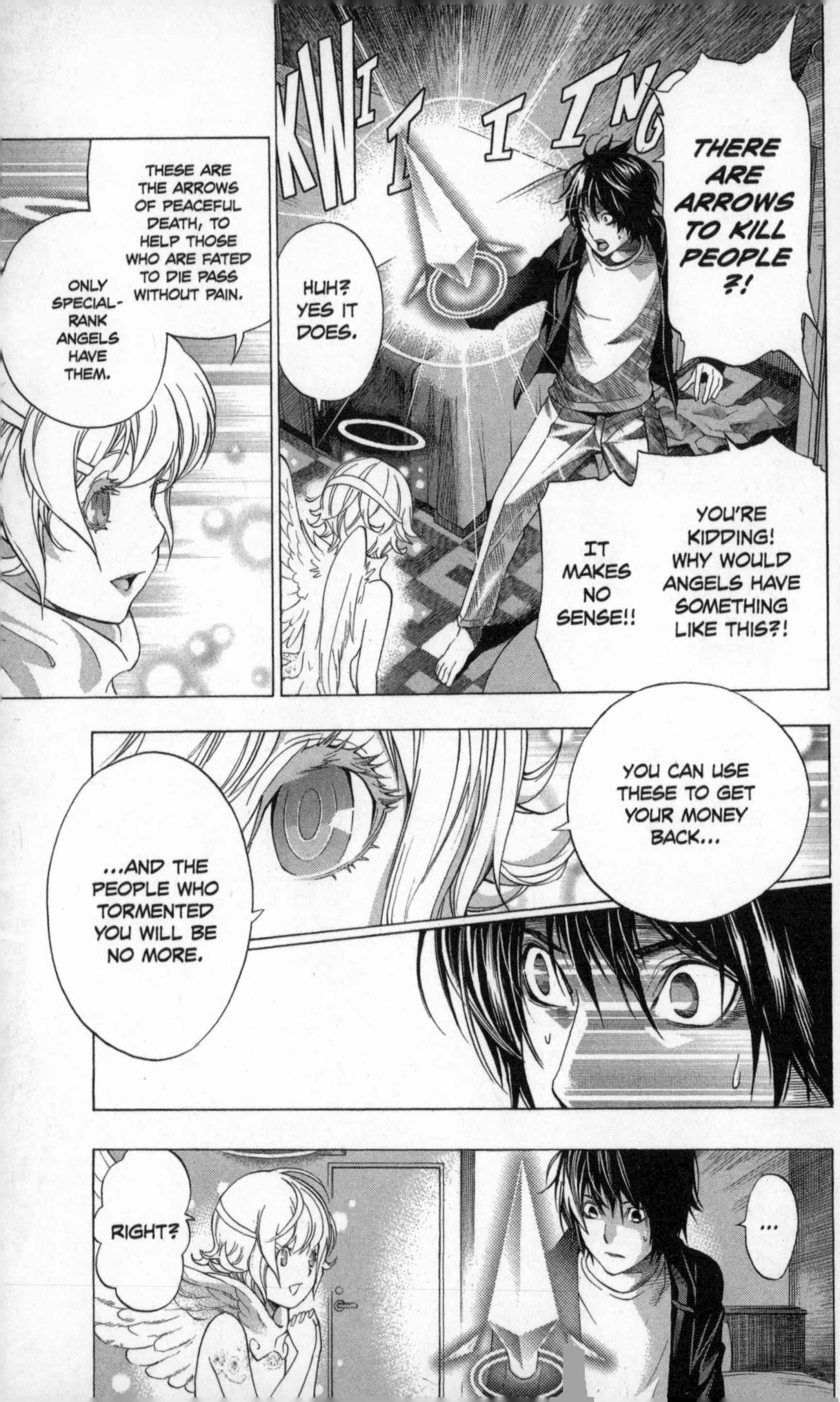
KWIIING
THERE ARE ARROWS TO KILL PEOPLE?!
YOU'RE KIDDING! WHY WOULD ANGELS HAVE SOMETHING LIKE THIS?!
IT MAKES NO SENSE!!
HUH? YES IT DOES.
THESE ARE THE ARROWS OF PEACEFUL DEATH, TO HELP THOSE WHO ARE FATED TO DIE PASS WITHOUT PAIN.
ONLY SPECIAL-RANK ANGELS HAVE THEM.
YOU CAN USE THESE TO GET YOUR MONEY BACK...
...AND THE PEOPLE WHO TORMENTED YOU WILL BE NO MORE.
...
RIGHT?

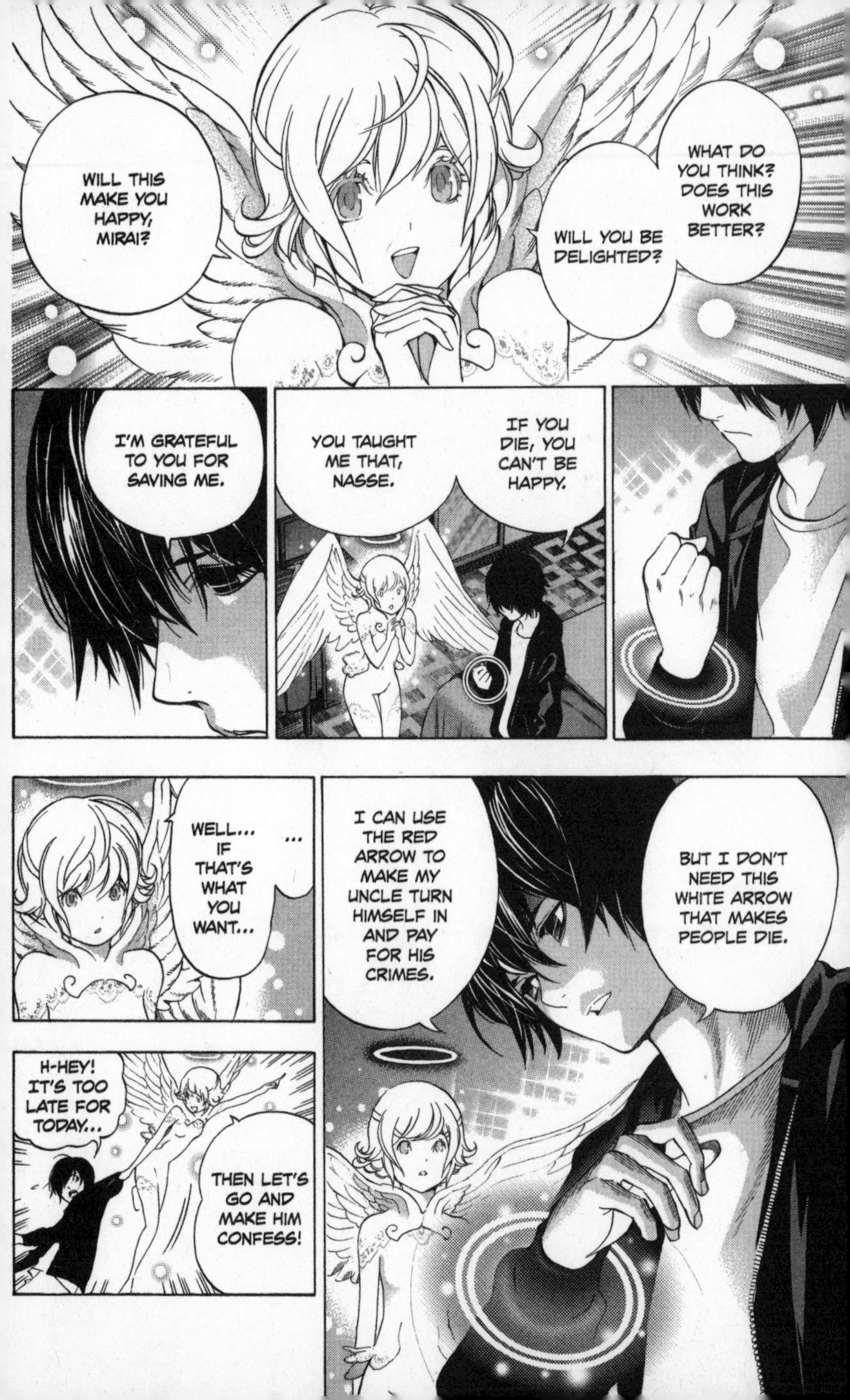
WHAT DO YOU THINK? DOES THIS WORK BETTER?
WILL YOU BE DELIGHTED?
WILL THIS MAKE YOU HAPPY, MIRAI?
IF YOU DIE, YOU CAN'T BE HAPPY.
YOU TAUGHT ME THAT, NASSE.
I'M GRATEFUL TO YOU FOR SAVING ME.
BUT I DON'T NEED THIS WHITE ARROW THAT MAKES PEOPLE DIE.
I CAN USE THE RED ARROW TO MAKE MY UNCLE TURN HIMSELF IN AND PAY FOR HIS CRIMES.
...
WELL... IF THAT'S WHAT YOU WANT...
THEN LET'S GO AND MAKE HIM CONFESS!
H-HEY! IT'S TOO LATE FOR TODAY...

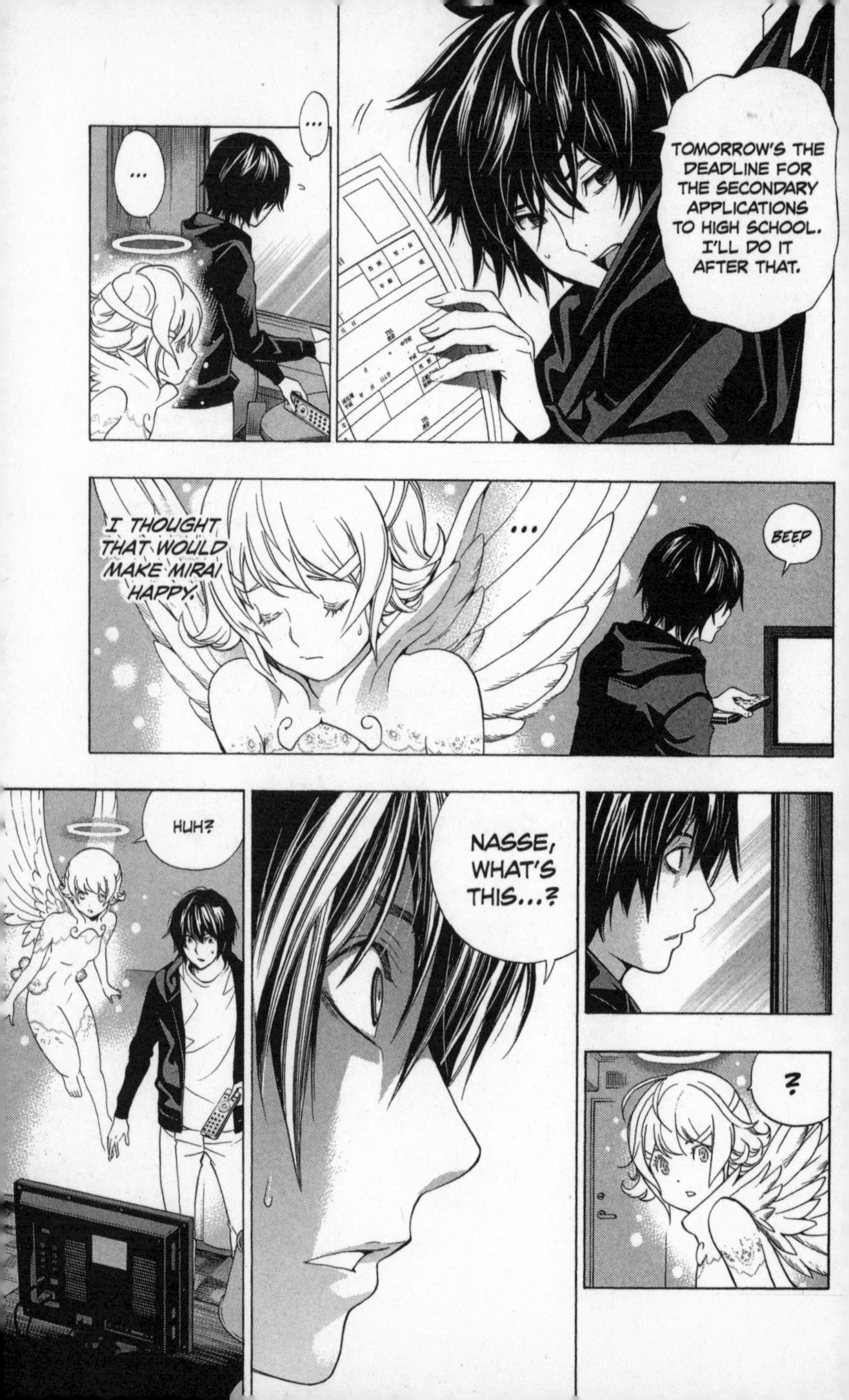
TOMORROW'S THE DEADLINE FOR THE SECONDARY APPLICATIONS TO HIGH SCHOOL. I'LL DO IT AFTER THAT.
...
...
BEEP
...
I THOUGHT THAT WOULD MAKE MIRAI HAPPY.
?
NASSE, WHAT'S THIS...?
HUH?

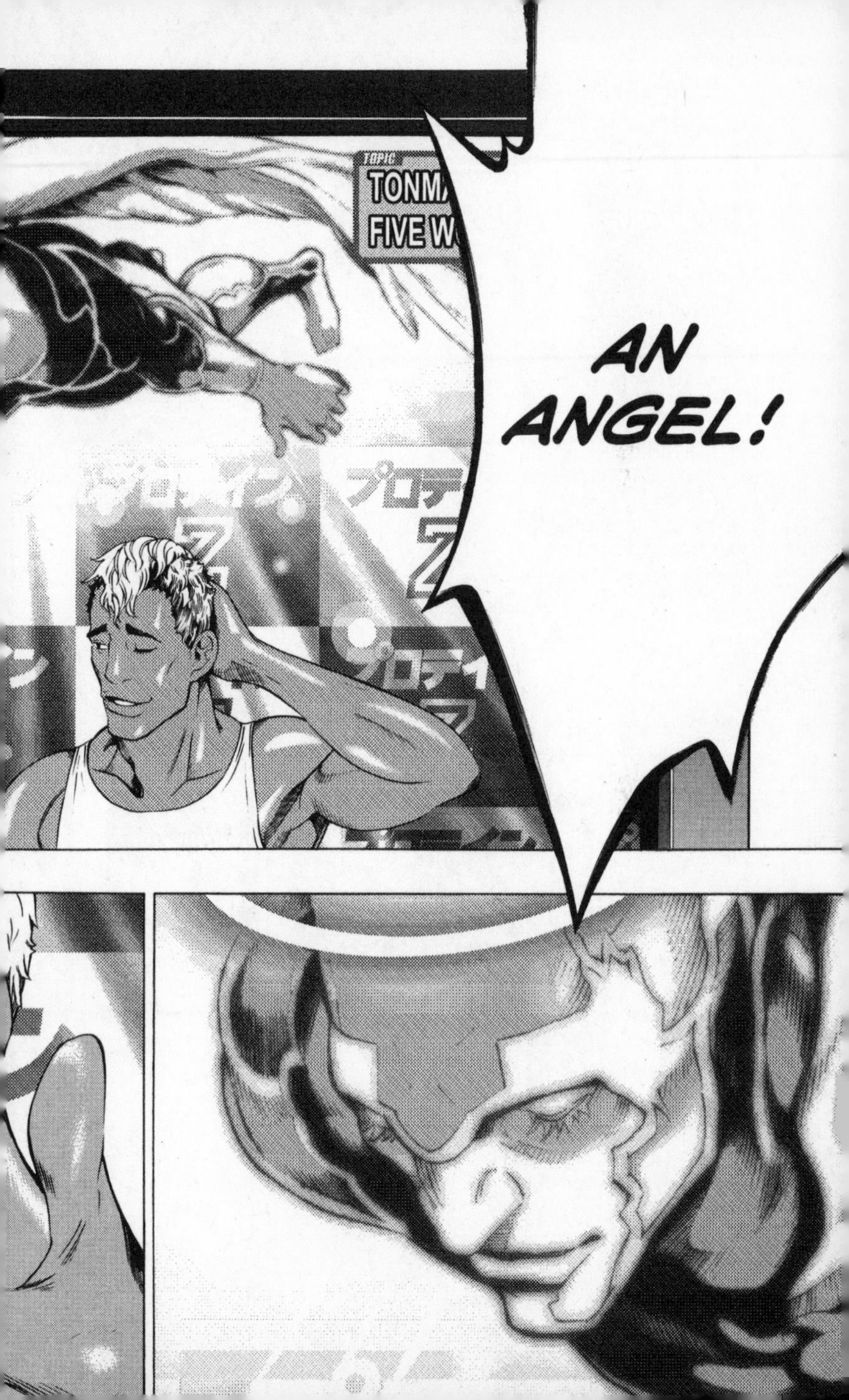
AN ANGEL!
TOPIC
TONMA
FIVE W

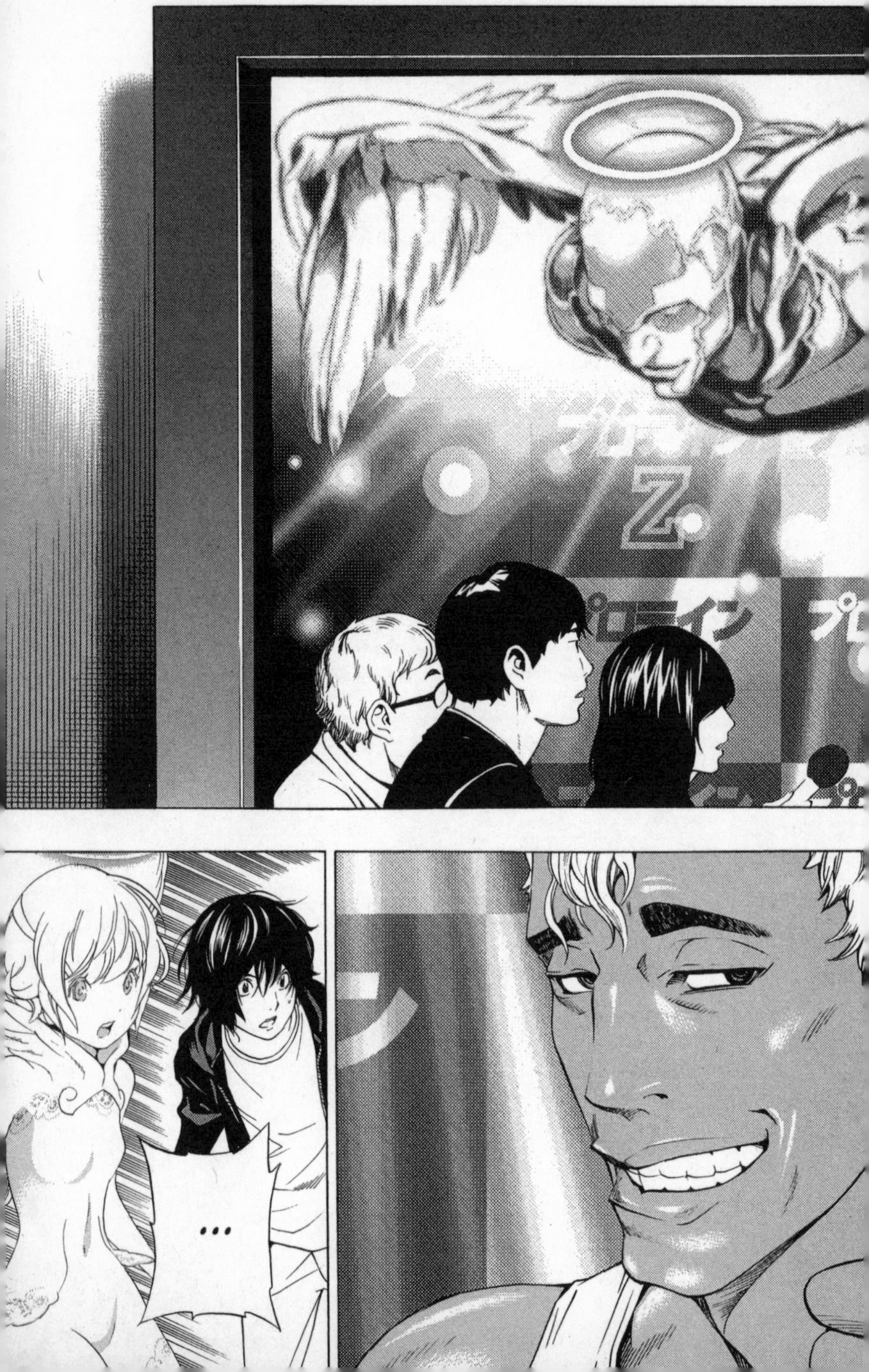
Z
...

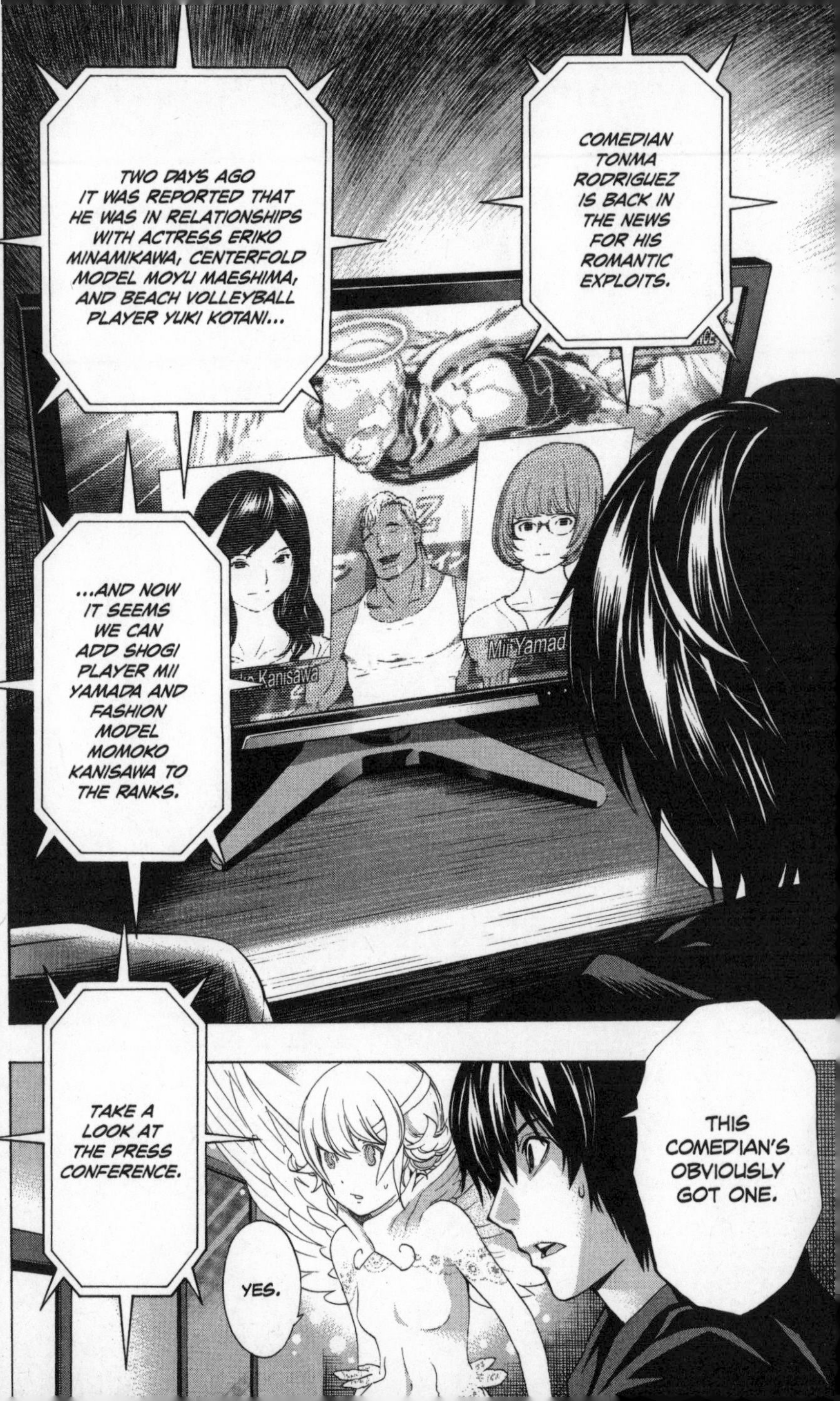
COMEDIAN TONMA RODRIGUEZ IS BACK IN THE NEWS FOR HIS ROMANTIC EXPLOITS.
TWO DAYS AGO IT WAS REPORTED THAT HE WAS IN RELATIONSHIPS WITH ACTRESS ERIKO MINAMIKAWA, CENTERFOLD MODEL MOYU MAESHIMA, AND BEACH VOLLEYBALL PLAYER YUKI KOTANI...
...AND NOW IT SEEMS WE CAN ADD SHOGI PLAYER MII YAMADA AND FASHION MODEL MOMOKO KANISAWA TO THE RANKS.
THIS COMEDIAN'S OBVIOUSLY GOT ONE.
TAKE A LOOK AT THE PRESS CONFERENCE.
YES.

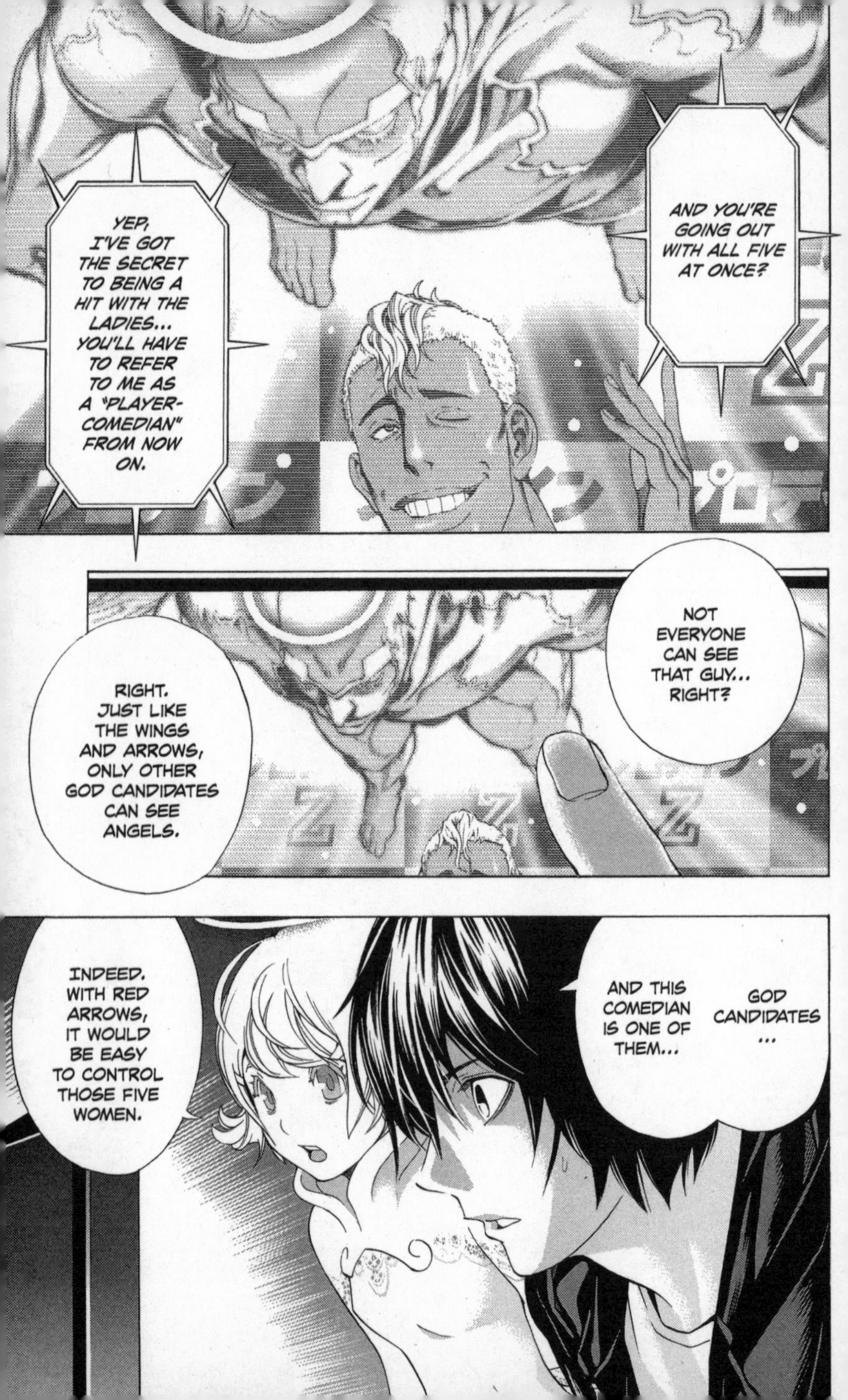
AND YOU'RE GOING OUT WITH ALL FIVE AT ONCE?
YEP, I'VE GOT THE SECRET TO BEING A HIT WITH THE LADIES... YOU'LL HAVE TO REFER TO ME AS A "PLAYER-COMEDIAN" FROM NOW ON.
NOT EVERYONE CAN SEE THAT GUY... RIGHT?
RIGHT. JUST LIKE THE WINGS AND ARROWS, ONLY OTHER GOD CANDIDATES CAN SEE ANGELS.
GOD CANDIDATES ...
AND THIS COMEDIAN IS ONE OF THEM...
INDEED. WITH RED ARROWS, IT WOULD BE EASY TO CONTROL THOSE FIVE WOMEN.

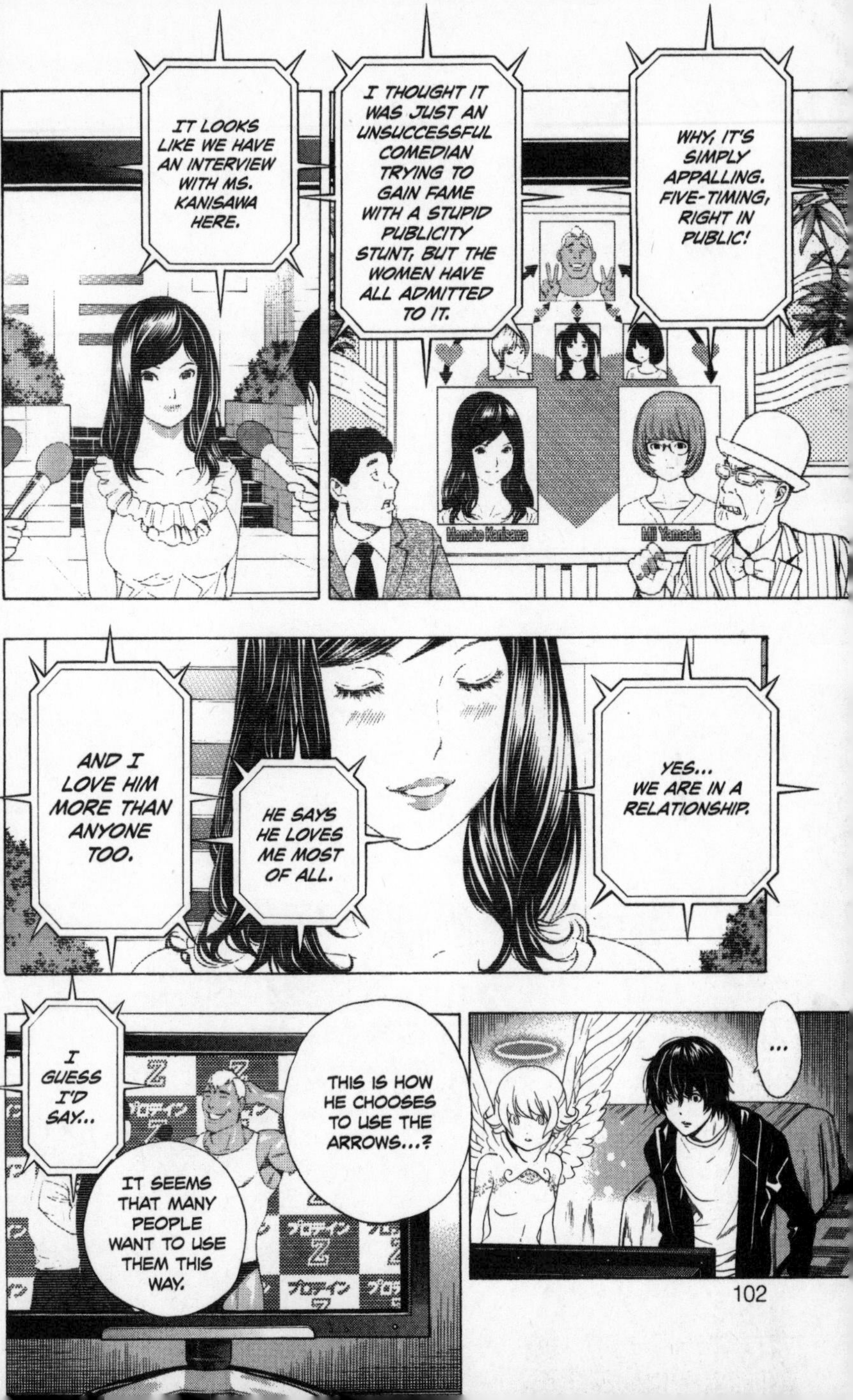
WHY, IT'S SIMPLY APPALLING. FIVE-TIMING, RIGHT IN PUBLIC!
I THOUGHT IT WAS JUST AN UNSUCCESSFUL COMEDIAN TRYING TO GAIN FAME WITH A STUPID PUBLICITY STUNT, BUT THE WOMEN HAVE ALL ADMITTED TO IT.
Mii Yamada
Momoko Kanisawa
IT LOOKS LIKE WE HAVE AN INTERVIEW WITH MS. KANISAWA HERE.
YES... WE ARE IN A RELATIONSHIP.
HE SAYS HE LOVES ME MOST OF ALL.
AND I LOVE HIM MORE THAN ANYONE TOO.
...
THIS IS HOW HE CHOOSES TO USE THE ARROWS...?
I GUESS I'D SAY...
IT SEEMS THAT MANY PEOPLE WANT TO USE THEM THIS WAY.

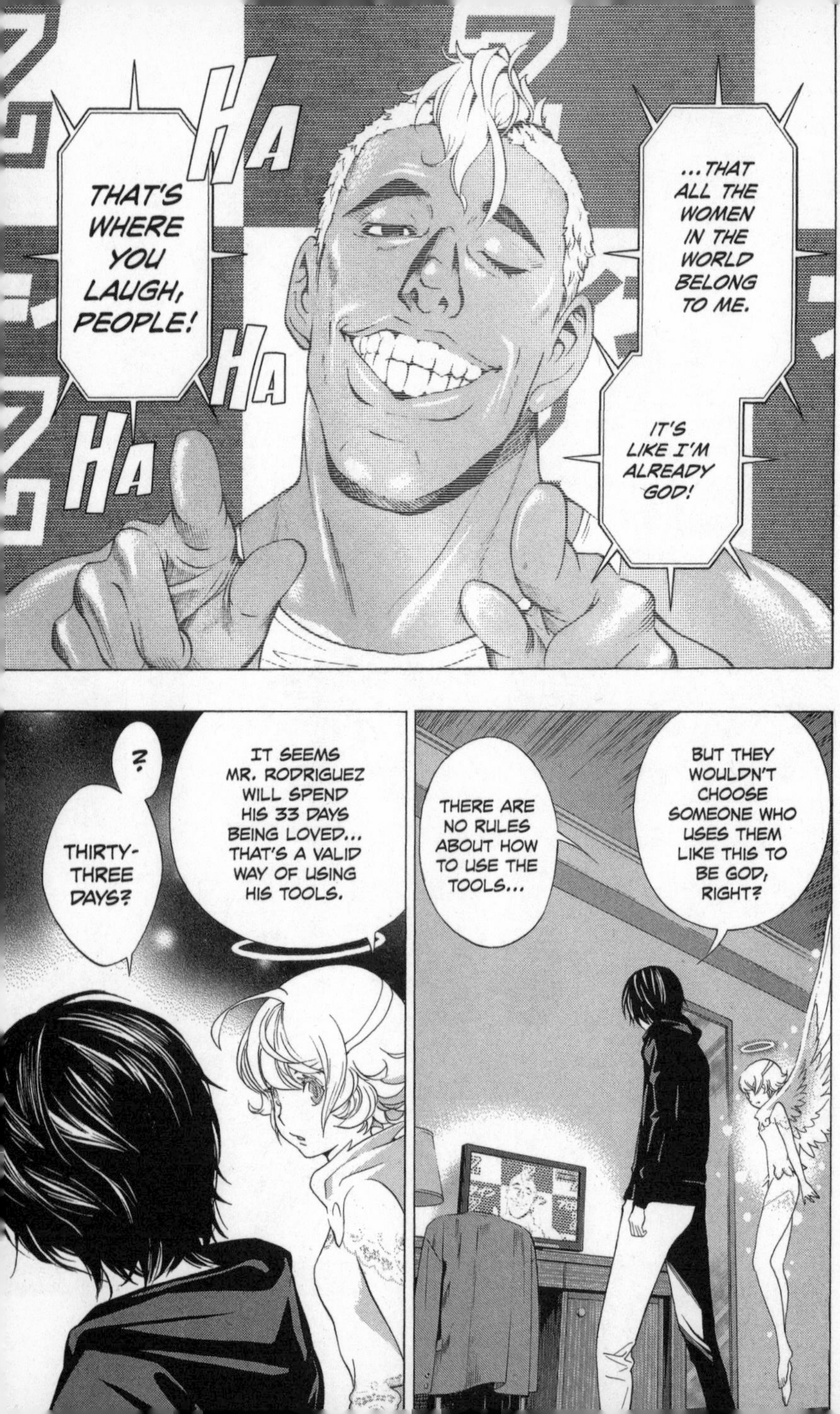
...THAT ALL THE WOMEN IN THE WORLD BELONG TO ME.
IT'S LIKE I'M ALREADY GOD!
HA
HA
HA
THAT'S WHERE YOU LAUGH, PEOPLE!
THERE ARE NO RULES ABOUT HOW TO USE THE TOOLS...
BUT THEY WOULDN'T CHOOSE SOMEONE WHO USES THEM LIKE THIS TO BE GOD, RIGHT?
IT SEEMS MR. RODRIGUEZ WILL SPEND HIS 33 DAYS BEING LOVED... THAT'S A VALID WAY OF USING HIS TOOLS.
?
THIRTY-THREE DAYS?

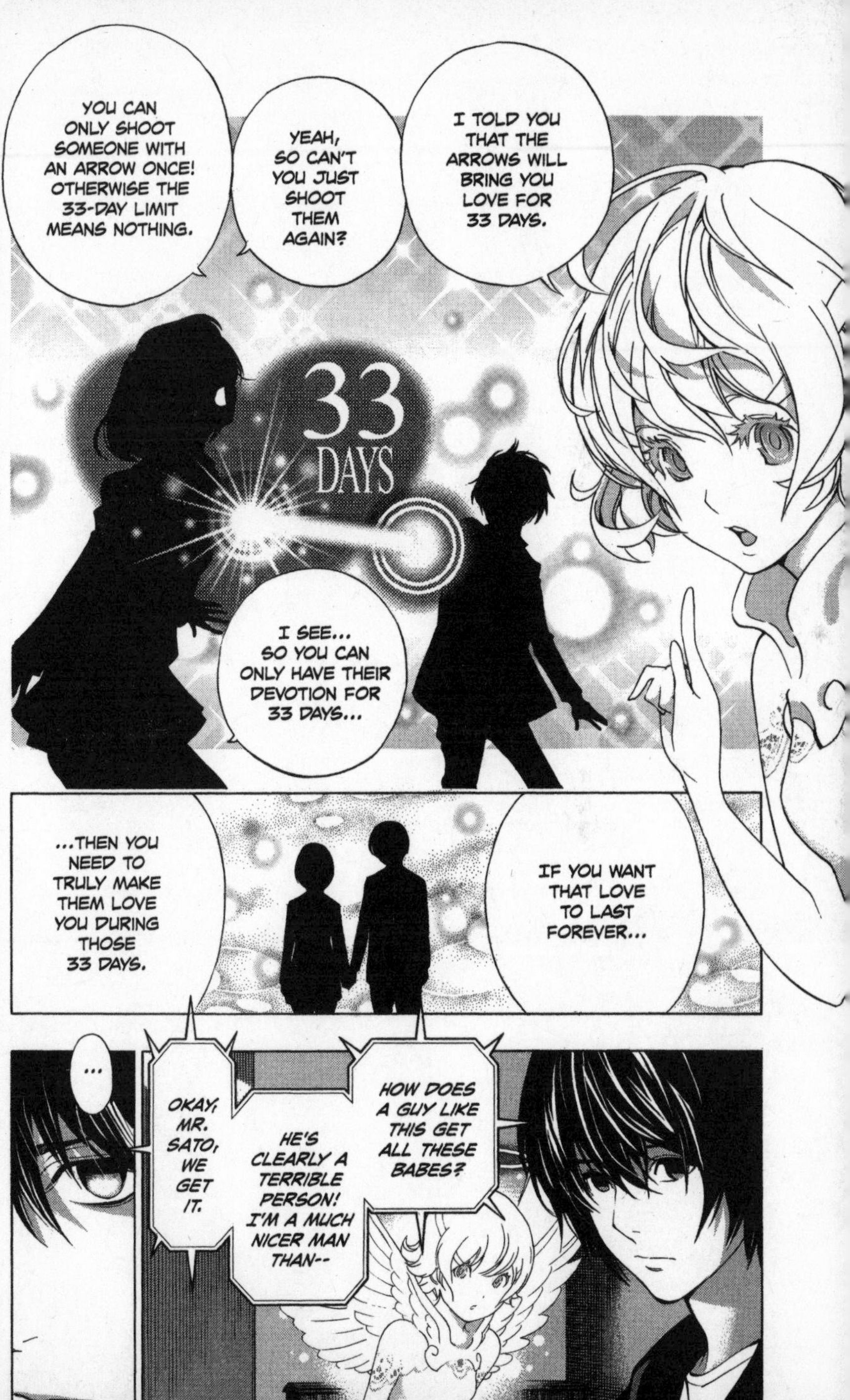
I TOLD YOU THAT THE ARROWS WILL BRING YOU LOVE FOR 33 DAYS.
YEAH, SO CAN'T YOU JUST SHOOT THEM AGAIN?
YOU CAN ONLY SHOOT SOMEONE WITH AN ARROW ONCE! OTHERWISE THE 33-DAY LIMIT MEANS NOTHING.
33 DAYS
I SEE... SO YOU CAN ONLY HAVE THEIR DEVOTION FOR 33 DAYS...
IF YOU WANT THAT LOVE TO LAST FOREVER...
...THEN YOU NEED TO TRULY MAKE THEM LOVE YOU DURING THOSE 33 DAYS.
HOW DOES A GUY LIKE THIS GET ALL THESE BABES?
HE'S CLEARLY A TERRIBLE PERSON! I'M A MUCH NICER MAN THAN--
OKAY, MR. SATO, WE GET IT.
...

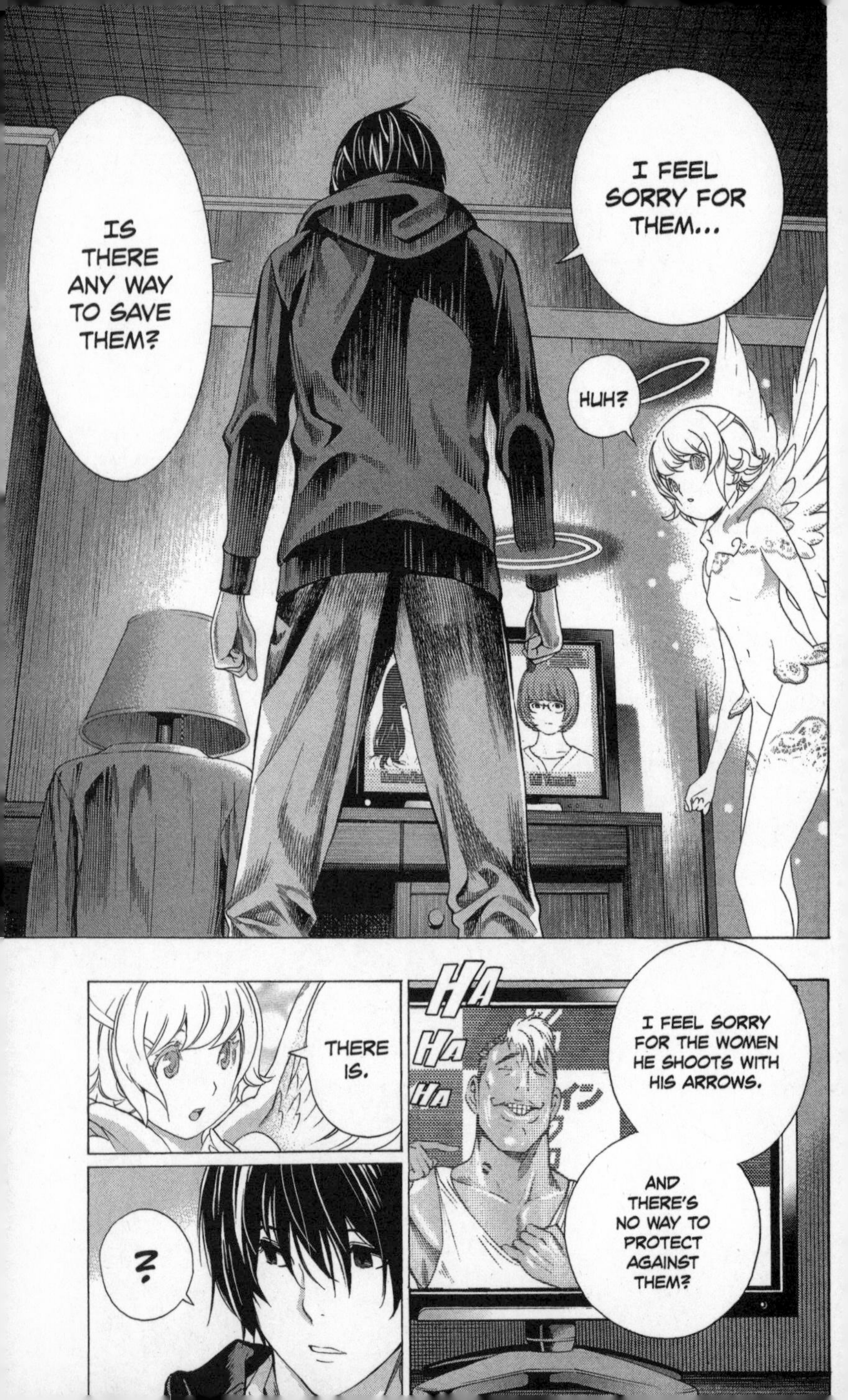
I FEEL SORRY FOR THEM...
IS THERE ANY WAY TO SAVE THEM?
HUH?
HA HA HA
I FEEL SORRY FOR THE WOMEN HE SHOOTS WITH HIS ARROWS.
AND THERE'S NO WAY TO PROTECT AGAINST THEM?
THERE IS.
?

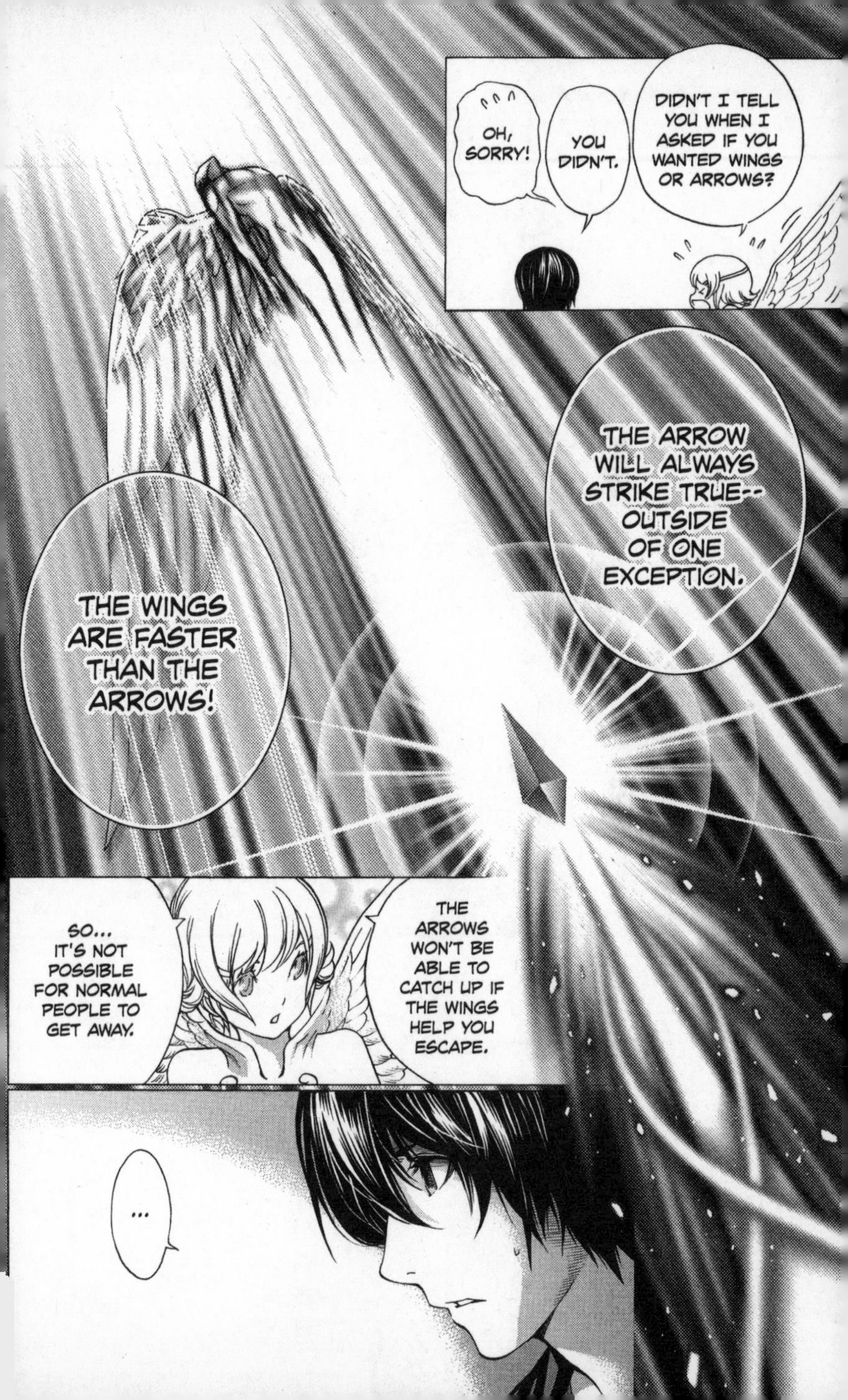
DIDN'T I TELL YOU WHEN I ASKED IF YOU WANTED WINGS OR ARROWS?
YOU DIDN'T.
OH, SORRY!
THE ARROW WILL ALWAYS STRIKE TRUE-- OUTSIDE OF ONE EXCEPTION.
THE WINGS ARE FASTER THAN THE ARROWS!
THE ARROWS WON'T BE ABLE TO CATCH UP IF THE WINGS HELP YOU ESCAPE.
SO... IT'S NOT POSSIBLE FOR NORMAL PEOPLE TO GET AWAY.
...

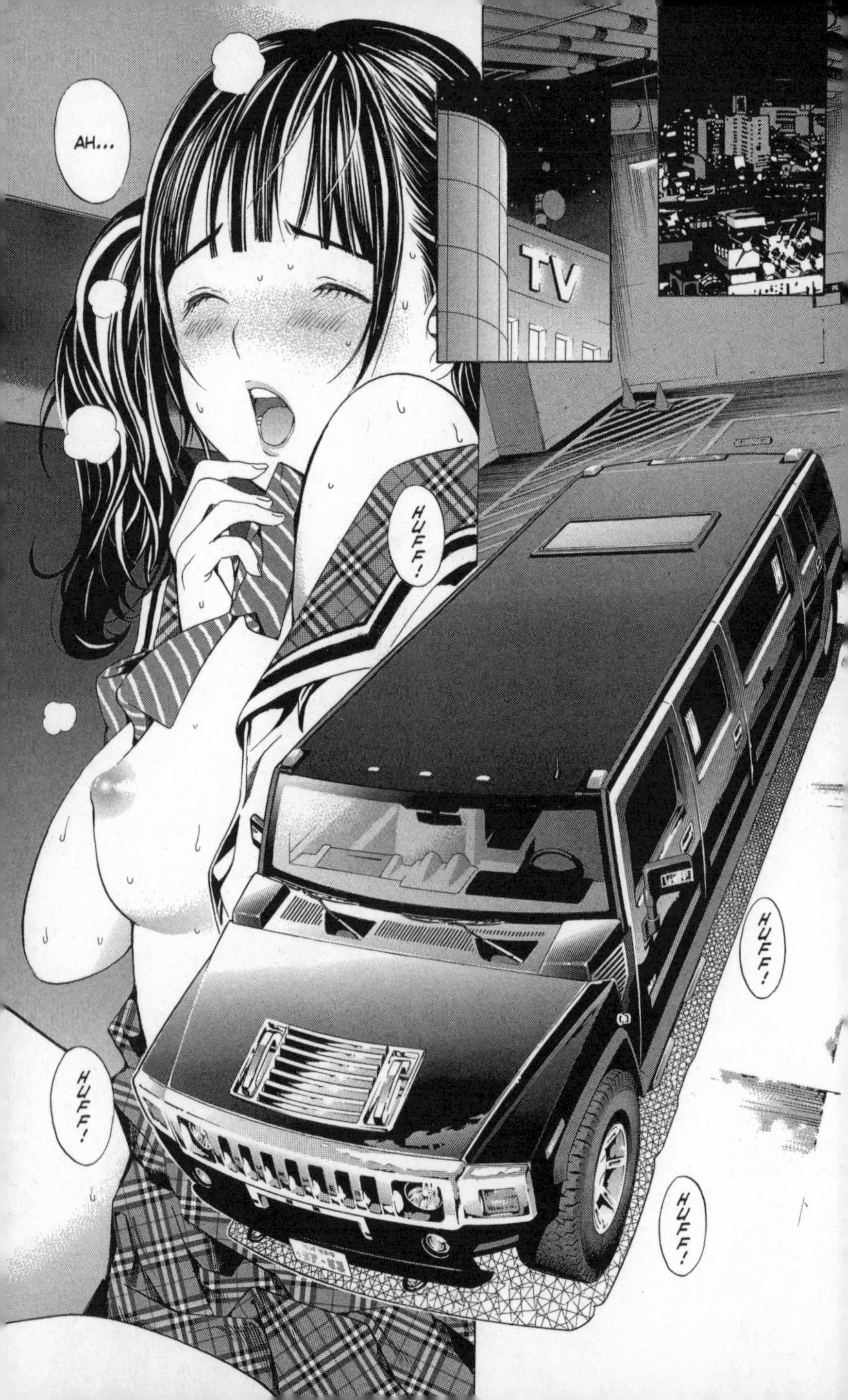
TV
AH...
HUFF!
HUFF!
HUFF!
HUFF!

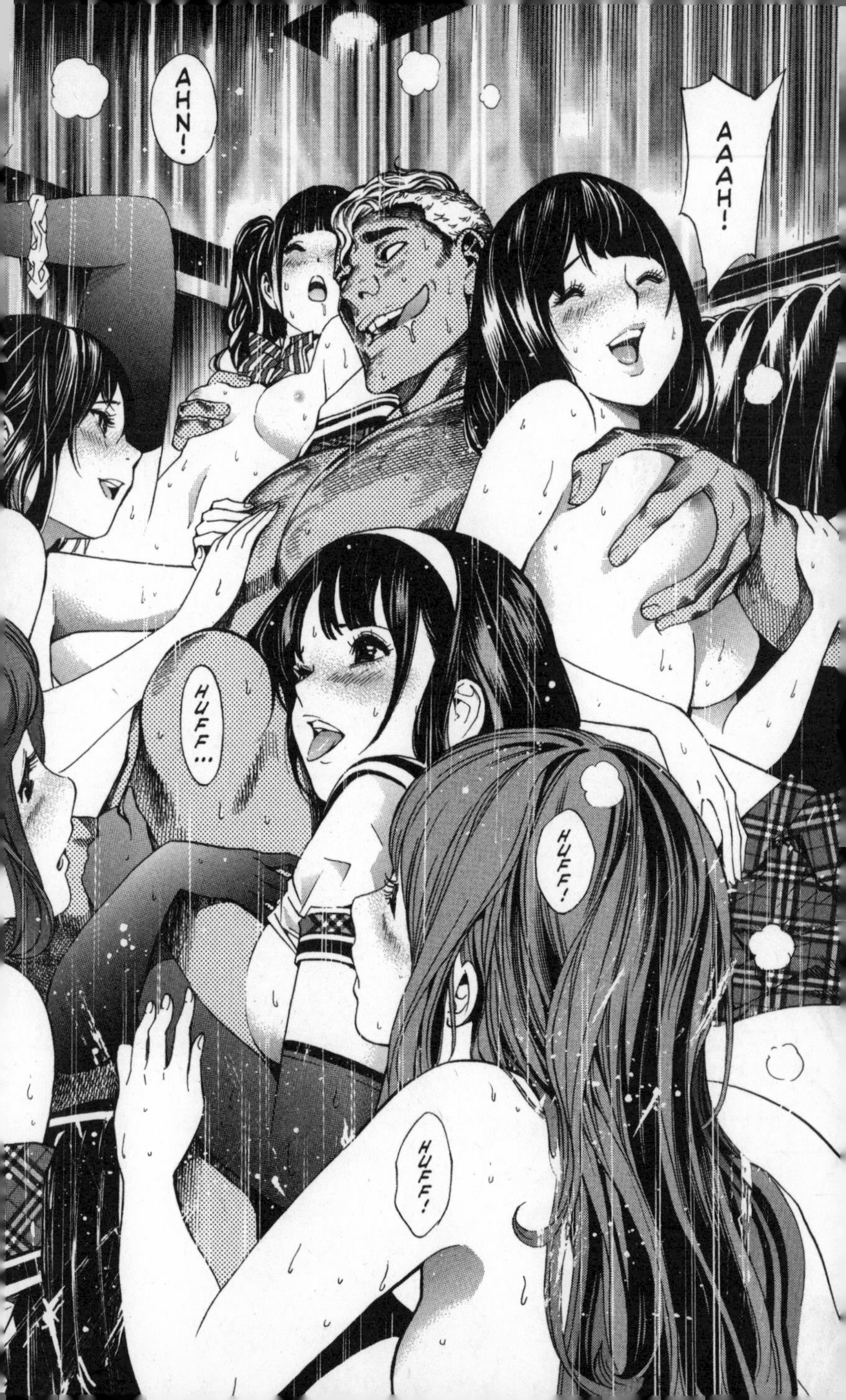
AAAAH!
AHN!
HUFF!
HUFF...
HUFF!

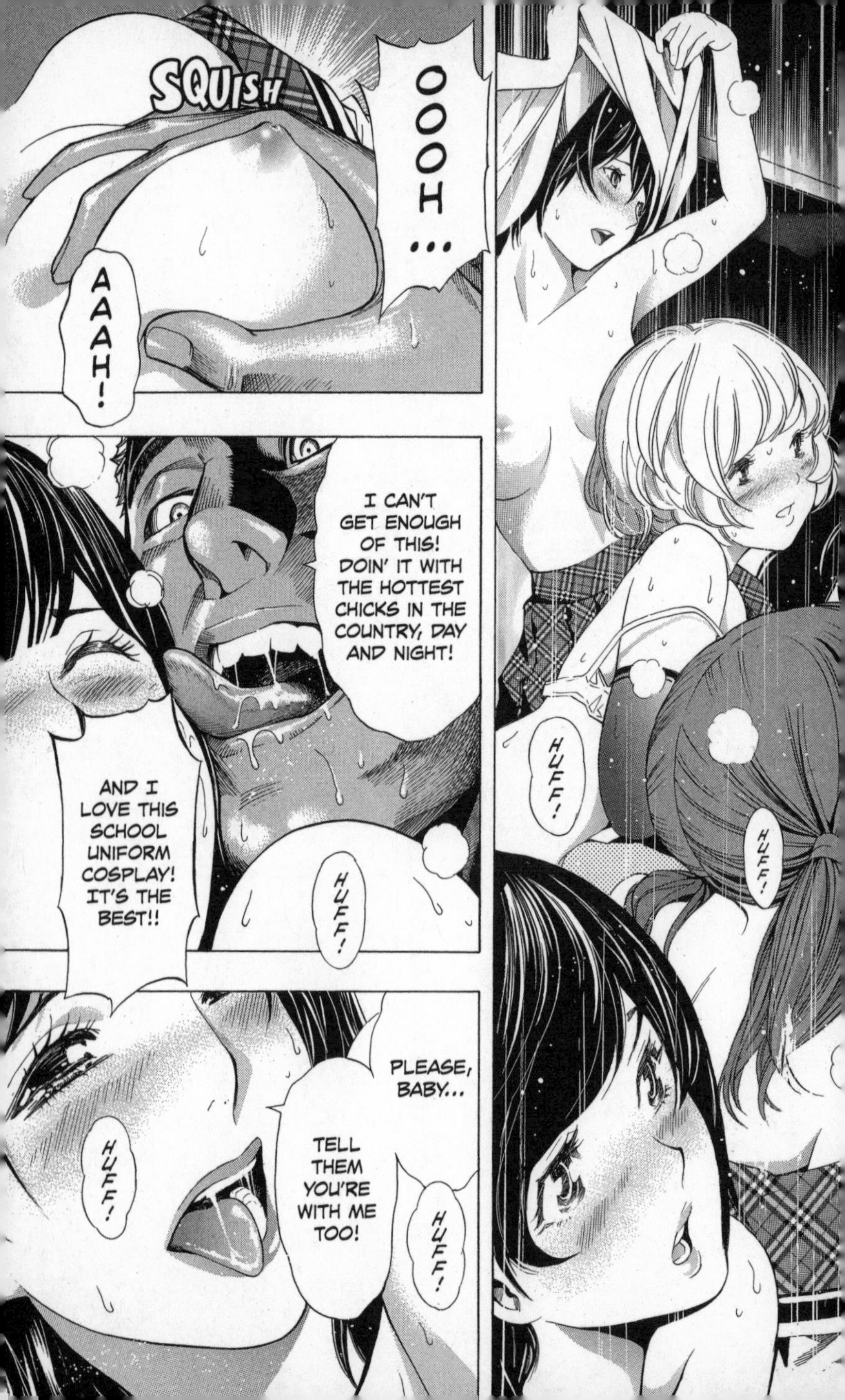
HUFF!
HUFF!
SQUISH
OOOH...
AAAH!
I CAN'T GET ENOUGH OF THIS! DOIN' IT WITH THE HOTTEST CHICKS IN THE COUNTRY, DAY AND NIGHT!
AND I LOVE THIS SCHOOL UNIFORM COSPLAY! IT'S THE BEST!!
HUFF!
PLEASE, BABY...
TELL THEM YOU'RE WITH ME TOO!
HUFF!
HUFF!

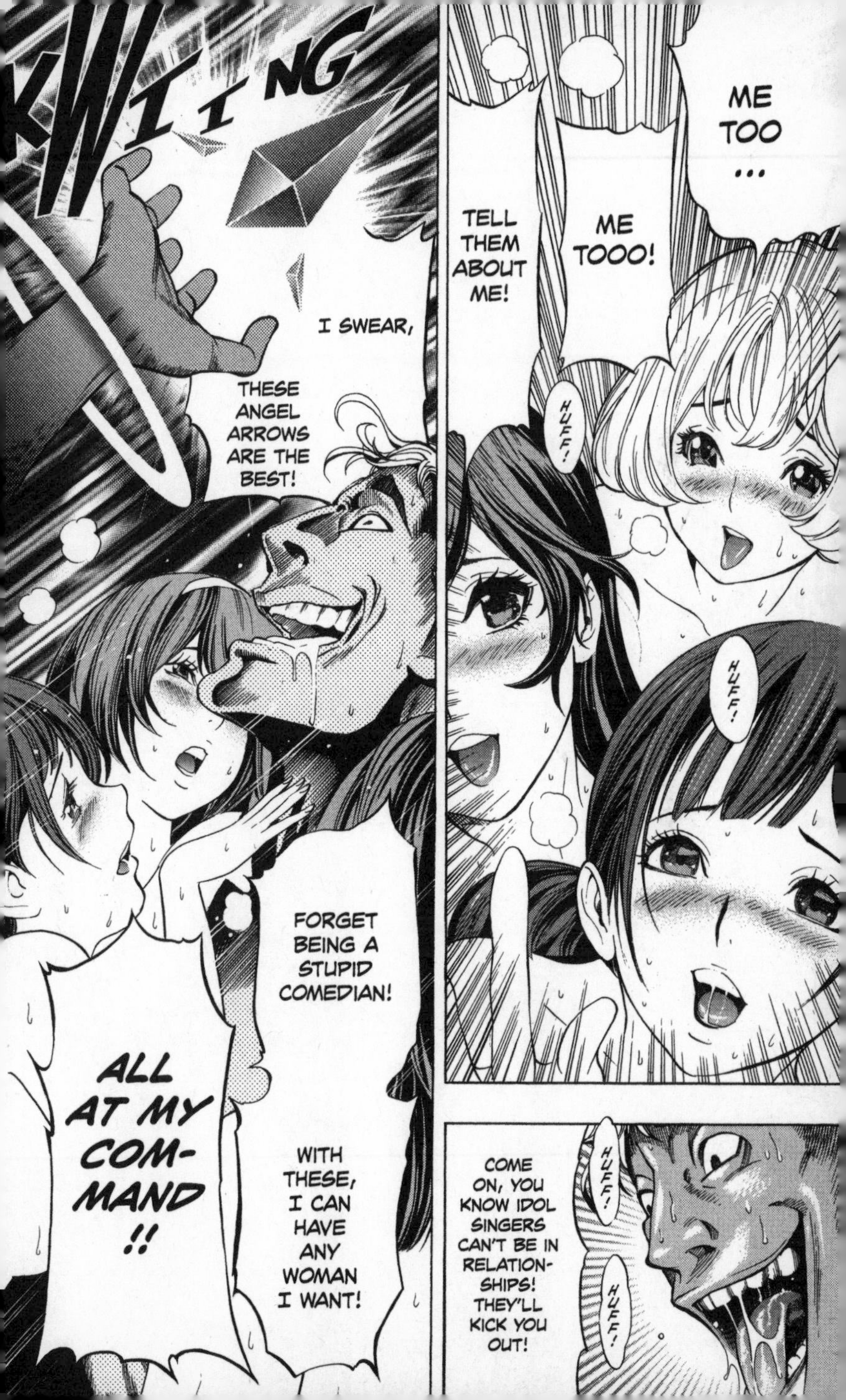
ME TOO...
ME TOOO!
TELL THEM ABOUT ME!
HUFF!
HUFF!
HUFF!
HUFF!
COME ON, YOU KNOW IDOL SINGERS CAN'T BE IN RELATION-SHIPS! THEY'LL KICK YOU OUT!
KWIING
I SWEAR,
THESE ANGEL ARROWS ARE THE BEST!
FORGET BEING A STUPID COMEDIAN!
WITH THESE, I CAN HAVE ANY WOMAN I WANT!
ALL AT MY COM-MAND!!

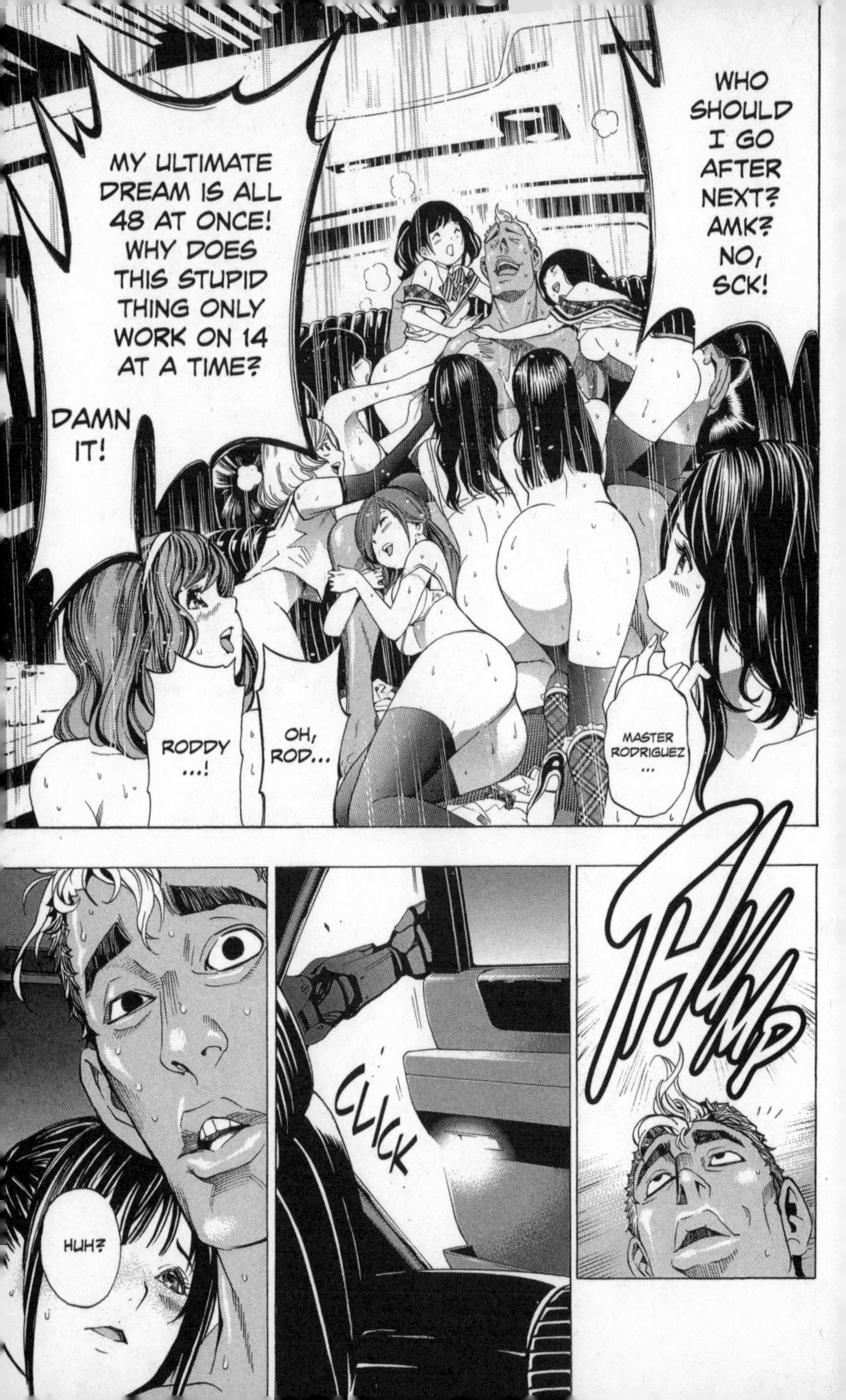
WHO SHOULD I GO AFTER NEXT? AMK? NO, SCK!
MY ULTIMATE DREAM IS ALL 48 AT ONCE! WHY DOES THIS STUPID THING ONLY WORK ON 14 AT A TIME?
DAMN IT!
MASTER RODRIGUEZ...
OH, ROD...
RODDY...!
THUMP
CLICK
HUH?

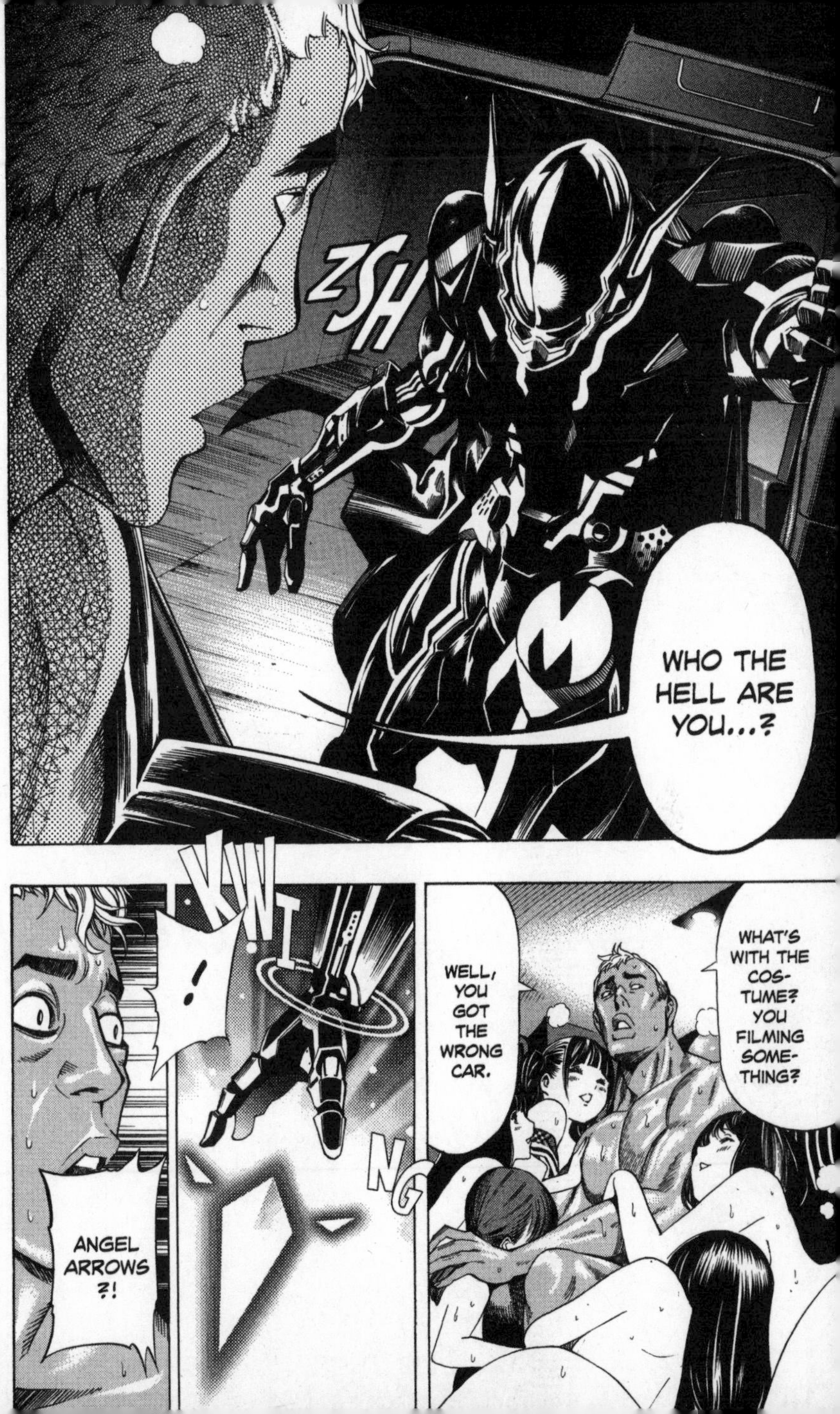
ZSH
WHO THE HELL ARE YOU...?
WHAT'S WITH THE COS-TUME? YOU FILMING SOME-THING?
WELL, YOU GOT THE WRONG CAR.
KWING
!
ANGEL ARROWS ?!

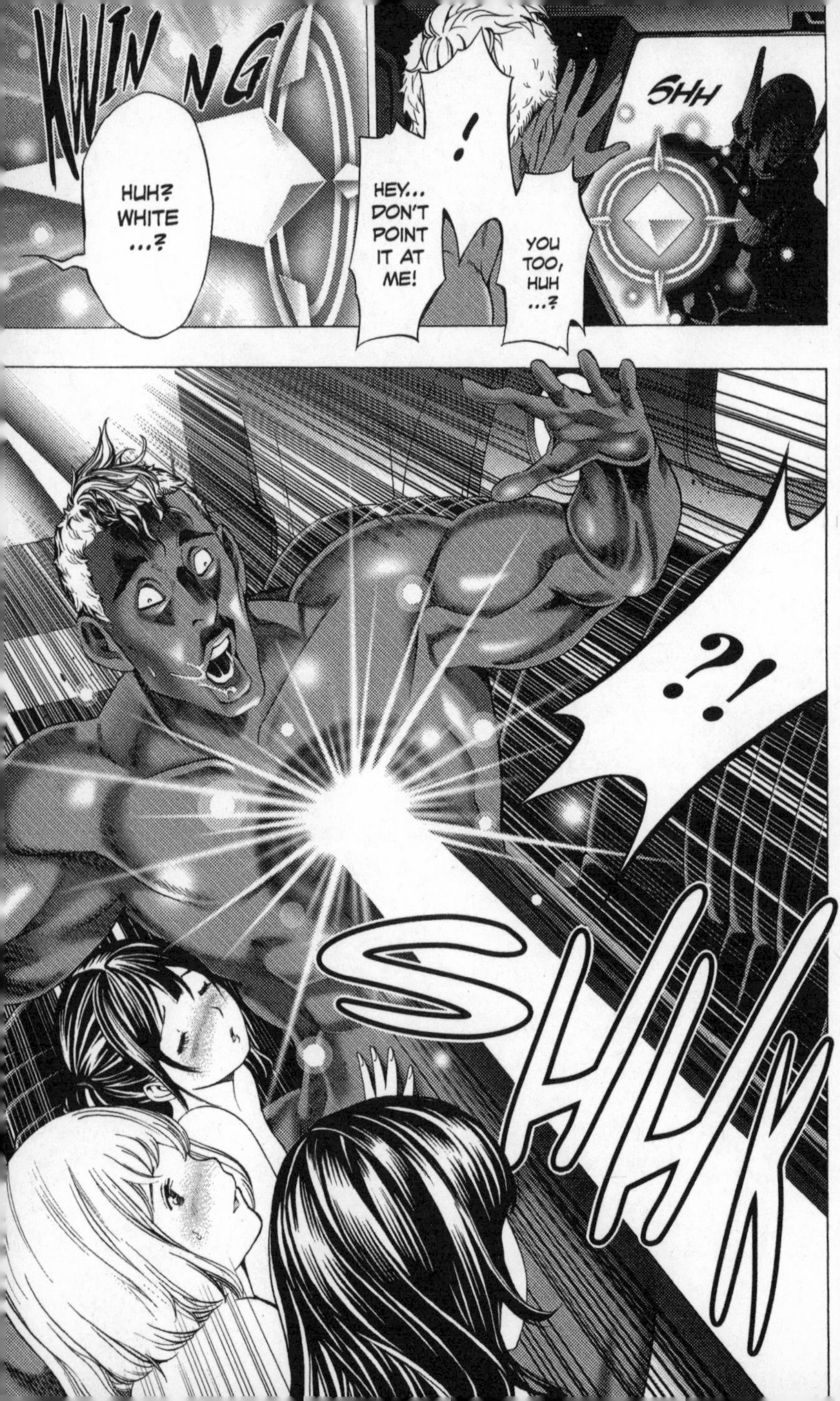
SHH
YOU TOO, HUH ...?
!
HEY... DON'T POINT IT AT ME!
KWIN NG
HUH? WHITE ...?
?!
SHHK

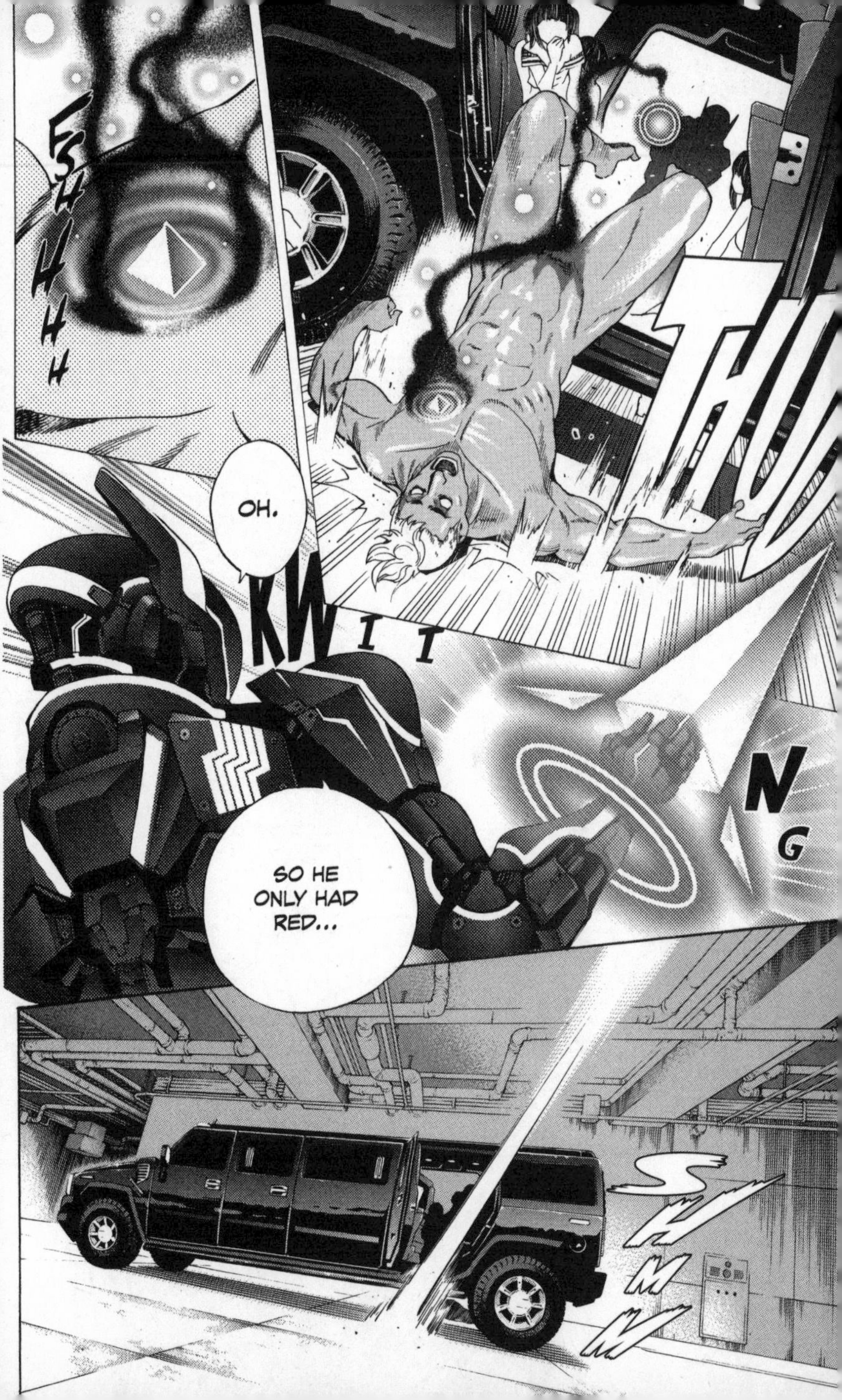
THU
FSHHHHHH
OH.
KWI I
NG
SO HE ONLY HAD RED...
SHMN

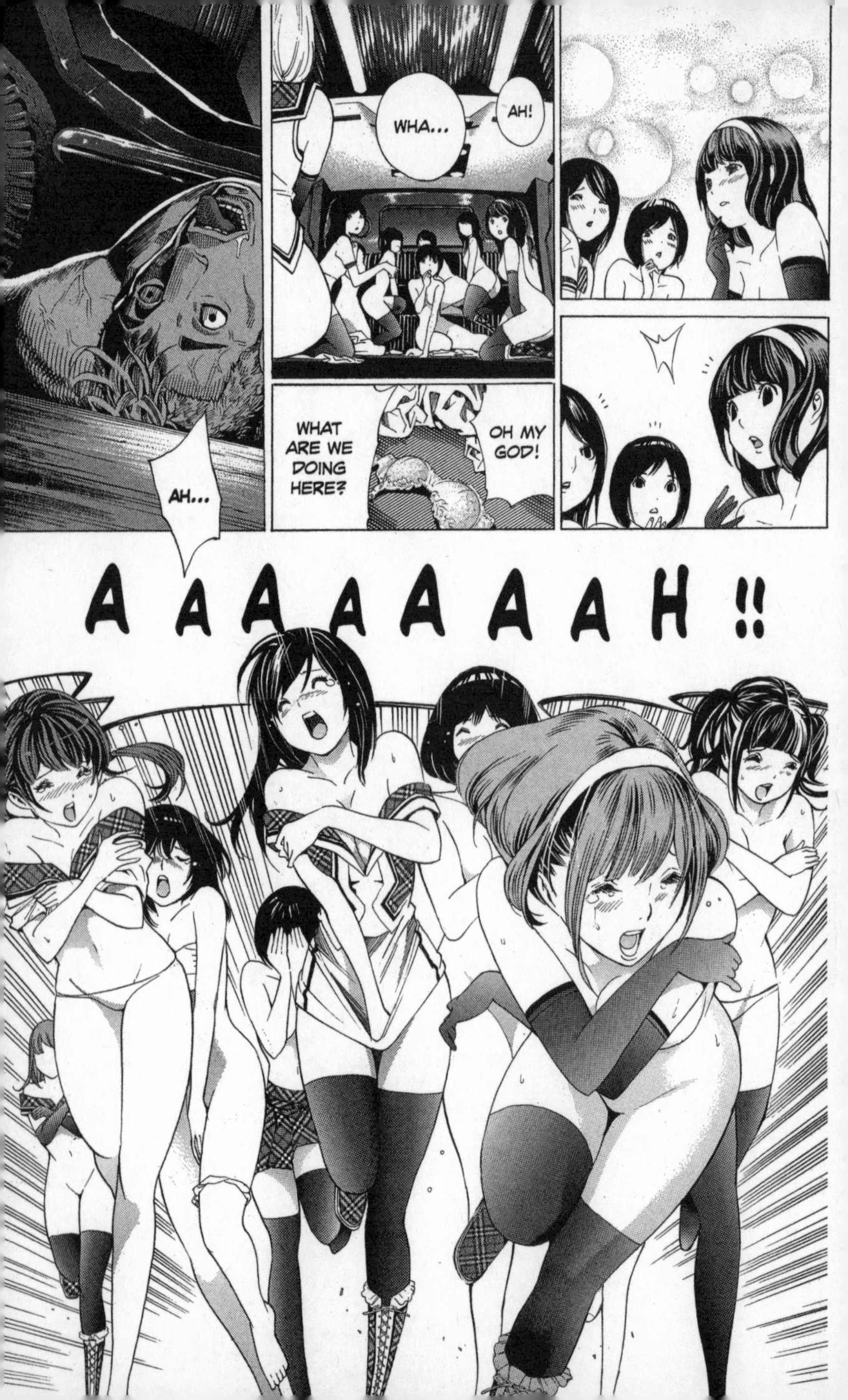
AH!
WHA...
OH MY GOD!
WHAT ARE WE DOING HERE?
AH...
AAAAAAAH!!

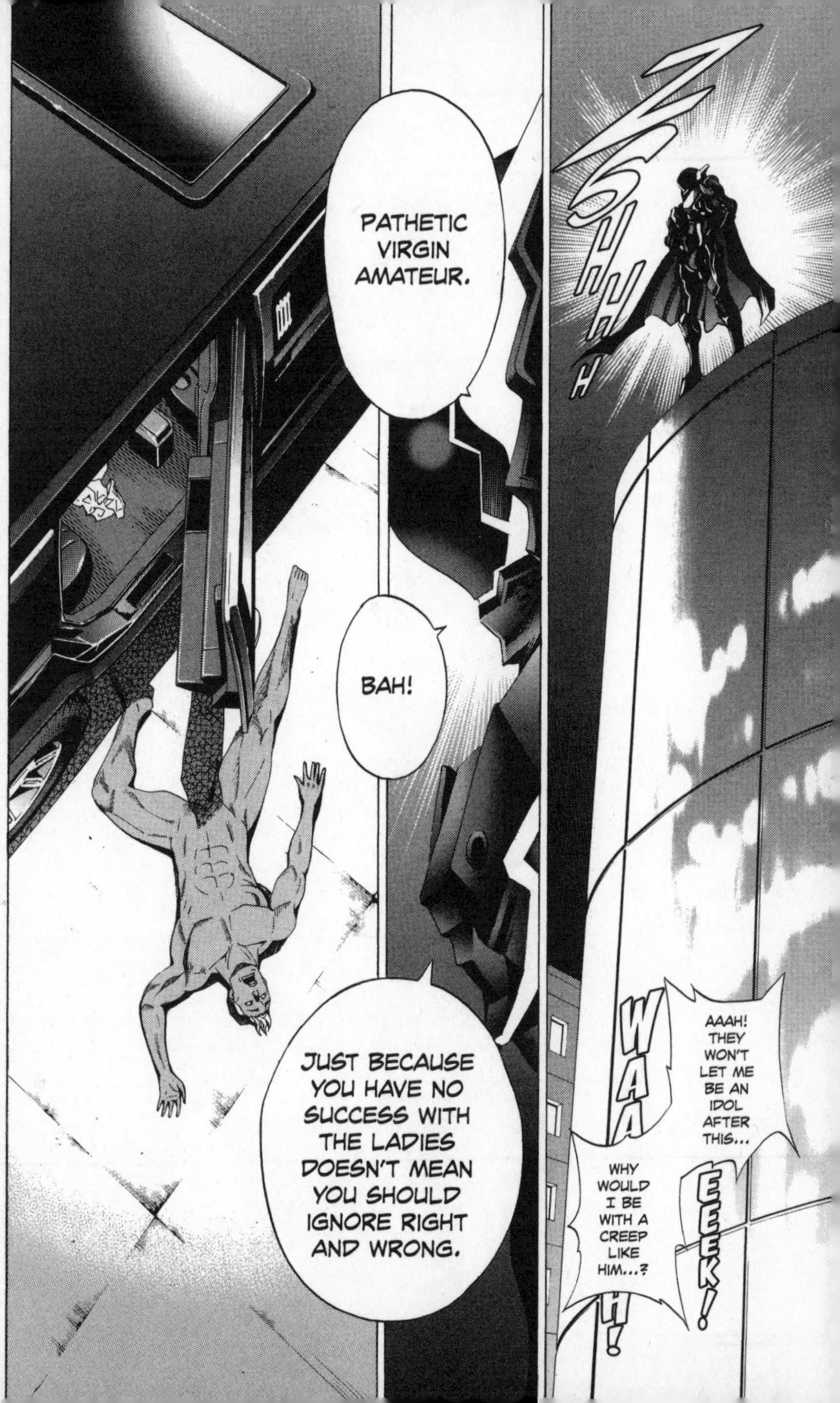
ZSHHHH
WAAH!
AAAH! THEY WON'T LET ME BE AN IDOL AFTER THIS...
WHY WOULD I BE WITH A CREEP LIKE HIM...?
EEEK!
PATHETIC VIRGIN AMATEUR.
BAH!
JUST BECAUSE YOU HAVE NO SUCCESS WITH THE LADIES DOESN'T MEAN YOU SHOULD IGNORE RIGHT AND WRONG.

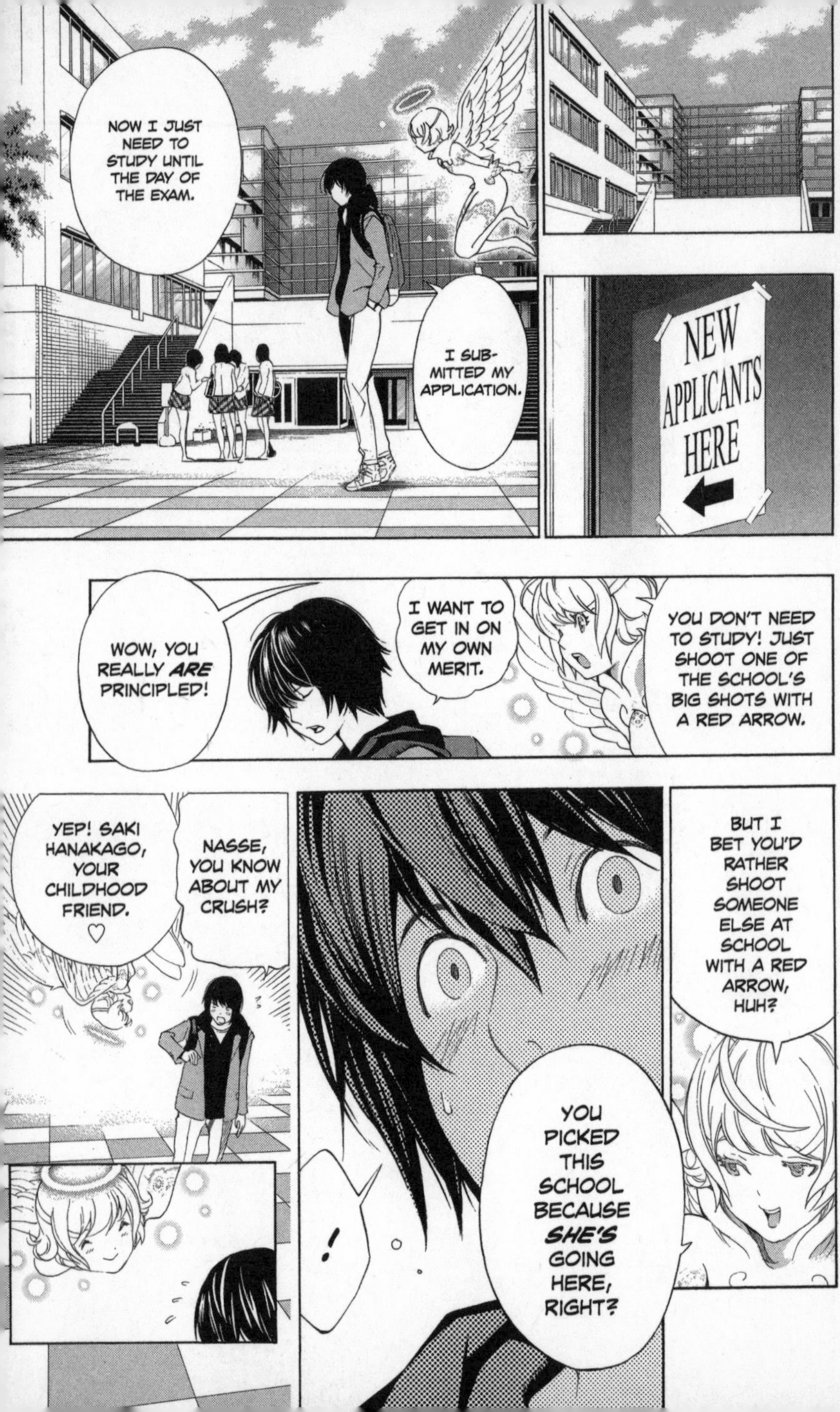
NEW APPLICANTS HERE
I SUB-MITTED MY APPLICATION.
NOW I JUST NEED TO STUDY UNTIL THE DAY OF THE EXAM.
YOU DON'T NEED TO STUDY! JUST SHOOT ONE OF THE SCHOOL'S BIG SHOTS WITH A RED ARROW.
I WANT TO GET IN ON MY OWN MERIT.
WOW, YOU REALLY *ARE* PRINCIPLED!
BUT I BET YOU'D RATHER SHOOT SOMEONE ELSE AT SCHOOL WITH A RED ARROW, HUH?
YOU PICKED THIS SCHOOL BECAUSE *SHE'S* GOING HERE, RIGHT?
!
NASSE, YOU KNOW ABOUT MY CRUSH?
YEP! SAKI HANAKAGO, YOUR CHILDHOOD FRIEND. ♡

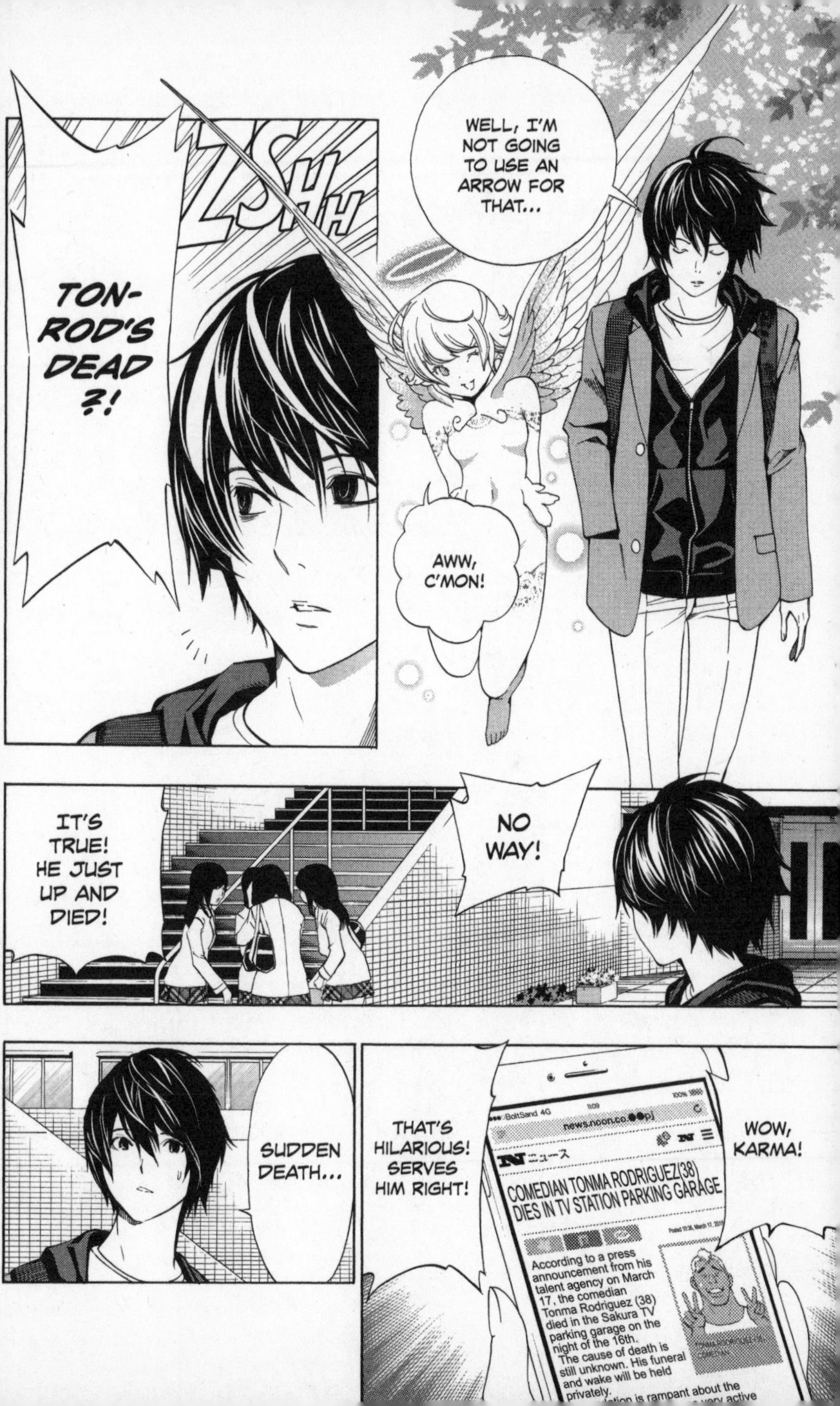
WELL, I'M NOT GOING TO USE AN ARROW FOR THAT...
AWW, C'MON!
ZSHH
TON-ROD'S DEAD ?!
NO WAY!
IT'S TRUE! HE JUST UP AND DIED!
WOW, KARMA!
THAT'S HILARIOUS! SERVES HIM RIGHT!
BoltSand 4G
news.noon.co.●●pj
ニュース
COMEDIAN TONMA RODRIGUEZ(38) DIES IN TV STATION PARKING GARAGE
According to a press announcement from his talent agency on March 17, the comedian Tonma Rodriguez (38) died in the Sakura TV parking garage on the night of the 16th.
The cause of death is still unknown. His funeral and wake will be held privately.
SUDDEN DEATH...

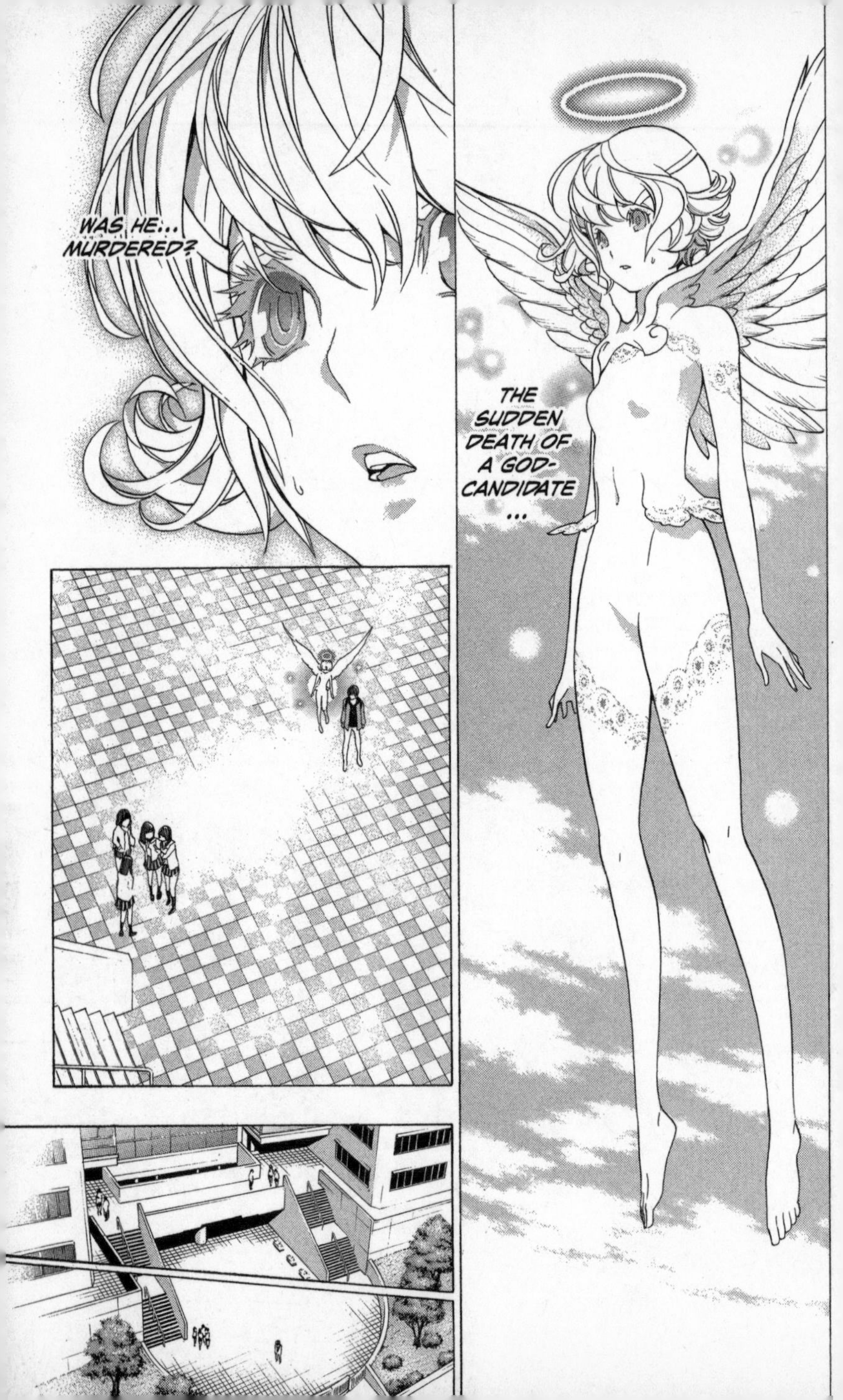
THE SUDDEN DEATH OF A GOD-CANDIDATE...
WAS HE... MURDERED?

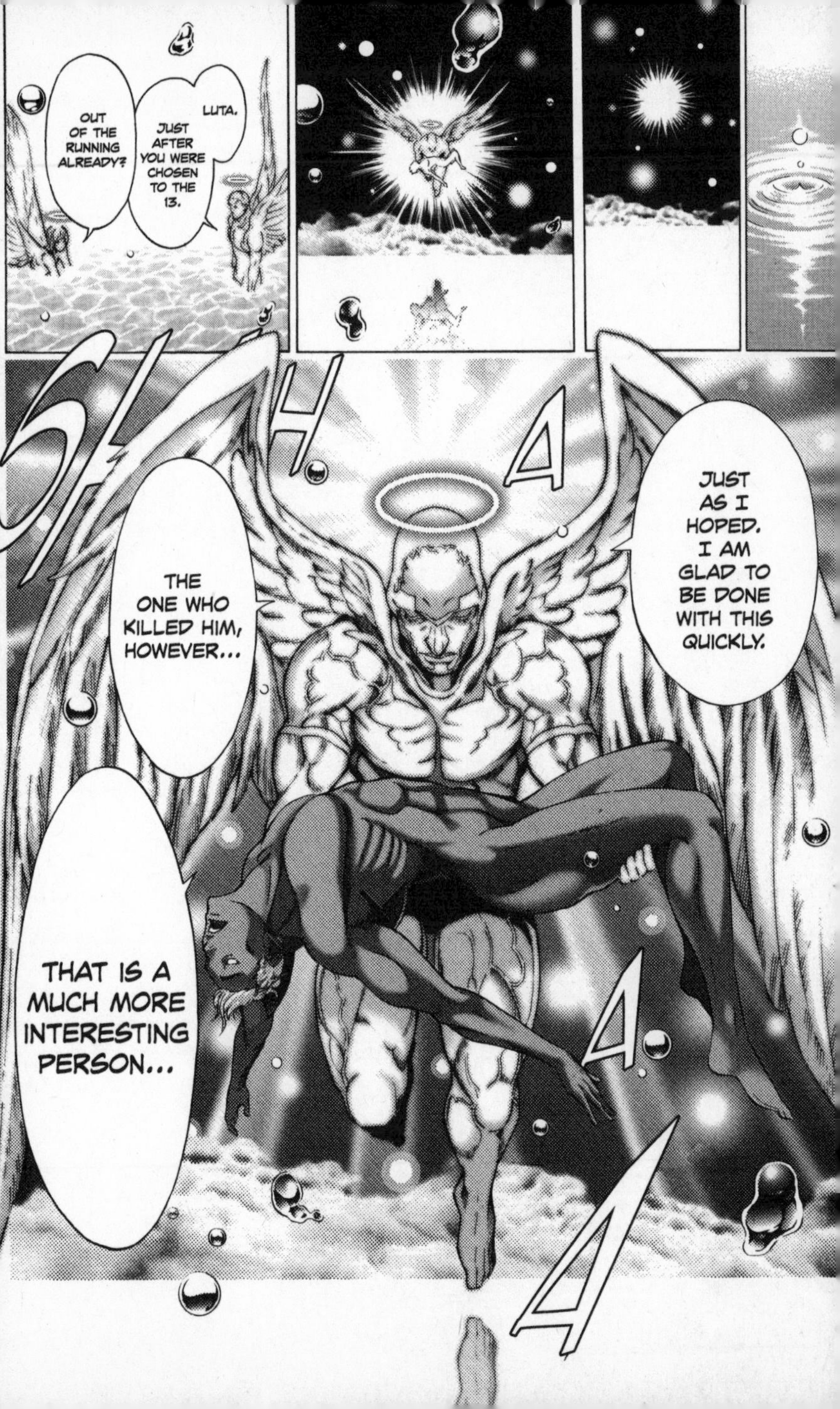
LUTA. JUST AFTER YOU WERE CHOSEN TO THE 13.
OUT OF THE RUNNING ALREADY?
JUST AS I HOPED. I AM GLAD TO BE DONE WITH THIS QUICKLY.
THE ONE WHO KILLED HIM, HOWEVER...
THAT IS A MUCH MORE INTERESTING PERSON...
SHHAAA

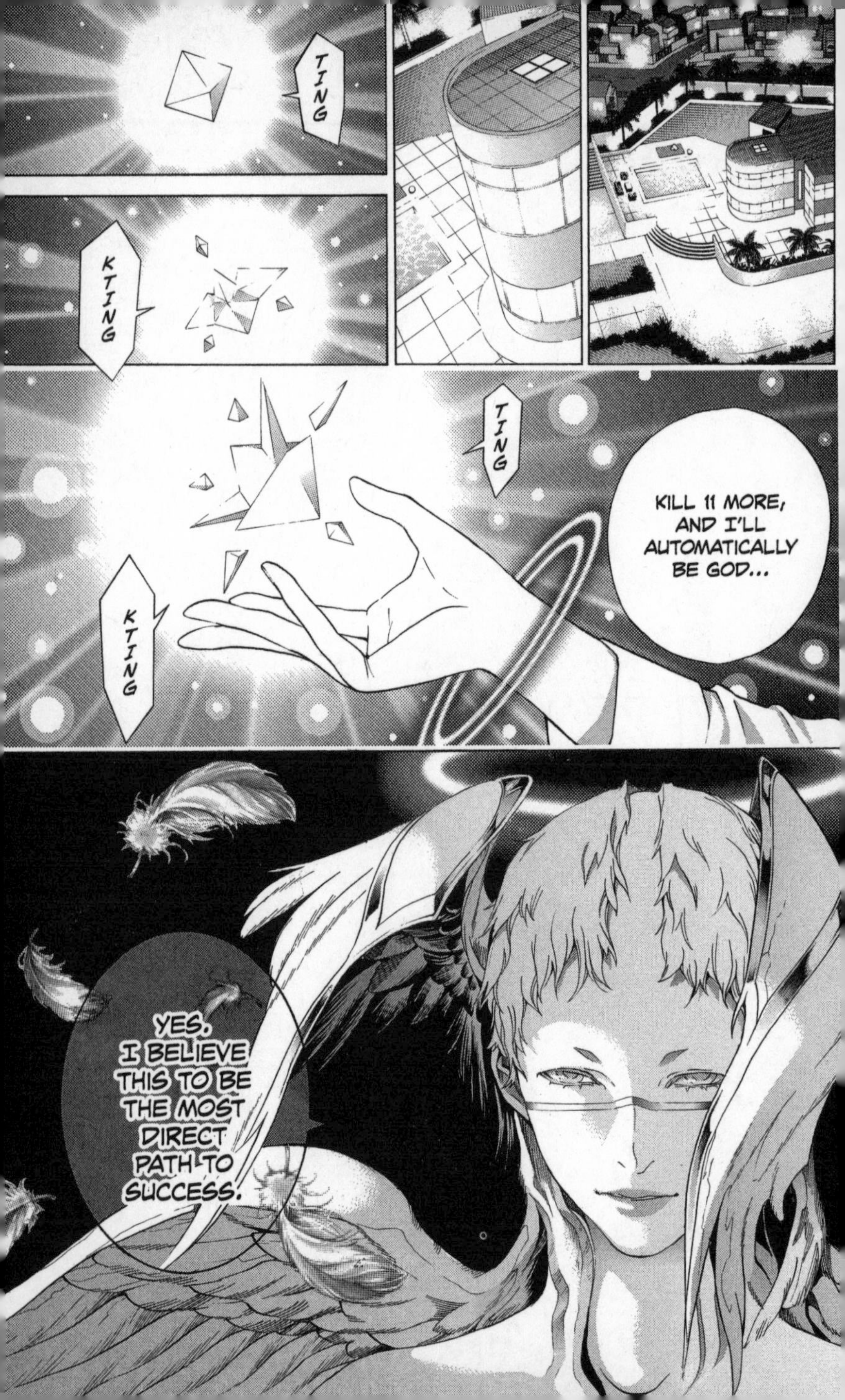
TING
KTING
TING
KILL 11 MORE, AND I'LL AUTOMATICALLY BE GOD...
KTING
YES. I BELIEVE THIS TO BE THE MOST DIRECT PATH TO SUCCESS.

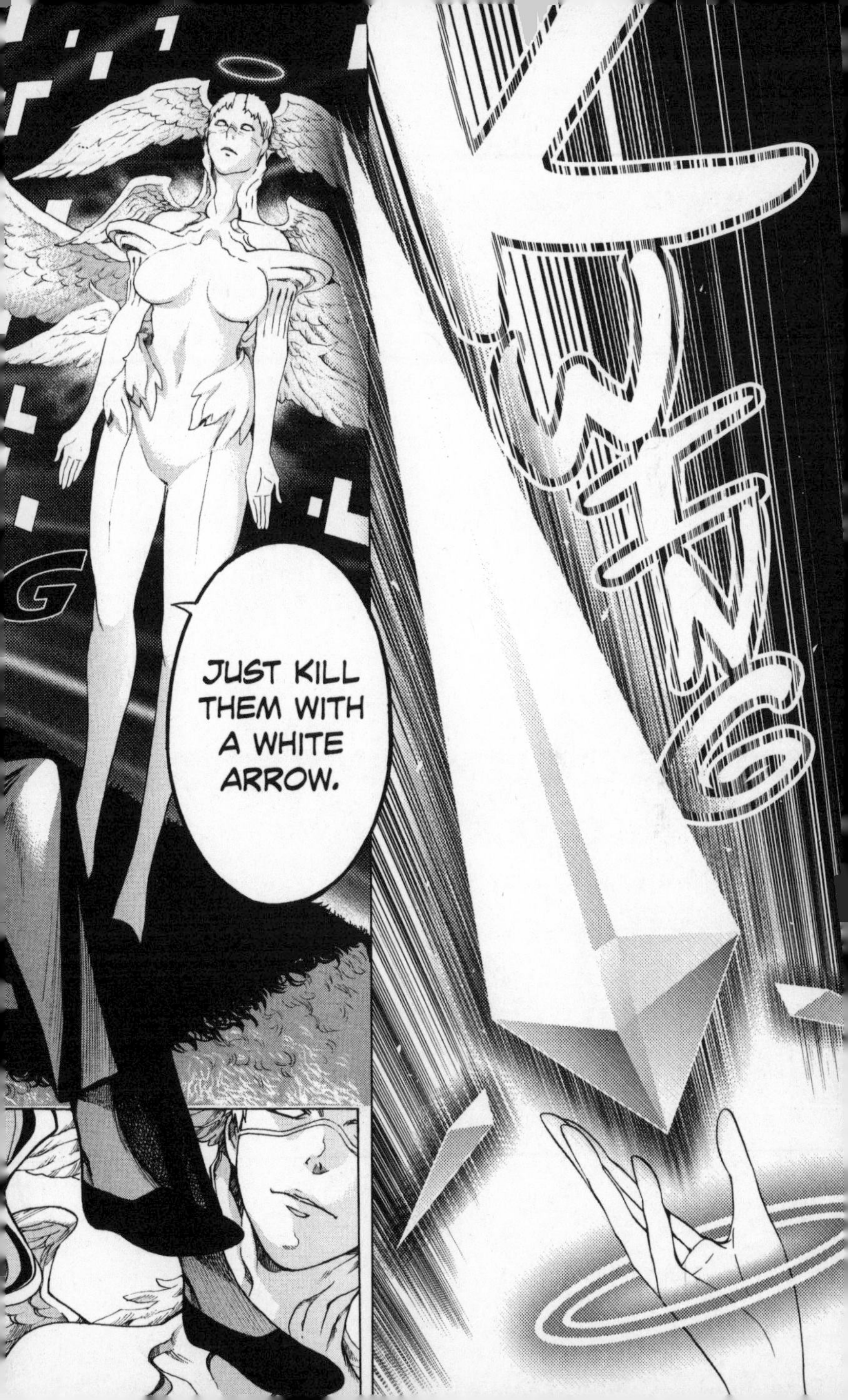
WHING
JUST KILL THEM WITH A WHITE ARROW.

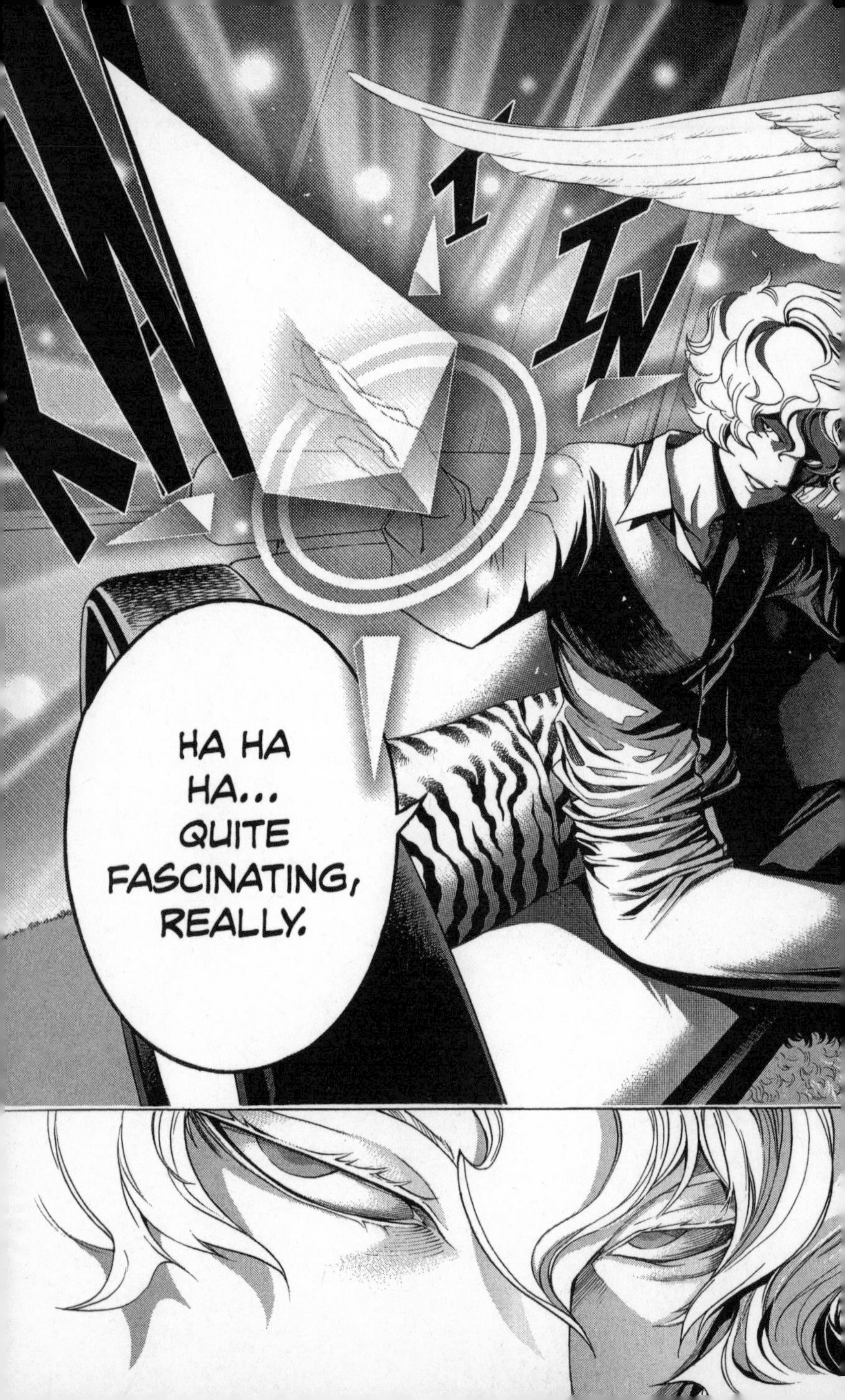
HA HA HA... QUITE FASCINATING, REALLY.

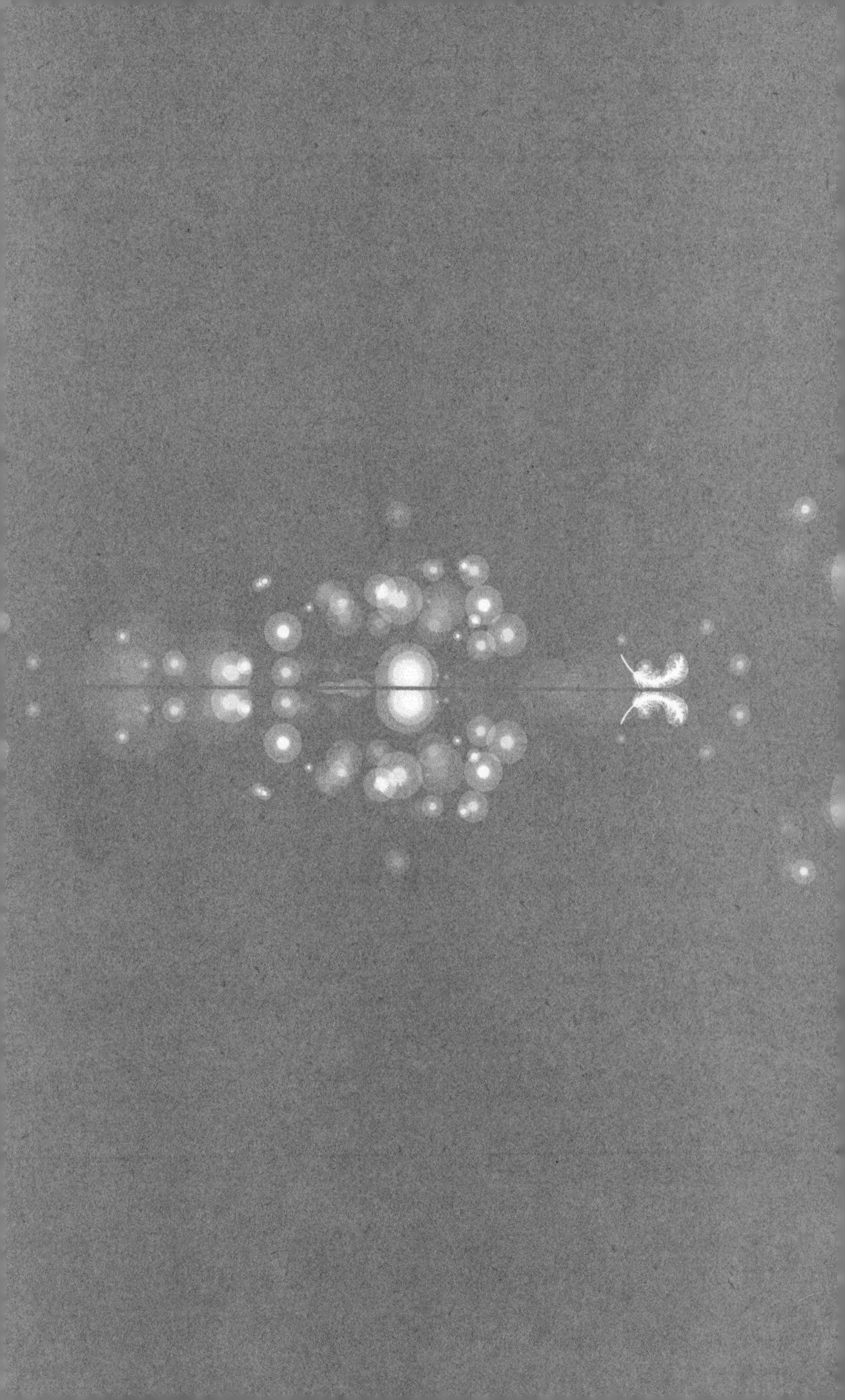

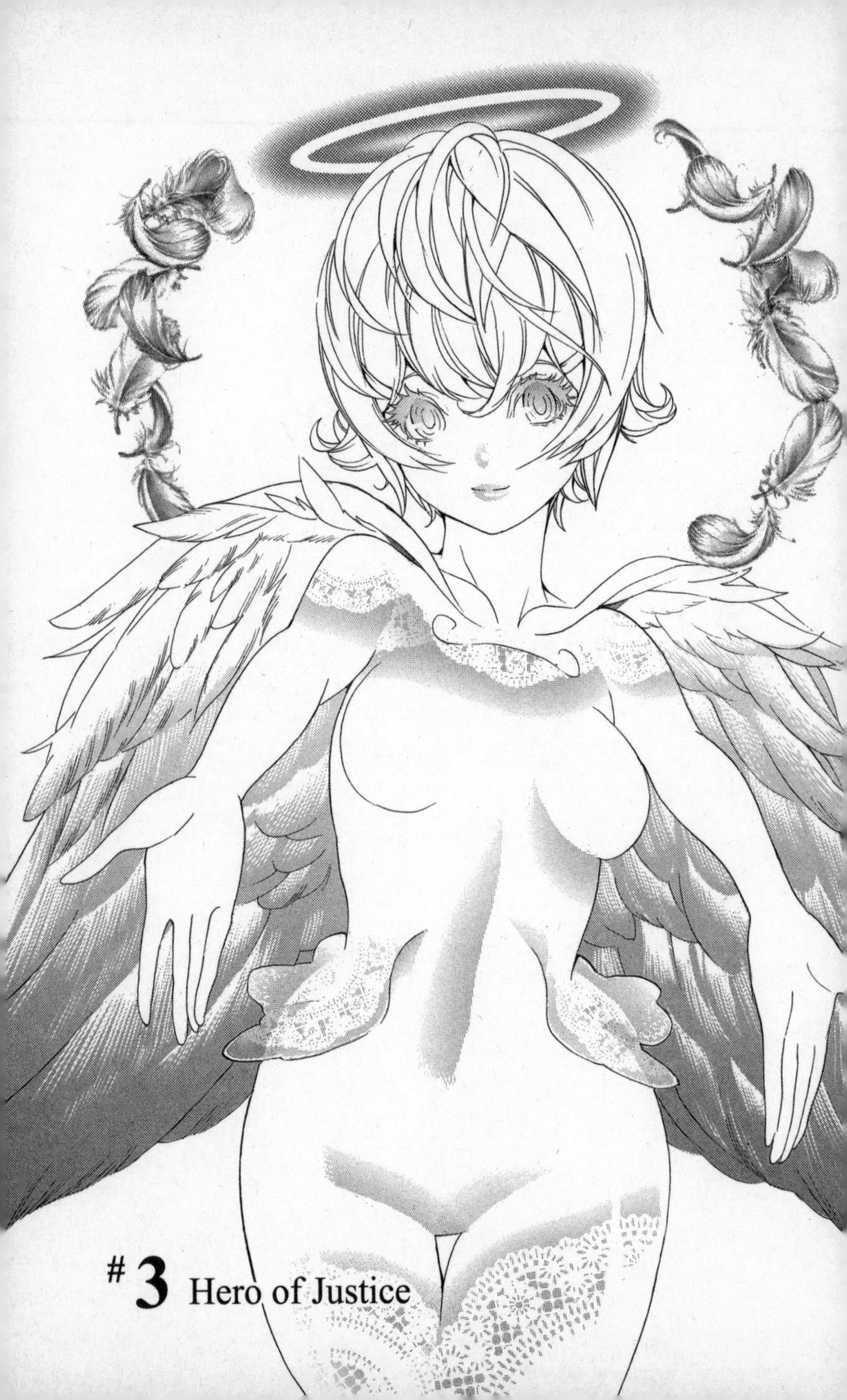

#3 Hero of Justice

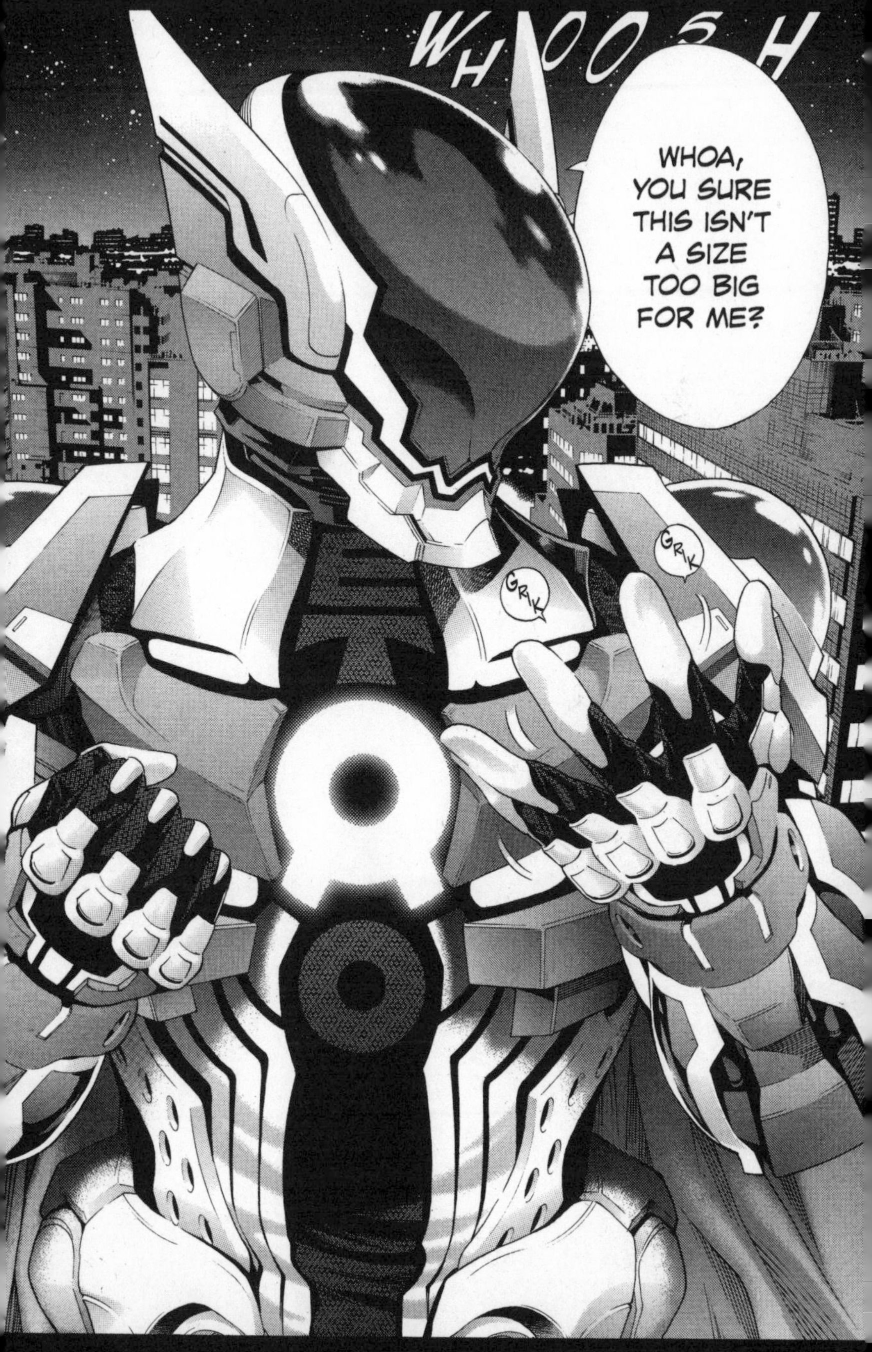
WHOOSH
WHOA, YOU SURE THIS ISN'T A SIZE TOO BIG FOR ME?
GRIK
GRIK

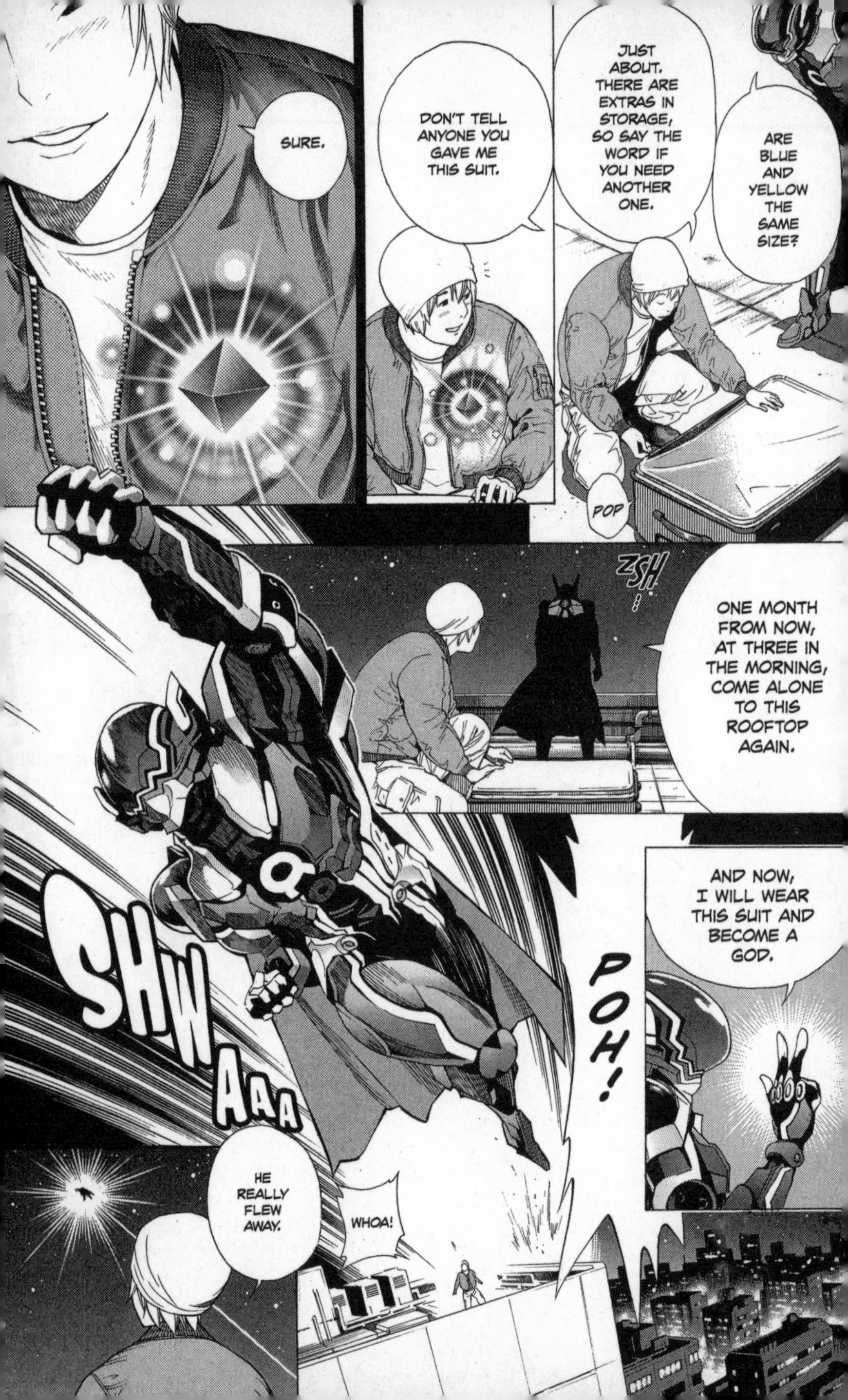
ARE BLUE AND YELLOW THE SAME SIZE?
JUST ABOUT. THERE ARE EXTRAS IN STORAGE, SO SAY THE WORD IF YOU NEED ANOTHER ONE.
POP
DON'T TELL ANYONE YOU GAVE ME THIS SUIT.
SURE.
ZSH!
ONE MONTH FROM NOW, AT THREE IN THE MORNING, COME ALONE TO THIS ROOFTOP AGAIN.
AND NOW, I WILL WEAR THIS SUIT AND BECOME A GOD.
SHWAAA
POH!
WHOA!
HE REALLY FLEW AWAY.

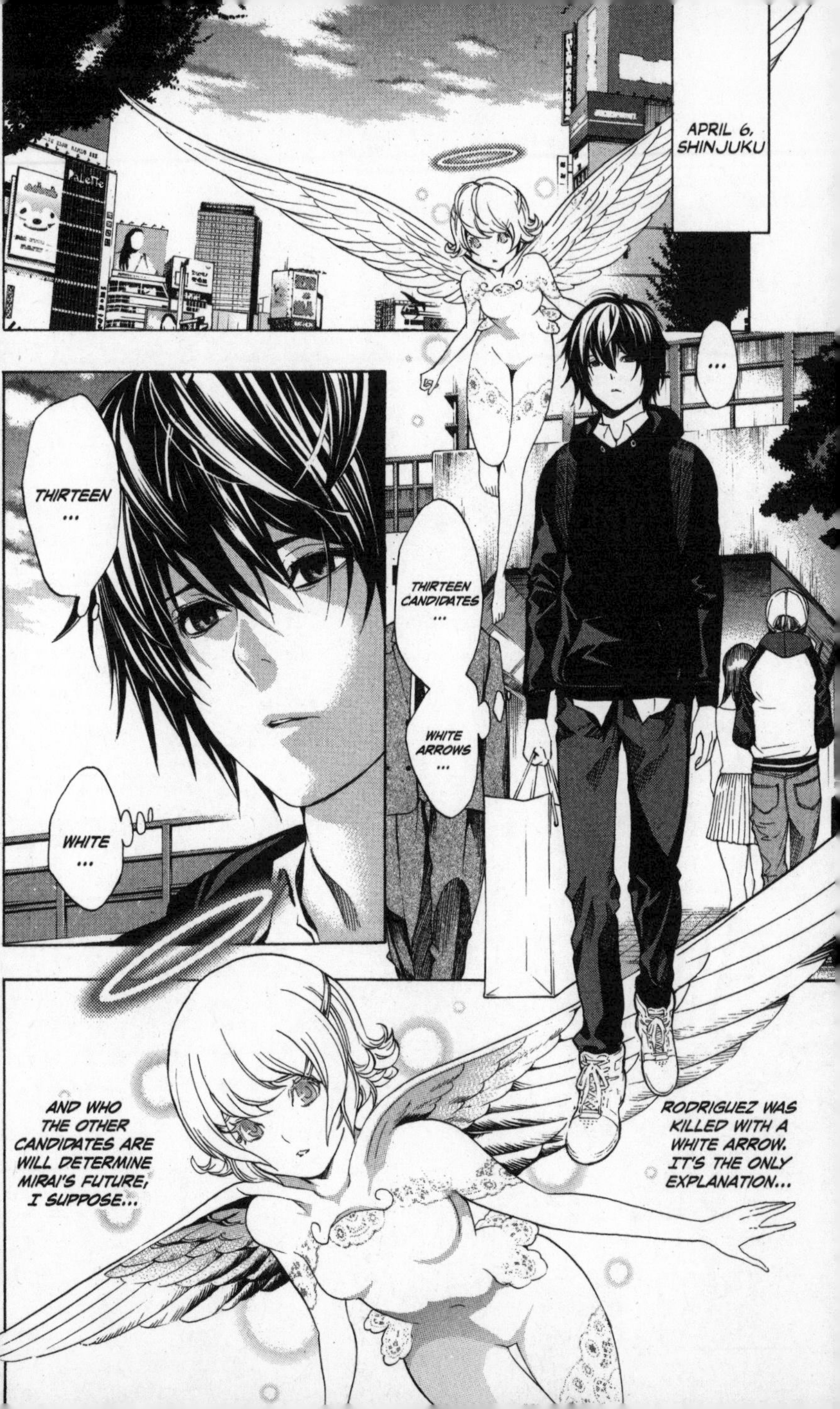
APRIL 6, SHINJUKU
...
THIRTEEN CANDIDATES ...
WHITE ARROWS ...
THIRTEEN ...
WHITE ...
RODRIGUEZ WAS KILLED WITH A WHITE ARROW. IT'S THE ONLY EXPLANATION...
AND WHO THE OTHER CANDIDATES ARE WILL DETERMINE MIRAI'S FUTURE, I SUPPOSE...

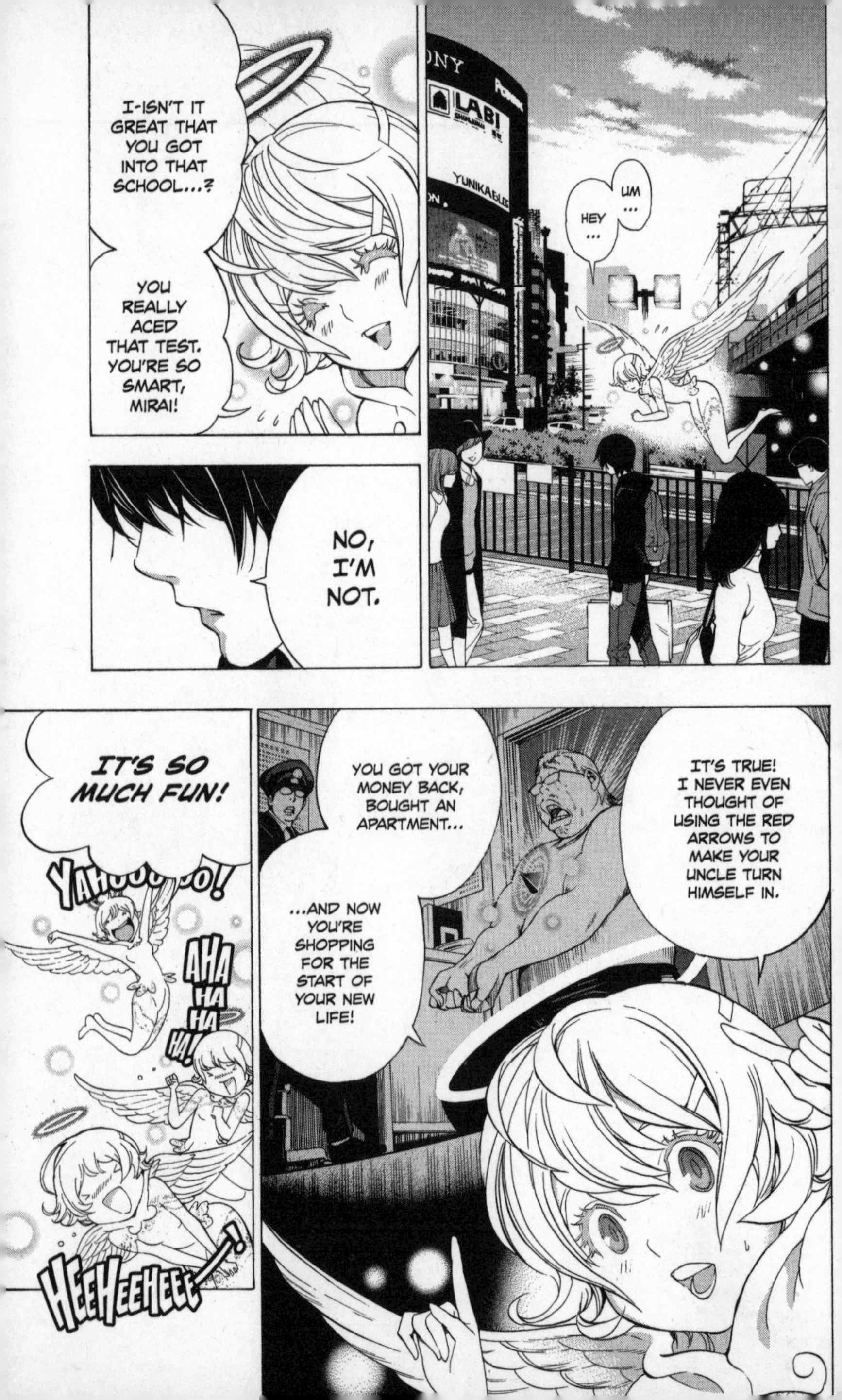
HEY ... UM ...
I-ISN'T IT GREAT THAT YOU GOT INTO THAT SCHOOL...?
YOU REALLY ACED THAT TEST. YOU'RE SO SMART, MIRAI!
NO, I'M NOT.
IT'S TRUE! I NEVER EVEN THOUGHT OF USING THE RED ARROWS TO MAKE YOUR UNCLE TURN HIMSELF IN.
YOU GOT YOUR MONEY BACK, BOUGHT AN APARTMENT...
...AND NOW YOU'RE SHOPPING FOR THE START OF YOUR NEW LIFE!
IT'S SO MUCH FUN!
YAHOOOOOO!
AHAHAHAHA!
HEEHEEHEEE

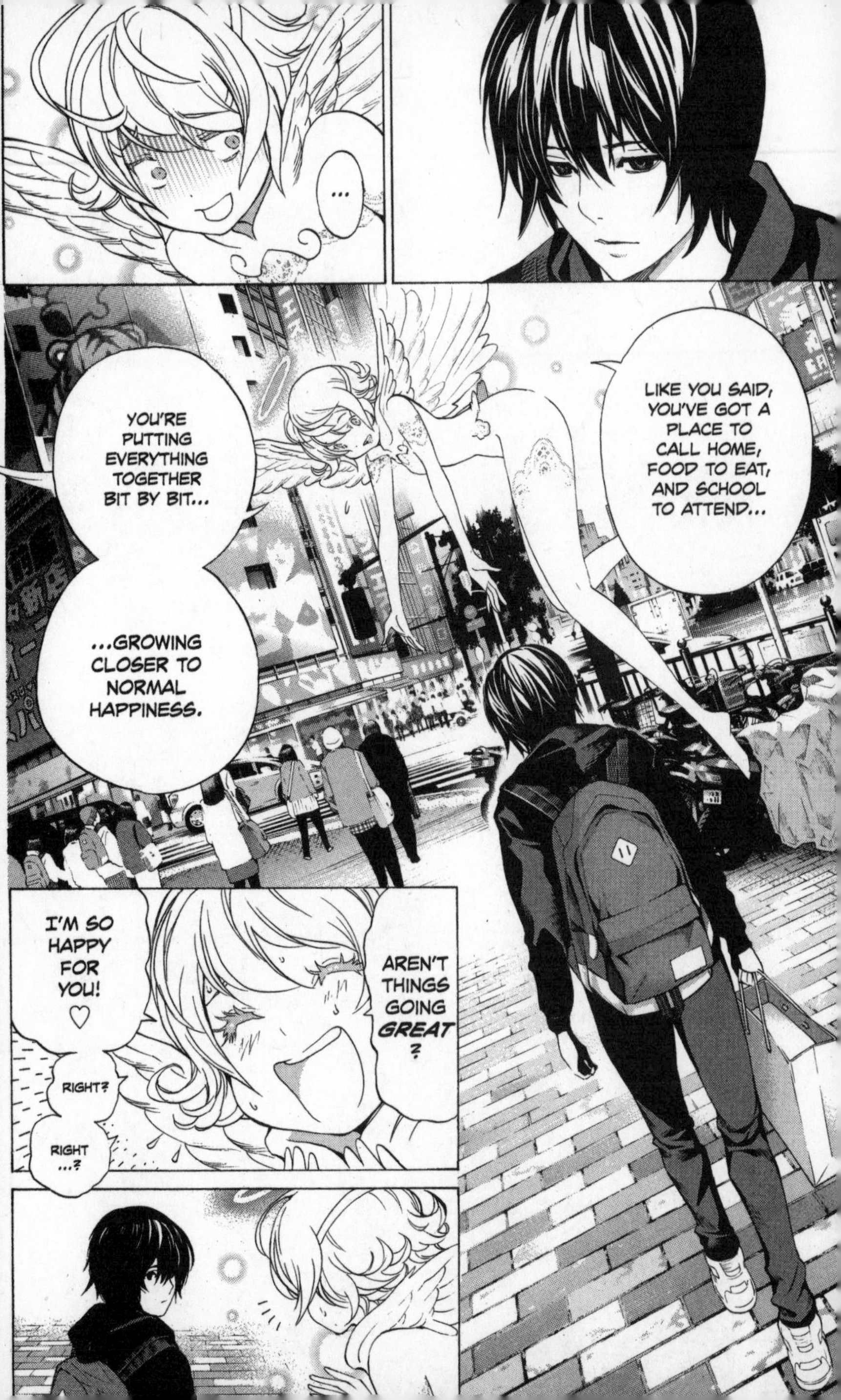
...
LIKE YOU SAID, YOU'VE GOT A PLACE TO CALL HOME, FOOD TO EAT, AND SCHOOL TO ATTEND...
YOU'RE PUTTING EVERYTHING TOGETHER BIT BY BIT...
...GROWING CLOSER TO NORMAL HAPPINESS.
AREN'T THINGS GOING *GREAT*?
I'M SO HAPPY FOR YOU! ♡
RIGHT?
RIGHT...?

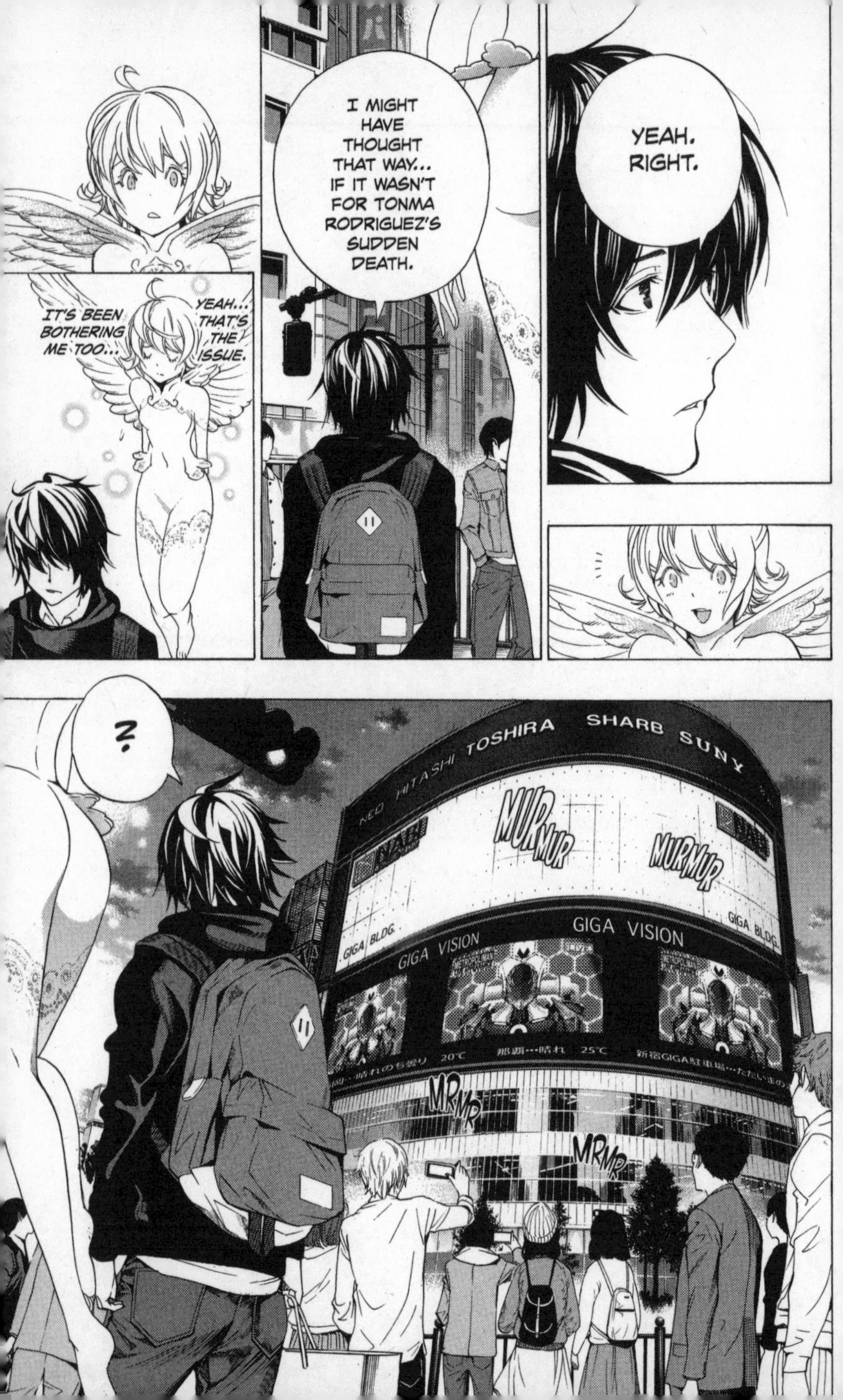
YEAH. RIGHT.
I MIGHT HAVE THOUGHT THAT WAY... IF IT WASN'T FOR TONMA RODRIGUEZ'S SUDDEN DEATH.
YEAH... THAT'S THE ISSUE.
IT'S BEEN BOTHERING ME TOO...
?
NEO HITASHI TOSHIRA SHARB SUNY
MURMUR
MURMUR
GIGA BLDG.
GIGA BLDG.
GIGA VISION
GIGA VISION
MRMR
MRMR

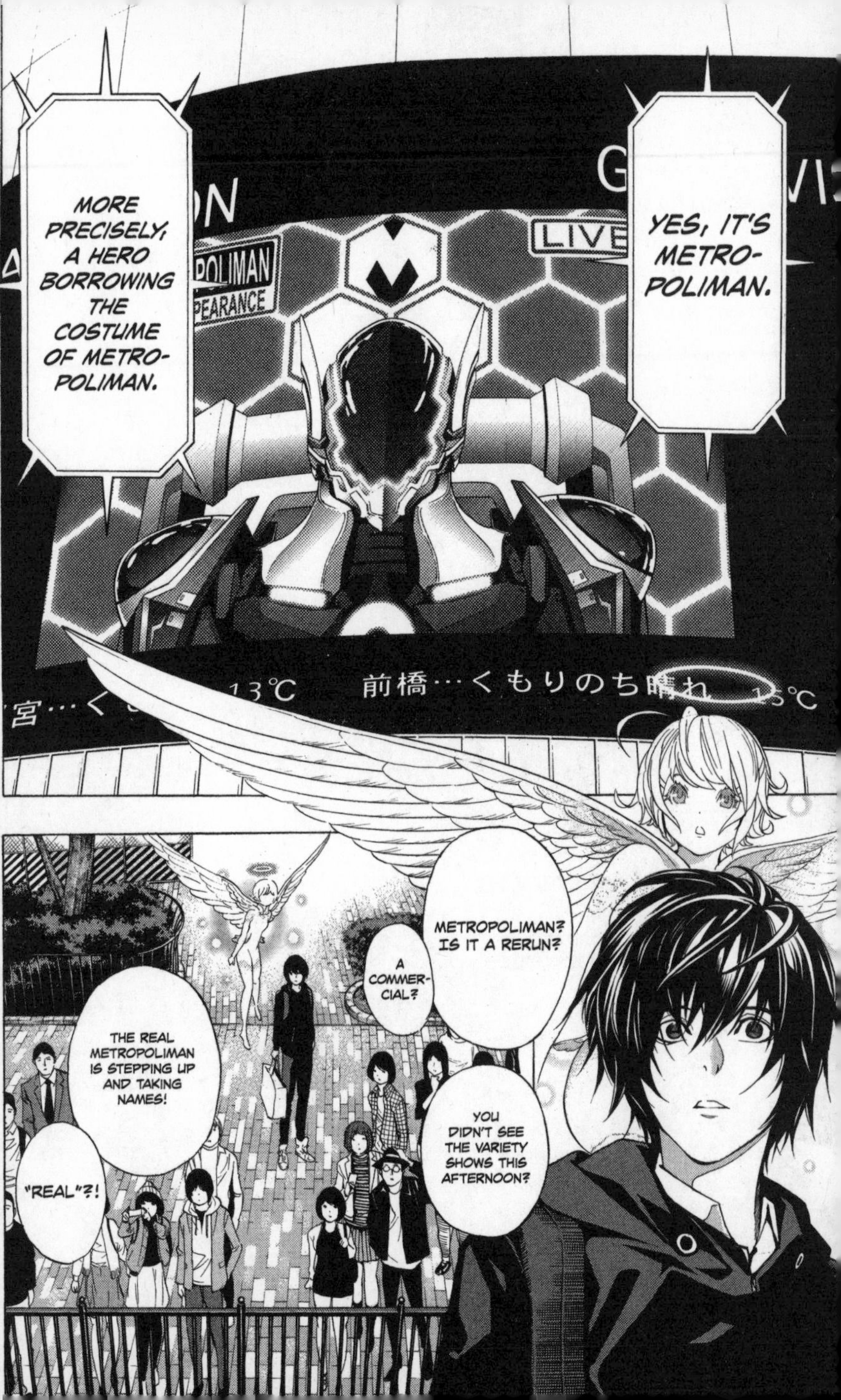
YES, IT'S METRO-POLIMAN.
LIVE
MORE PRECISELY, A HERO BORROWING THE COSTUME OF METRO-POLIMAN.
13℃
前橋…くもりのち晴れ
METROPOLIMAN? IS IT A RERUN?
A COMMERCIAL?
YOU DIDN'T SEE THE VARIETY SHOWS THIS AFTERNOON?
THE REAL METROPOLIMAN IS STEPPING UP AND TAKING NAMES!
"REAL"?!

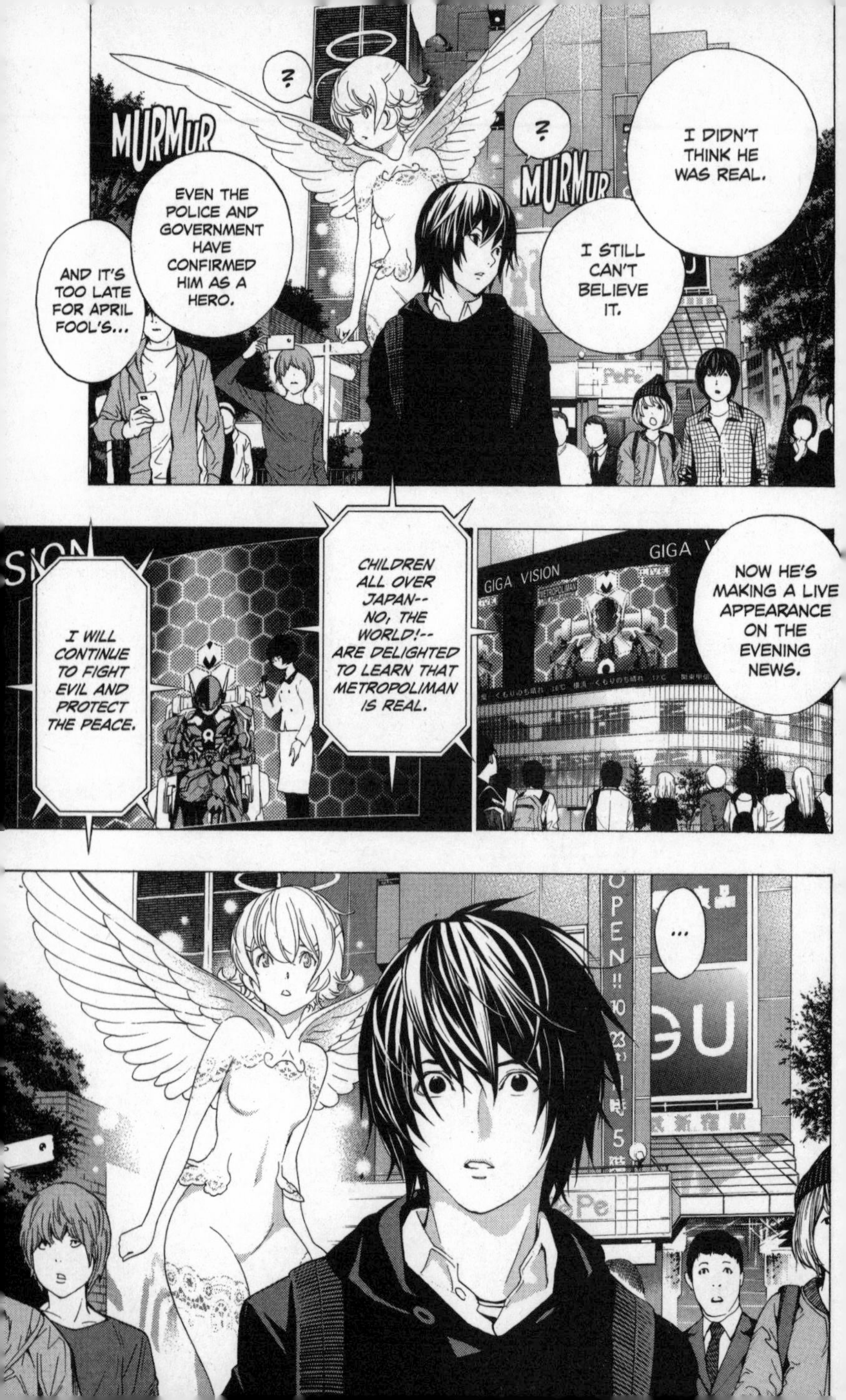
I DIDN'T THINK HE WAS REAL.
?
MURMUR
I STILL CAN'T BELIEVE IT.
?
MURMUR
EVEN THE POLICE AND GOVERNMENT HAVE CONFIRMED HIM AS A HERO.
AND IT'S TOO LATE FOR APRIL FOOL'S...
GIGA VISION
NOW HE'S MAKING A LIVE APPEARANCE ON THE EVENING NEWS.
CHILDREN ALL OVER JAPAN-- NO, THE WORLD!-- ARE DELIGHTED TO LEARN THAT METROPOLIMAN IS REAL.
I WILL CONTINUE TO FIGHT EVIL AND PROTECT THE PEACE.
...
OPEN!!
GU

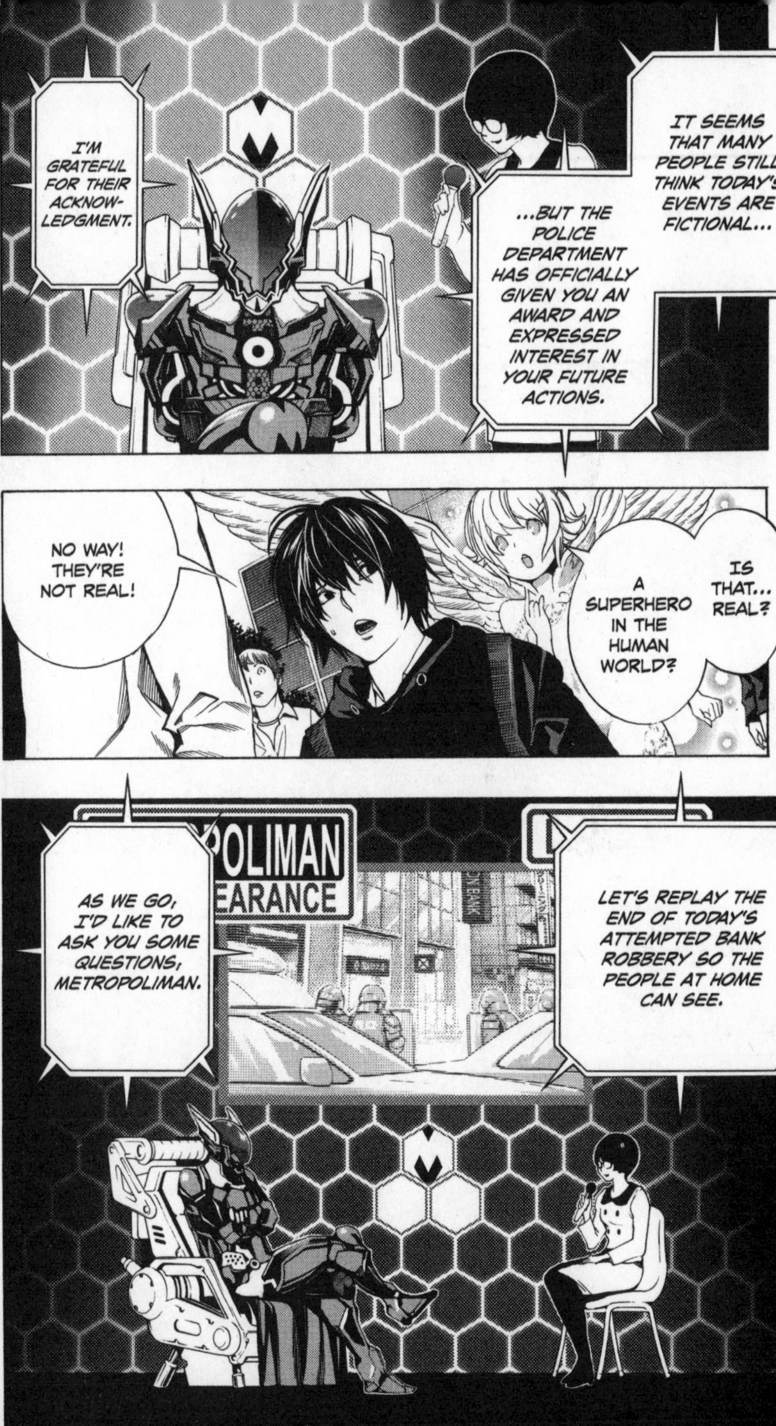
IT SEEMS THAT MANY PEOPLE STILL THINK TODAY'S EVENTS ARE FICTIONAL...
...BUT THE POLICE DEPARTMENT HAS OFFICIALLY GIVEN YOU AN AWARD AND EXPRESSED INTEREST IN YOUR FUTURE ACTIONS.
I'M GRATEFUL FOR THEIR ACKNOW-LEDGMENT.
IS THAT... REAL?
A SUPERHERO IN THE HUMAN WORLD?
NO WAY! THEY'RE NOT REAL!
LET'S REPLAY THE END OF TODAY'S ATTEMPTED BANK ROBBERY SO THE PEOPLE AT HOME CAN SEE.
POLIMAN
EARANCE
AS WE GO, I'D LIKE TO ASK YOU SOME QUESTIONS, METROPOLIMAN.

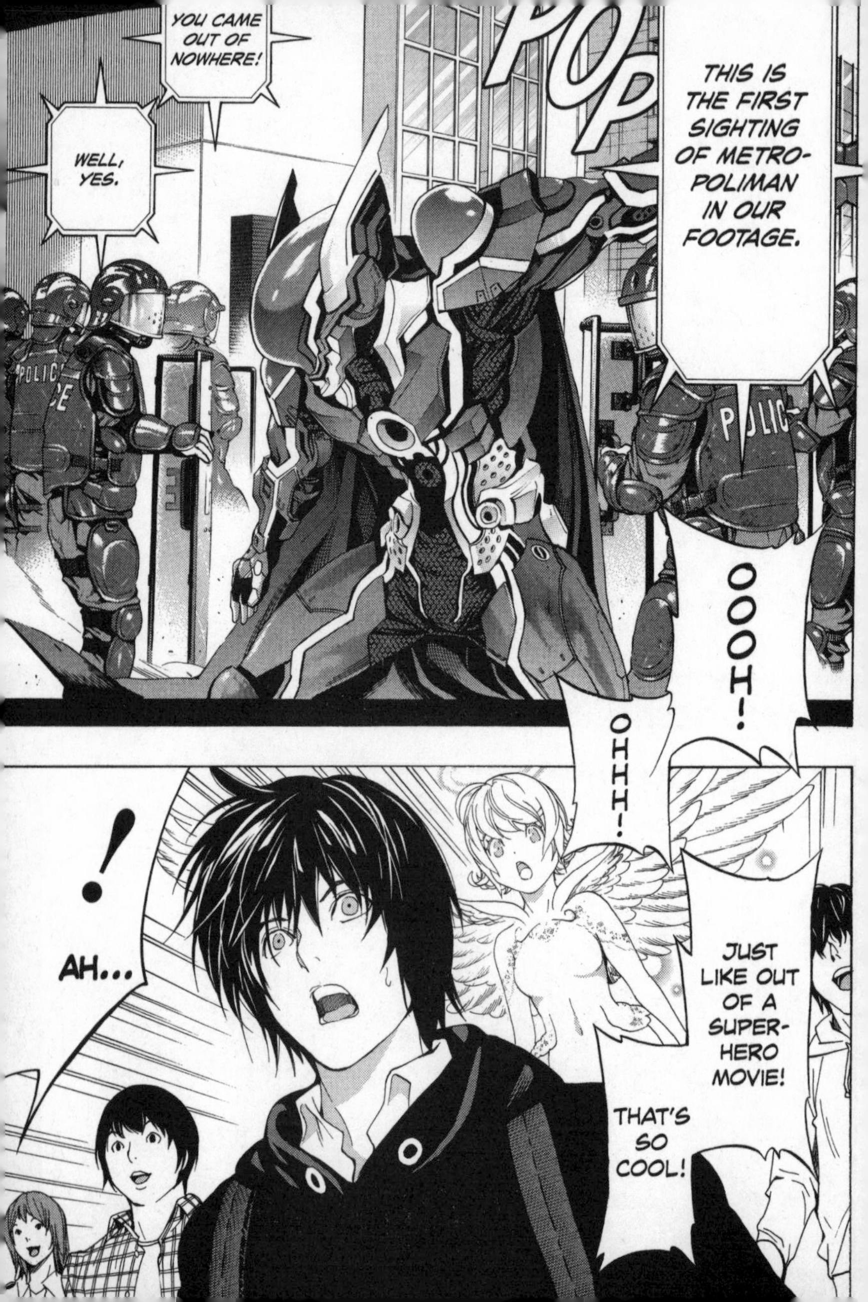
THIS IS THE FIRST SIGHTING OF METRO-POLIMAN IN OUR FOOTAGE.
POP
YOU CAME OUT OF NOWHERE!
WELL, YES.
OOOOH!
OHHH!
JUST LIKE OUT OF A SUPER-HERO MOVIE!
THAT'S SO COOL!
!
AH...

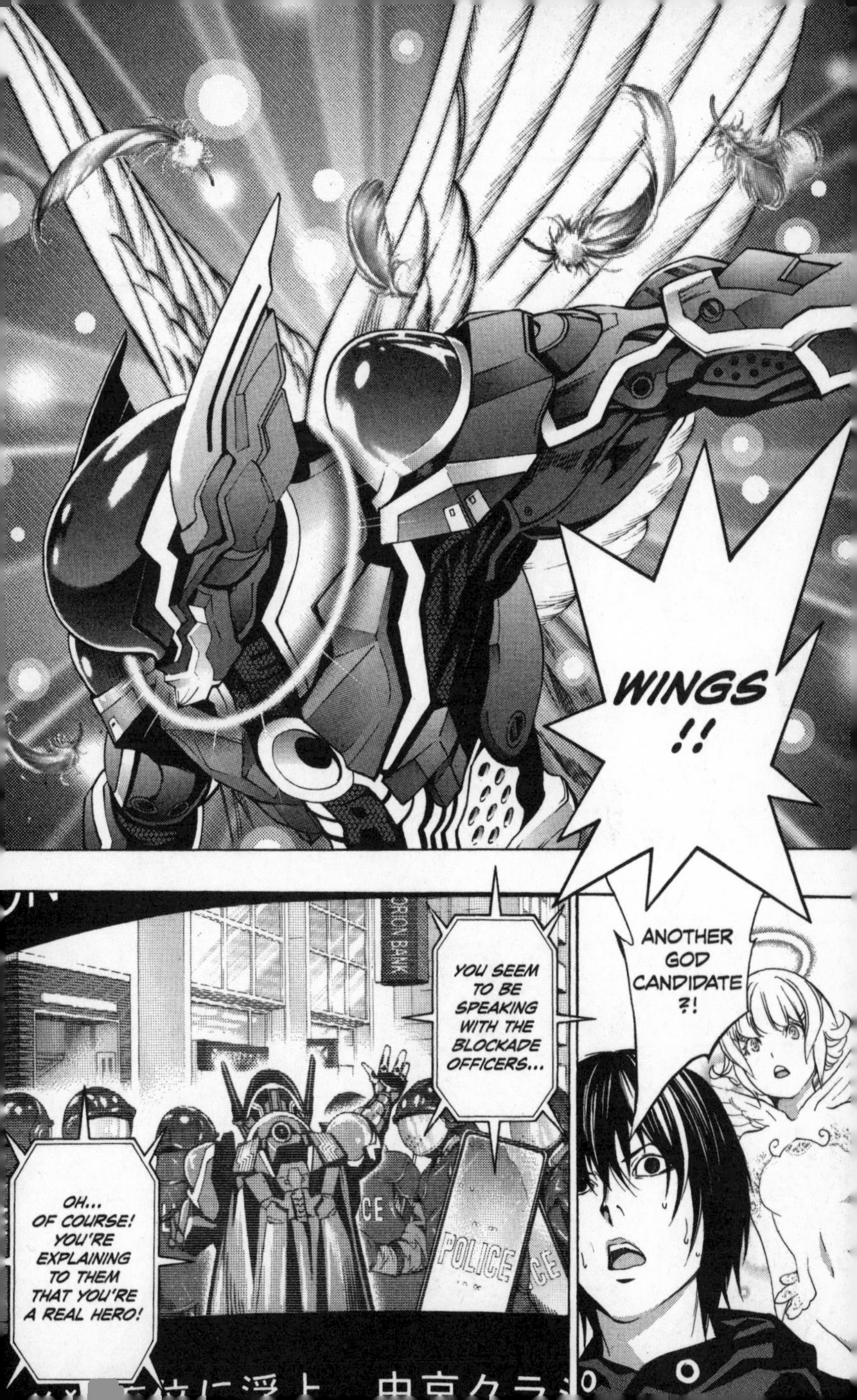
WINGS!!
ANOTHER GOD CANDIDATE?!
ORION BANK
YOU SEEM TO BE SPEAKING WITH THE BLOCKADE OFFICERS...
OH... OF COURSE! YOU'RE EXPLAINING TO THEM THAT YOU'RE A REAL HERO!
POLICE

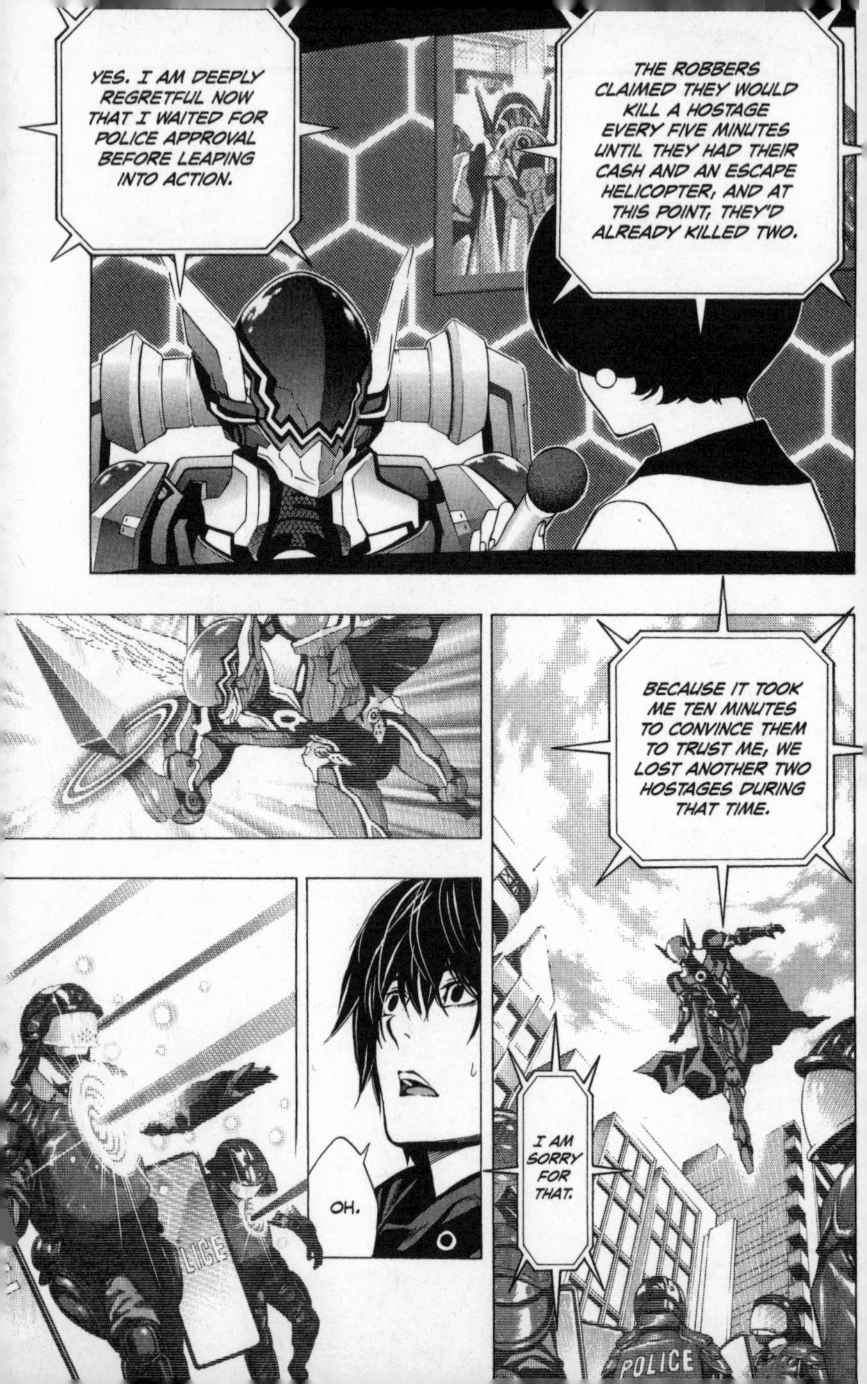
YES. I AM DEEPLY REGRETFUL NOW THAT I WAITED FOR POLICE APPROVAL BEFORE LEAPING INTO ACTION.
THE ROBBERS CLAIMED THEY WOULD KILL A HOSTAGE EVERY FIVE MINUTES UNTIL THEY HAD THEIR CASH AND AN ESCAPE HELICOPTER, AND AT THIS POINT, THEY'D ALREADY KILLED TWO.
BECAUSE IT TOOK ME TEN MINUTES TO CONVINCE THEM TO TRUST ME, WE LOST ANOTHER TWO HOSTAGES DURING THAT TIME.
I AM SORRY FOR THAT.
POLICE
OH.
LICE

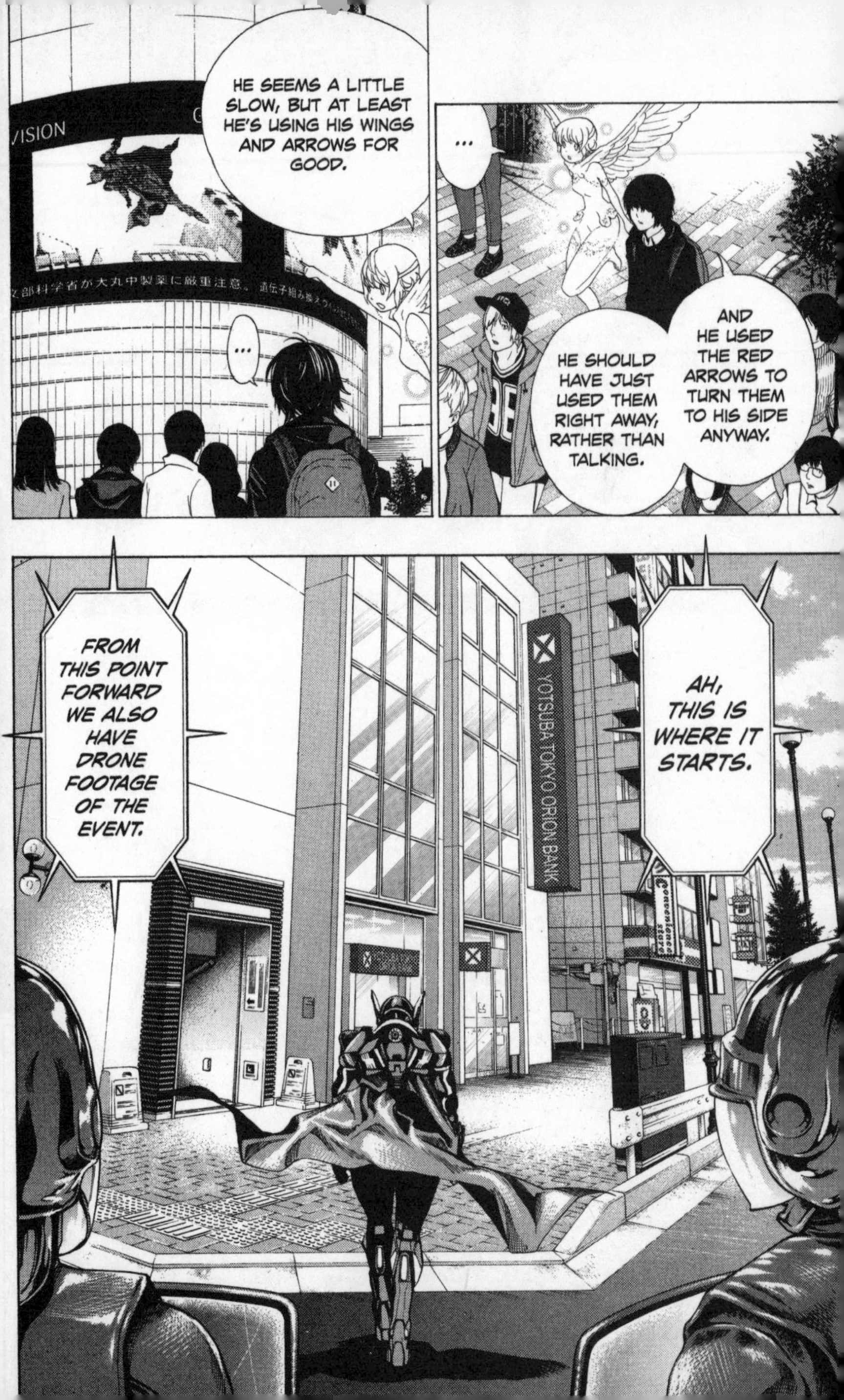
...
AND HE USED THE RED ARROWS TO TURN THEM TO HIS SIDE ANYWAY.
HE SHOULD HAVE JUST USED THEM RIGHT AWAY, RATHER THAN TALKING.
HE SEEMS A LITTLE SLOW, BUT AT LEAST HE'S USING HIS WINGS AND ARROWS FOR GOOD.
VISION
文部科学省が大丸中製薬に厳重注意。
...
AH, THIS IS WHERE IT STARTS.
YOTSUBA TOKYO ORION BANK
FROM THIS POINT FORWARD WE ALSO HAVE DRONE FOOTAGE OF THE EVENT.

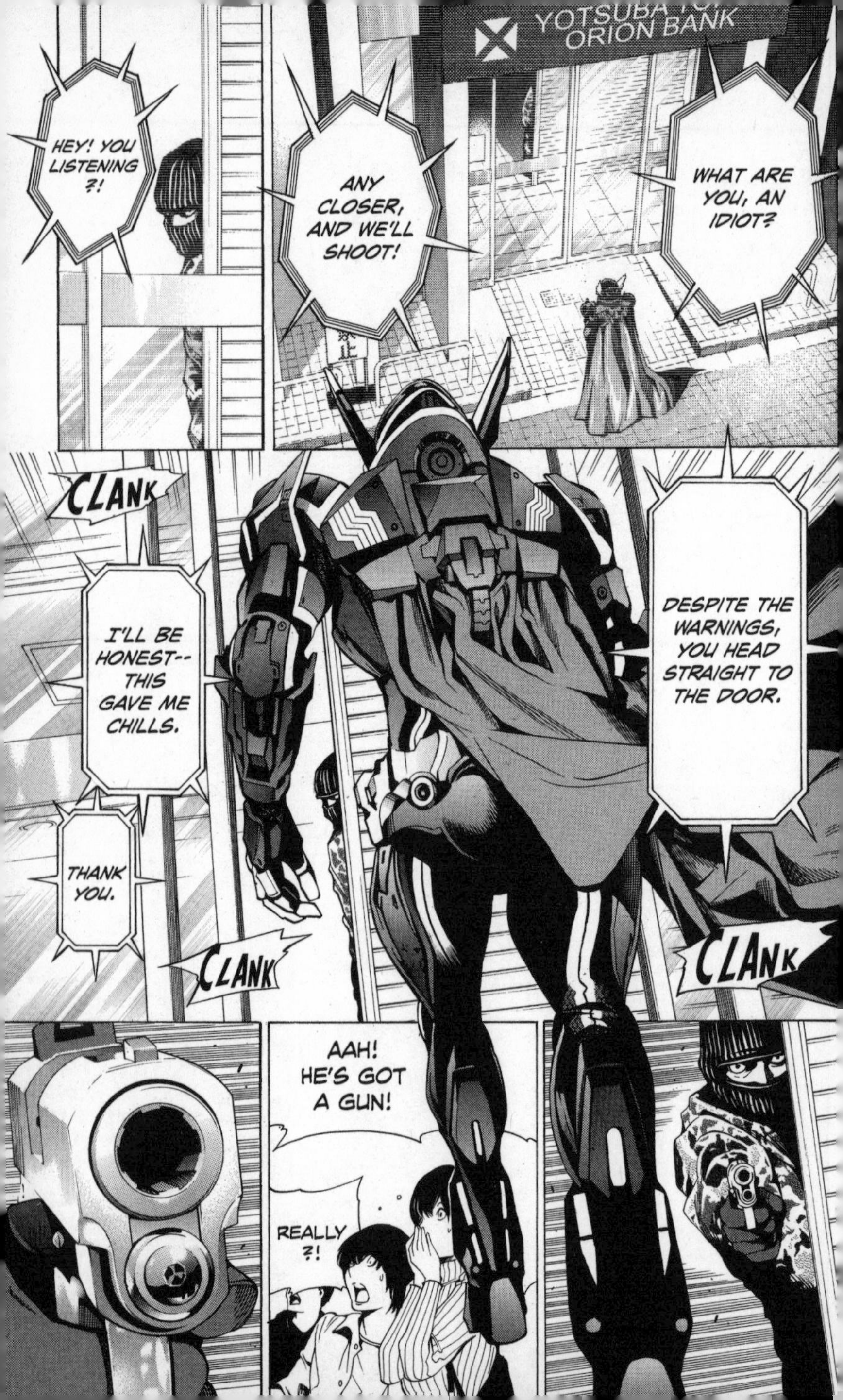
YOTSUBA
ORION BANK
WHAT ARE YOU, AN IDIOT?
ANY CLOSER, AND WE'LL SHOOT!
HEY! YOU LISTENING ?!
CLANK
DESPITE THE WARNINGS, YOU HEAD STRAIGHT TO THE DOOR.
CLANK
I'LL BE HONEST-- THIS GAVE ME CHILLS.
THANK YOU.
CLANK
AAH! HE'S GOT A GUN!
REALLY ?!

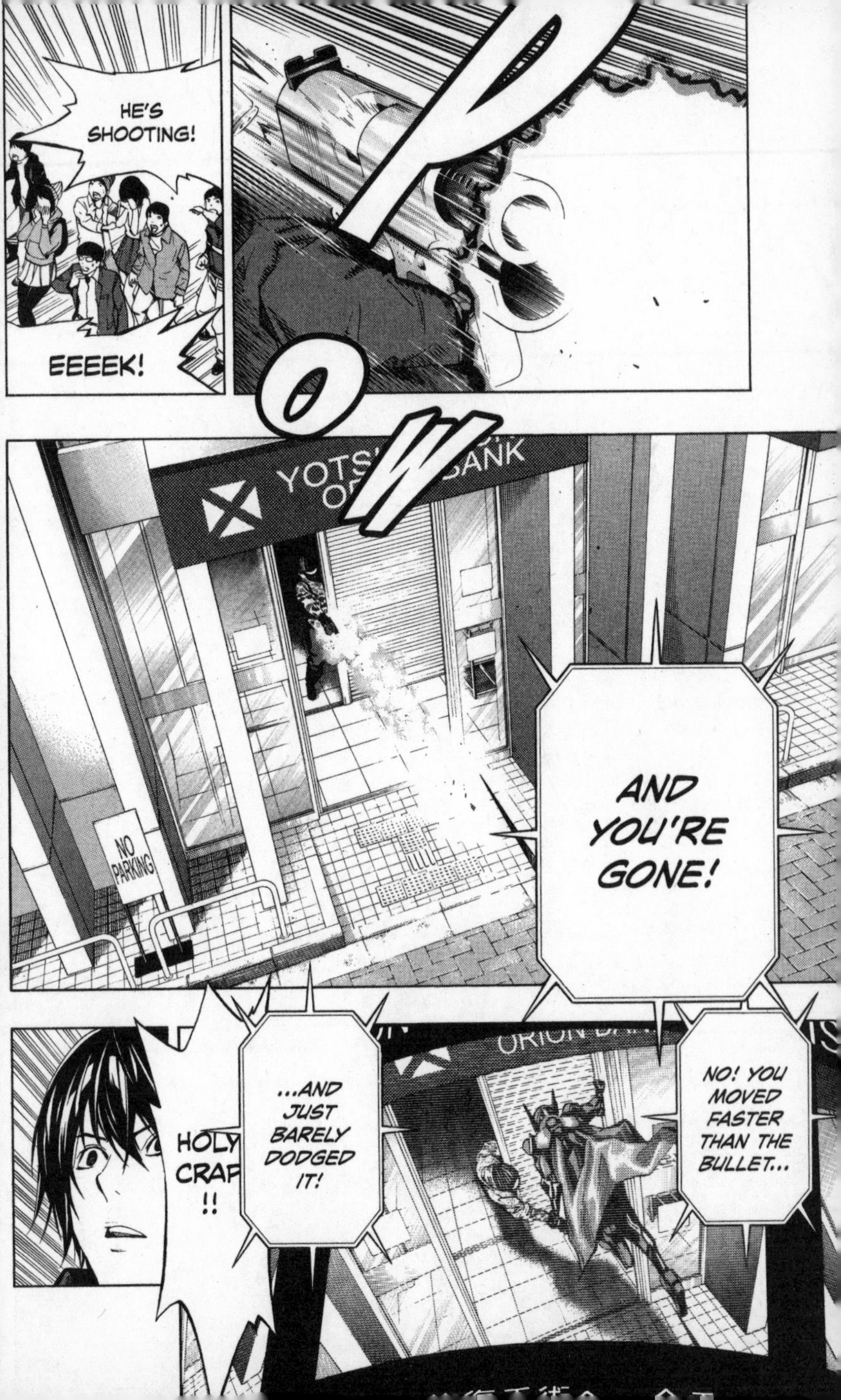
HE'S SHOOTING!
EEEEK!
NO PARKING
AND YOU'RE GONE!
NO! YOU MOVED FASTER THAN THE BULLET...
...AND JUST BARELY DODGED IT!
HOLY CRAP!!

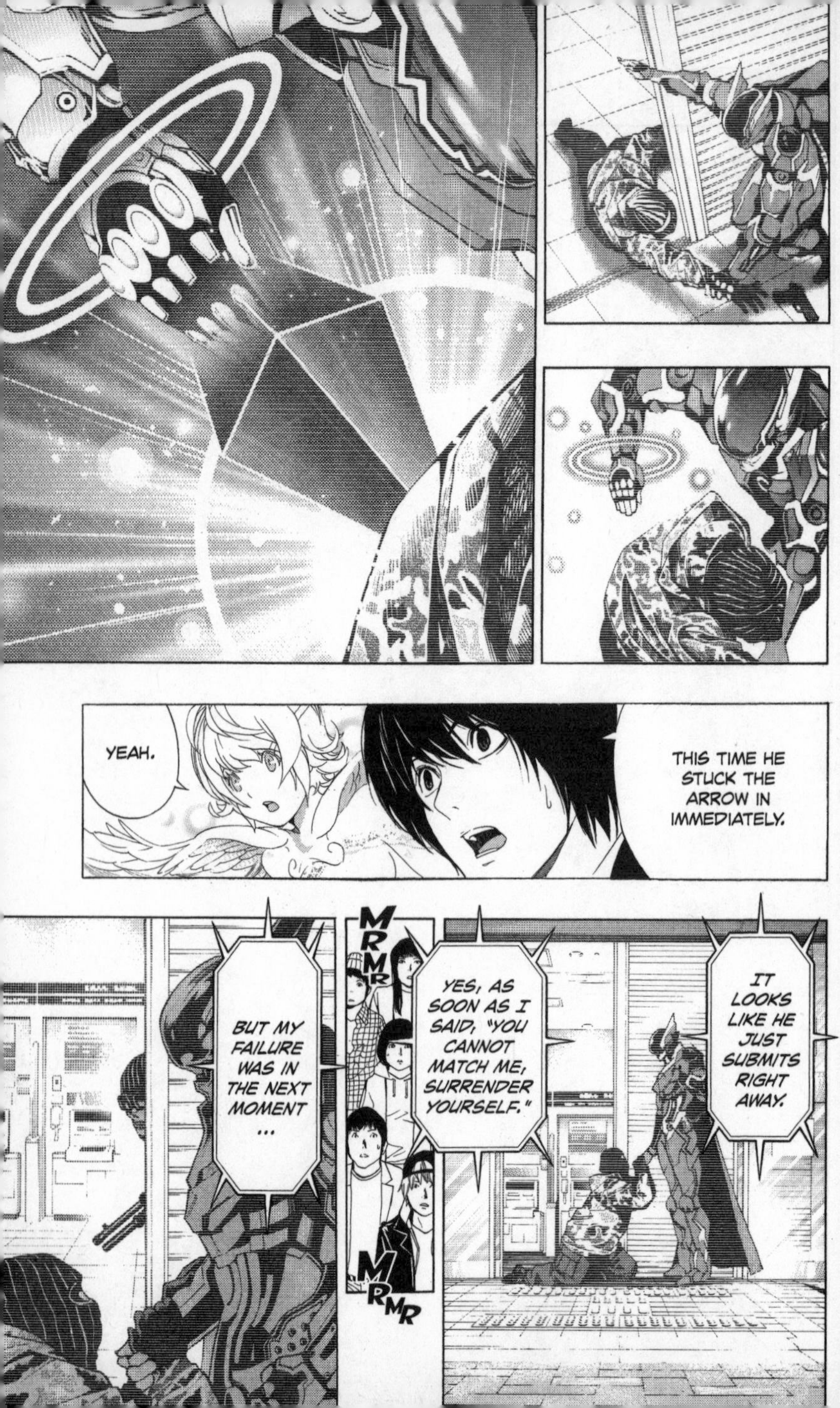
THIS TIME HE STUCK THE ARROW IN IMMEDIATELY.
YEAH.
IT LOOKS LIKE HE JUST SUBMITS RIGHT AWAY.
YES, AS SOON AS I SAID, "YOU CANNOT MATCH ME, SURRENDER YOURSELF."
MRMR
MRMR
BUT MY FAILURE WAS IN THE NEXT MOMENT ...

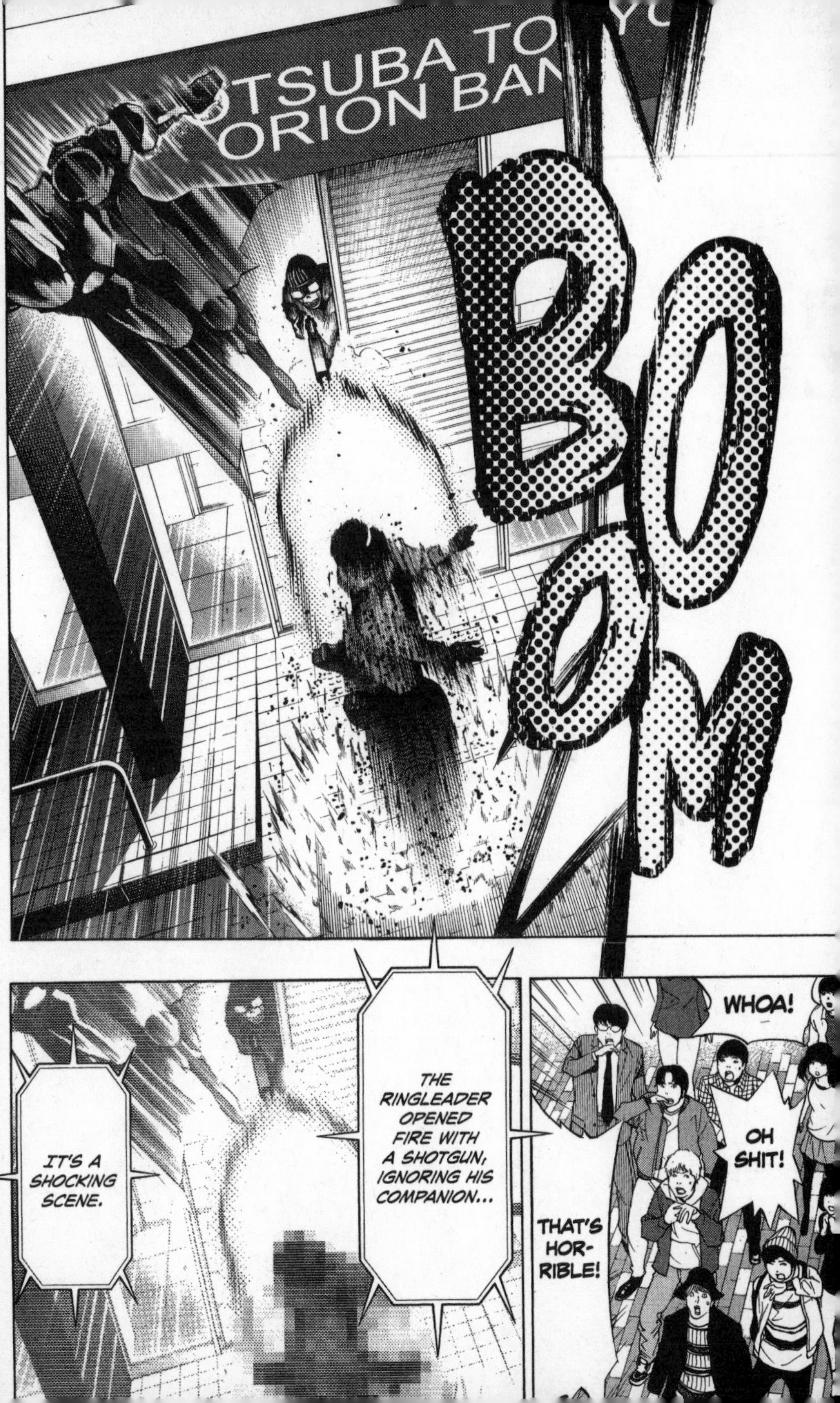
BOOM
WHOA!
OH SHIT!
THAT'S HOR-RIBLE!
THE RINGLEADER OPENED FIRE WITH A SHOTGUN, IGNORING HIS COMPANION...
IT'S A SHOCKING SCENE.

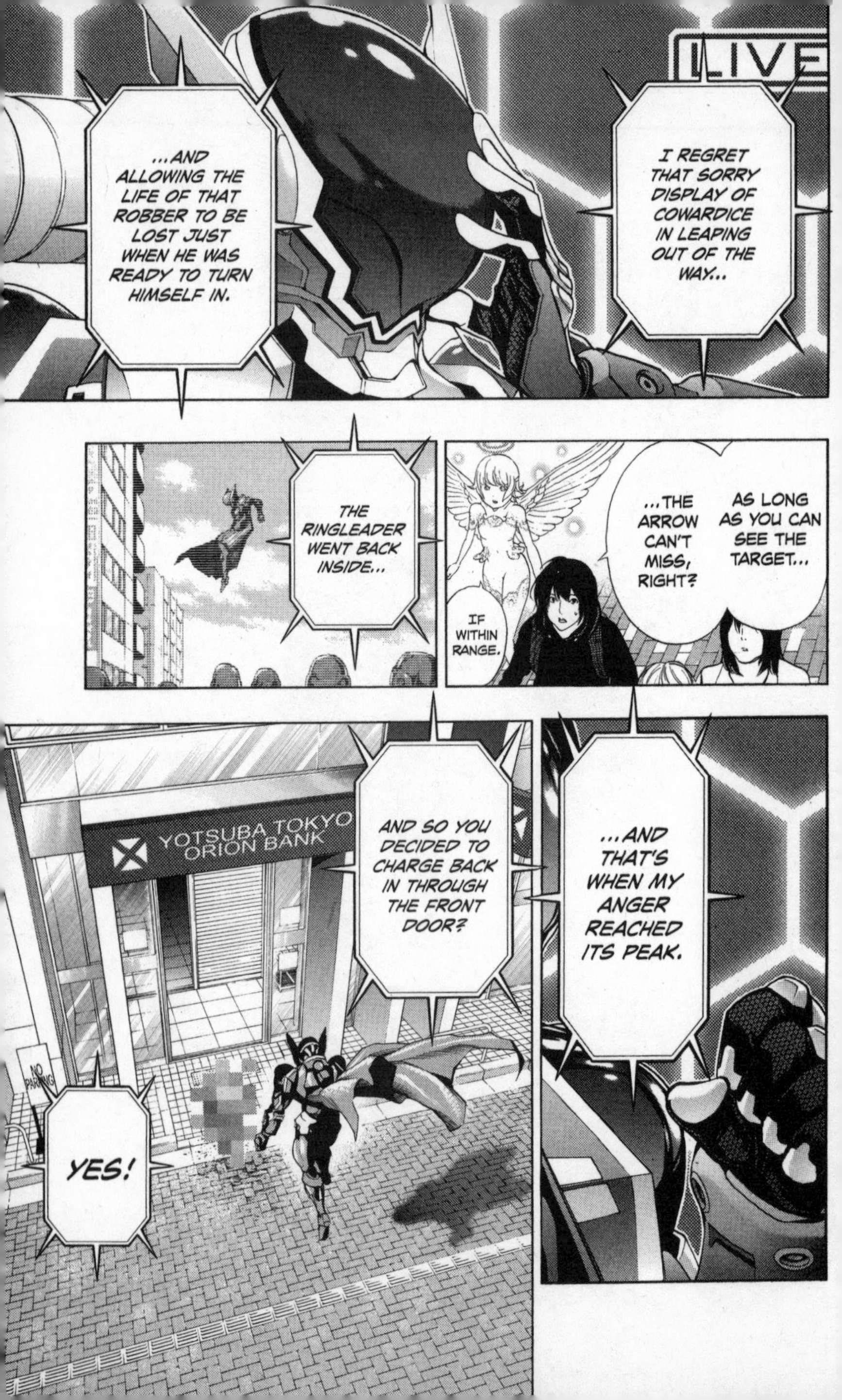
LIVE
I REGRET THAT SORRY DISPLAY OF COWARDICE IN LEAPING OUT OF THE WAY...
...AND ALLOWING THE LIFE OF THAT ROBBER TO BE LOST JUST WHEN HE WAS READY TO TURN HIMSELF IN.
AS LONG AS YOU CAN SEE THE TARGET...
...THE ARROW CAN'T MISS, RIGHT?
IF WITHIN RANGE.
THE RINGLEADER WENT BACK INSIDE...
...AND THAT'S WHEN MY ANGER REACHED ITS PEAK.
AND SO YOU DECIDED TO CHARGE BACK IN THROUGH THE FRONT DOOR?
YOTSUBA TOKYO ORION BANK
NO PARKING
YES!

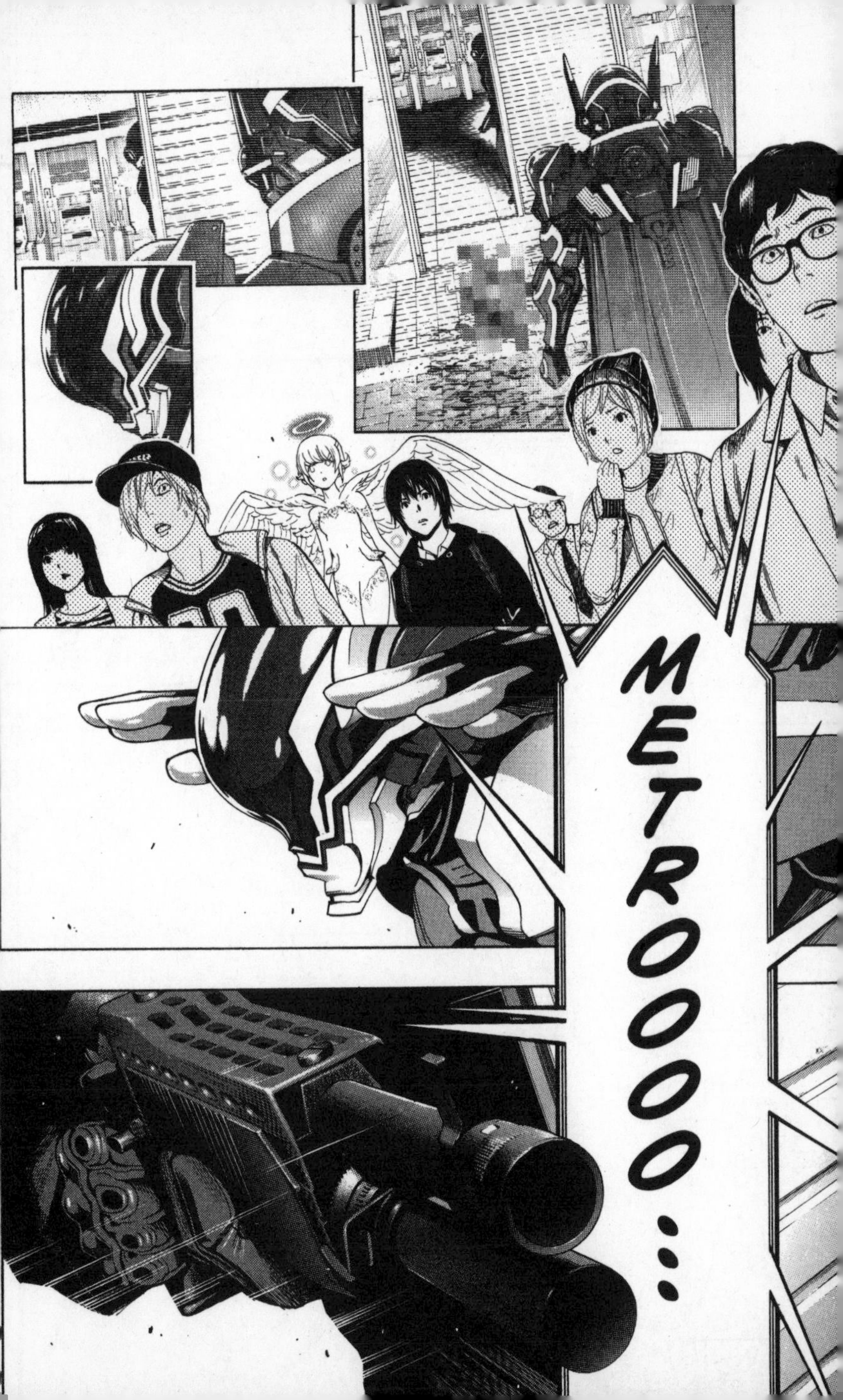
METROOOO...

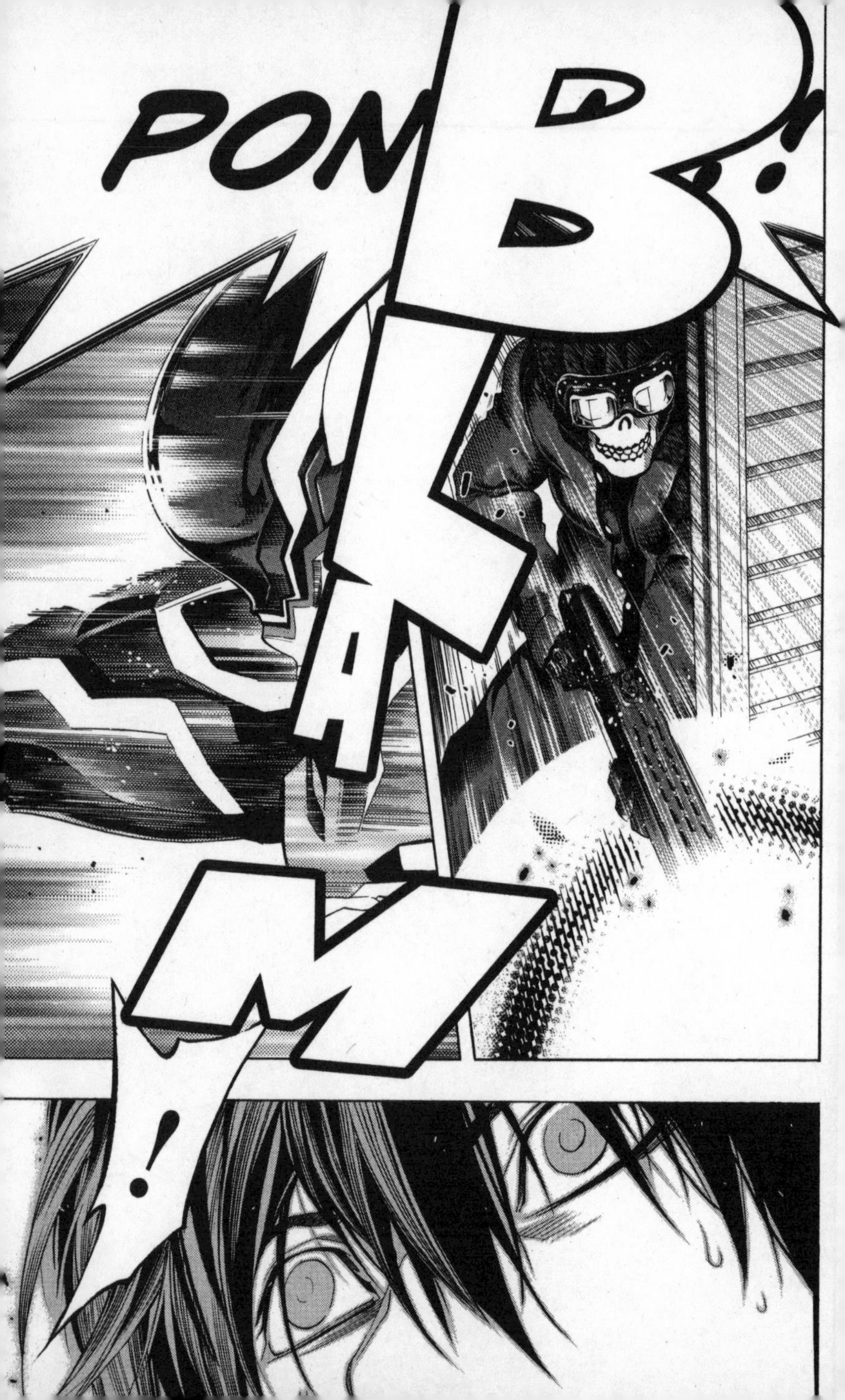

PON
BAM!!

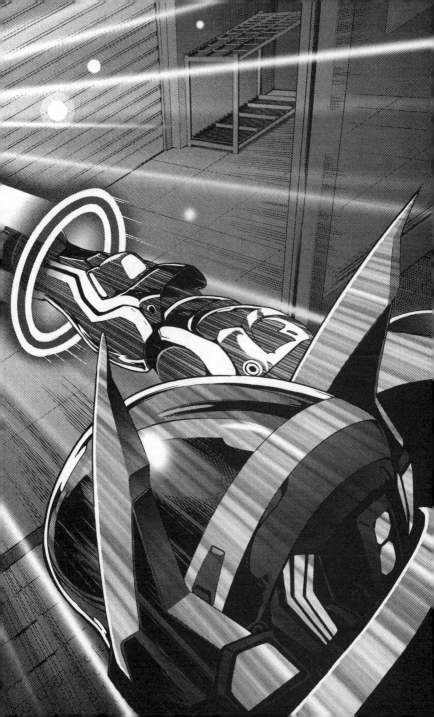

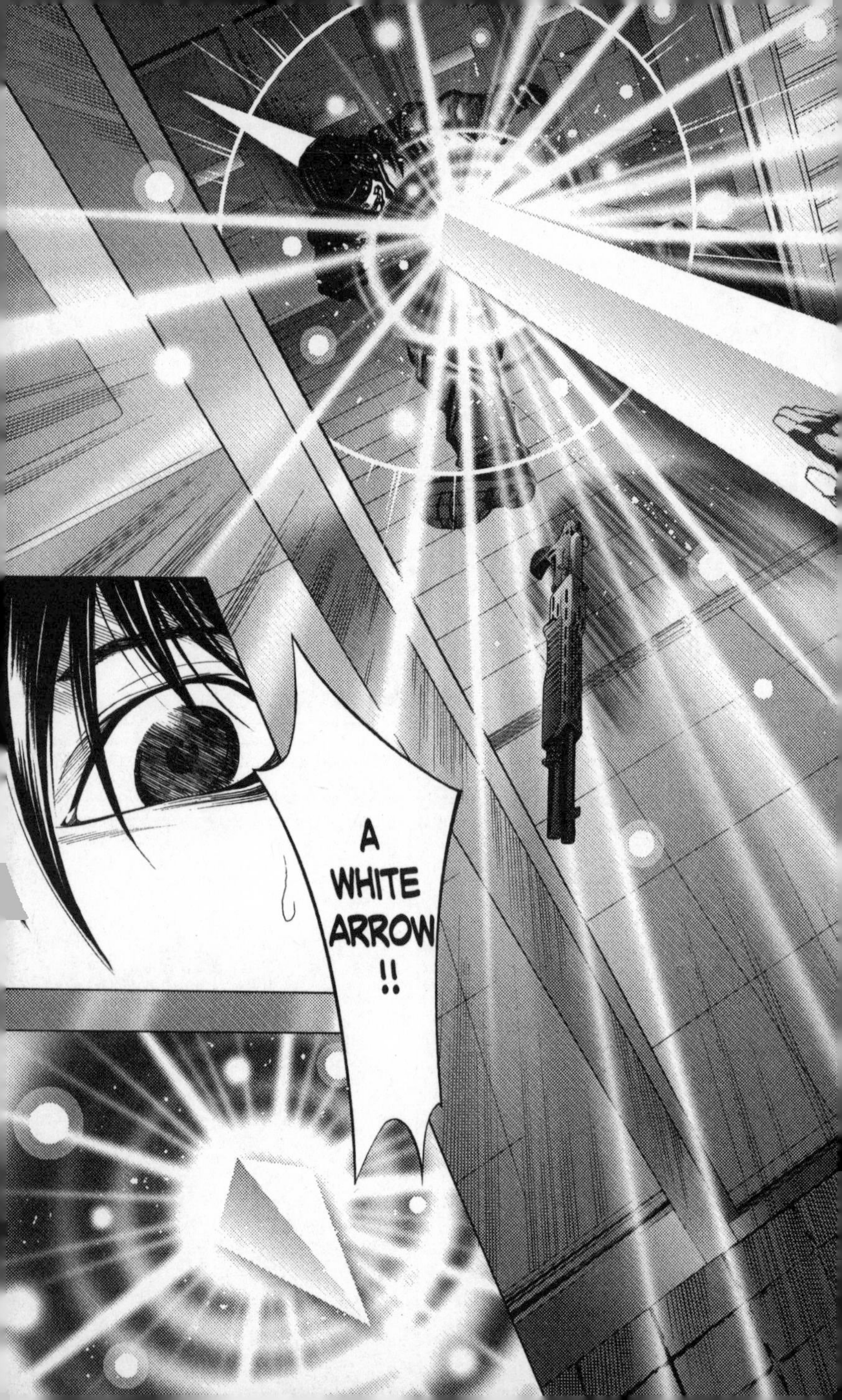
A WHITE ARROW !!

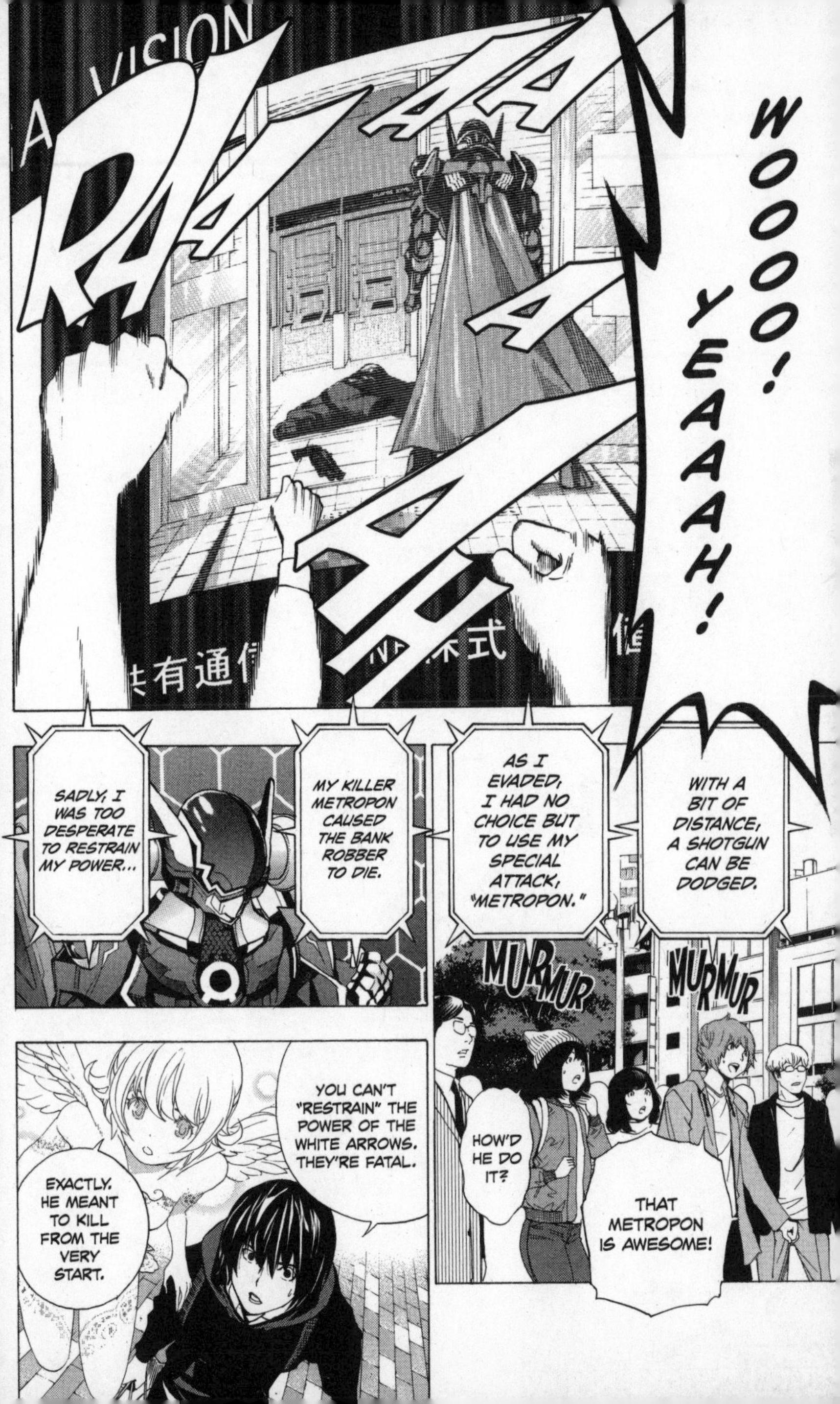
A VISION
RAAAAAH
WOOOO! YEAAAAH!
WITH A BIT OF DISTANCE, A SHOTGUN CAN BE DODGED.
AS I EVADED, I HAD NO CHOICE BUT TO USE MY SPECIAL ATTACK, "METROPON."
MURMUR
MURMUR
HOW'D HE DO IT?
THAT METROPON IS AWESOME!
MY KILLER METROPON CAUSED THE BANK ROBBER TO DIE.
SADLY, I WAS TOO DESPERATE TO RESTRAIN MY POWER...
YOU CAN'T "RESTRAIN" THE POWER OF THE WHITE ARROWS. THEY'RE FATAL.
EXACTLY. HE MEANT TO KILL FROM THE VERY START.

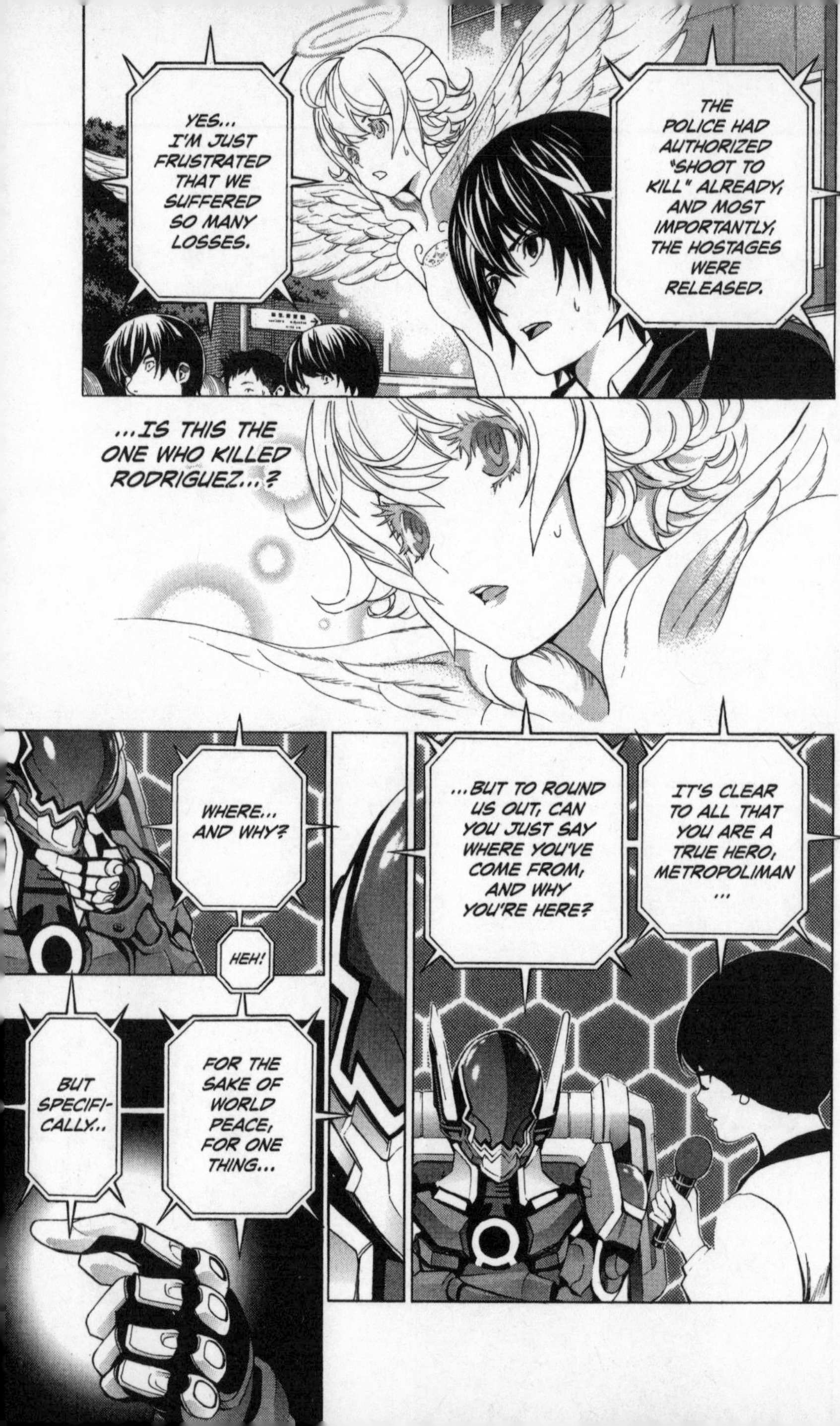
THE POLICE HAD AUTHORIZED "SHOOT TO KILL" ALREADY, AND MOST IMPORTANTLY, THE HOSTAGES WERE RELEASED.
YES... I'M JUST FRUSTRATED THAT WE SUFFERED SO MANY LOSSES.
...IS THIS THE ONE WHO KILLED RODRIGUEZ...?
IT'S CLEAR TO ALL THAT YOU ARE A TRUE HERO, METROPOLIMAN...
...BUT TO ROUND US OUT, CAN YOU JUST SAY WHERE YOU'VE COME FROM, AND WHY YOU'RE HERE?
WHERE... AND WHY?
HEH!
FOR THE SAKE OF WORLD PEACE, FOR ONE THING...
BUT SPECIFI-CALLY...

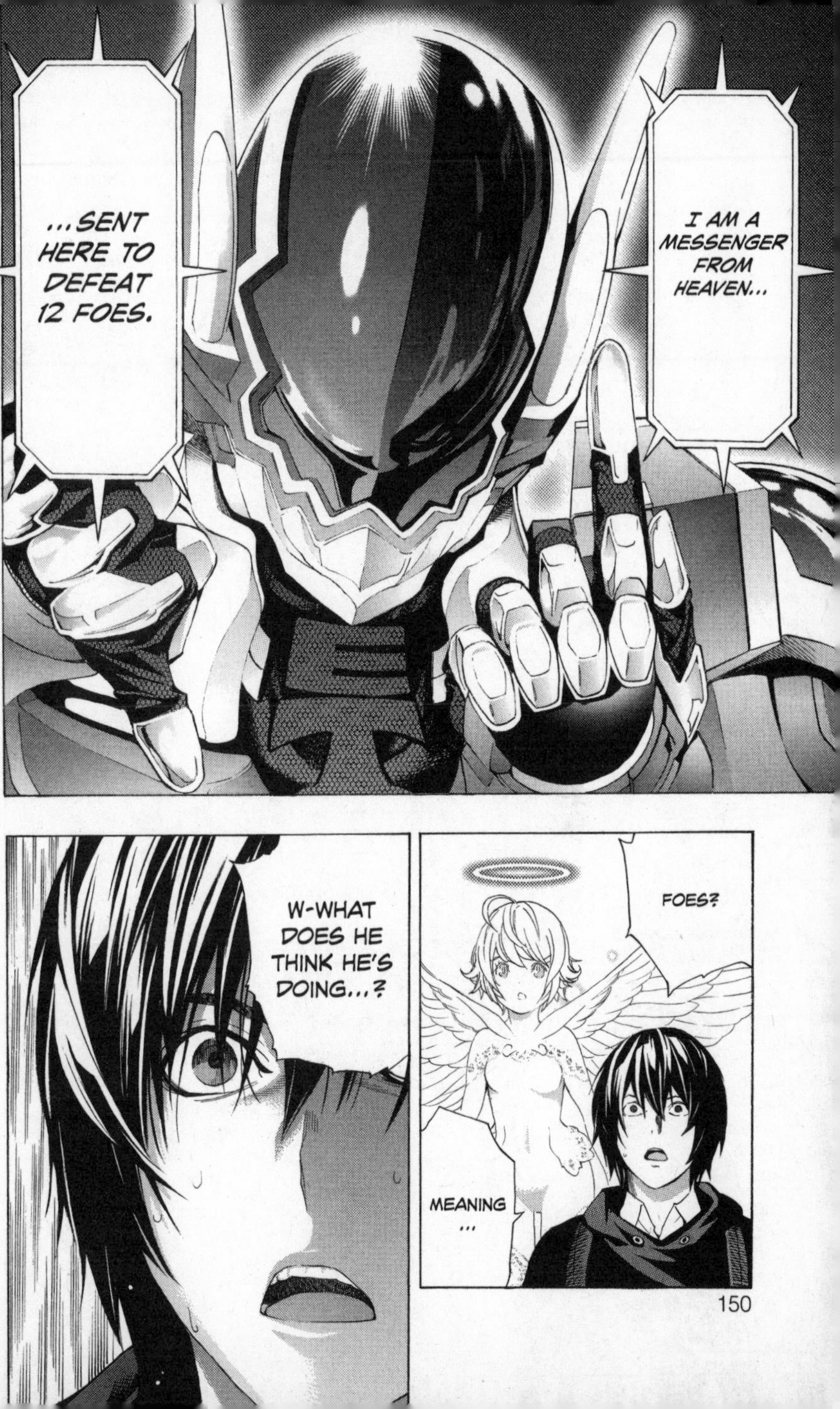
I AM A MESSENGER FROM HEAVEN...
...SENT HERE TO DEFEAT 12 FOES.
FOES?
MEANING ...
W-WHAT DOES HE THINK HE'S DOING...?

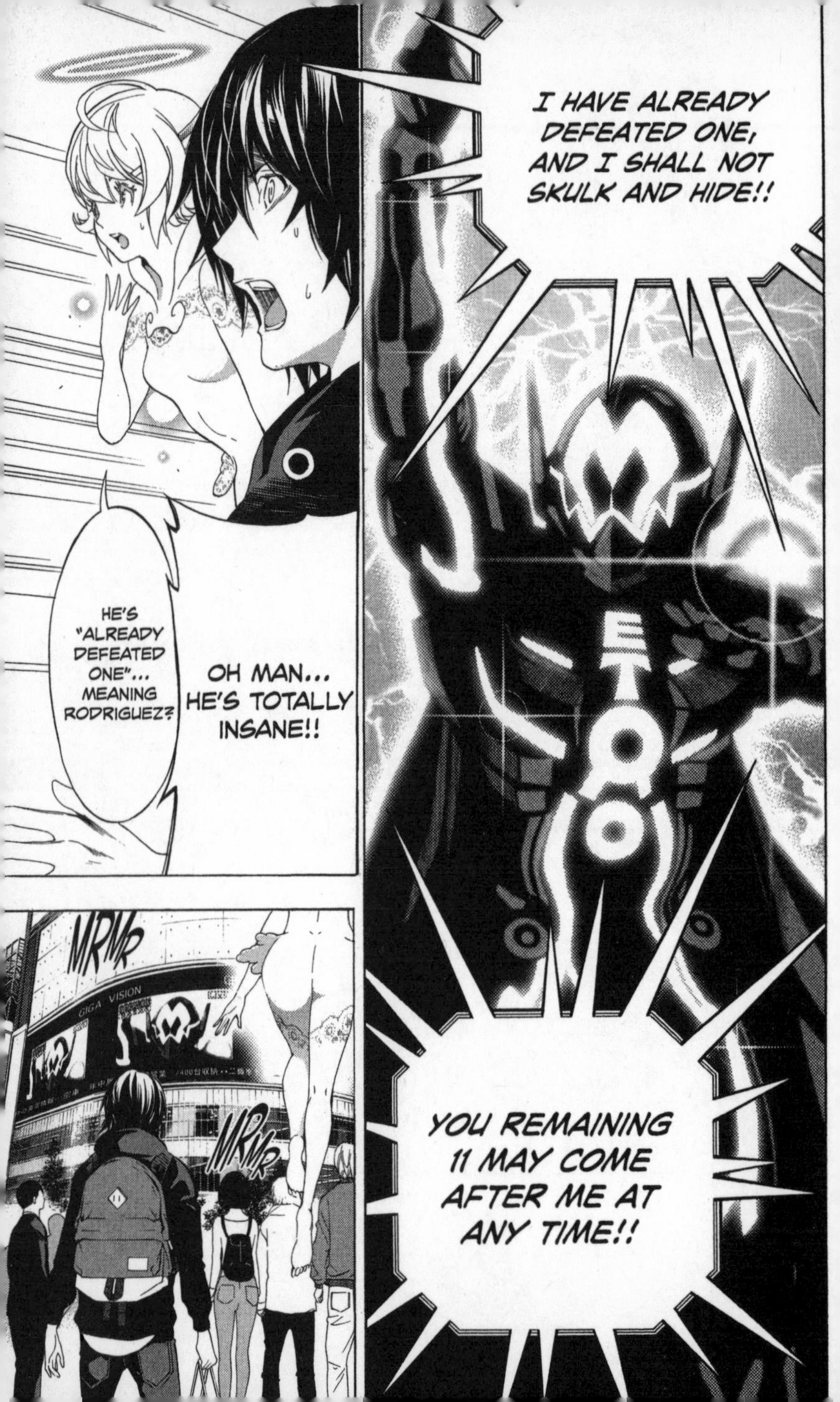
I HAVE ALREADY DEFEATED ONE, AND I SHALL NOT SKULK AND HIDE!!
YOU REMAINING 11 MAY COME AFTER ME AT ANY TIME!!
HE'S "ALREADY DEFEATED ONE"... MEANING RODRIGUEZ?
OH MAN... HE'S TOTALLY INSANE!!
MRMR
GIGA VISION
MRMR

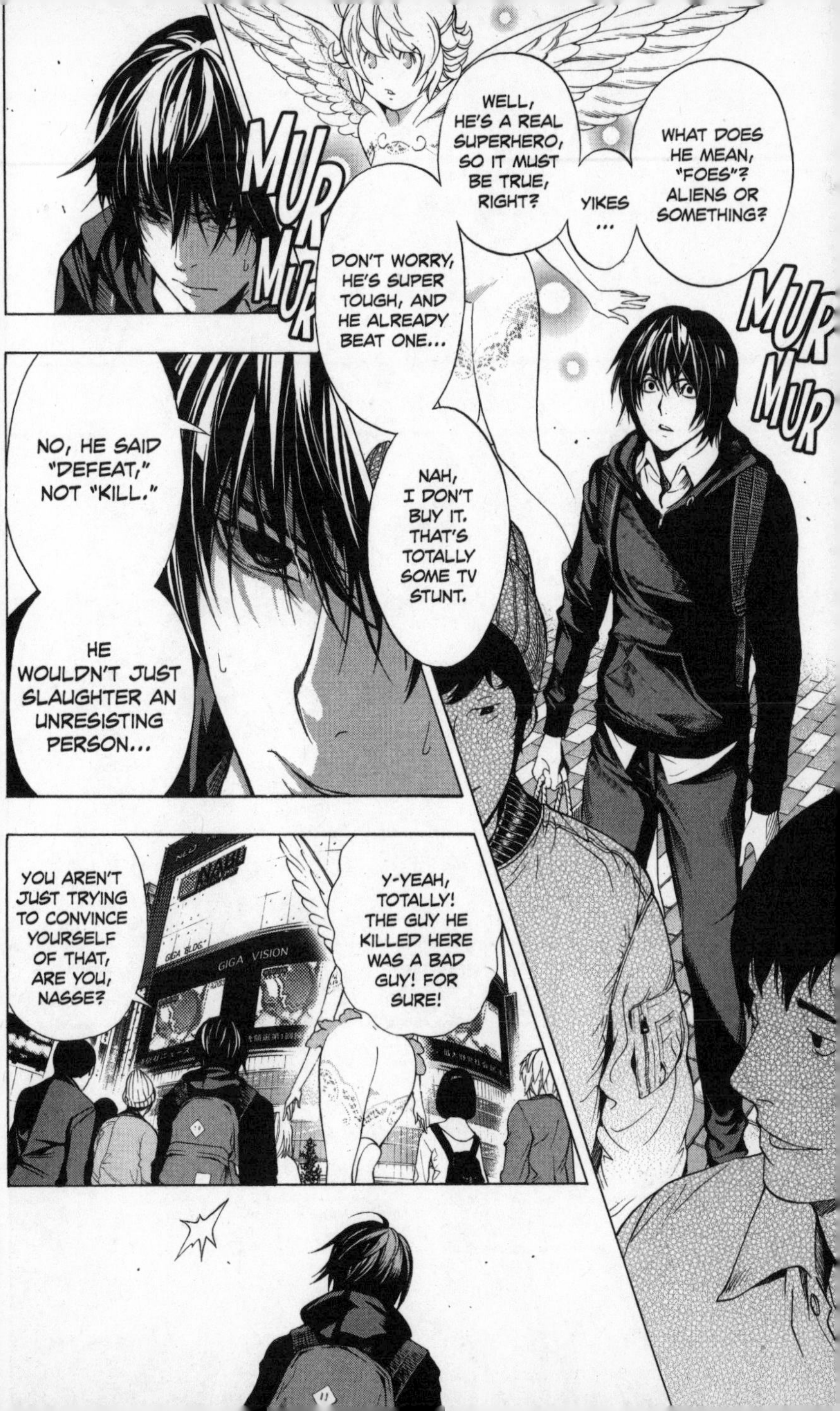
WHAT DOES HE MEAN, "FOES"? ALIENS OR SOMETHING?
YIKES ...
WELL, HE'S A REAL SUPERHERO, SO IT MUST BE TRUE, RIGHT?
MUR MUR
DON'T WORRY, HE'S SUPER TOUGH, AND HE ALREADY BEAT ONE...
NAH, I DON'T BUY IT. THAT'S TOTALLY SOME TV STUNT.
MUR MUR
NO, HE SAID "DEFEAT," NOT "KILL."
HE WOULDN'T JUST SLAUGHTER AN UNRESISTING PERSON...
Y-YEAH, TOTALLY! THE GUY HE KILLED HERE WAS A BAD GUY! FOR SURE!
GIGA VISION
YOU AREN'T JUST TRYING TO CONVINCE YOURSELF OF THAT, ARE YOU, NASSE?

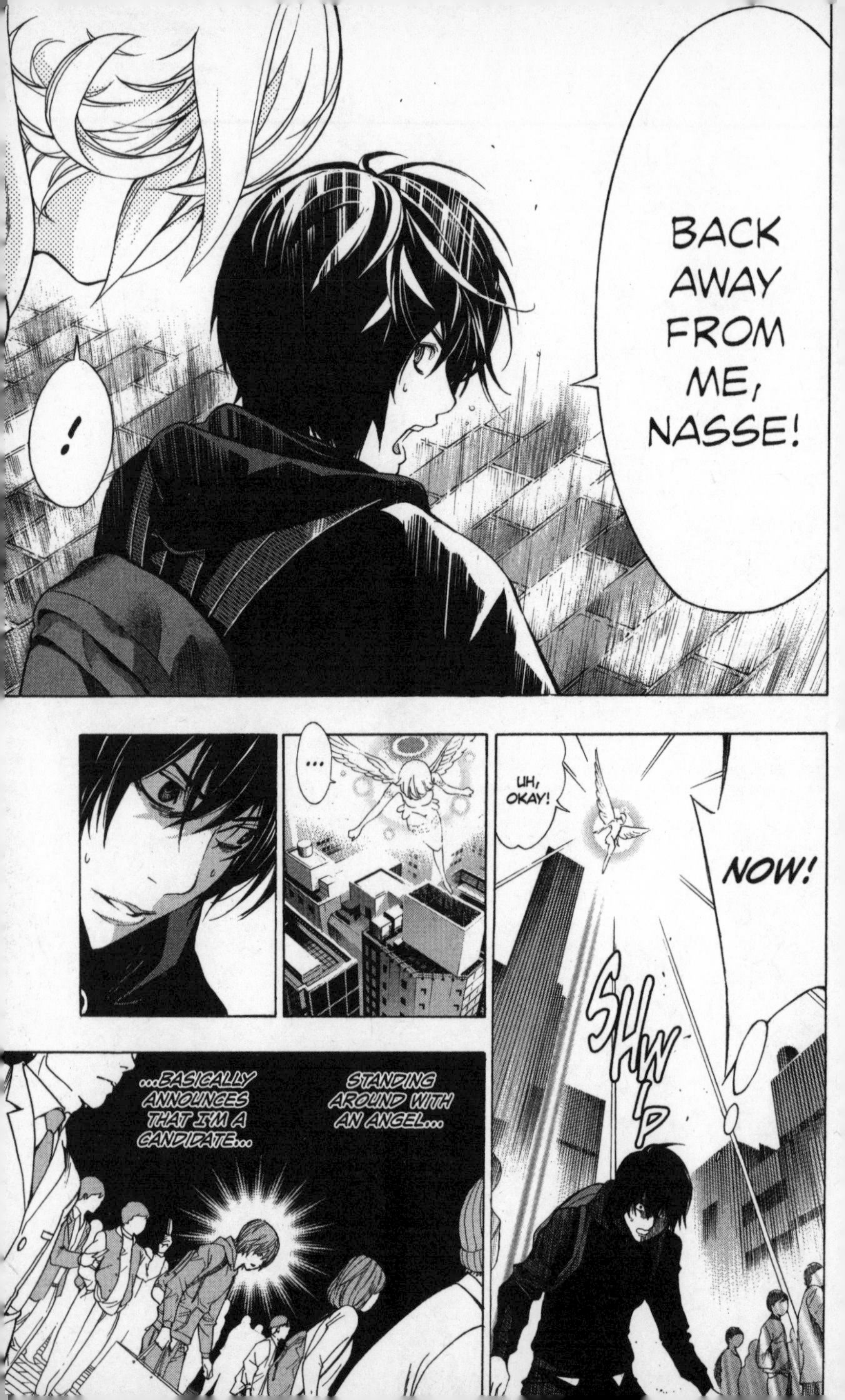
BACK AWAY FROM ME, NASSE!
!
NOW!
UH, OKAY!
SHWIP
...
STANDING AROUND WITH AN ANGEL...
...BASICALLY ANNOUNCES THAT I'M A CANDIDATE...

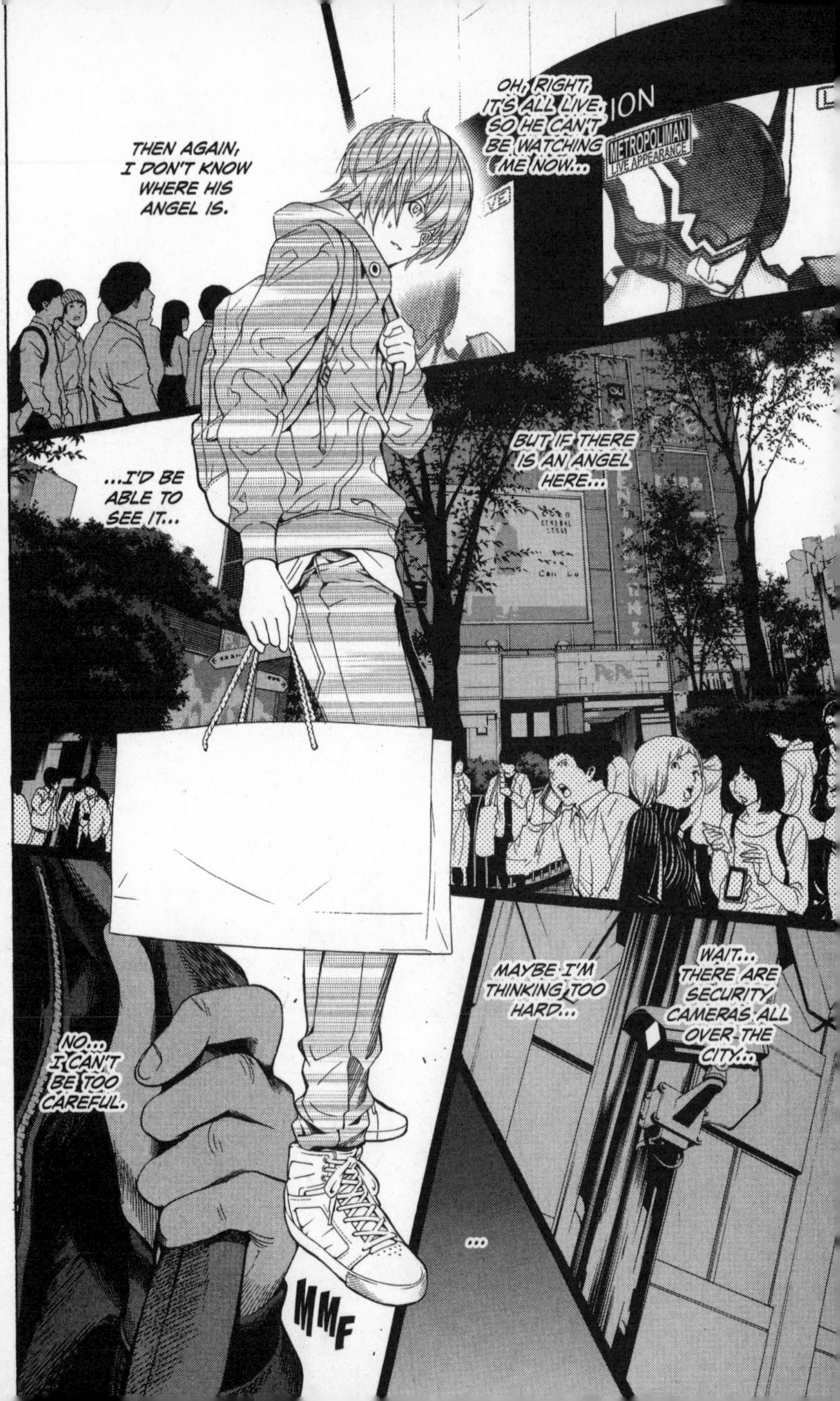
ION
METROPOLIMAN
LIVE APPEARANCE
OH, RIGHT, IT'S ALL LIVE, SO HE CAN'T BE WATCHING ME NOW...
THEN AGAIN, I DON'T KNOW WHERE HIS ANGEL IS.
BUT IF THERE IS AN ANGEL HERE...
...I'D BE ABLE TO SEE IT...
WAIT... THERE ARE SECURITY CAMERAS ALL OVER THE CITY...
MAYBE I'M THINKING TOO HARD...
...
NO... I CAN'T BE TOO CAREFUL.
MMF

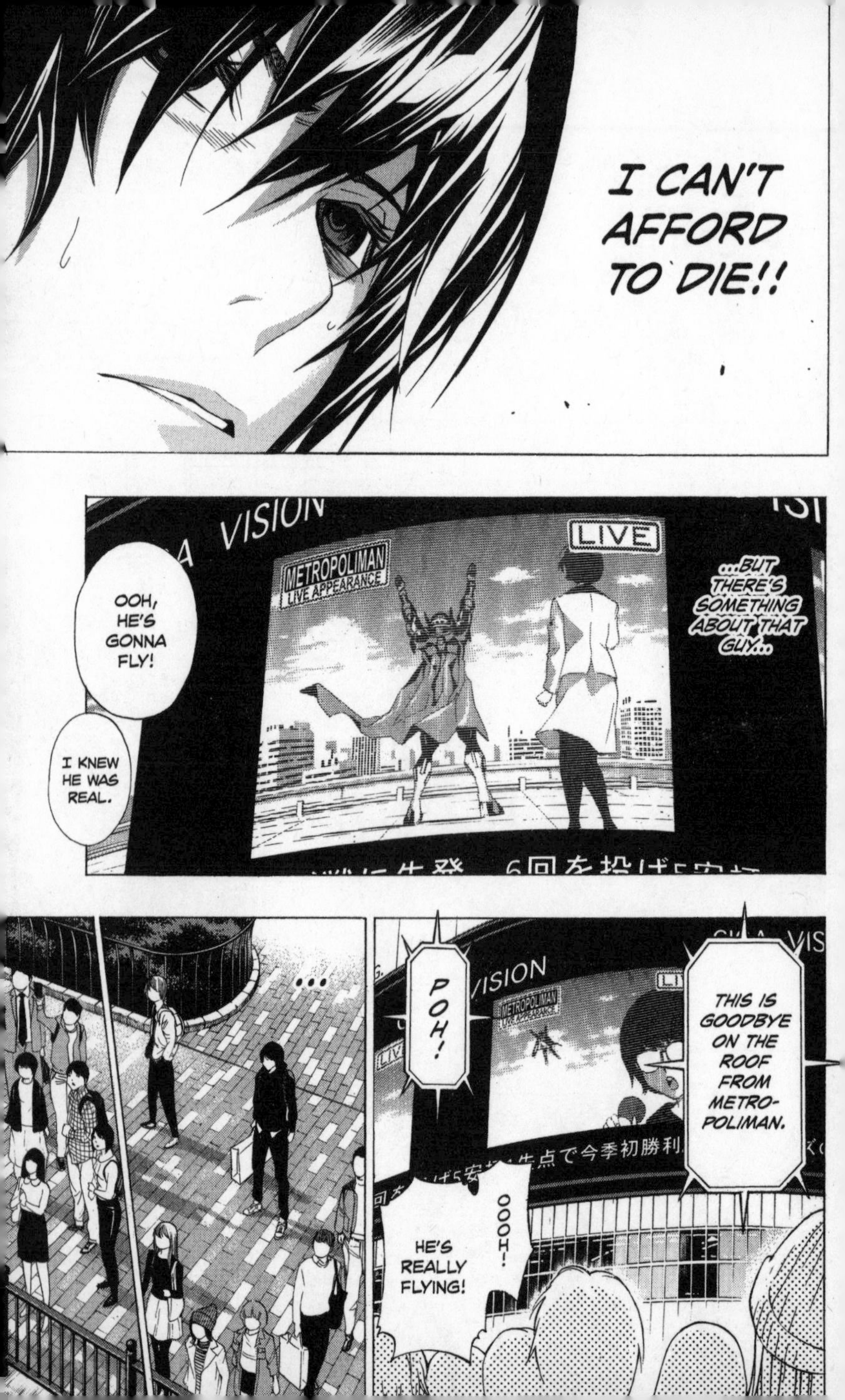

I CAN'T AFFORD TO DIE!!
...BUT THERE'S SOMETHING ABOUT THAT GUY...
LIVE
VISION
METROPOLIMAN
LIVE APPEARANCE
OOH, HE'S GONNA FLY!
I KNEW HE WAS REAL.
THIS IS GOODBYE ON THE ROOF FROM METRO-POLIMAN.
POH!
VISION
METROPOLIMAN
LIVE APPEARANCE
OOOOH!
HE'S REALLY FLYING!
...

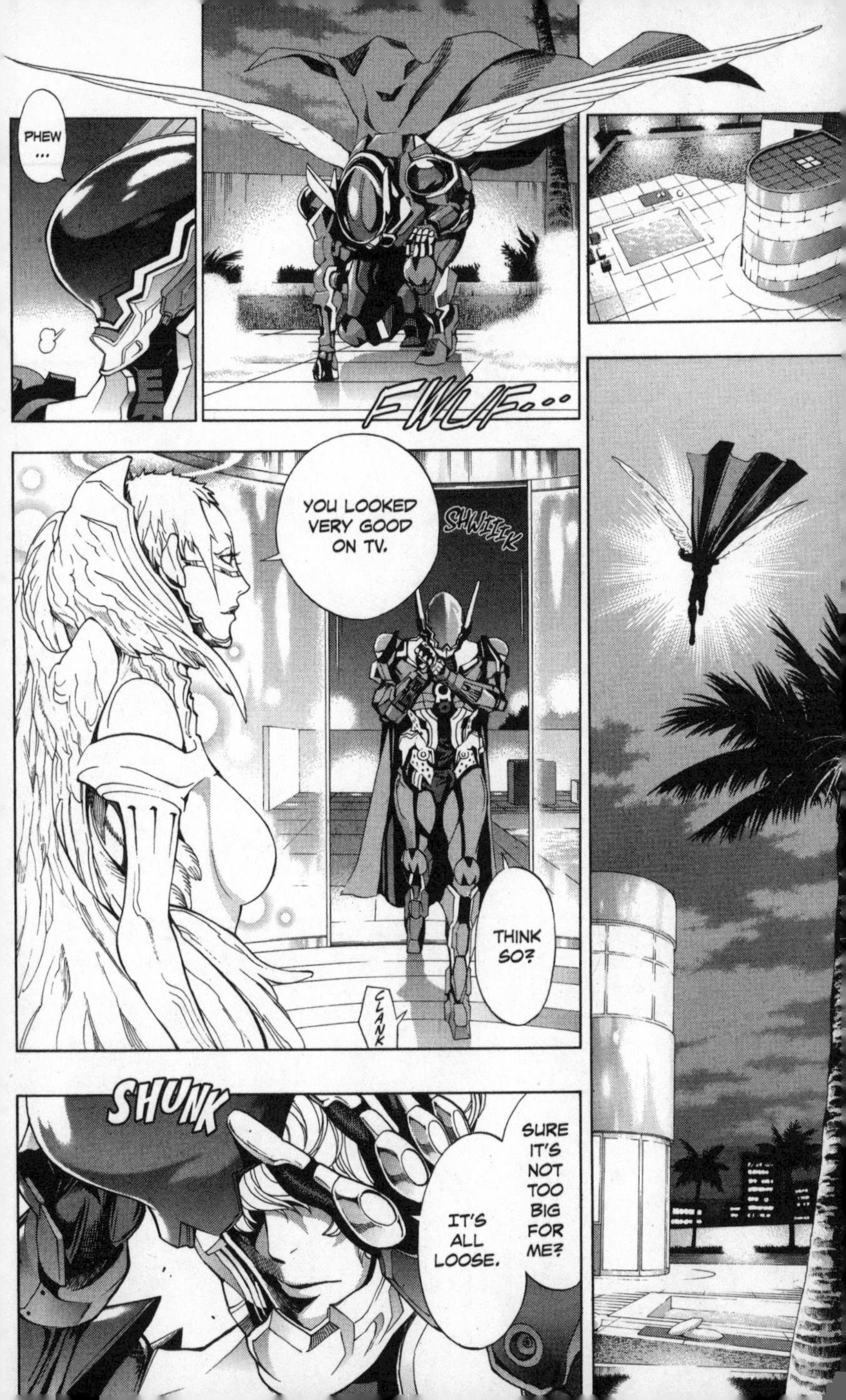
FWUF...
PHEW ...
SHWIIIK
YOU LOOKED VERY GOOD ON TV.
THINK SO?
CLANK
SHUNK
SURE IT'S NOT TOO BIG FOR ME?
IT'S ALL LOOSE.

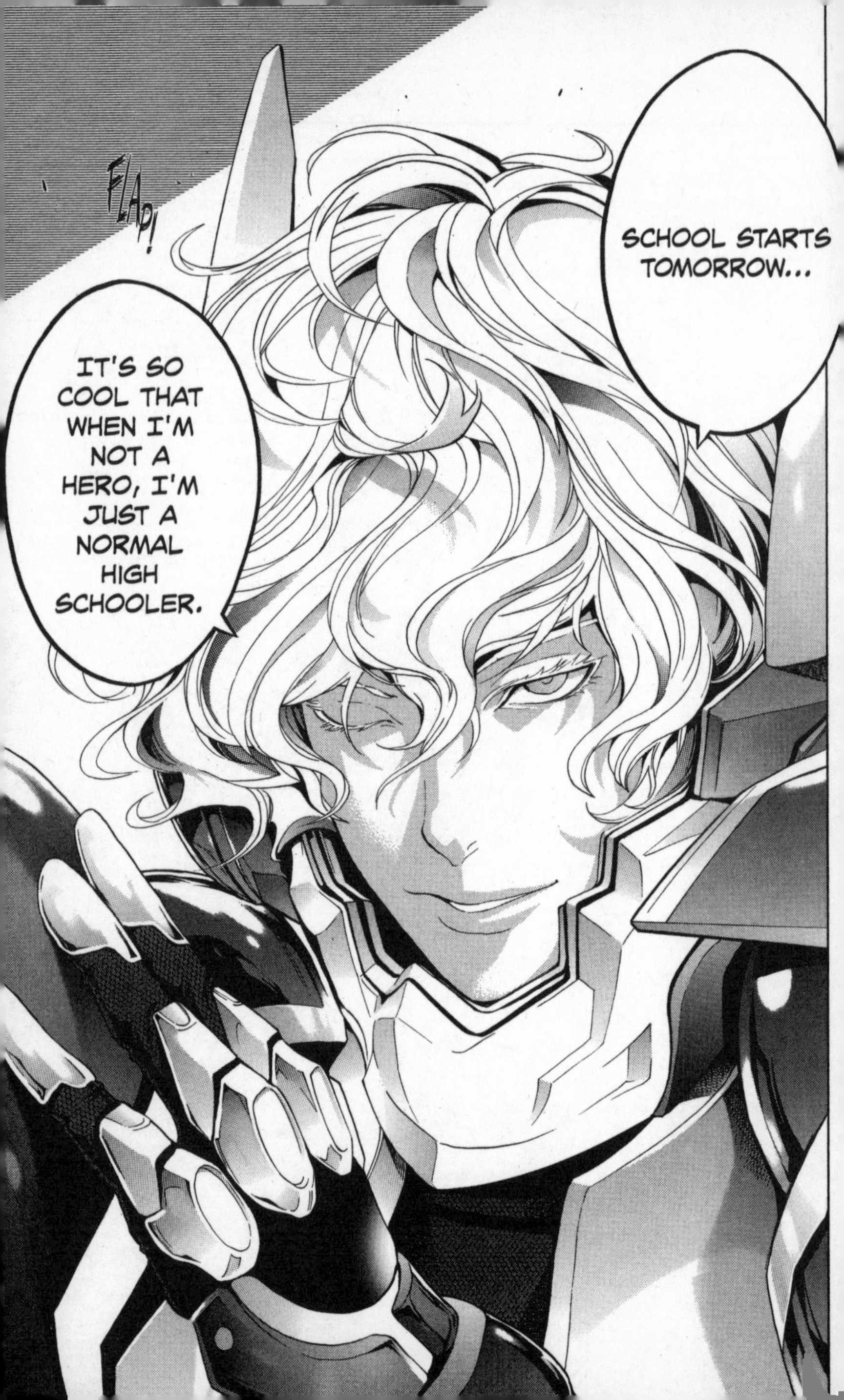
SCHOOL STARTS TOMORROW...
FLAP!
IT'S SO COOL THAT WHEN I'M NOT A HERO, I'M JUST A NORMAL HIGH SCHOOLER.

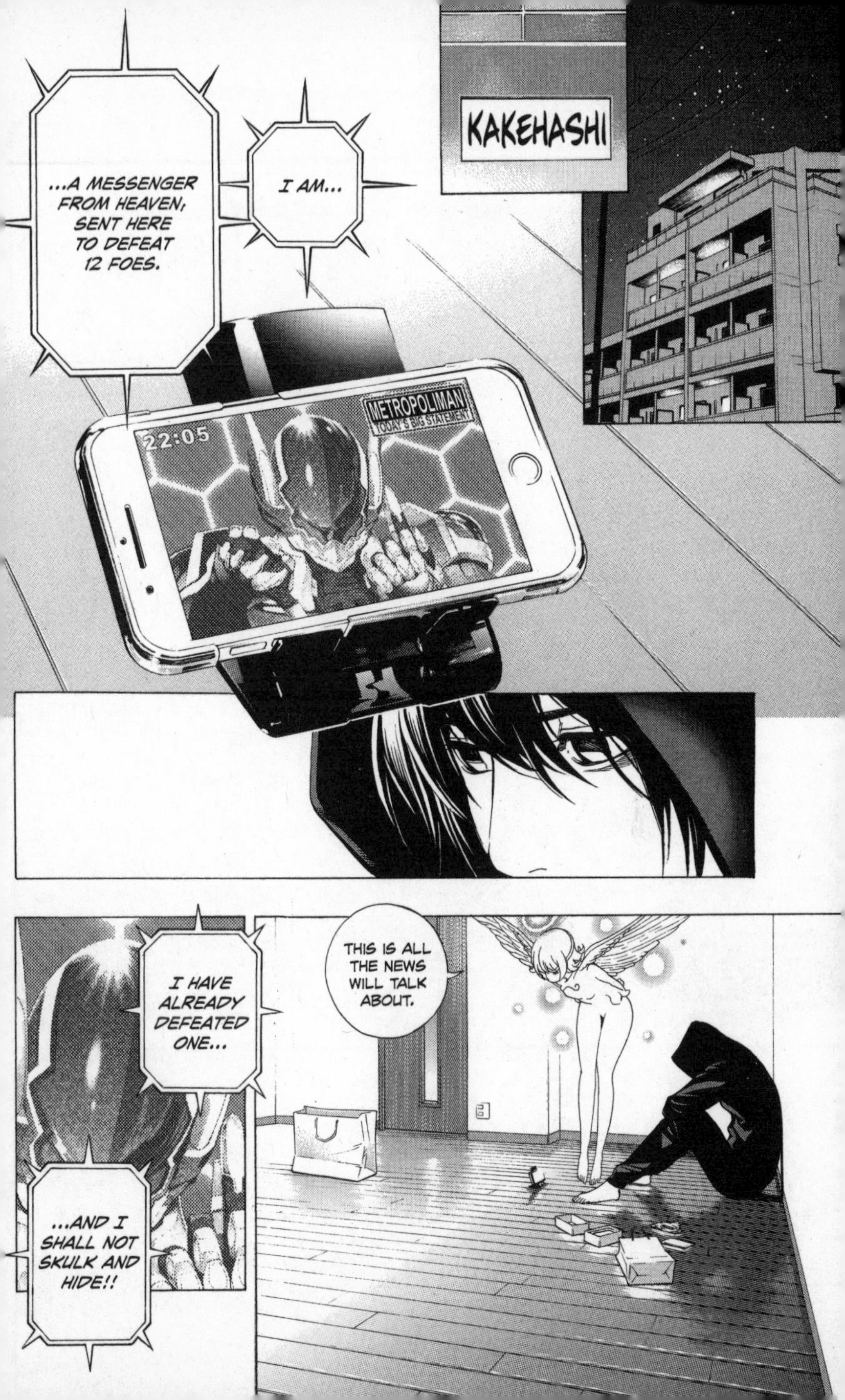
KAKEHASHI
I AM...
...A MESSENGER FROM HEAVEN, SENT HERE TO DEFEAT 12 FOES.
METROPOLIMAN
TODAY'S BIG STATEMENT
22:05
THIS IS ALL THE NEWS WILL TALK ABOUT.
I HAVE ALREADY DEFEATED ONE...
...AND I SHALL NOT SKULK AND HIDE!!

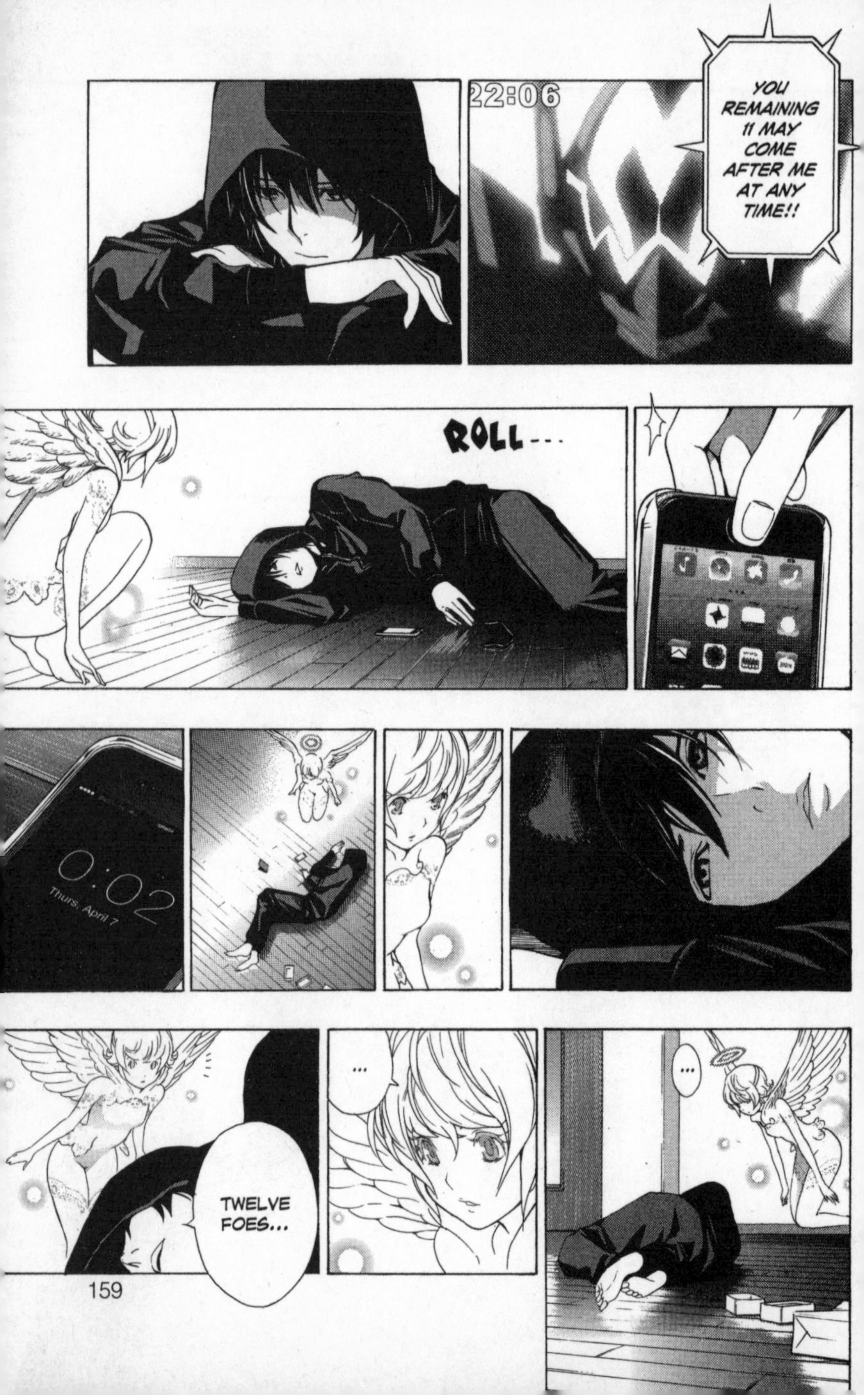
22:06
YOU REMAINING 11 MAY COME AFTER ME AT ANY TIME!!
ROLL...
0:02
Thurs, April 7
...
...
TWELVE FOES...

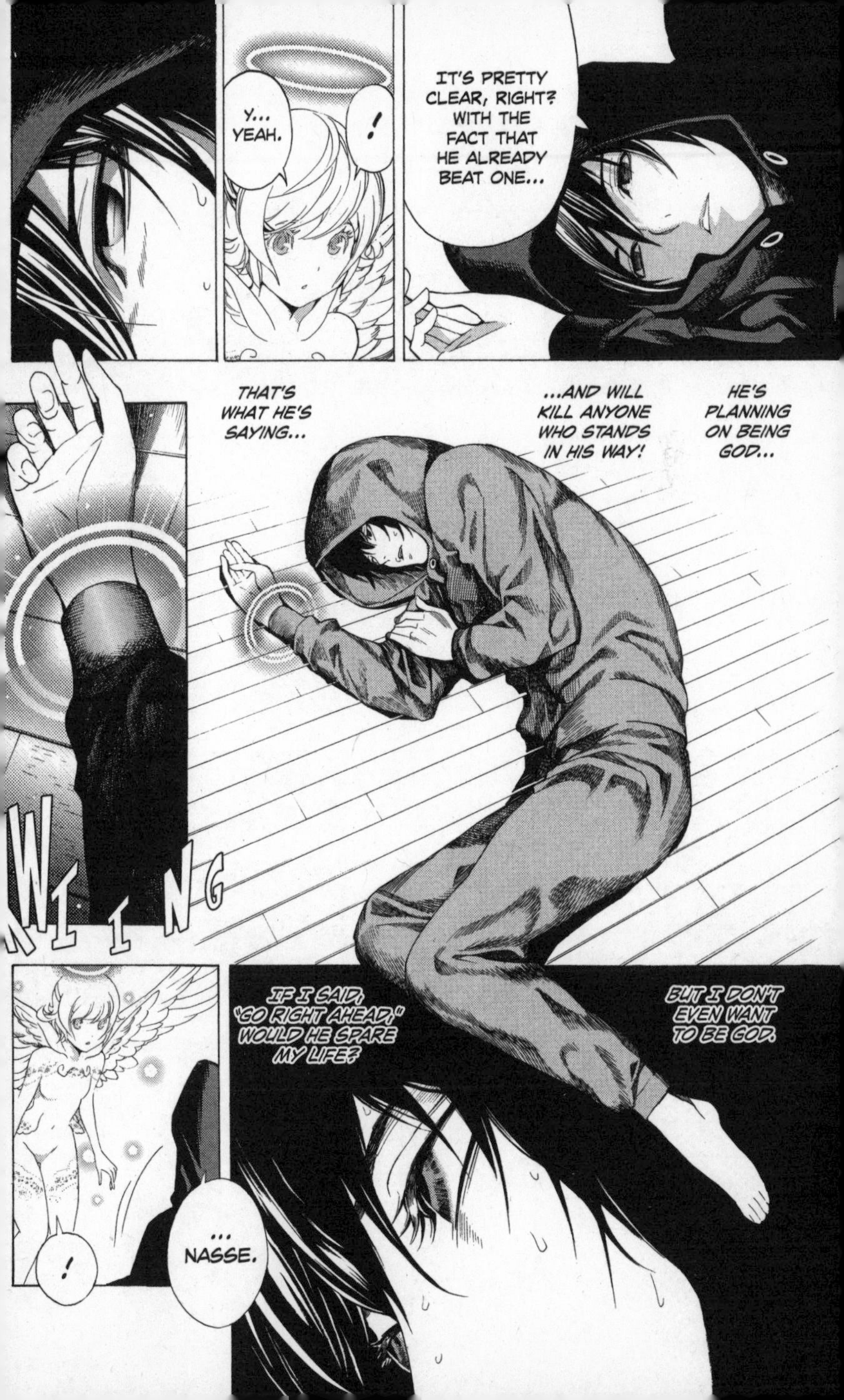
IT'S PRETTY CLEAR, RIGHT? WITH THE FACT THAT HE ALREADY BEAT ONE...
!
Y... YEAH.
HE'S PLANNING ON BEING GOD...
...AND WILL KILL ANYONE WHO STANDS IN HIS WAY!
THAT'S WHAT HE'S SAYING...
WIING
BUT I DON'T EVEN WANT TO BE GOD.
IF I SAID, "GO RIGHT AHEAD," WOULD HE SPARE MY LIFE?
... NASSE.
!

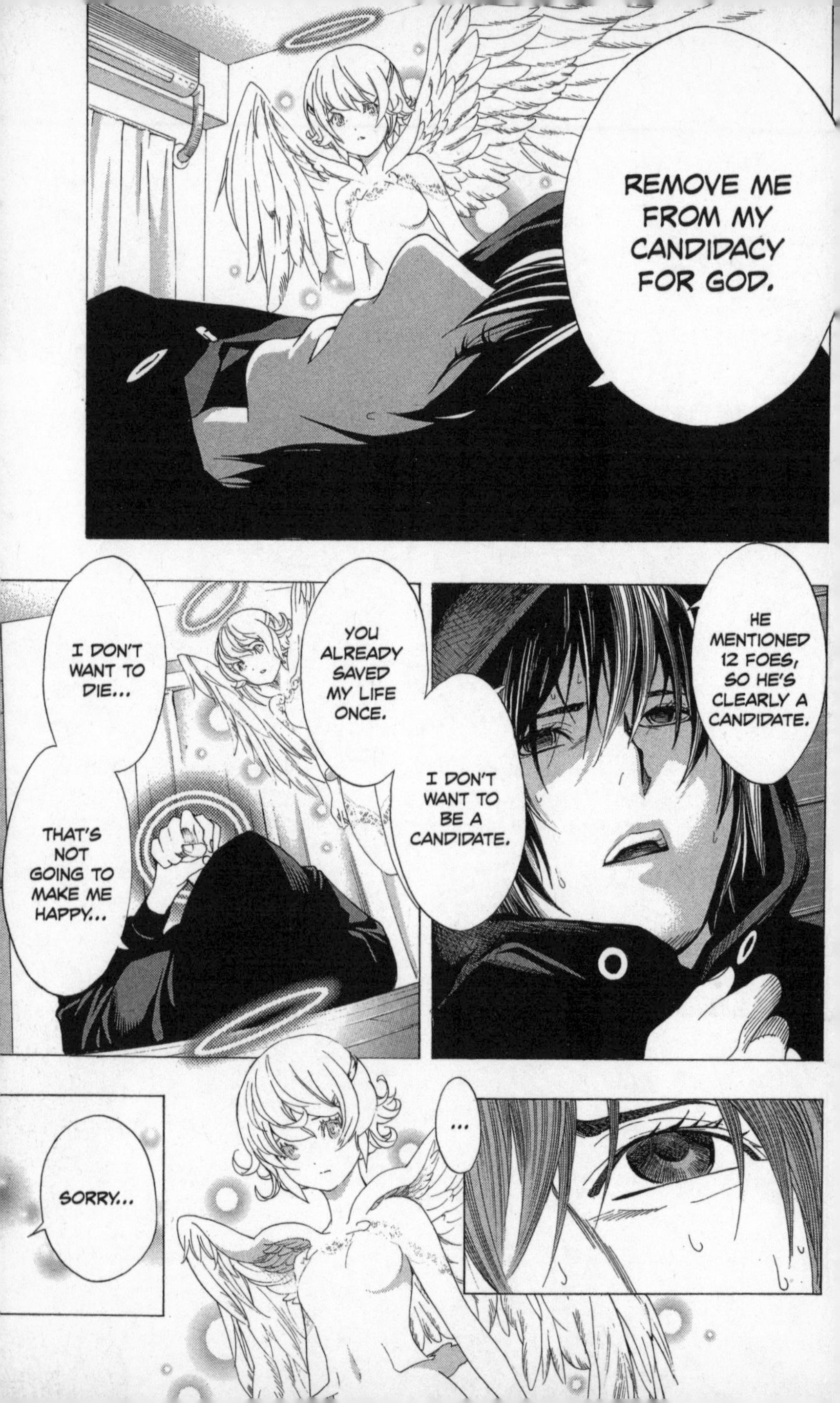
REMOVE ME FROM MY CANDIDACY FOR GOD.
HE MENTIONED 12 FOES, SO HE'S CLEARLY A CANDIDATE.
YOU ALREADY SAVED MY LIFE ONCE.
I DON'T WANT TO BE A CANDIDATE.
I DON'T WANT TO DIE...
THAT'S NOT GOING TO MAKE ME HAPPY...
...
SORRY...

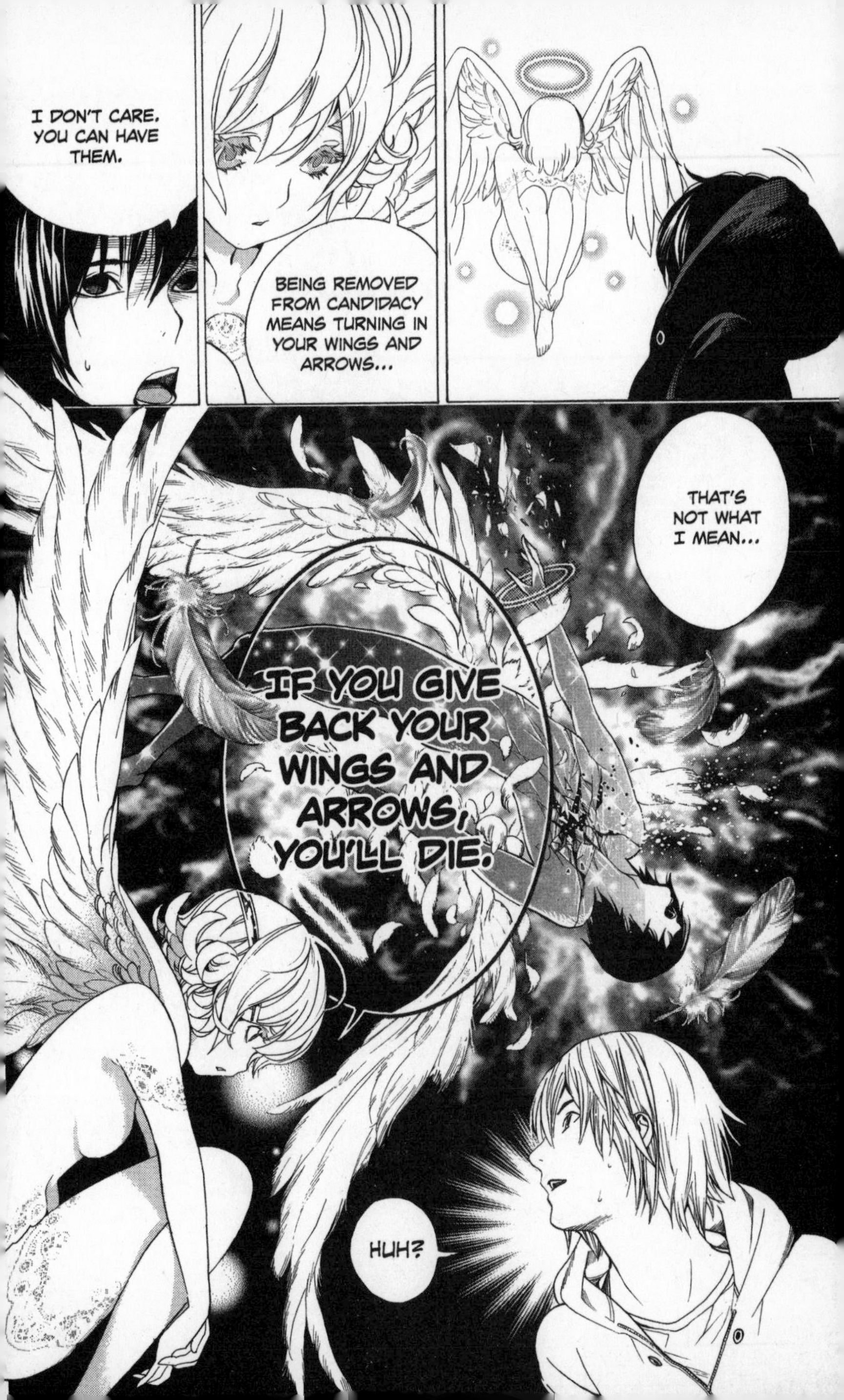
BEING REMOVED FROM CANDIDACY MEANS TURNING IN YOUR WINGS AND ARROWS...
I DON'T CARE. YOU CAN HAVE THEM.
THAT'S NOT WHAT I MEAN...
IF YOU GIVE BACK YOUR WINGS AND ARROWS, YOU'LL DIE.
HUH?

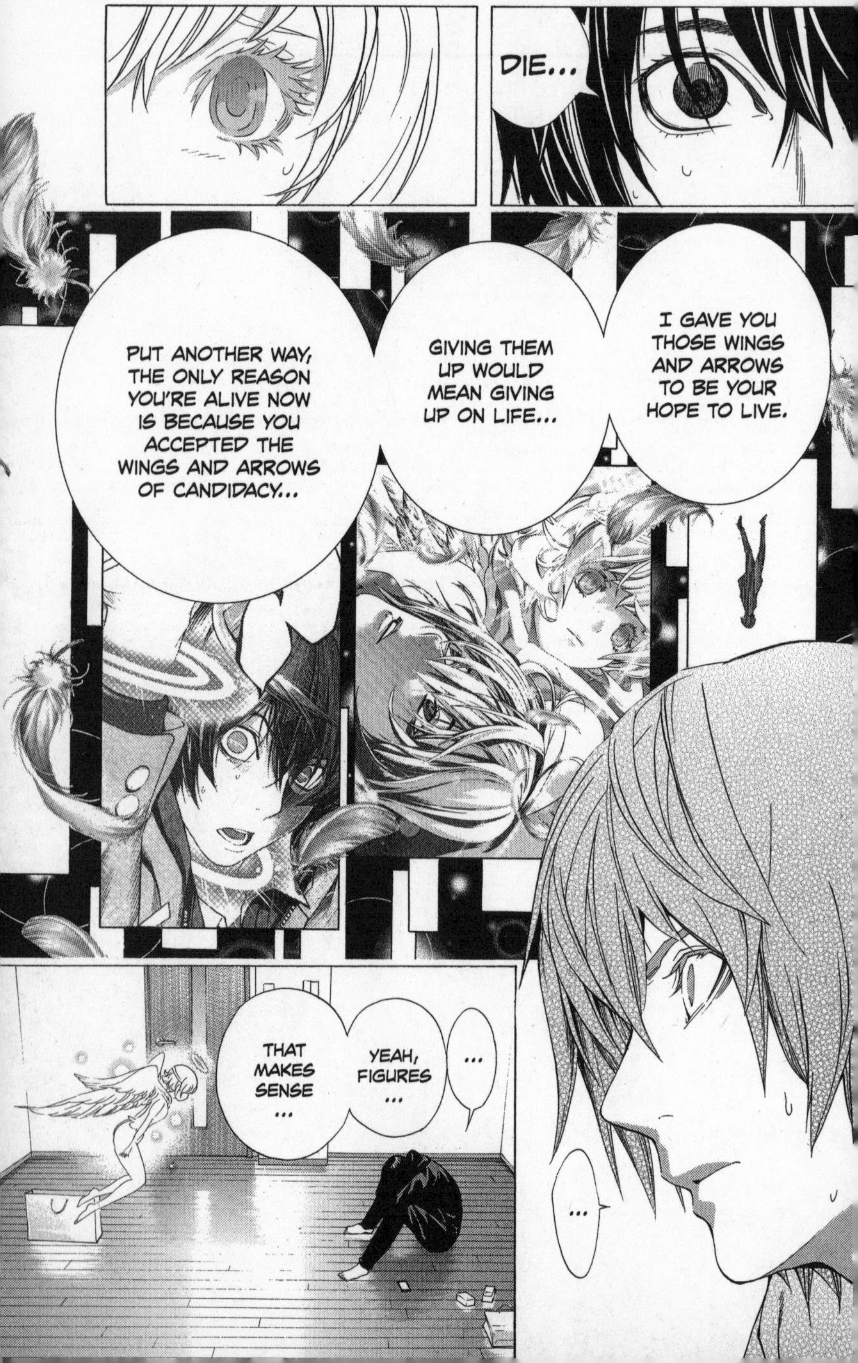

DIE...
I GAVE YOU THOSE WINGS AND ARROWS TO BE YOUR HOPE TO LIVE.
GIVING THEM UP WOULD MEAN GIVING UP ON LIFE...
PUT ANOTHER WAY, THE ONLY REASON YOU'RE ALIVE NOW IS BECAUSE YOU ACCEPTED THE WINGS AND ARROWS OF CANDIDACY...
...
...
YEAH, FIGURES...
THAT MAKES SENSE...

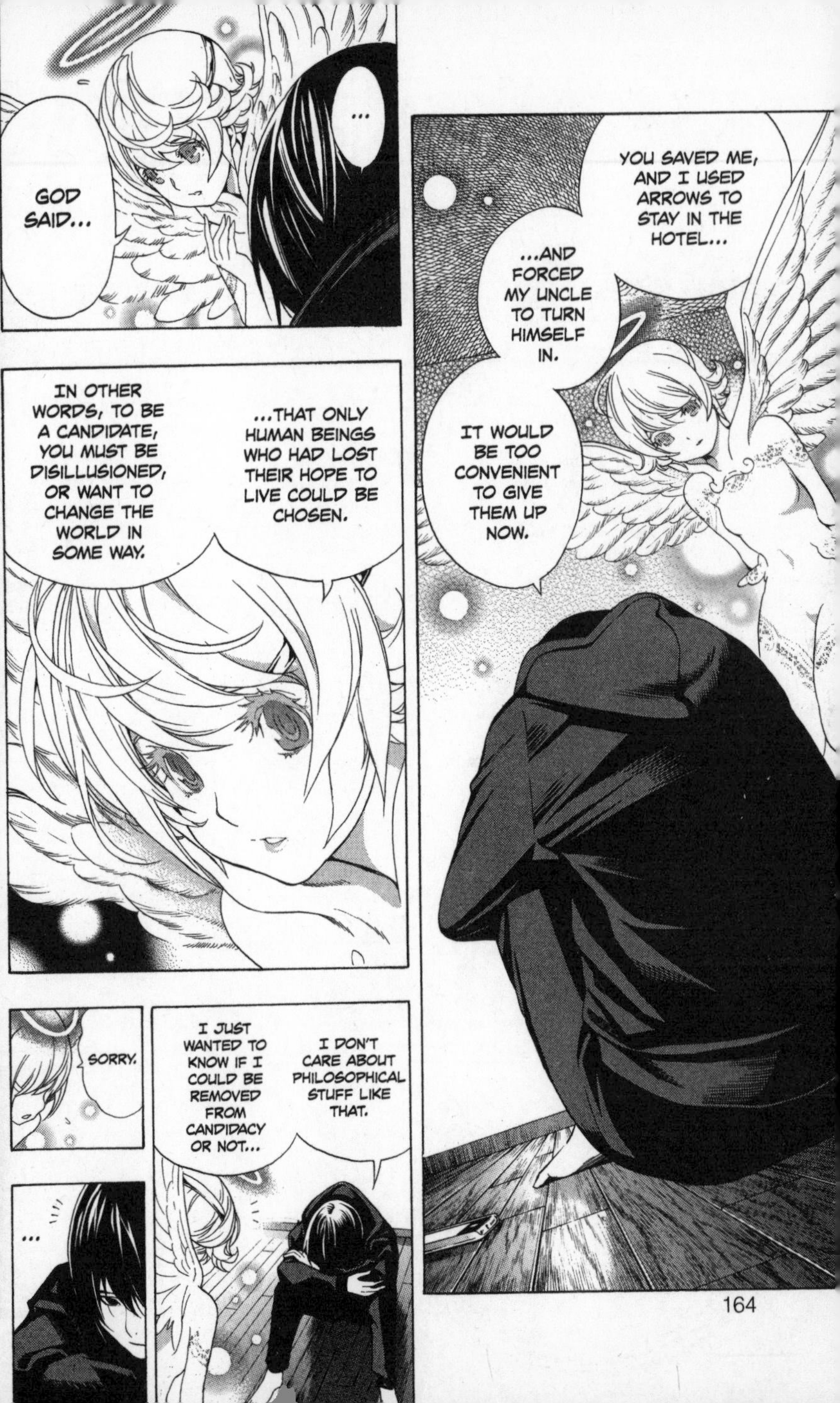
...
GOD SAID...
...THAT ONLY HUMAN BEINGS WHO HAD LOST THEIR HOPE TO LIVE COULD BE CHOSEN.
IN OTHER WORDS, TO BE A CANDIDATE, YOU MUST BE DISILLUSIONED, OR WANT TO CHANGE THE WORLD IN SOME WAY.
I DON'T CARE ABOUT PHILOSOPHICAL STUFF LIKE THAT.
I JUST WANTED TO KNOW IF I COULD BE REMOVED FROM CANDIDACY OR NOT...
SORRY.
...
YOU SAVED ME, AND I USED ARROWS TO STAY IN THE HOTEL...
...AND FORCED MY UNCLE TO TURN HIMSELF IN.
IT WOULD BE TOO CONVENIENT TO GIVE THEM UP NOW.

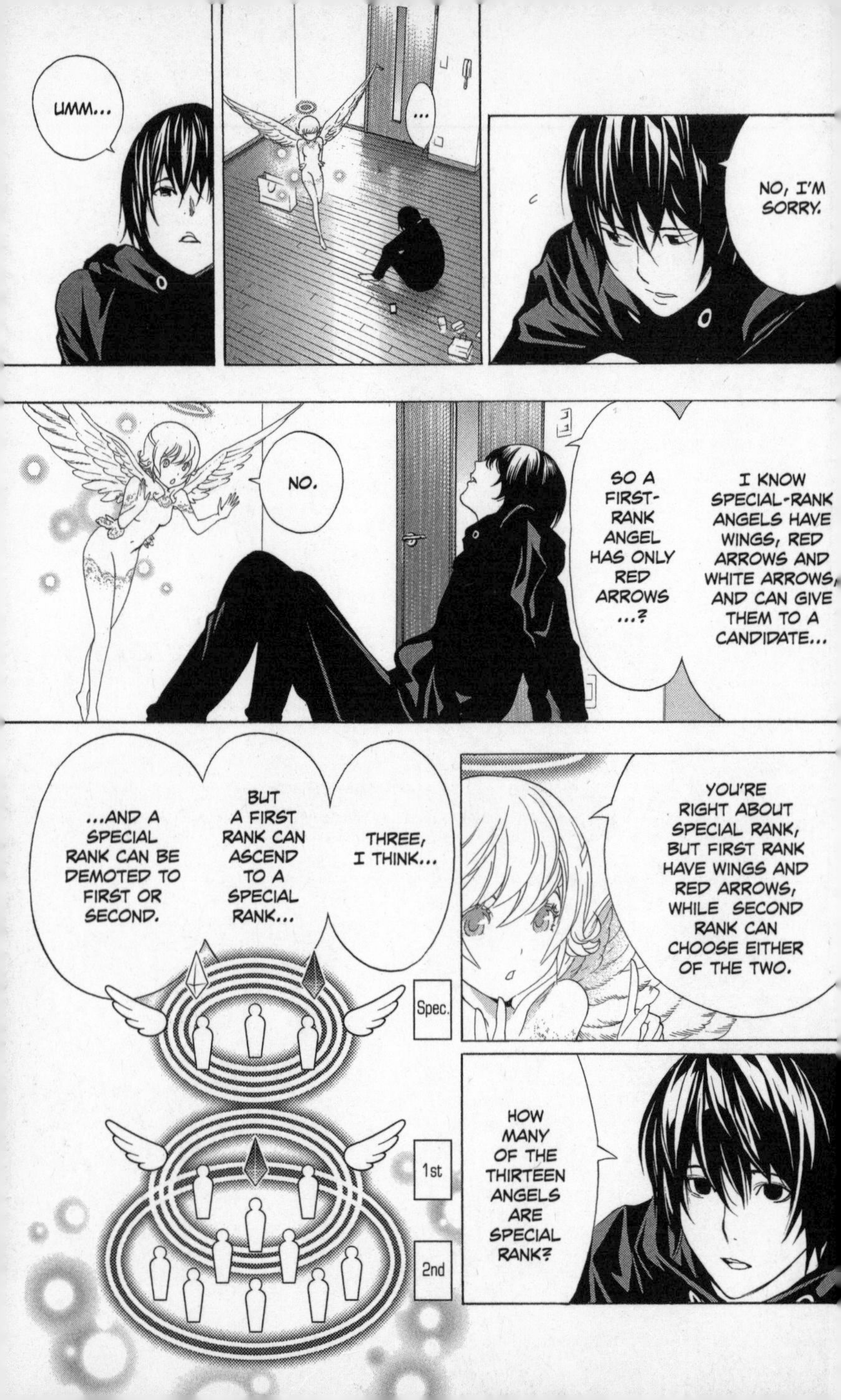
NO, I'M SORRY.
...
UMM...
I KNOW SPECIAL-RANK ANGELS HAVE WINGS, RED ARROWS AND WHITE ARROWS, AND CAN GIVE THEM TO A CANDIDATE...
SO A FIRST-RANK ANGEL HAS ONLY RED ARROWS ...?
NO.
YOU'RE RIGHT ABOUT SPECIAL RANK, BUT FIRST RANK HAVE WINGS AND RED ARROWS, WHILE SECOND RANK CAN CHOOSE EITHER OF THE TWO.
HOW MANY OF THE THIRTEEN ANGELS ARE SPECIAL RANK?
THREE, I THINK...
BUT A FIRST RANK CAN ASCEND TO A SPECIAL RANK...
...AND A SPECIAL RANK CAN BE DEMOTED TO FIRST OR SECOND.
Spec.
1st
2nd

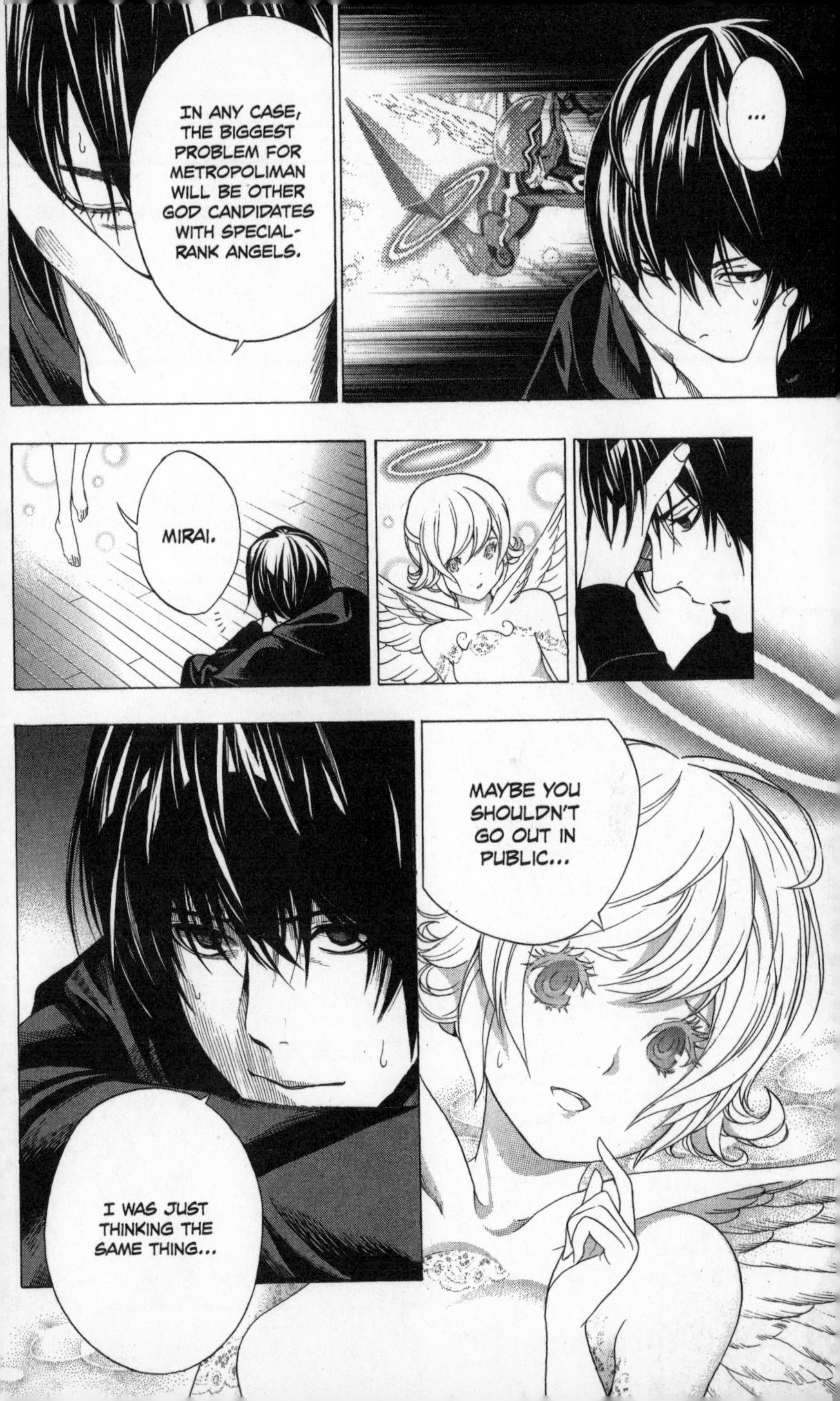
...
IN ANY CASE, THE BIGGEST PROBLEM FOR METROPOLIMAN WILL BE OTHER GOD CANDIDATES WITH SPECIAL-RANK ANGELS.
MIRAI.
MAYBE YOU SHOULDN'T GO OUT IN PUBLIC...
I WAS JUST THINKING THE SAME THING...

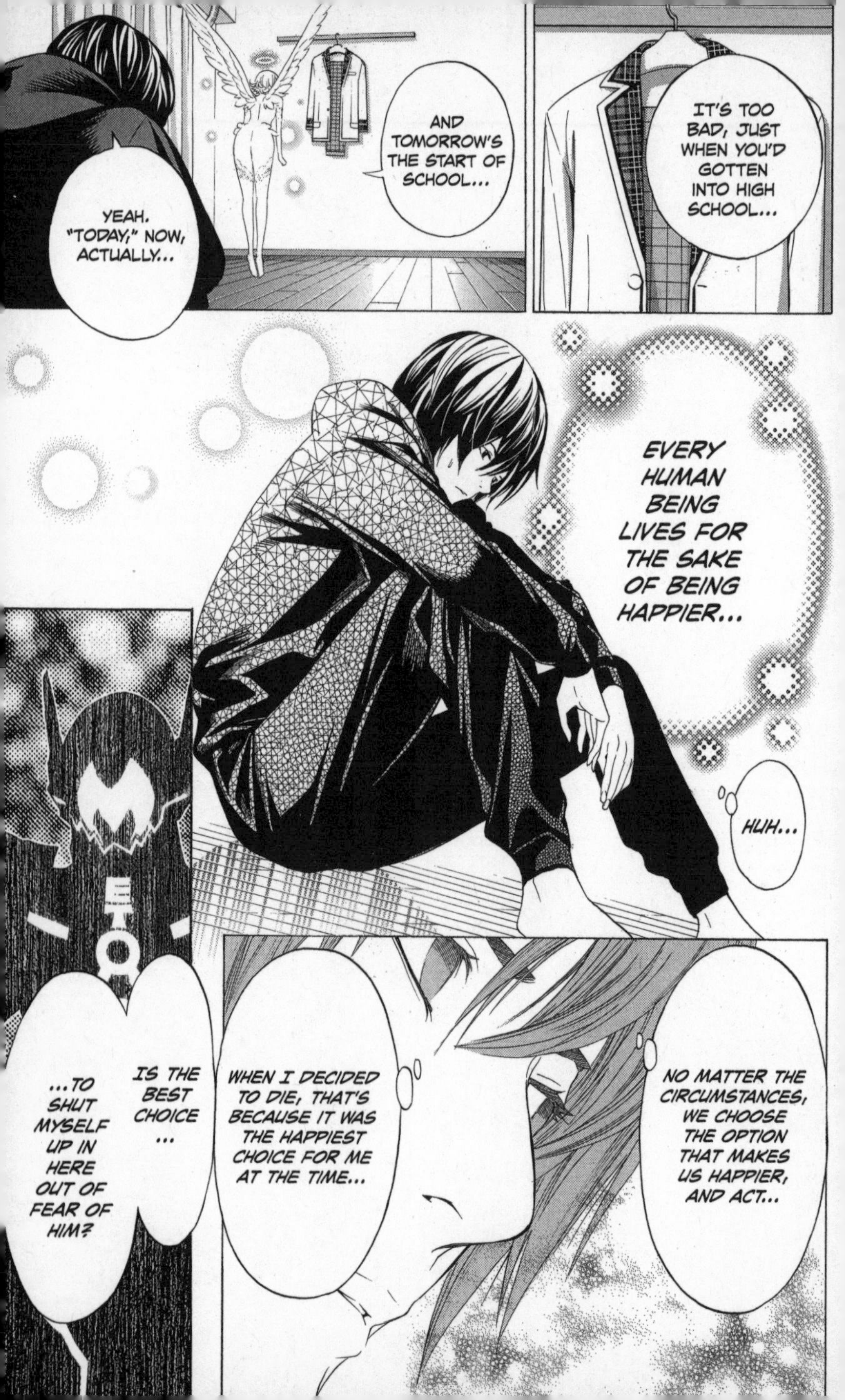
IT'S TOO BAD, JUST WHEN YOU'D GOTTEN INTO HIGH SCHOOL...
AND TOMORROW'S THE START OF SCHOOL...
YEAH. "TODAY," NOW, ACTUALLY...
EVERY HUMAN BEING LIVES FOR THE SAKE OF BEING HAPPIER...
HUH...
NO MATTER THE CIRCUMSTANCES, WE CHOOSE THE OPTION THAT MAKES US HAPPIER, AND ACT...
WHEN I DECIDED TO DIE, THAT'S BECAUSE IT WAS THE HAPPIEST CHOICE FOR ME AT THE TIME...
IS THE BEST CHOICE...
...TO SHUT MYSELF UP IN HERE OUT OF FEAR OF HIM?

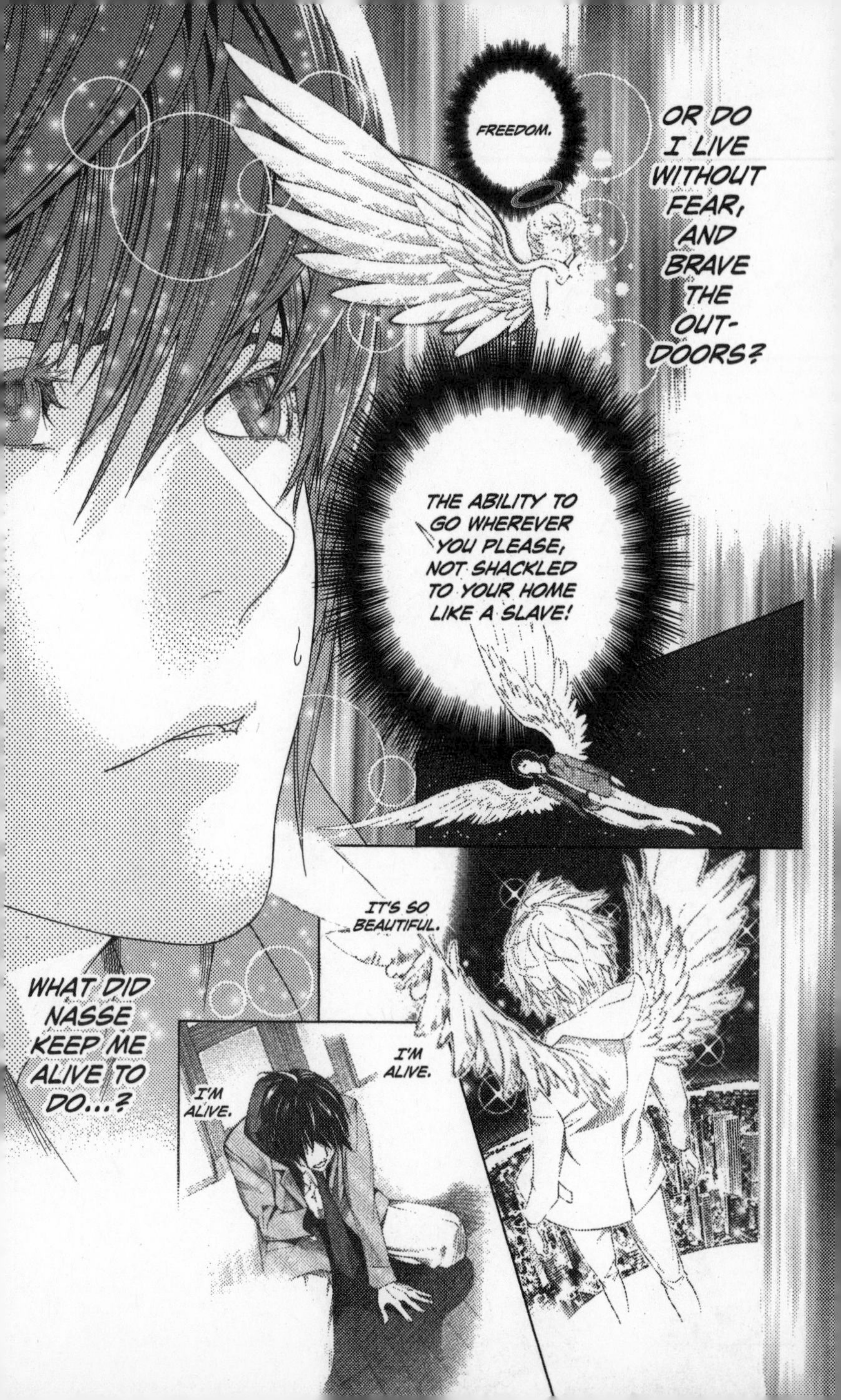
OR DO I LIVE WITHOUT FEAR, AND BRAVE THE OUT-DOORS?
FREEDOM.
THE ABILITY TO GO WHEREVER YOU PLEASE, NOT SHACKLED TO YOUR HOME LIKE A SLAVE!
IT'S SO BEAUTIFUL.
I'M ALIVE.
I'M ALIVE.
WHAT DID NASSE KEEP ME ALIVE TO DO...?

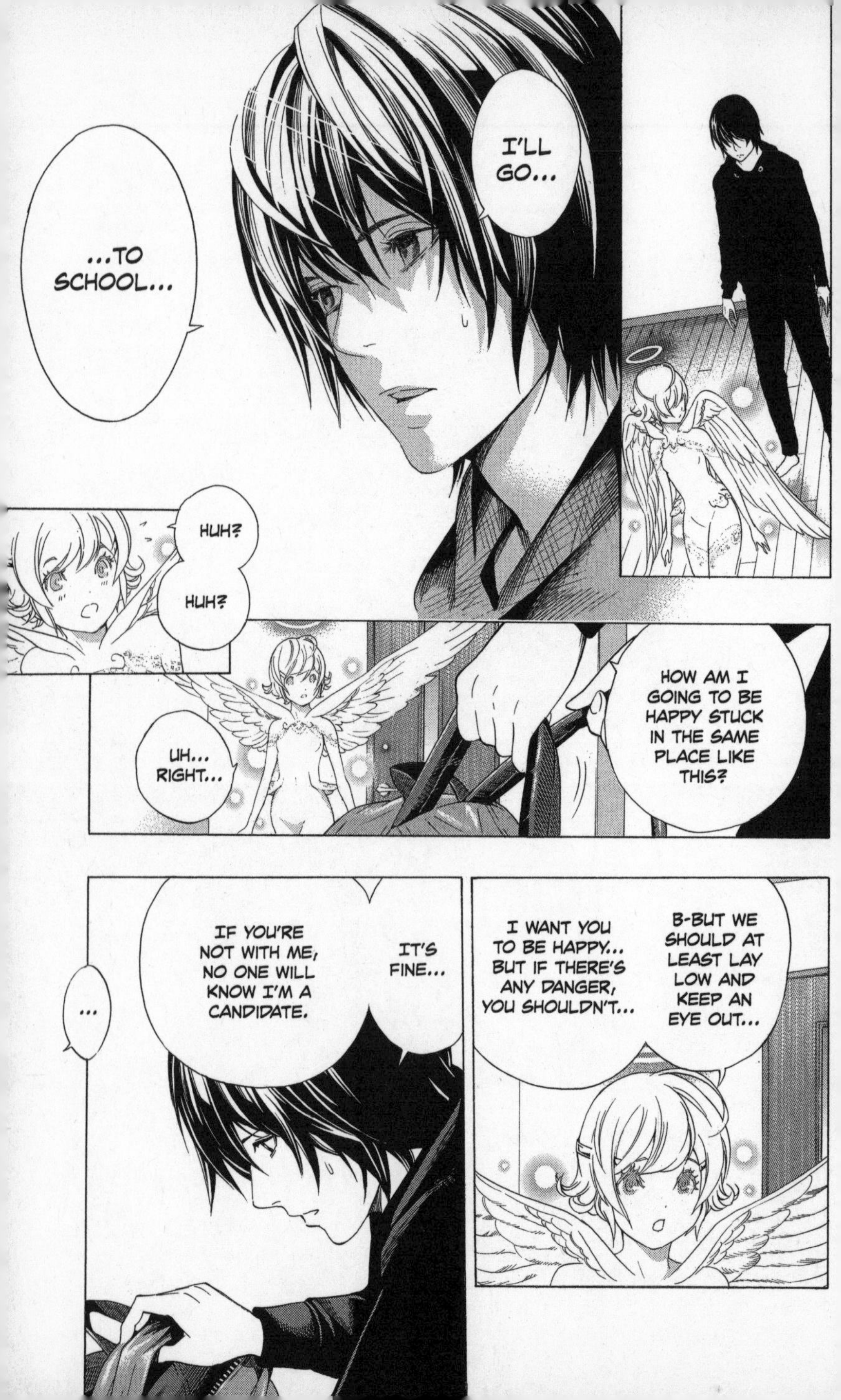
I'LL GO...
...TO SCHOOL...
HUH?
HUH?
HOW AM I GOING TO BE HAPPY STUCK IN THE SAME PLACE LIKE THIS?
UH... RIGHT...
B-BUT WE SHOULD AT LEAST LAY LOW AND KEEP AN EYE OUT...
I WANT YOU TO BE HAPPY... BUT IF THERE'S ANY DANGER, YOU SHOULDN'T...
IT'S FINE...
IF YOU'RE NOT WITH ME, NO ONE WILL KNOW I'M A CANDIDATE.
...

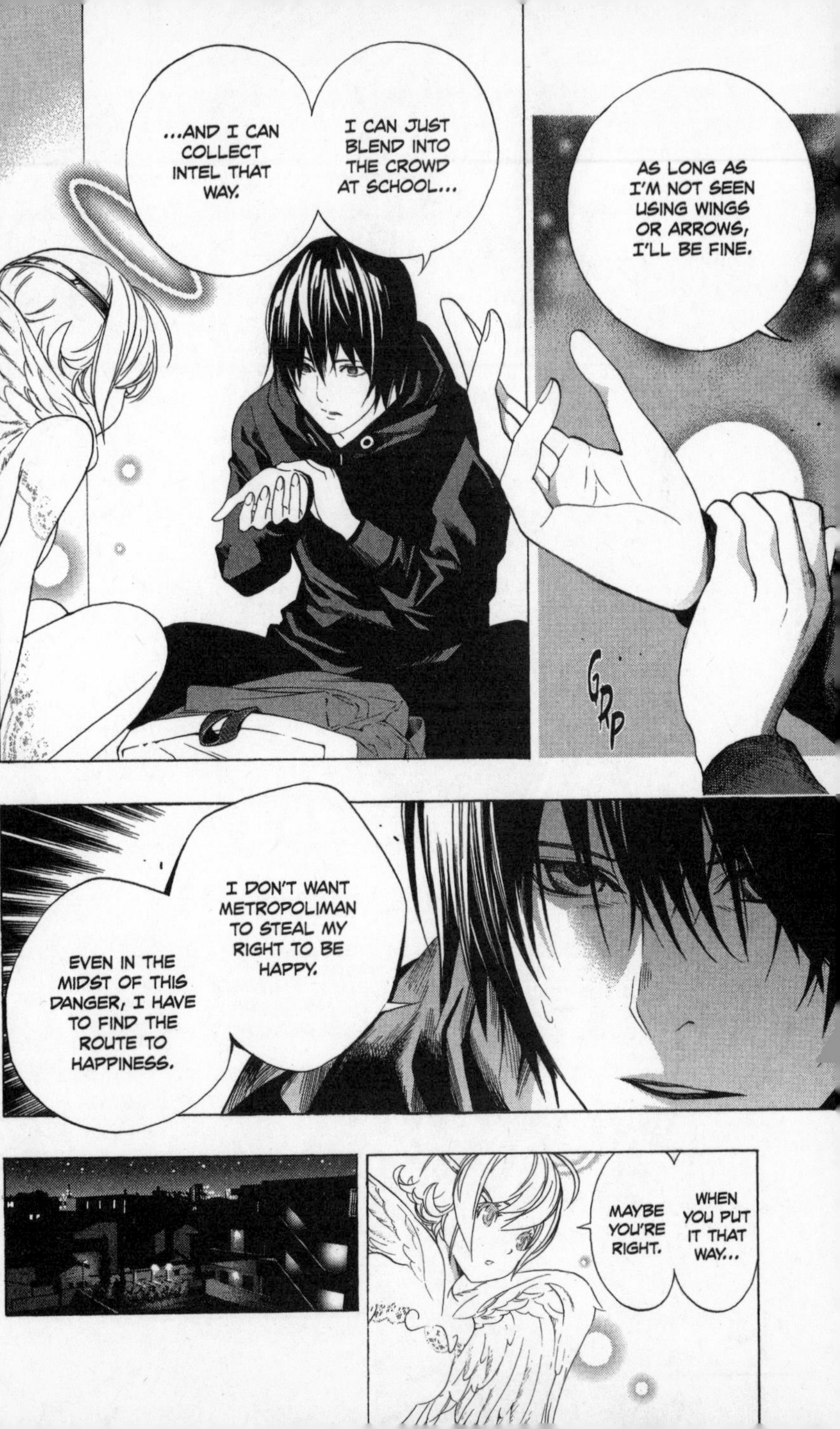
AS LONG AS I'M NOT SEEN USING WINGS OR ARROWS, I'LL BE FINE.
GRP
I CAN JUST BLEND INTO THE CROWD AT SCHOOL...
...AND I CAN COLLECT INTEL THAT WAY.
I DON'T WANT METROPOLIMAN TO STEAL MY RIGHT TO BE HAPPY.
EVEN IN THE MIDST OF THIS DANGER, I HAVE TO FIND THE ROUTE TO HAPPINESS.
WHEN YOU PUT IT THAT WAY...
MAYBE YOU'RE RIGHT.

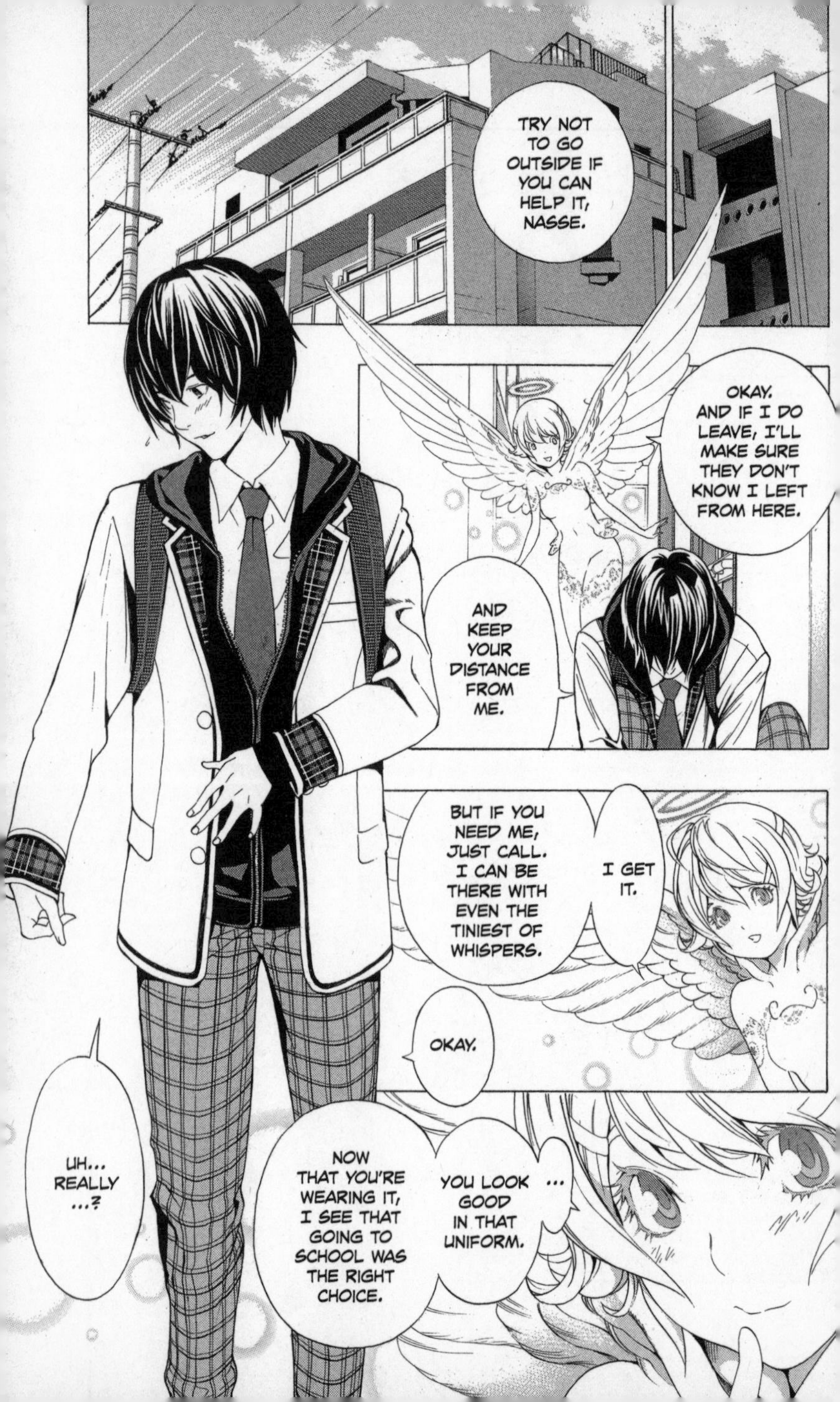
TRY NOT TO GO OUTSIDE IF YOU CAN HELP IT, NASSE.
OKAY. AND IF I DO LEAVE, I'LL MAKE SURE THEY DON'T KNOW I LEFT FROM HERE.
AND KEEP YOUR DISTANCE FROM ME.
I GET IT.
BUT IF YOU NEED ME, JUST CALL. I CAN BE THERE WITH EVEN THE TINIEST OF WHISPERS.
OKAY.
...
YOU LOOK GOOD IN THAT UNIFORM.
NOW THAT YOU'RE WEARING IT, I SEE THAT GOING TO SCHOOL WAS THE RIGHT CHOICE.
UH... REALLY ...?

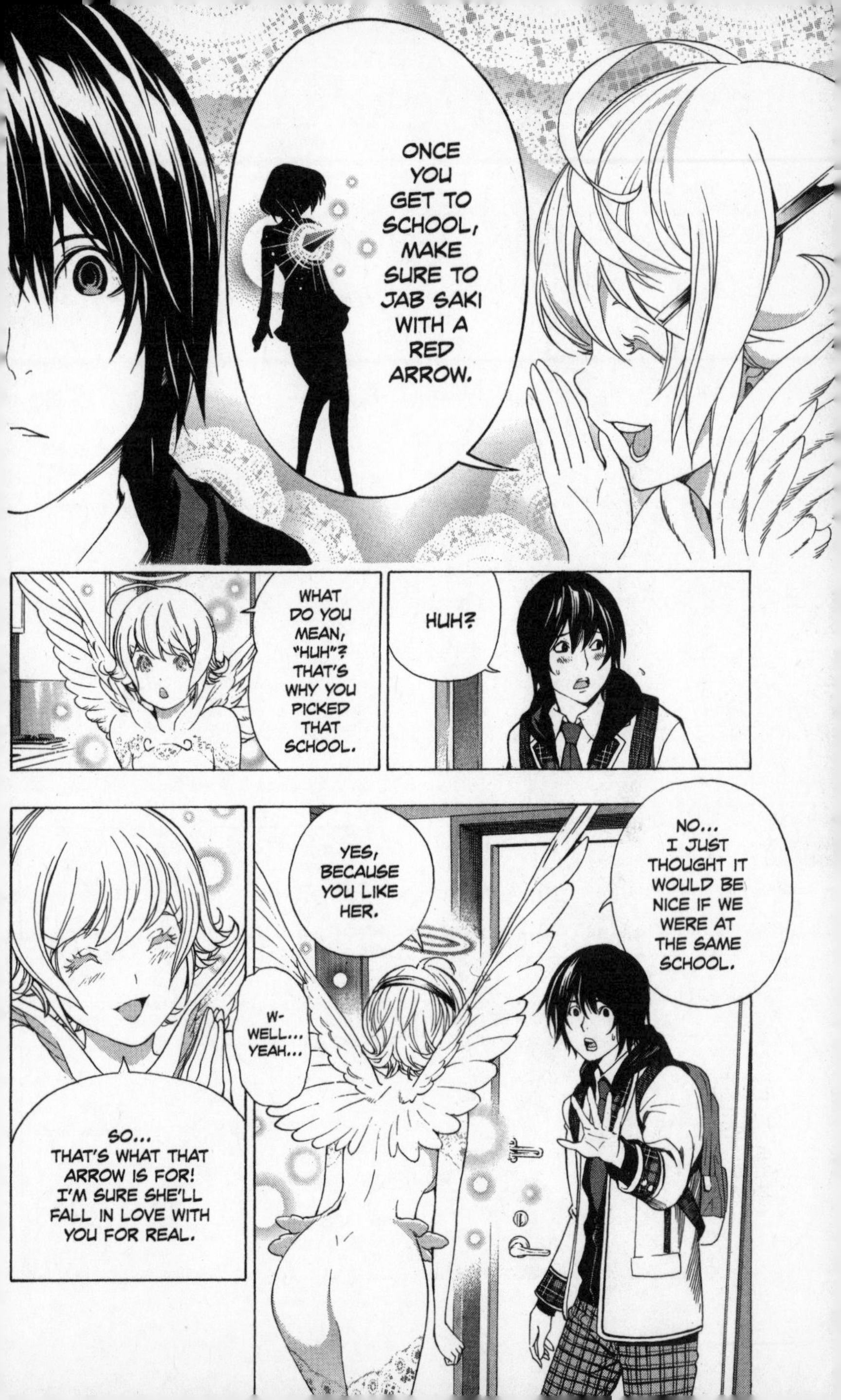

ONCE YOU GET TO SCHOOL, MAKE SURE TO JAB SAKI WITH A RED ARROW.
HUH?
WHAT DO YOU MEAN, "HUH"? THAT'S WHY YOU PICKED THAT SCHOOL.
NO... I JUST THOUGHT IT WOULD BE NICE IF WE WERE AT THE SAME SCHOOL.
YES, BECAUSE YOU LIKE HER.
W-WELL... YEAH...
SO... THAT'S WHAT THAT ARROW IS FOR! I'M SURE SHE'LL FALL IN LOVE WITH YOU FOR REAL.

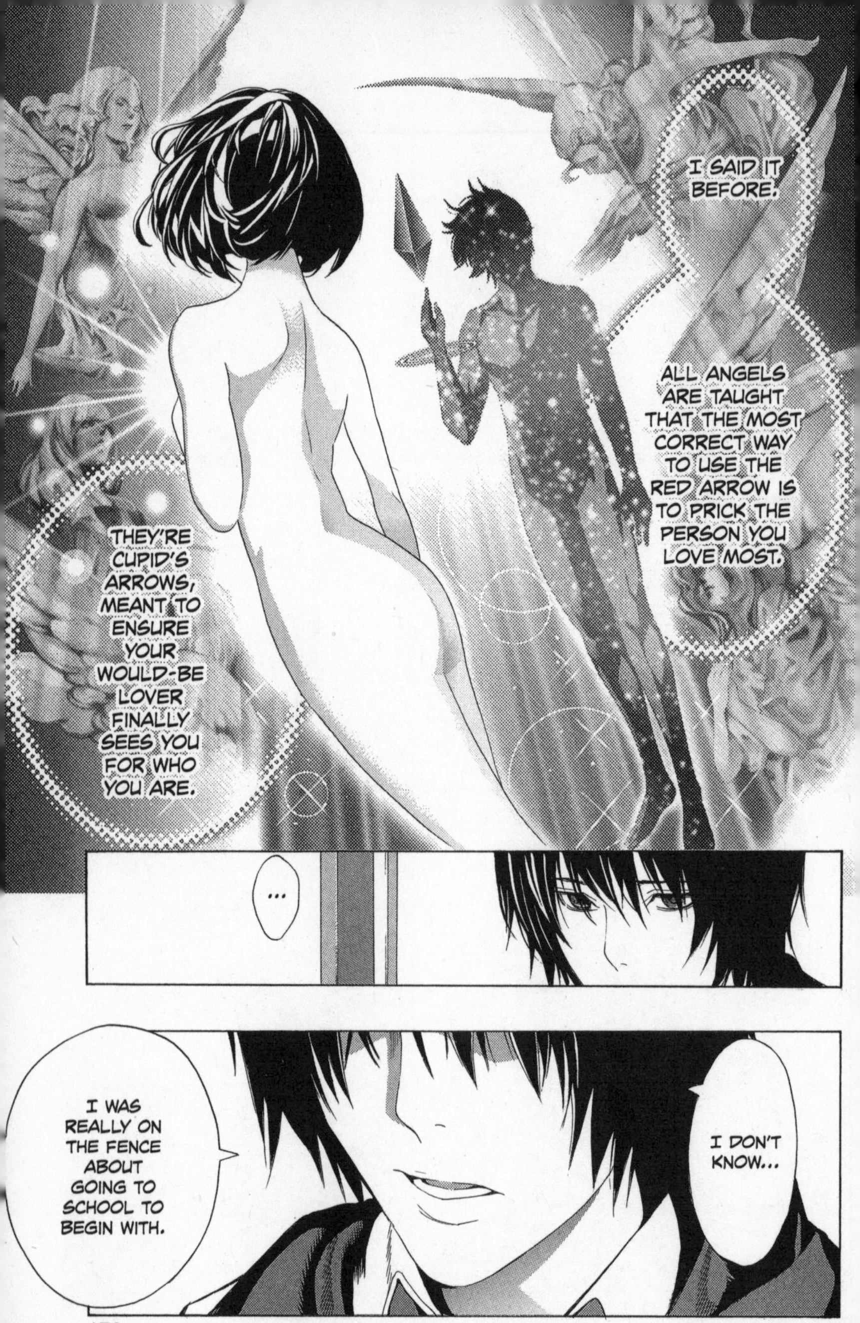
I SAID IT BEFORE.
ALL ANGELS ARE TAUGHT THAT THE MOST CORRECT WAY TO USE THE RED ARROW IS TO PRICK THE PERSON YOU LOVE MOST.
THEY'RE CUPID'S ARROWS, MEANT TO ENSURE YOUR WOULD-BE LOVER FINALLY SEES YOU FOR WHO YOU ARE.
...
I DON'T KNOW...
I WAS REALLY ON THE FENCE ABOUT GOING TO SCHOOL TO BEGIN WITH.

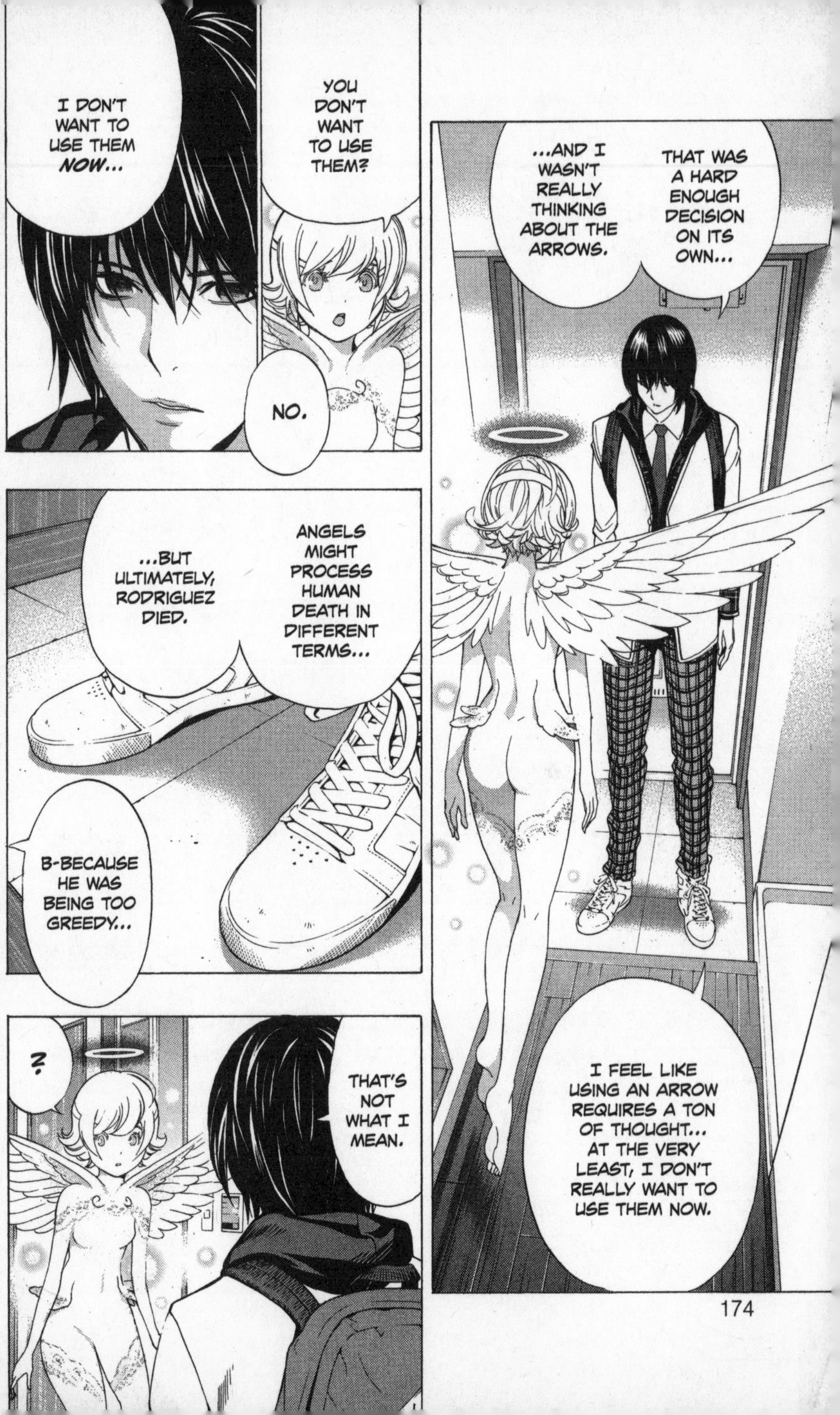
THAT WAS A HARD ENOUGH DECISION ON ITS OWN...
...AND I WASN'T REALLY THINKING ABOUT THE ARROWS.
I FEEL LIKE USING AN ARROW REQUIRES A TON OF THOUGHT... AT THE VERY LEAST, I DON'T REALLY WANT TO USE THEM NOW.
YOU DON'T WANT TO USE THEM?
NO.
I DON'T WANT TO USE THEM *NOW*...
ANGELS MIGHT PROCESS HUMAN DEATH IN DIFFERENT TERMS...
...BUT ULTIMATELY, RODRIGUEZ DIED.
B-BECAUSE HE WAS BEING TOO GREEDY...
THAT'S NOT WHAT I MEAN.
?

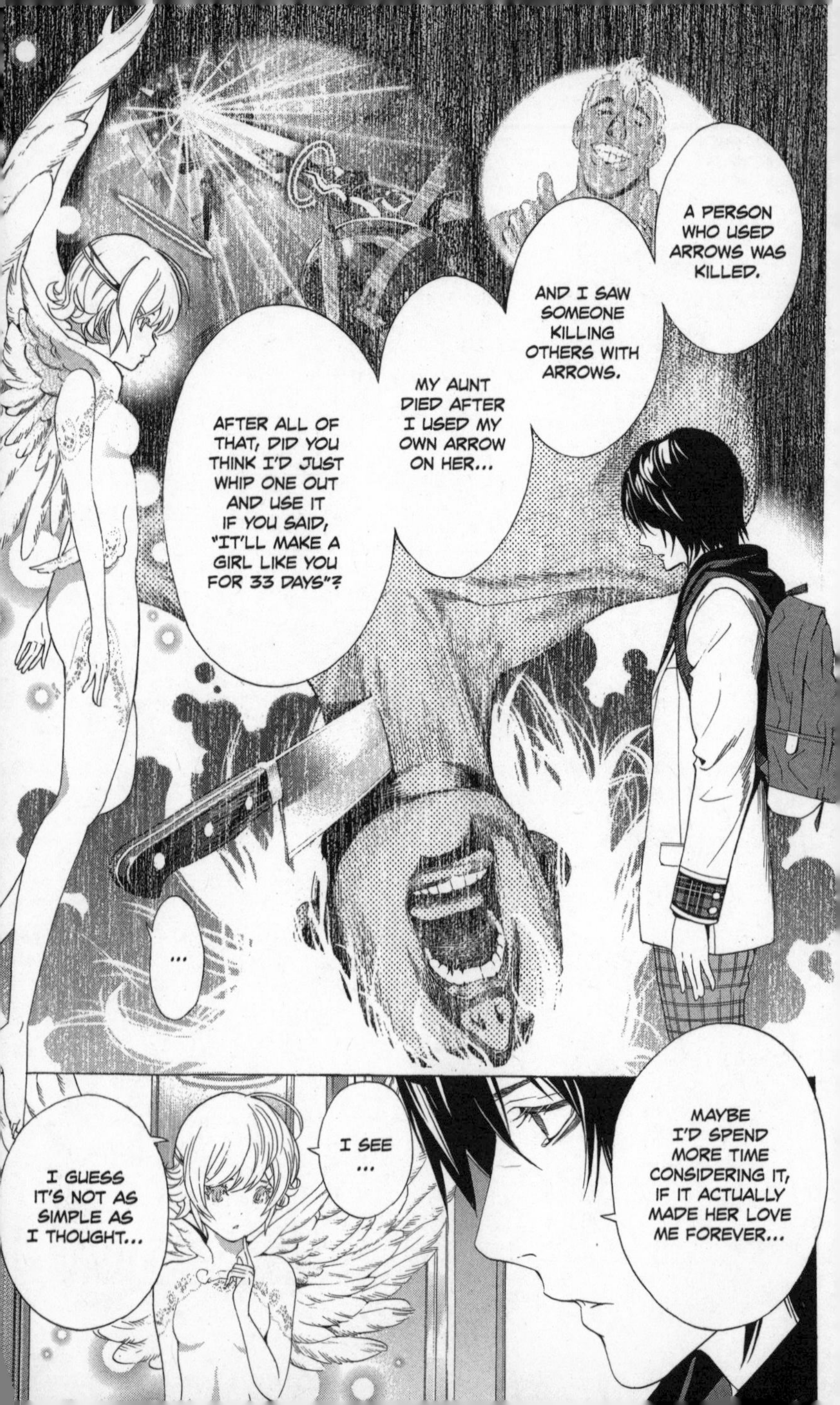
A PERSON WHO USED ARROWS WAS KILLED.
AND I SAW SOMEONE KILLING OTHERS WITH ARROWS.
MY AUNT DIED AFTER I USED MY OWN ARROW ON HER...
AFTER ALL OF THAT, DID YOU THINK I'D JUST WHIP ONE OUT AND USE IT IF YOU SAID, "IT'LL MAKE A GIRL LIKE YOU FOR 33 DAYS"?
...
MAYBE I'D SPEND MORE TIME CONSIDERING IT, IF IT ACTUALLY MADE HER LOVE ME FOREVER...
I SEE ...
I GUESS IT'S NOT AS SIMPLE AS I THOUGHT...

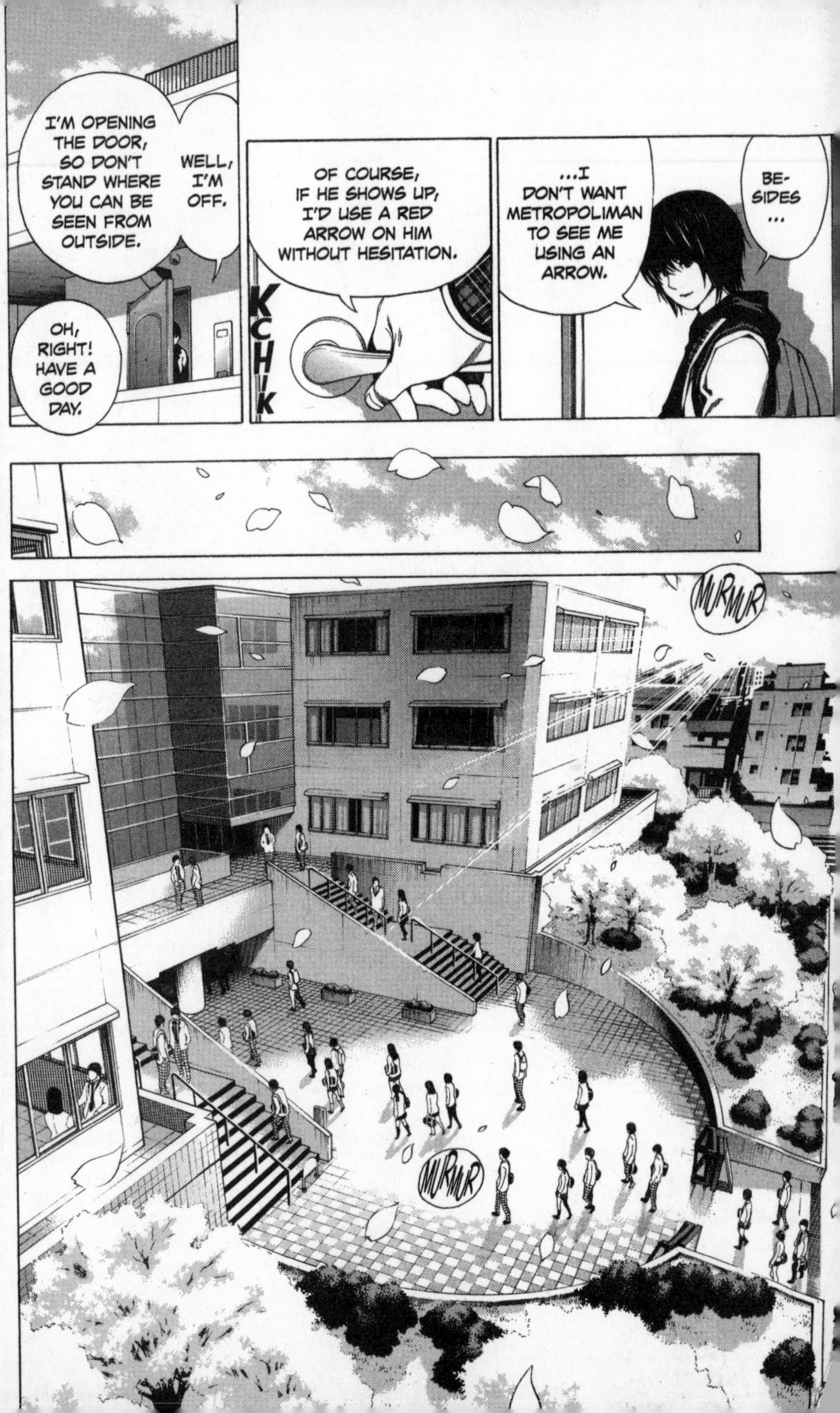
BE-SIDES ...
...I DON'T WANT METROPOLIMAN TO SEE ME USING AN ARROW.
OF COURSE, IF HE SHOWS UP, I'D USE A RED ARROW ON HIM WITHOUT HESITATION.
KCHIK
WELL, I'M OFF.
I'M OPENING THE DOOR, SO DON'T STAND WHERE YOU CAN BE SEEN FROM OUTSIDE.
OH, RIGHT! HAVE A GOOD DAY.
MURMUR
MURMUR

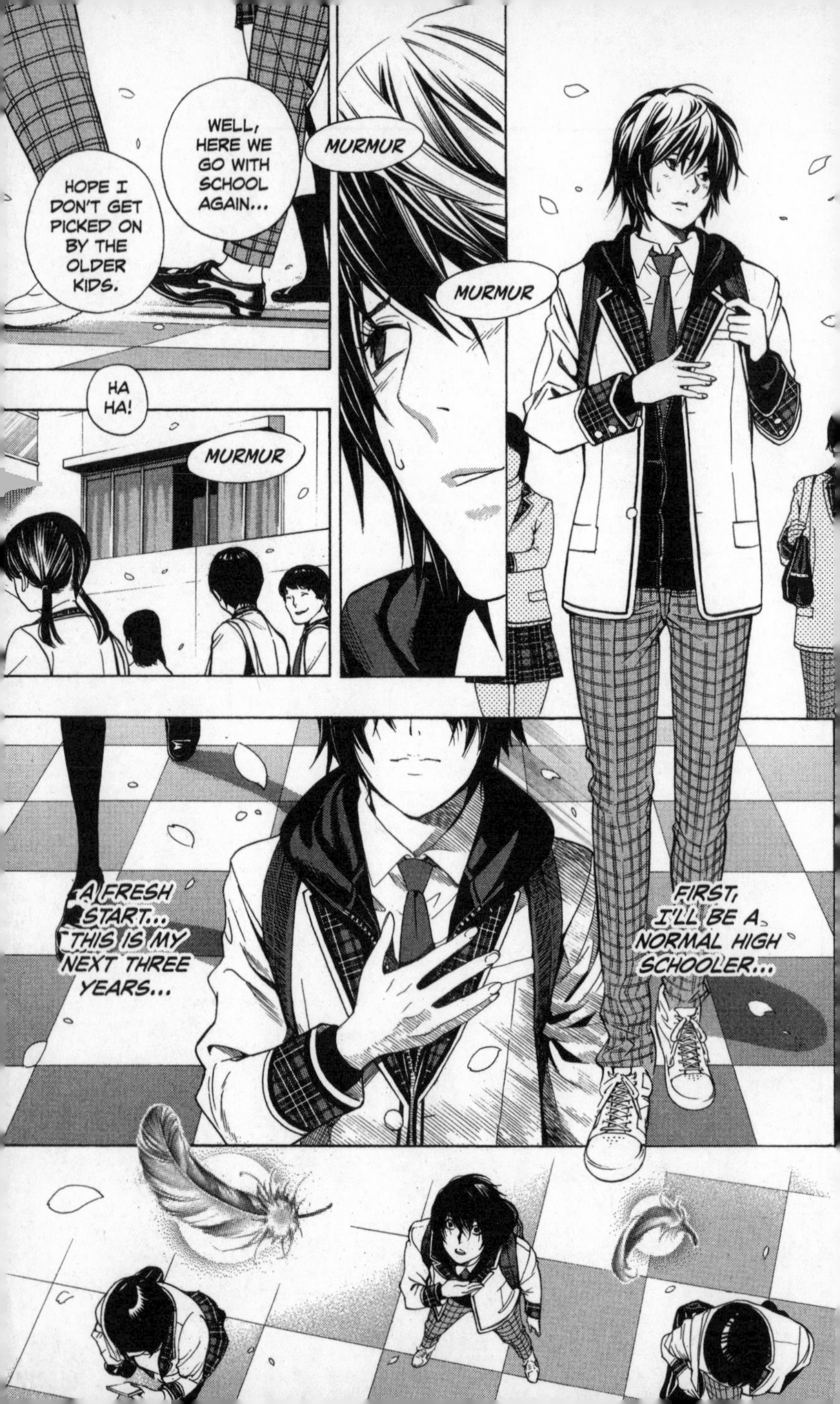
MURMUR
MURMUR
WELL, HERE WE GO WITH SCHOOL AGAIN...
HOPE I DON'T GET PICKED ON BY THE OLDER KIDS.
HA HA!
MURMUR
FIRST, I'LL BE A NORMAL HIGH SCHOOLER...
A FRESH START... THIS IS MY NEXT THREE YEARS...

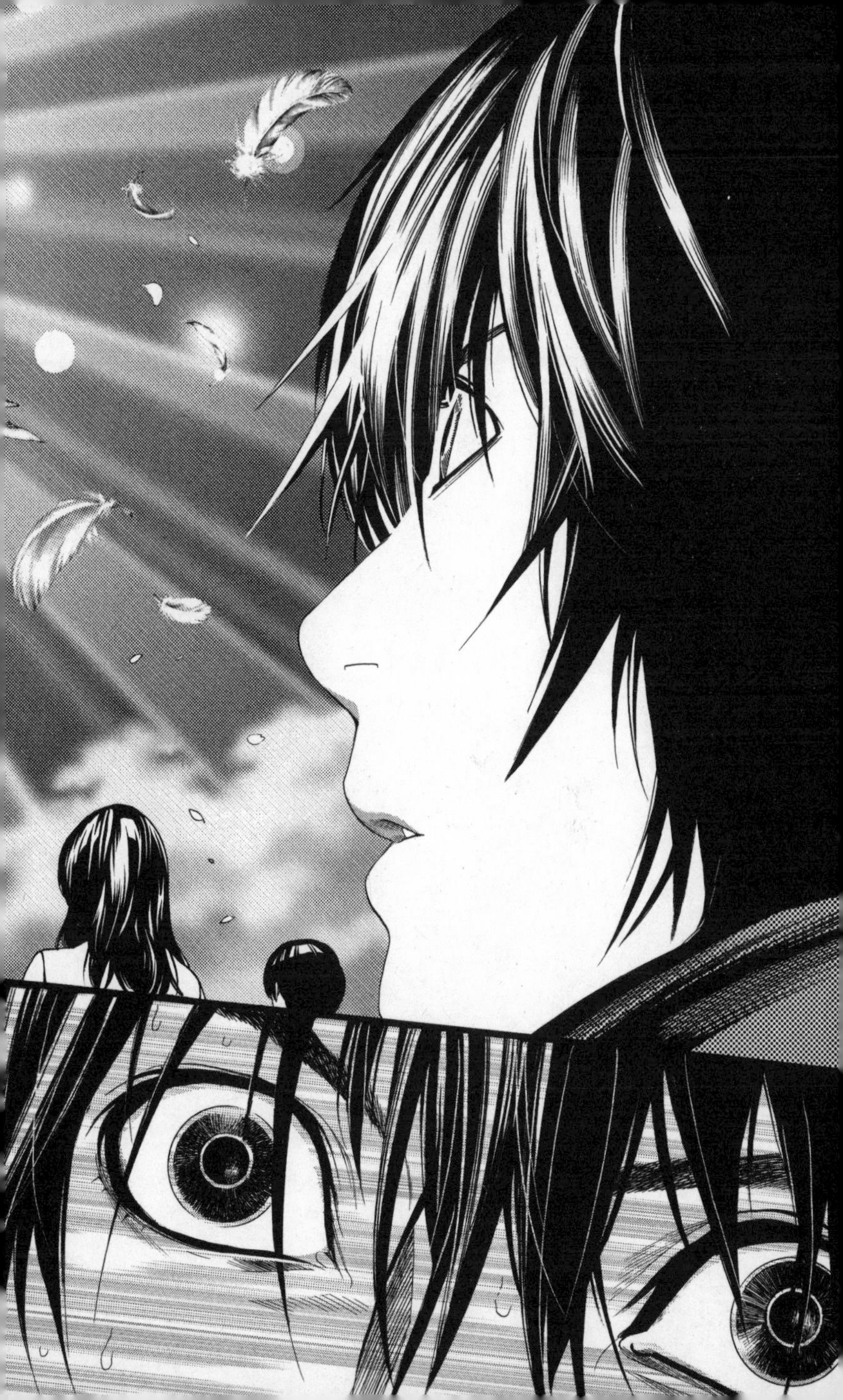

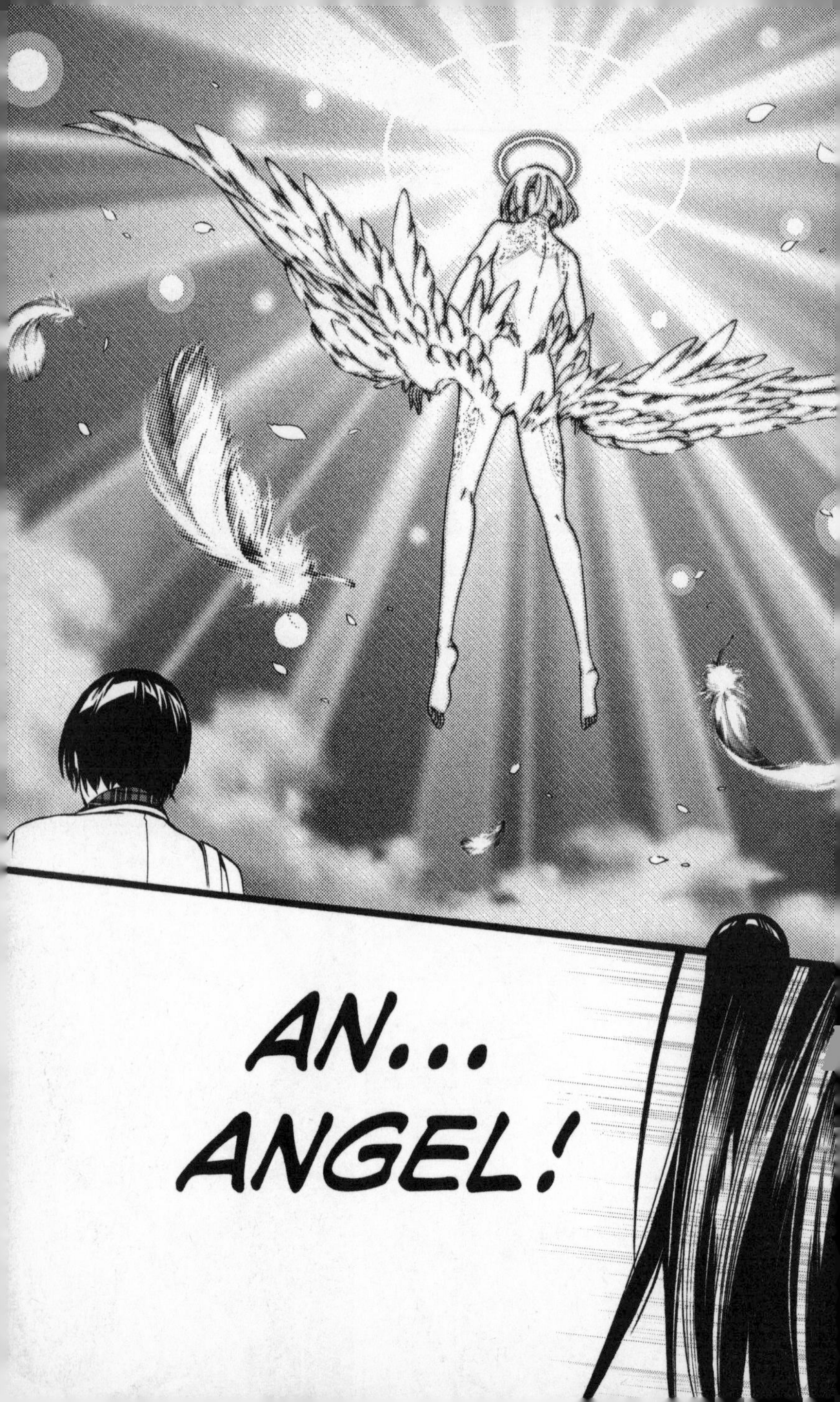
AN... ANGEL!

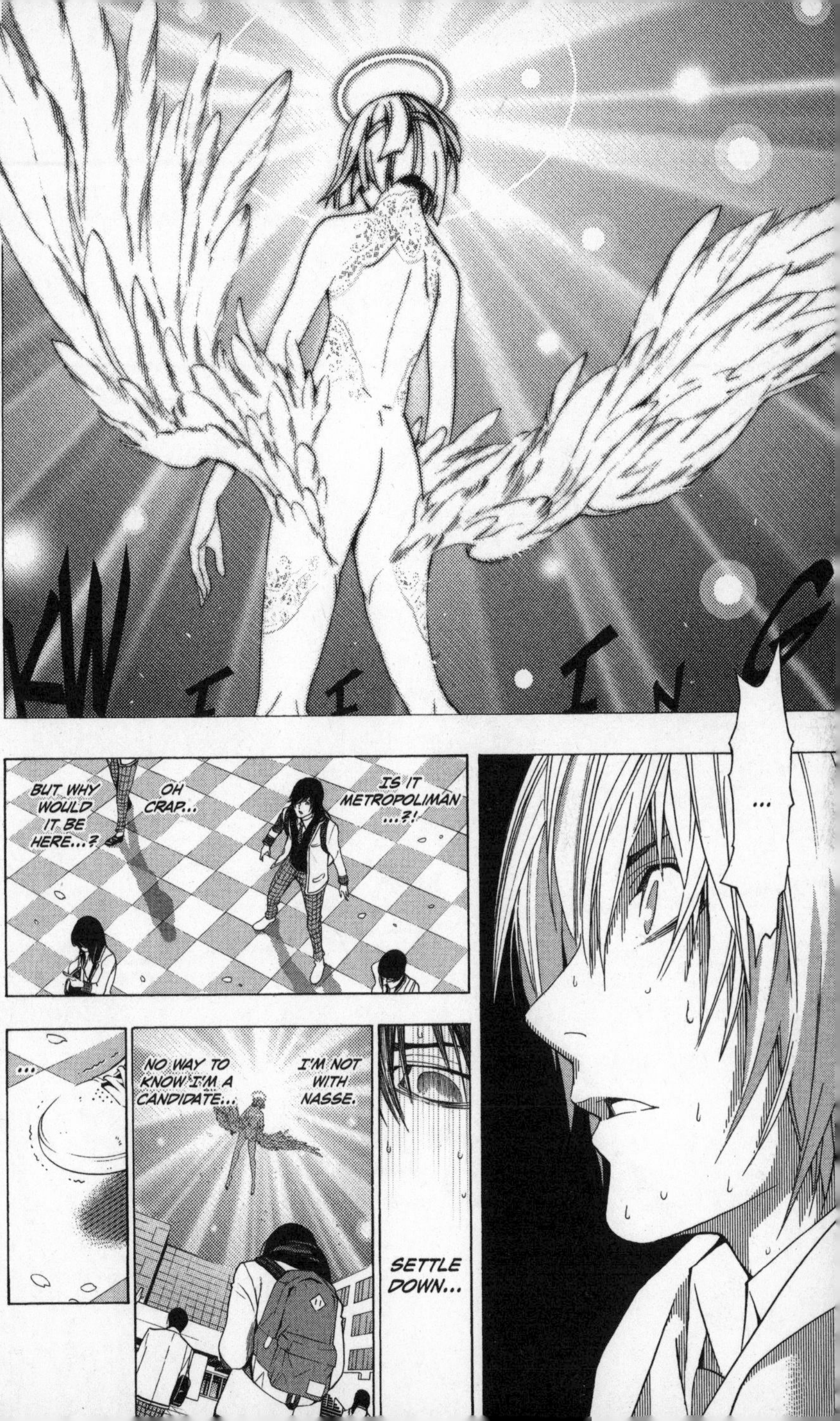
KWIING
...
IS IT METROPOLIMAN ...?!
OH CRAP...
BUT WHY WOULD IT BE HERE...?
SETTLE DOWN...
I'M NOT WITH NASSE.
NO WAY TO KNOW I'M A CANDIDATE...
...

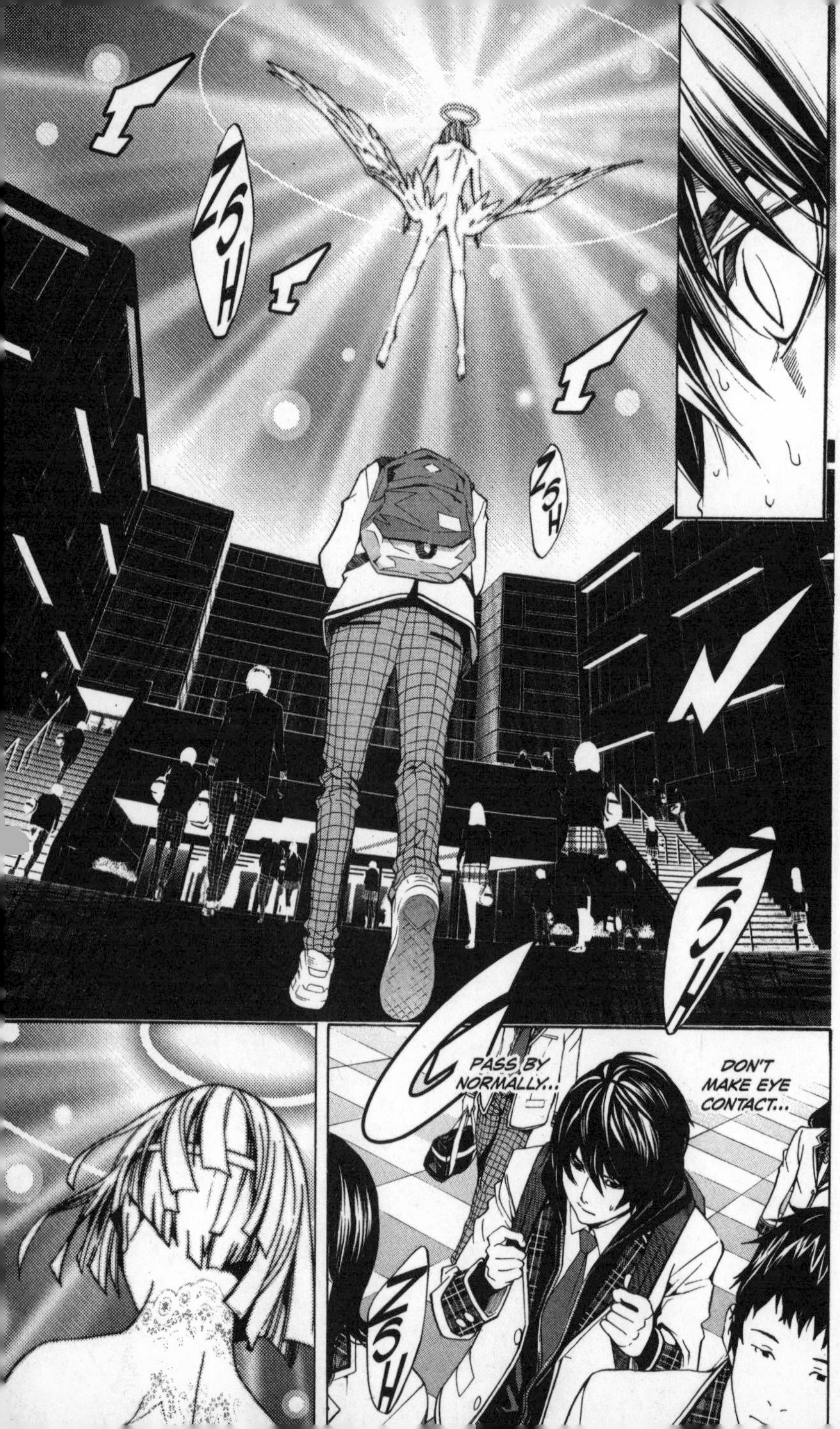
ZSH
ZSH
ZSH
DON'T MAKE EYE CONTACT...
PASS BY NORMALLY...
ZSH

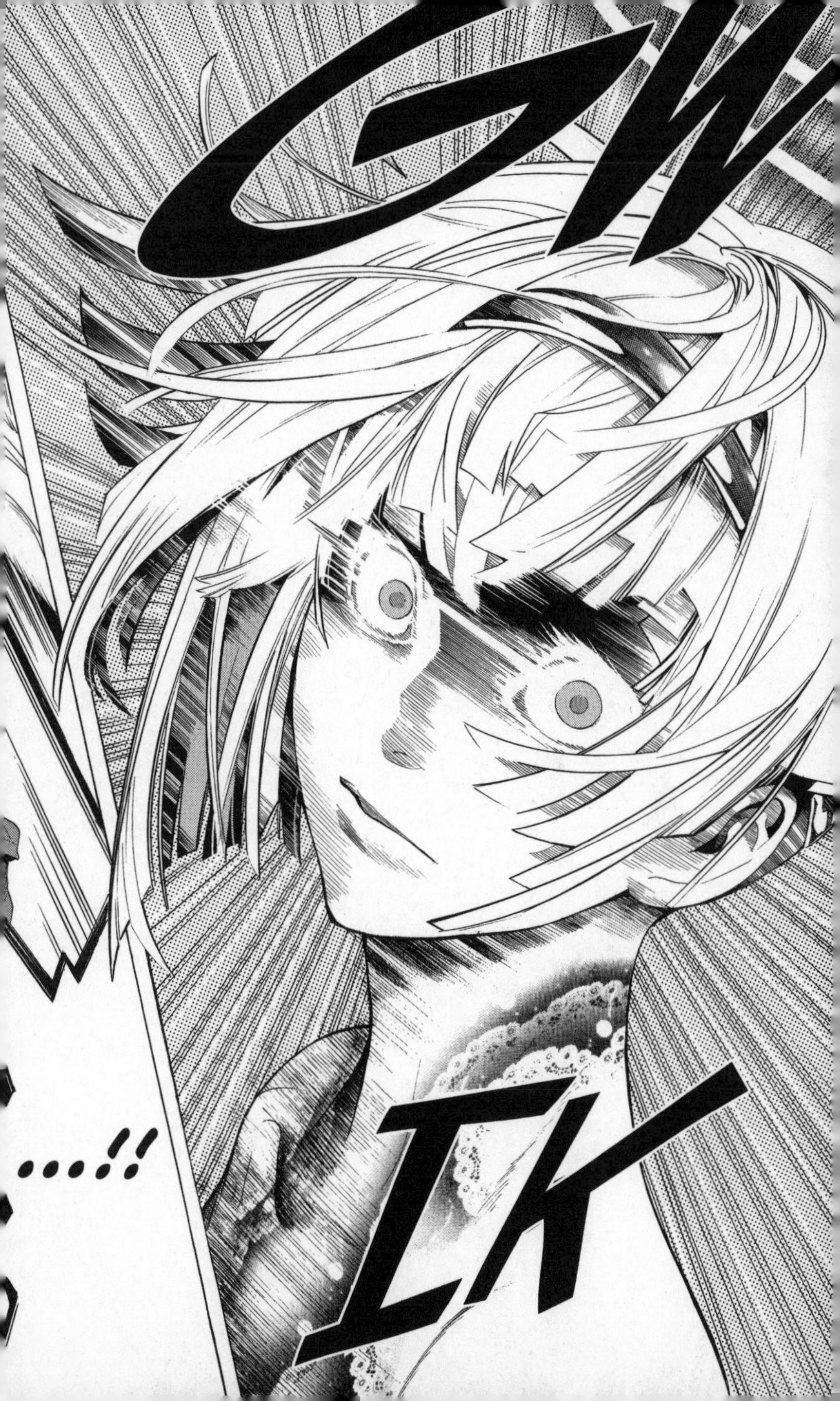
GW
IK
...!!

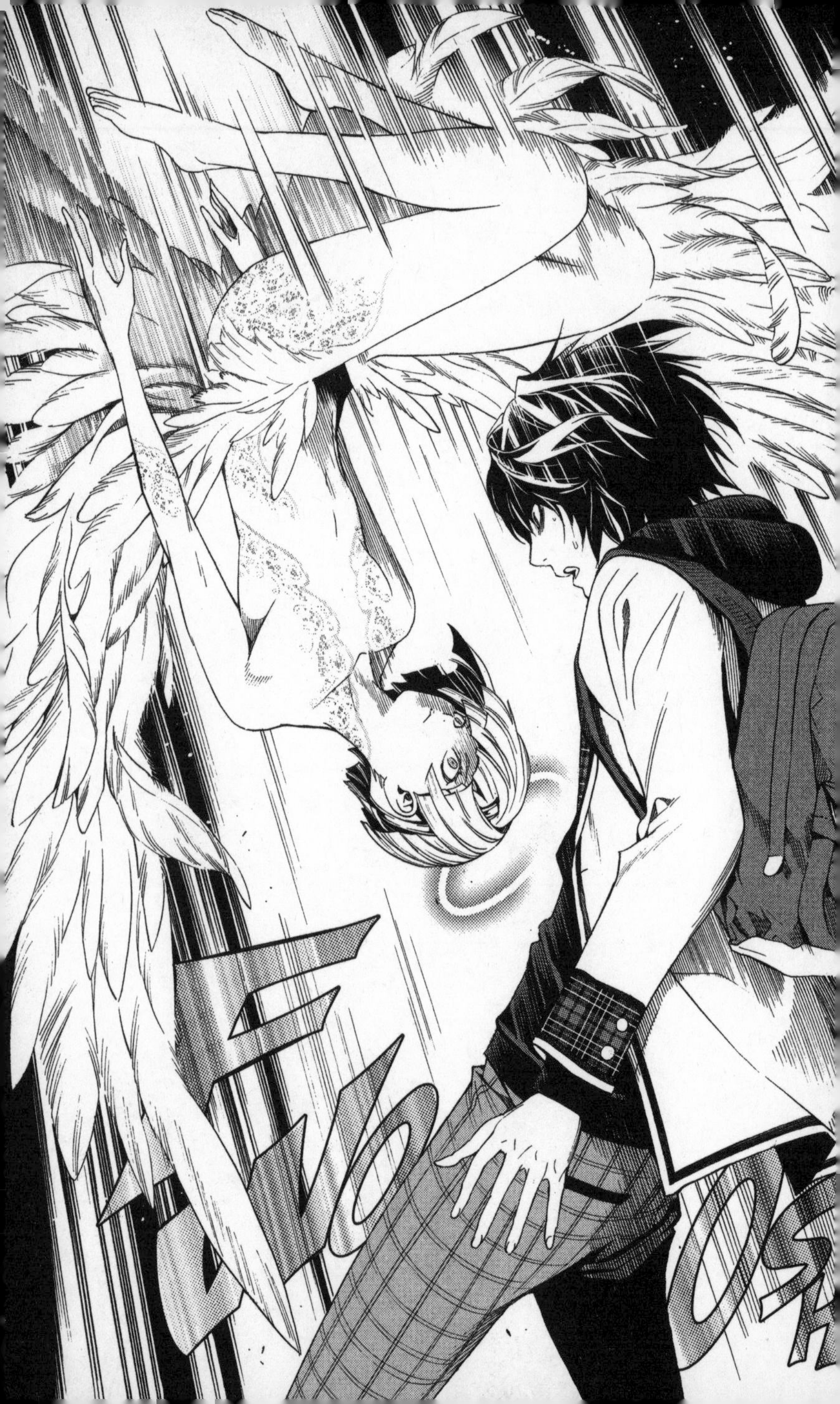
FWOOSH

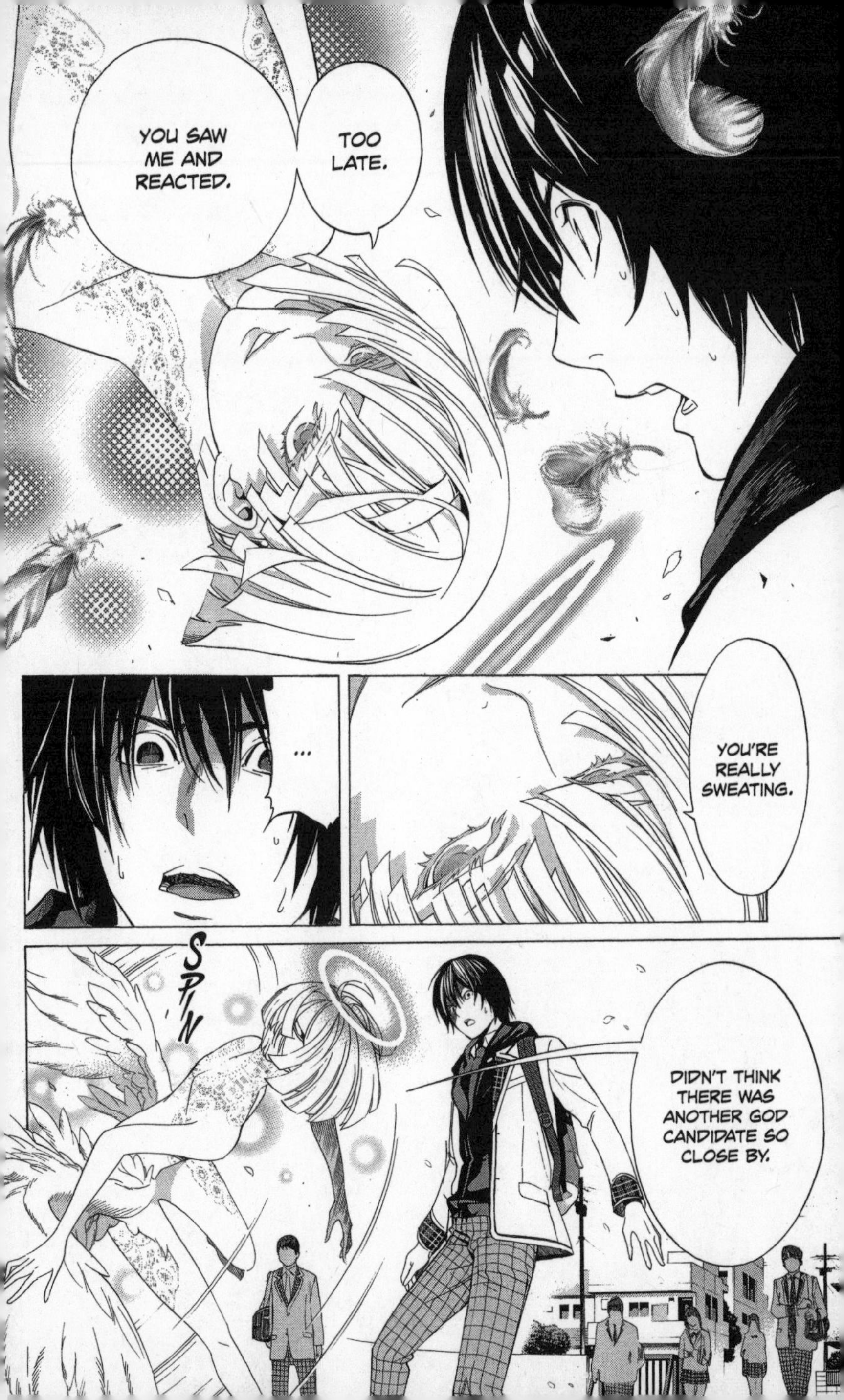
TOO LATE.
YOU SAW ME AND REACTED.
YOU'RE REALLY SWEATING.
...
DIDN'T THINK THERE WAS ANOTHER GOD CANDIDATE SO CLOSE BY.
SPIN

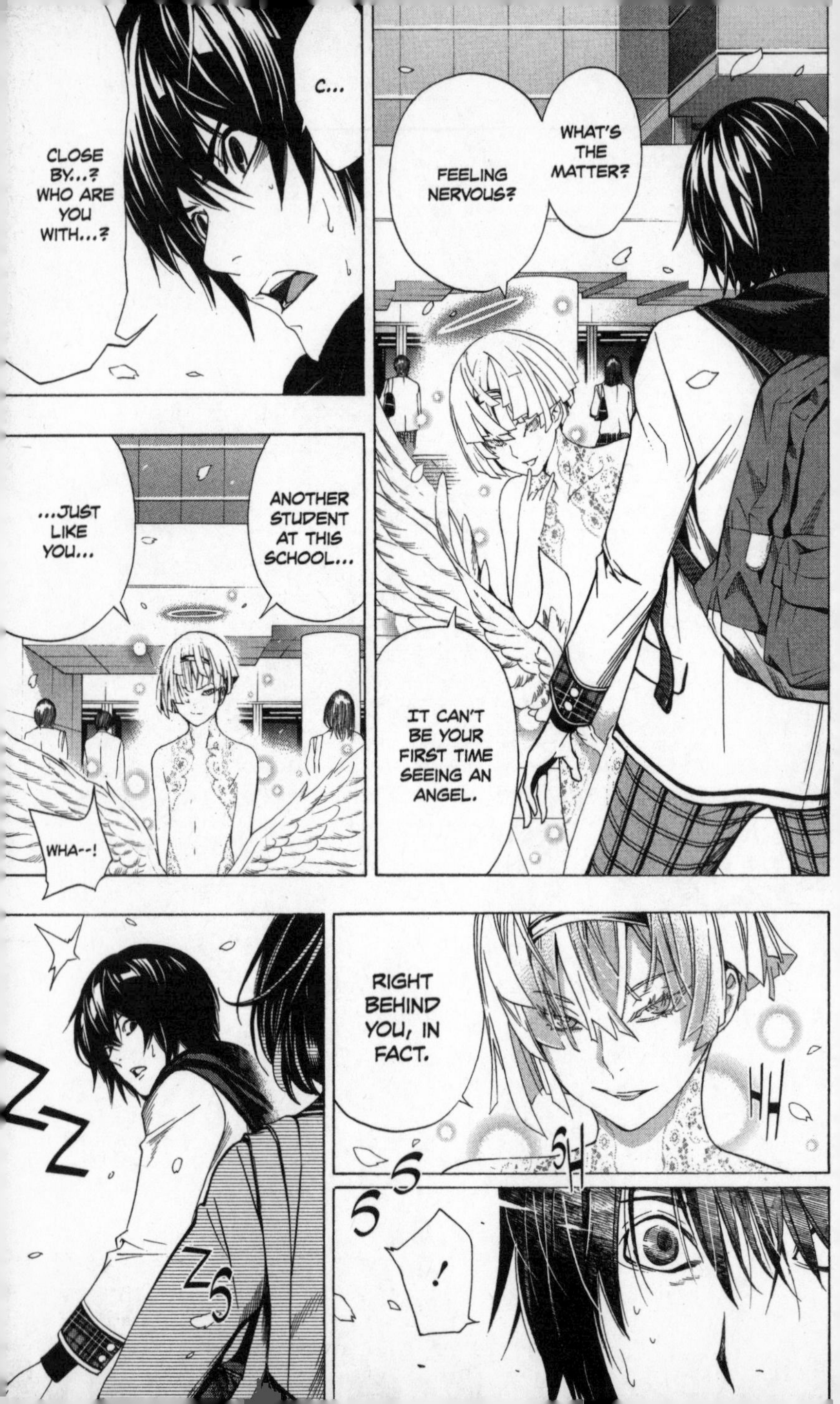
WHAT'S THE MATTER?
FEELING NERVOUS?
IT CAN'T BE YOUR FIRST TIME SEEING AN ANGEL.
C...
CLOSE BY...? WHO ARE YOU WITH...?
ANOTHER STUDENT AT THIS SCHOOL...
...JUST LIKE YOU...
WHA--!
RIGHT BEHIND YOU, IN FACT.
HH
SH
SS
!
ZZ
ZS

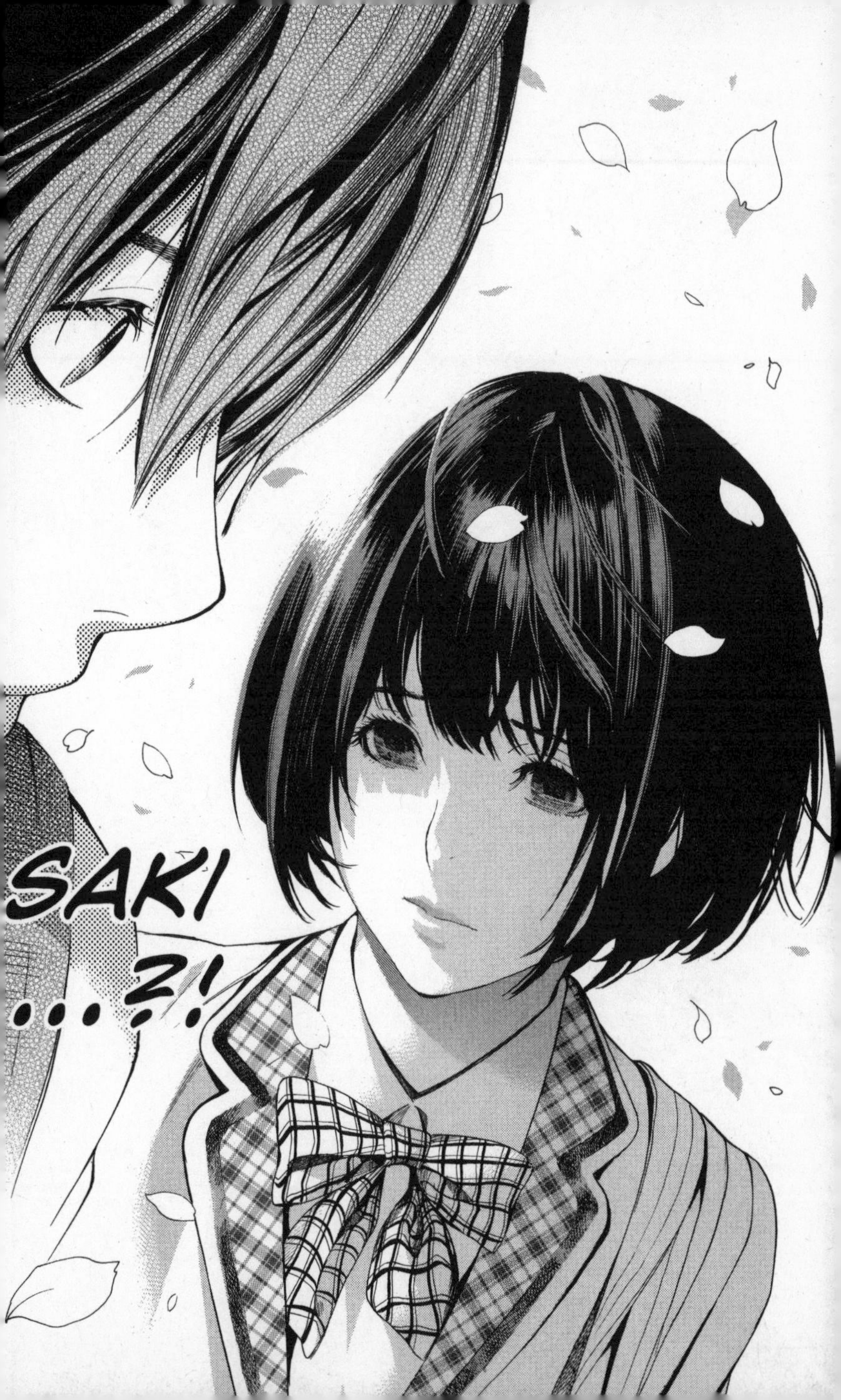
SAKI …?!

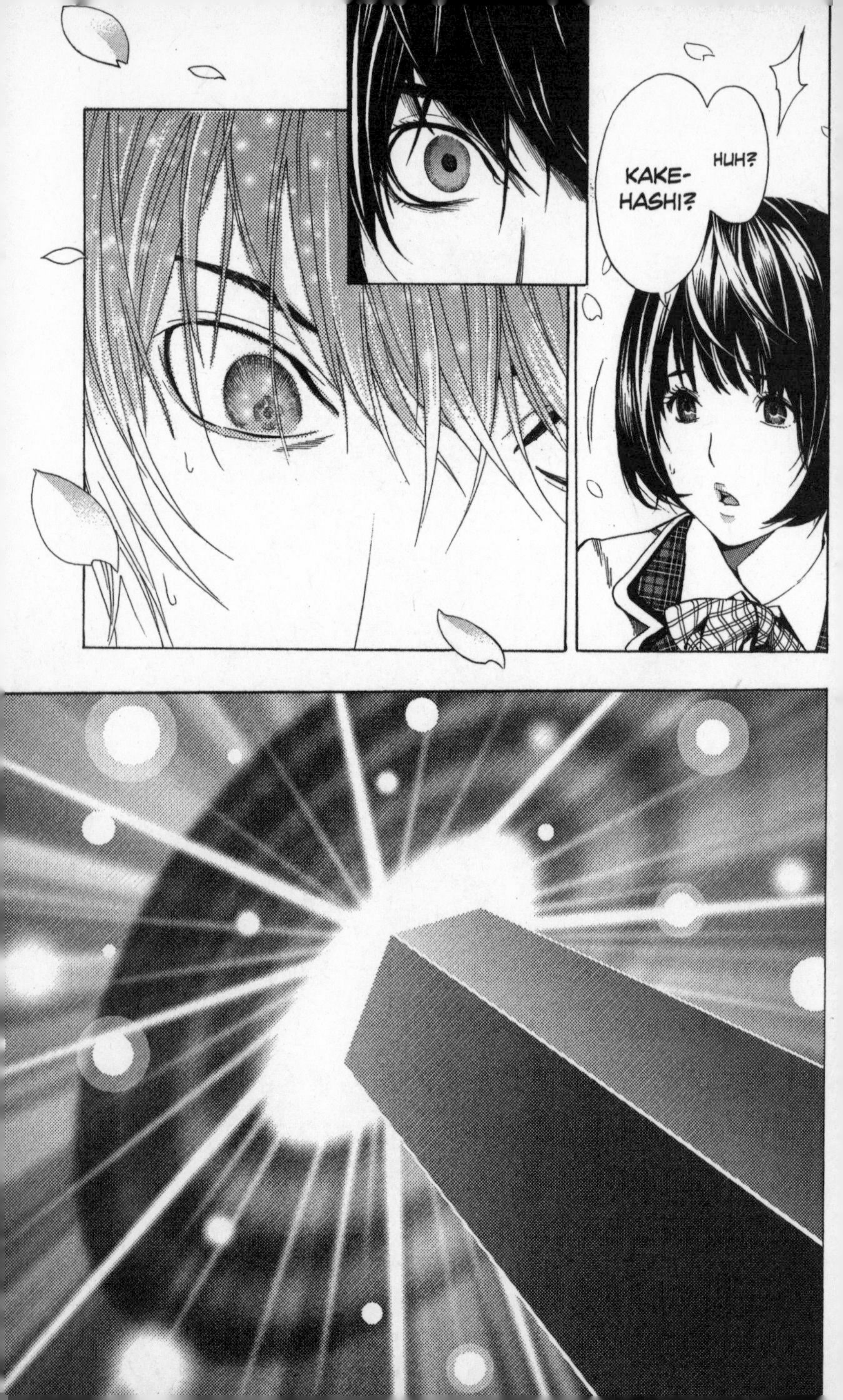
HUH?
KAKE-HASHI?

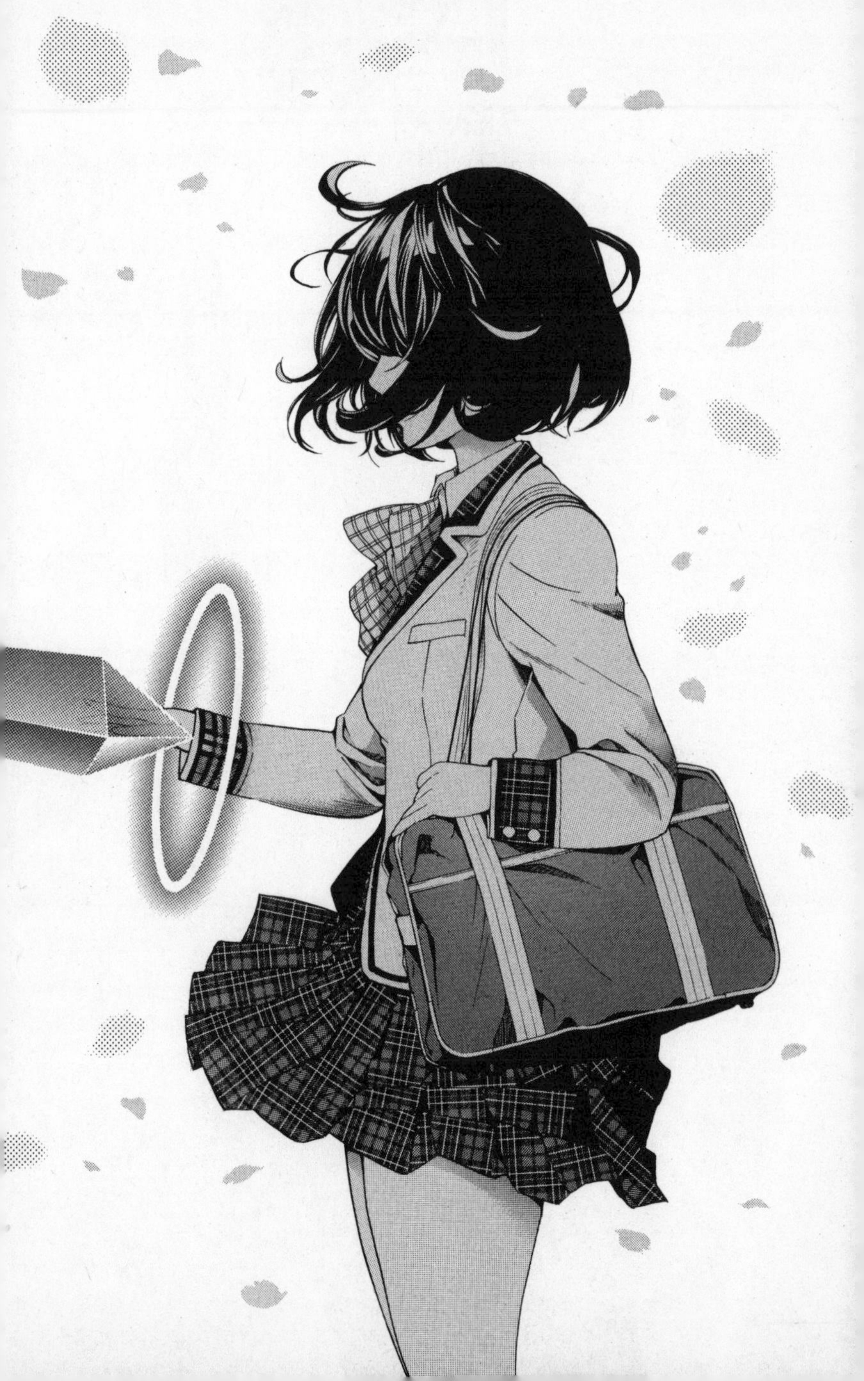

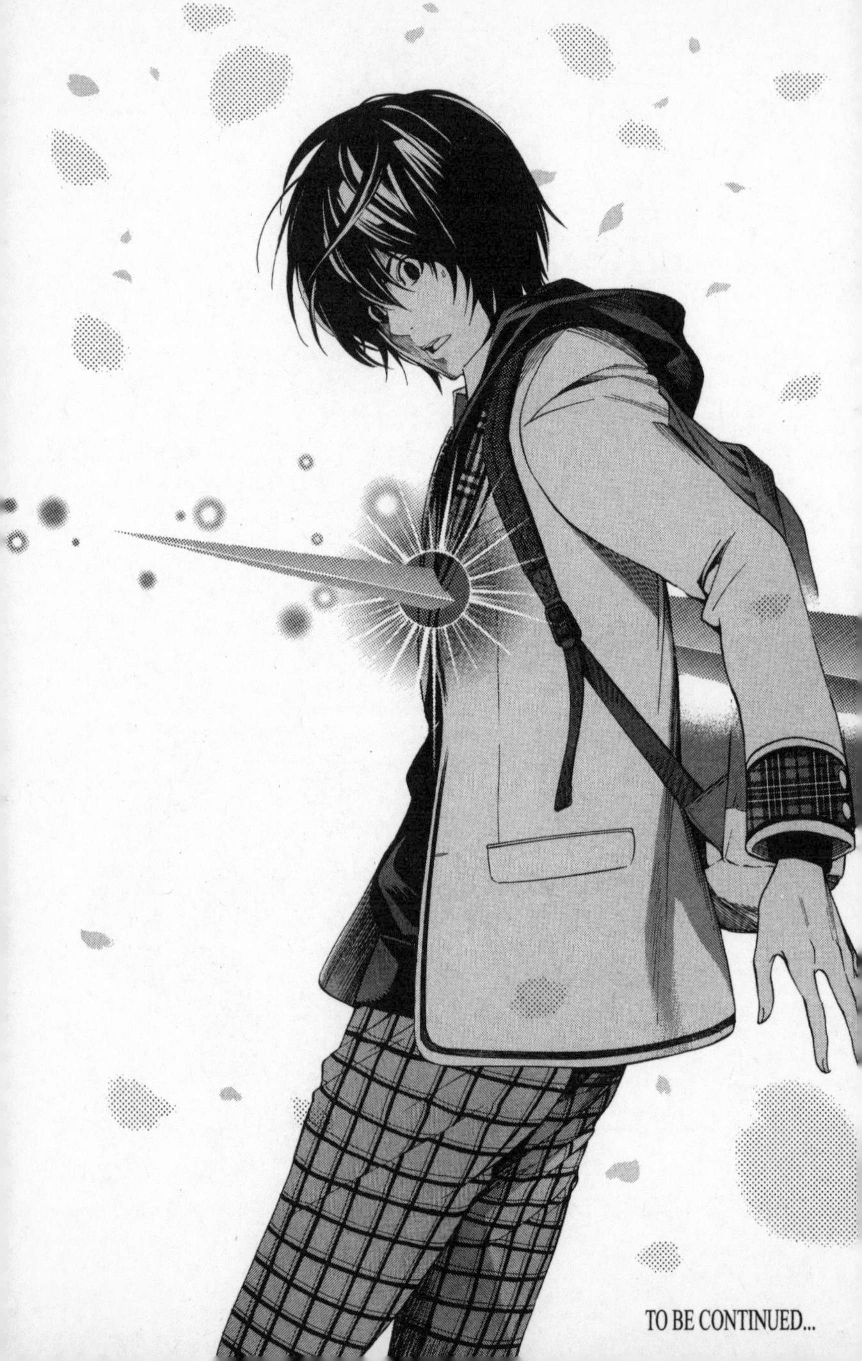

TO BE CONTINUED...

T s u g u mi **O** h b **a**

Born in Tokyo, Tsugumi Ohba is the author
of the hit series *Death Note* and *Bakuman*。

Ta **k** e **sh i** O b a **ta**

Takeshi Obata was born in 1969 in Niigata,
Japan, and first achieved international
recognition as the artist of the wildly popular
Shonen Jump title *Hikaru no Go*, which won the
2003 Tezuka Osamu Cultural Prize: Shinsei
"New Hope" Award and the 2000 Shogakukan
Manga Award. He went on to illustrate the smash
hit *Death Note* as well as the hugely successful
manga *Bakuman*。 and *All You Need Is Kill*.

PLATINVM END

VOLUME 1
SHONEN JUMP Manga Edition

STORY Tsugumi Ohba
ART Takeshi Obata

TRANSLATION Stephen Paul
TOUCH-UP ART & LETTERING James Gaubatz
DESIGN Shawn Carrico
EDITOR Alexis Kirsch

ORIGINAL COVER DESIGN Narumi Noriko

First published in Japan in 2015 by SHUEISHA Inc., Tokyo.
English translation rights arranged by SHUEISHA Inc.

Printed in the U.S.A.

Published by VIZ Media, LLC
P.O. Box 77010
San Francisco, CA 94107

10 9 8 7 6 5 4 3 2 1
First printing, October 2016

www.viz.com www.shonenjump.com

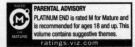

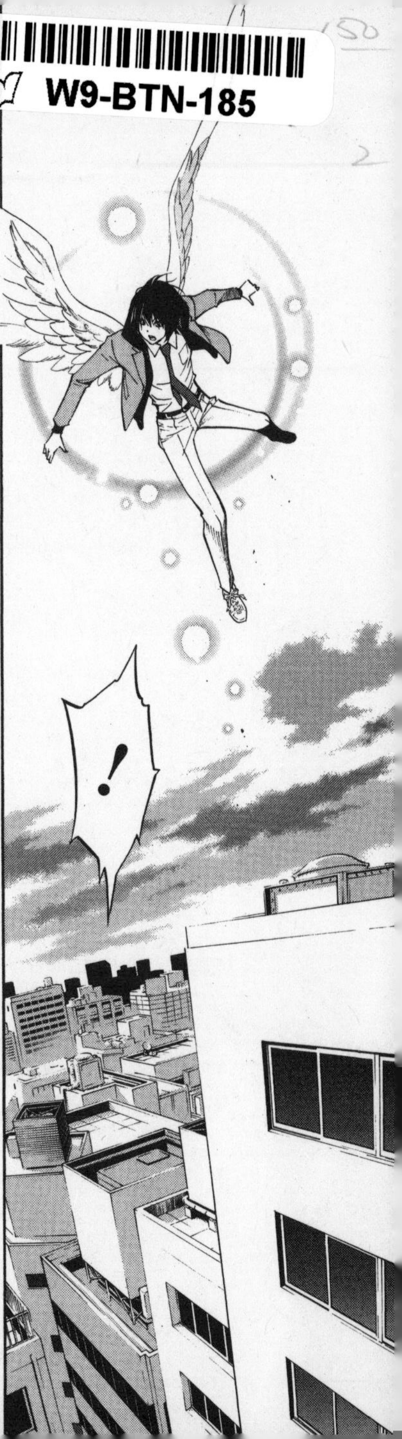
!

YOU'RE READING THE
WRONG WAY!

PLATINUM END
reads from right to left,
starting in the upper-right
corner. Japanese is read
from right to left, meaning
that action, sound effects
and word-balloon order
are completely reversed
from English order.

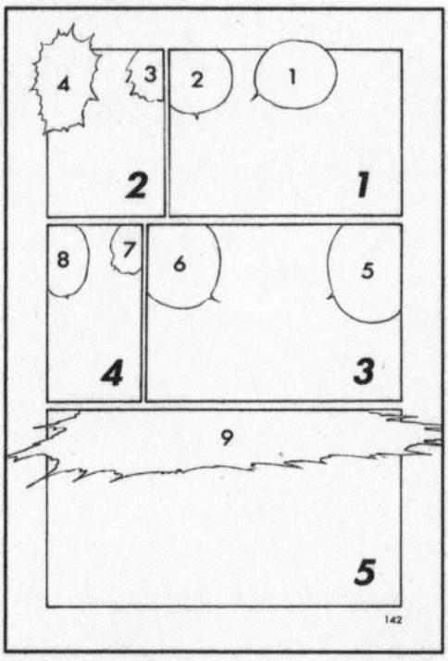
1
2
3
4
5
6
7
8
9
142